Almost All About Unit Roots
Foundations, Developments, and Applications

Many economic theories depend on the presence or absence of a unit root for their validity, and econometric and statistical theories undergo considerable changes when unit roots are present. Thus, knowledge about unit roots has become very important, necessitating an extensive, compact, and nontechnical book on this subject. This book introduces the literature on unit roots in a comprehensive manner to both students and empirical and theoretical researchers in economics and other areas. In providing a clear, complete, and critical discussion of the unit root literature, In Choi covers a wide range of topics, including uniform confidence interval construction, unit root tests allowing structural breaks, mildly explosive processes, exuberance testing, fractionally integrated processes, seasonal unit roots, and panel unit root testing. Extensive, up to date, and readily accessible, this book is a comprehensive reference source on unit roots for both students and researchers.

In Choi is a professor of economics at Sogang University in Seoul, Korea. His research focus has been on time series and panel data analysis, and he has published numerous articles in leading journals in economics and statistics. He is a Fellow of the *Journal of Econometrics* and has received the Plura Scripsit Award from *Econometric Theory* and the Chongram Award from the Korean Economic Association. He is currently an associate editor of the *Journal of Business and Economic Statistics*.

Themes in Modern Econometrics

Series Editor
PETER C. B. PHILLIPS, *Sterling Professor of Economics, Yale University*

Themes in Modern Econometrics provides an organized sequence of advanced textbooks in econometrics aimed directly at the student population and is the first series in the discipline to have this as its express aim. Written at a level accessible to those who have completed an introductory course in econometrics, each book addresses topics and themes that students and researchers encounter daily. All areas of econometrics are covered within the series. Particular emphasis is given to theory fundamentals and practical implementation in breaking research areas that are relevant to empirical applications. Each book stands alone as an authoritative survey in its own right. The distinct emphasis throughout is on pedagogic excellence and accessibility.

Recent Books in the Series
Granularity Theory with Applications to Finance and Insurance (2014) PATRICK GAGLIARDINI *and* CHRISTIAN GOURIÉROUX
Econometric Modeling with Time Series (2012) VANCE MARTIN, STAN HURN, *and* DAVID HARRIS
Economic Modeling and Inference (2007) JEAN-PIERRE FLORENSE, VELAYOUDOM MARIMOUTOU, *and* ANNE PEGUIN-FEISSOLLE; *Translated by* JOSEF PERKTOLD *and* MARINE CARRASCO
Introduction to the Mathematical and Statistical Foundations of Econometrics (2004) HERMAN J. BIERENS
Applied Time Series Econometrics (2004) HELMUT LÜTKEPOHL *and* MARKUS KRÄTZIG
Semiparametric Regression for the Applied Econometrician (2003) ADONIS YATCHEW
The Econometric Analysis of Seasonal Time Series (2001) ERIC GHYSELS *and* DENISE R. OSBORN
Econometrics of Qualitative Dependent Variables (2000) CHRISTIAN GOURIEROUX *Translated by* PAUL B. KLASSEN
Nonparametric Econometrics (1999) ADRIAN PAGAN *and* AMAN ULLAH
Generalized Method of Moments Estimation (1999) *Edited by* LÁSZLÓ MÁTYÁS
Unit Roots, Cointegration, and Structural Change (1999) G. S. MADDALA *and* IN-MOO KIM
Time Series and Dynamic Models (1997) CHRISTIAN GOURIEROUX *and* ALAIN MONFORT; *Translated and edited by* GIAMPIERO GALLO
Statistics and Econometric Models: Volumes 1 and 2 (1995) CHRISTIAN GOURIÉROUX *and* ALAIN MONFORT; *Translated by* QUANG VUONG

ALMOST ALL ABOUT UNIT ROOTS

Foundations, Developments, and Applications

IN CHOI
Sogang University, Korea

CAMBRIDGE
UNIVERSITY PRESS

CAMBRIDGE
UNIVERSITY PRESS

University Printing House, Cambridge CB2 8BS, United Kingdom

One Liberty Plaza, 20th Floor, New York, NY 10006, USA

477 Williamstown Road, Port Melbourne, VIC 3207, Australia

314-321, 3rd Floor, Plot 3, Splendor Forum, Jasola District Centre, New Delhi - 110025, India

103 Penang Road, #05-06/07, Visioncrest Commercial, Singapore 238467

Cambridge University Press is part of the University of Cambridge.

It furthers the University's mission by disseminating knowledge in the pursuit of education, learning and research at the highest international levels of excellence.

www.cambridge.org
Information on this title: www.cambridge.org/9781107097339

First published 2015

A catalogue record for this publication is available from the British Library

Library of Congress Cataloging in Publication data
Choi, In, 1958–
Almost all about unit roots : foundations, developments, and applications / In Choi.
    pages cm. – (Themes in modern econometrics)
Includes bibliographical references and index.
ISBN 978-1-107-09733-9 (hardback) – ISBN 978-1-107-48250-0 (pbk.)
1. Econometrics.   2. Economics – Statistical methods.   3. Social sciences – Statistical methods.   I. Title.
HB139.C4797   2015
330.01´5195–dc23   2014037527

ISBN 978-1-107-09733-9 Hardback
ISBN 978-1-107-48250-0 Paperback

In memory of

my father Mr. Suk Whan Choi

Contents

Contents

Foreword

Socioeconomic trends figure prominently in media discussion and the financial pages of newspapers. They dominate data, guide policy decisions, and attract intense interest that extends well beyond the subject matter of economics and finance. In spite of this widespread influence trends are poorly understood. They are the inscrutable Hamlet of econometrics. No one really knows what they will do next.

During the 1980s econometrics embarked on a revolutionary journey that opened up a new understanding of the stochastic properties of trend. The unit root revolution changed the way the profession thought about trend by emphasizing the role of random elements in the trend mechanism and by formulating a technically well-defined concept of long-run behavior that did not remove randomness. By the 1990s, functional limit laws, stochastic integrals, and functionals of stochastic processes had overtaken econometrics in a firestorm that swept away earlier methods. New symbols of limit theory forever changed the pages of the mainline economics journals. New thinking penetrated econometric teaching and empirical practice. And a vast literature of applied economic analysis was born that demonstrated surprising sophistication in its use of modern econometric technology and nonstandard limit theory.

The implications of this unit root revolution have been enormous. The methodology exported itself throughout the social and business sciences with concomitant changes in thinking that acknowledged the ubiquitous presence of nonstationarity in data. The methods now reach into the natural sciences in areas as diverse as paleoclimatology and biodiversity with datasets that span hundreds of millions of years rather than the decades and centuries of economic data.

The single most important tool in the development of a theory for nonstationary time series was the use of limit laws on function spaces, first brilliantly exposited by Patrick Billingsley in his monograph *Convergence of Probability Measures,* published in 1968. Measure theoretic principles in metric spaces

xvi   **Foreword**

underpinned all the foundations of this major work. Appropriately, Billingsley's author index reference to the mathematician Paul Halmos (who wrote a classic treatise on measure theory) read quite simply as "a.e." (almost everywhere).

Fittingly too, Choi's volume on nonstationarity in the Themes in Modern Econometrics series is entitled *Almost All About Unit Roots*. The world of unit roots has exploded since the 1990s when the last generation of textbooks on the subject were written. Choi escorts us into this excitingly complex arena of research and empirical findings with a text that reaches out to the non-specialist and practitioner, while providing for the specialist a guidebook to the expanding universe of literature that has come to define the discipline of unit root econometrics.

The unit root revolution was a revolution in thinking about economic time series and trends that massively changed the conduct of empirical research and supported the emergence of the field of financial econometrics. The excitement of this transformation of econometrics lives on in the latest work of the profession, which this volume seeks to reveal.

One of the laws of modern econometrics is that "no one understands trends, but everyone sees them in the data." This volume by Choi will help readers learn how unit root econometrics enabled us to tackle the curiously inscrutable phenomenon of trend by marshalling new scientific methods of function space limit theory and inference.

Peter C. B. Phillips
January 2015

Preface

There has been much research conducted on nonstationary time series in the last few decades, and the related literature continues to expand. Research on nonstationary time series can be categorized into two areas: unit roots and cointegration. The literature on unit roots dates back to White (1958), and methods related to unit roots are now popular among economists and other social scientists. The concept of cointegration was developed by Engle and Granger (1987), and the techniques for cointegration have been accepted as standard tools in economics and other areas.

The aim of this book is to introduce the literature on unit roots in a comprehensive manner to both students and empirical and theoretical researchers in economics and other areas. The literature on nonstationary time series is now so huge that it seems difficult, if not impossible, to include all the related topics in a single monograph. Therefore, this book focuses on unit roots.

This book takes the approach of discussing as many papers as possible in presenting developments in the literature on unit roots. Yet it emphasizes important works that either contain novel ideas or have been cited often. By reading this book, the student or researcher can understand major developments in the literature on unit roots and related areas. The papers covered in this book were published in more than 30 major journals in econometrics, statistics, and other branches of social science up to 2013. A few unpublished papers and book chapters are also included.

This book is ideal for graduate students and researchers in economics, finance, political science, sociology, statistics, and other areas who want to learn about unit roots as they conduct their empirical research projects or theoretical research on unit roots. Material in this book can be taught in graduate-level courses on time series analysis along with more conventional textbooks such as Brockwell and Davies (1991), Hamilton (1994), and Fuller (1976). This book is also useful as a reference for researchers interested in nonstationary time series analysis. For those who are interested in theoretical aspects of unit roots, this book provides an up-to-date literature survey and suggests some open questions. To understand this book fully, the reader must have some knowledge of time series analysis at the level of, for example, Brockwell and Davies (1991). There are excellent books that deal with unit roots, such as Banerjee, Dolado, Galbraith, and Hendry (1993); Hatanaka (1996); Maddala and Kim (1998); and Patterson (2010, 2011). However, the first three of these books were written more than 15 years ago and do not reflect recent contributions to the literature on unit roots. The books by Patterson focus on conventional methods of unit root testing. In contrast, this book contains up-to-date and comprehensive research results about unit roots and therefore is complementary to them.

I am thankful to many people who have guided me in my development as a researcher and helped me while I was writing this book. I am grateful to Professors Peter Phillips, Don Andrews, Matthew Shapiro, Vassilis Hajivassiliou, Benedikt Pötscher, and David Pollard, who taught me econometrics, statistics, and probability at Yale. In particular, Professor Peter Phillips, as my thesis advisor, led me into the research area of nonstationary time series. He showed me how to do research, how to teach, and how hard academicians should work to achieve their goals. I owe much to him for what I am now as a researcher and educator. In fact, without his encouragement, I would not have dared to start writing this book. He, as well as four anonymous reviewers, provided very helpful comments on previous versions of this book. Those comments greatly improved the book, for which I am truly thankful. I also thank him for his insightful foreword for this book. I first learned econometrics from Professor Ki-Jun Jeong, then at Seoul National University. His course was challenging for most undergraduate students at that time, but I became interested in econometrics despite its difficulty. I appreciate his serious teaching. Part of this book was written while I was visiting the University of Leeds and the University of Bonn. I thank Professors Jörg Breitung, Martin Carter, Matei Demetrescu, Christian Pigorsch, Kevin Reilly, and Yongcheol Shin for their hospitality. Minchul Yum (now a graduate student at the Ohio State University) gathered the papers covered in this book, and I thank him for his diligent efforts. John Morris read the entire manuscript carefully and suggested grammatical corrections and stylistic improvements, which I deeply appreciate. The research reported in this book was supported by the National Research Foundation of Korea (project #NRF-2010-342-B00006), which I gratefully acknowledge. Last, but most important, I thank my wife Joanne Jung-un Han for her enduring support for the last 25 years. Indeed, I can live a happy personal life and a productive professional one thanks to her presence.

In Choi
Seoul, Korea
September 2013

Abbreviations and Notation

The following abbreviations and notations are used throughout this book.

AR	autoregressive
ARCH	autoregressive conditional heteroskedasticity
ARIMA	autoregressive integrated moving average
ARMA	autoregressive moving average
cdf	cumulative density function
CLT	central limit theorem
DGP	data-generating process
FCLT	functional central limit theorem
GARCH	generalized autoregressive conditional heteroskedasticity
GLS	generalized least squares
GMM	generalized method of moments
HPD	highest posterior density
i.i.d., iid	independent and identically distributed
IV	instrumental variables
LAD	least absolute deviation
LM	Lagrange multiplier
LR	likelihood ratio
MA	moving average
MLE	maximum likelihood estimator
OLS	ordinary least squares
pdf	probability density function
SUR	seemingly unrelated regression
VAR	vector autoregression
$[x]$	integer not greater than x
$1\{A\}$	indicator function taking value one when A is true and zero otherwise

$\Rightarrow$	weak convergence
$\xrightarrow{p}$	convergence in probability
B	backward-shift operator (i.e., $B^m X_t = X_{t-m}$ for an integer m)
Δ^d	$\Delta^d X_t = (1 - B)^d X_t$
$X_t = \mathrm{I}(d)$	$\Delta^d X_t$ is a stationary process

1 Introduction

This chapter starts with a discussion of the motivation and scope of this book. Then, it introduces properties of unit root processes, relations between social science and unit roots, and some basic technical tools related to inferences on unit roots. It also provides an overview of subsequent chapters. Discussions on preliminary concepts and basic tools are brief because of the nature of this book, and the reader is referred to more specialized books such as Brockwell and Davis (1991), Davidson (1994), Hamilton (1994), Fuller (1976), and Serfling (1980).

1.1 Motivation and Scope of This Book

The last two decades or so have seen significant developments in the literature on unit roots. By the early 1980s, only a handful of papers had been written about unit roots, mostly by Professor Wayne Fuller and his coauthors. In those days, researchers in social science seldom used unit root tests for their empirical studies, and it was hard to find a graduate course on time series analysis offered by departments related to social science. Todays, the situation is radically different: there are many theoretical papers about unit roots, as the reference section of this book attests, and various procedures designed for testing for a unit root are often used in social science, particularly in economics. Naturally, commercial software for econometrics and statistics has incorporated many of the methods developed in the literature on unit roots.

Because so many unit root tests had been developed by the 1990s, some even thought that efforts dedicated to unit roots were excessive and unwarranted, as Maddala and Kim (1998, p. 488) succinctly quipped, "What we do not need is more unit root tests (each of which uses the Nelson–Plosser data as a guinea pig)." Nonetheless, because no one can predict with confidence the future direction of the world of knowledge, research on unit roots has continued to expand.

1

The main vehicle for the massive theoretical developments in unit root regressions and testing has been the functional central limit theory (FCLT) that Phillips (1986, 1987a) first introduced to the literature on unit roots. Although White (1958) and Dickey and Fuller (1979) developed asymptotic theory for the AR(1) model with a unit root, their methods require a normality assumption and are difficult to use for other types of regressions involving nonstationary regressors. By contrast, the FCLT allows us to employ general assumptions on the DGP of the model in use and can be applied to various linear and nonlinear regression models. In this sense, it is fair to say that the FCLT of Phillips (1986, 1987a) has played a pivotal role in the developments of limit theory for regressions with nonstationary time series.

There are several reasons why unit roots are important in economics, other disciplines of social science, and statistics. First, the validity of many economic propositions hinges on the presence or absence of unit roots. For example, real exchange rates should not have a unit root for the relative purchasing power parity to hold as discussed in Subsection 1.3.3. Some other examples are also given in Section 1.3. This is one of the reasons why unit root tests are so often used in economics.

Second, regressions and VARs require knowing about the univariate properties of the variables in use. If the variables are stationary, conventional theories on regressions and VARs can be used. But if they have a unit root, regressions can be spurious (cf. Granger and Newbold, 1974) unless those variables are cointegrated. In a VAR system, the presence of unit roots invites a host of nontrivial issues for such standard VAR procedures as the causality test, impulse response analysis, and forecast error variance decomposition, as analyzed in Toda and Phillips (1993) and Phillips (1998). Using differenced data is not necessarily the best option for conducting VAR analysis. Thus, testing for a unit root has almost always preceded regressions and VARs in economics, political science, and sociology, and those test results have routinely been reported. Because unit roots appear to be present at many key time series in social science (e.g., GDP, nominal interest rates, exchange rates, consumer sentiments, presidential approval rates, etc.), such preliminary specification testing has been performed faithfully in empirical time series analysis. In addition, a way of testing for cointegration or spuriousness of regressions is to check the presence of a unit root in the OLS residuals as suggested by Engle and Granger (1987). Unit root tests are again used for this purpose, although asymptotic theory for such tests is not dealt with in this book.

Third, as subsequent chapters show, diverse econometric and statistical theories have been applied to the AR model with unit roots. For many theoretical researchers, unit roots have been an important means with which they could test their econometric and statistical theories. Moreover, the level of generality, strength, and usefulness of those theories can be assessed when they are applied to the AR model with unit roots, which makes the model important to theorists in econometrics and statistics. The reader can learn about those theories from this book, which is an added benefit that this book can provide beyond knowledge on unit roots.

In light of the well-accepted importance of unit roots, it is no wonder that many researchers in social science and statistics want to learn about them. Indeed, knowledge on unit roots has become so essential for modern time series analysis that performing empirical time series analysis and understanding empirical literatures in social science are virtually impossible without it. But for those who want to study the literature on unit roots, it is difficult to know where to start because the literature is now so immense. Finding specific information on unit roots for each researcher's purposes is also hard for the same reason. These difficulties motivate an extensive, compact, nontechnical, and up-to-date book on unit roots. This book rests on this motivation and will be useful to those who want to study the literature on unit roots. From this book, the reader will be able to obtain the most comprehensive and up-to-date information on unit roots that he or she can then use to conduct empirical and theoretical research on unit roots.

This book covers research papers on unit roots from 1958 to the present time. The oldest paper this book discusses is White (1958) (see Subsection 2.2.1), and the most recent one is Gao and Robinson (2013) (see Subsection 4.2.2). More space is given to important papers such as those by Dickey and Fuller (1979) and Phillips (1987a), but lesser known papers are also discussed in detail if they are deemed to be based on novel and useful ideas. Because there are so many papers in the area of univariate unit roots alone, those on cointegration and multivariate unit roots are not included in this book and relegated to future works. This book may look incomplete because of this feature, but this choice was necessary to keep its length within reasonable bounds. This book tries to cover as many papers as possible to provide comprehensive information on unit roots to the reader and to record the developments of the literature on unit roots. Undoubtedly, however, some papers must have been neglected. This makes it necessary to put the word "almost" in the title of this book. But let me emphasize that I made a genuine effort to make this book as comprehensive as possible.

1.2 Properties of Unit Root Processes

The characteristic equation of the AR(1) model,

$$y_t = \alpha y_{t-1} + u_t, (t = 2, \ldots, T),$$

where $\{u_t\}$ is a white noise process with variance σ_u^2, is written as

$$1 - \alpha z = 0.$$

When the root of this equation is 1 or -1, the process is said to have a unit root. That is, if $\alpha = \pm 1$, $\{y_t\}$ has a unit root. In most applications in economics, the main concern is whether the coefficient α is equal to one. Hence, discussions in this section revolve around the case of $\alpha = 1$.

When $\alpha = 1$, $y_t = \sum_{i=1}^{t} u_i + y_0$, although we may write $y_t = \sum_{i=0}^{\infty} \alpha^i u_{t-i}$ when $|\alpha| < 1$. These representations can be used to show that the stochastic properties of $\{y_t\}$ with $\alpha = 1$ are remarkably different from those of $\{y_t\}$ with $|\alpha| < 1$. Engle and Granger (1987) summarize them as follows.

(i) When $\alpha = 1$, $\text{Var}(y_t) \to \infty$ as $t \to \infty$ once y_0 is assumed to be a constant. When $|\alpha| < 1$, however, $\text{Var}(y_t) = \frac{\sigma_u^2}{1-\alpha^2}$ for all t. These imply that the data become more variable as we collect more of them when $\alpha = 1$. But the data will move within a fixed range when $|\alpha| < 1$.

(ii) When $\alpha = 1$, an innovation (i.e., u_{t-i}, $i \geq 0$) has a permanent effect on the value of y_t that does not die out as the stochastic process progresses toward the future. When $|\alpha| < 1$, an innovation will lose its effect on the value of y_t eventually as we move forward into the future.

(iii) When $\alpha = 1$, $f_{yy}(0) = \infty$ where $f_{yy}(\cdot)$ denotes the spectral density of $\{y_t\}$. This means that $\{y_t\}$ has a strong long-run component. When $|\alpha| < 1$, the spectral density is finite at all frequencies.

(iv) When $\alpha = 1$, the expected time between crossings of $y = 0$ is infinite. Thus, $\{y_t\}$ has no tendency to return to its theoretical mean. When $|\alpha| < 1$, the expected time between crossings of $y = 0$ is finite, which implies that the process moves around its mean and has a tendency of mean reversion.

(v) When $\alpha = 1$, the theoretical autocorrelation at lag k converges to 1 for all k as $t \to \infty$. This means that the autocorrelation does not allow conventional interpretations when $\alpha = 1$. When $|\alpha| < 1$, the autocorrelation decreases steadily in magnitude as k increases.

In addition to these properties, the coefficient α also affects the variance of the forecasting error. Suppose that we forecast $y_{T+1}, y_{T+2}, \ldots$, with a known value of the coefficient α. Then the optimal forecasts are $\hat{y}_{T+1} = \alpha y_T$, $\hat{y}_{T+2} = \alpha \hat{y}_{T+1}, \ldots$, and the forecast error is defined by

$$y_{T+1} - \hat{y}_{T+1} = u_{T+1}$$

$$y_{T+2} - \hat{y}_{T+2} = u_{T+2} + \alpha u_{T+1}$$

$$\vdots$$

Thus, denoting the forecasting horizon as h, the variance of the forecasting error is $\sigma_u^2(1 + \alpha^2 + \cdots + \alpha^{2(h-1)})$ when $|\alpha| < 1$. But when $\alpha = 1$, it is $h\sigma_u^2$, which grows linearly with h, and is larger than that for the case $|\alpha| < 1$. This indicates that it becomes difficult to predict the future observations precisely when $\alpha = 1$.

We have assumed so far that $\{u_t\}$ is a white noise process. But essentially the same results hold true when $\{u_t\}$ is a stationary and invertible ARMA process, indicating that an ARMA model with a unit root has properties quite different from that without it.

1.3 Economics and Unit Roots

Discussions in the previous section indicate that the unit root case has quite distinctive characteristics. It is no wonder that researchers have exerted so much effort to study the AR process with a unit root. However, these characteristics alone do not explain the huge interest in the unit root AR model in the economics literature. This section delves into why the unit root case has attracted so much attention from economists.

1.3.1 Nelson and Plosser (1982)

It was Nelson and Plosser (1982) who brought the issue of nonstationarity to the forefront of economic research.[1] They investigated whether macroeconomic time series are characterized as stationary fluctuations around a deterministic trend or as unit root processes with drift. Using historical time series for the United States, they could not reject the hypothesis of a unit root with drift for most of them. Using these findings and an unobserved components model for output, they conclude that "macroeconomic models that focus on monetary disturbances as a source of purely transitory fluctuations may never be successful in explaining a large fraction of output variation and that stochastic variation due to real factors is an essential element of any model of macro-economic fluctuations" (Nelson and Plosser, 1982, p. 139). In other words, they interpret presence of a unit root or a high level of persistence in real GNP as supporting evidence for real-business-cycle theory. However, this interpretation does not seem to be universally accepted. Romer (2001, p. 210) writes,

> Keynesian models do not require that persistence be low. To begin with, although they attribute the bulk of short-run fluctuations to aggregate demand disturbances, they do not assume that the processes that drive long-run growth

---

[1] Before Nelson and Plosser (1982) published their research, Altonji and Ashenfelter (1980) also applied the Dickey-Fuller test to the annual real wage data of the United States and the United Kingdom and could not reject the null hypothesis of a unit root.

follow a deterministic trend; thus they allow at least one part of output movements to be highly persistent. More importantly, the part of fluctuations that
is due to aggregate demand movements may also be persistent.

In other words, according to Romer, the presence of a unit root in real GDP
should not be construed as evidence against Keynesian business-cycle models.

Some ascribed Nelson and Plosser's (1982) results to the low power of
Dickey and Fuller's (1979) test they used, which prompted further studies
seeking to improve the power of unit root tests (see Section 2.4). Nelson and
Plosser's dataset was used extensively as an experimental object for some time
whenever someone invented a new unit root test, and its extended version
is used in Schotman and van Dijk (1991b). Subsequent similar studies have
generally confirmed Nelson and Plosser's empirical results. However, as is seen
in Sections 3.2 and 4.6, unit root tests accommodating structural changes and
a Bayesian approach can yield somewhat different results.

1.3.2 Cointegration

Engle and Granger (1987) define that an $I(1)$ multiple time series $\{X_t\}$ is cointegrated if there exists a vector γ such that $\{\gamma' X_t\}$ becomes $I(0)$. The vector
γ denotes a statistical equilibrium relationship among the elements of $\{X_t\}$
because $\{\gamma' X_t\}$ tends to return to its mean while each element of $\{X_t\}$ does not
possess such a property. The concept of cointegration and related econometric tools have often been used in economics to model statistical equilibrium
relationships among economic variables and to verify those relationships. In
cointegration analysis, the first step is to test whether the variables of interest
have a unit root. Thus, without exceptions, unit root tests are used in applications of cointegration, serving as specification tests, the results of which are
used for subsequent analysis.

1.3.3 Purchasing Power Parity Hypothesis

The absolute law of one price postulates that the same good should have the
same price across countries and is expressed by the relation

$$P_{it} = S_t P_{it}^*, \tag{1.1}$$

where P_{it} is the price of good i in terms of the domestic currency at time t, S_t
is the domestic price of a unit of foreign currency at time t, and P_{it}^* is the price
of good i in terms of the foreign currency at time t. Taking natural logarithms
of relation (1.1), we obtain

$$p_{it} = s_t + p_{it}^*,$$

where lowercase letters denote the logarithms of the corresponding capital letters. Summing all the traded goods in each country with weights γ_i yields a relation

$$p_t = s_t + p_t^*, \tag{1.2}$$

where $p_t = \sum_{i=1}^{N} \gamma_i p_{it}$, $p_t^* = \sum_{i=1}^{N} \gamma_i p_{it}^*$, and $\sum_{i=1}^{N} \gamma_i = 1$. Because p_t and p_t^* can be considered as national price levels,[2] equation (1.2) indicates that the exchange rate is determined by the price levels of both countries and is called the absolute purchasing power parity (PPP) relation. The relative PPP hypothesis postulates that

$$\Delta p_t = \Delta s_t + \Delta p_t^*. \tag{1.3}$$

That is, changes in the nominal exchange rate should match those of the national price levels. The relative PPP holds if $q_t = s_t - p_t + p_t^*$, called the real exchange rate, is a constant. In reality, it is hard to expect that this relation holds in every t. But if relation (1.3) provides a reasonably good approximation to the real world, $\{q_t\}$ should be a stationary process with possibly a nonzero mean. In other words, there should not be a unit root in the real exchange rate $\{q_t\}$ for the relative PPP to hold. Empirical studies employing unit root tests have generally been unable to reject the null hypothesis of a unit root for real exchange rates (see section 3 of Sarno and Taylor, 2002).

1.3.4 Asset Prices

Samuelson (1965) shows that asset prices in an informationally efficient market follow the martingale process, which means that returns are unpredictable and that asset prices have a unit root. Although some evidence has emerged for the predictability of stock returns at a long horizon when variables such as term spread, dividend yield, and earnings/price ratio are used (e.g., Lettau and Ludvigson, 2001), it is now empirically well accepted that asset prices have a unit root. In a consumption-based asset pricing model without dividends, asset prices also follow the martingale process if investors are risk-neutral and if the discount factor is equal to one (see Cochrane, 2005, pp. 24–25).

1.3.5 Relative Mean Reversion in International Stock Markets

Mean reversion of asset prices refers to their tendency to return to a trend path. Fama and French (1988) and Poterba and Summers (1988) are the first works

---

[2] In practice, countries use different baskets of goods to formulate price indices. Moreover, it is more common to use arithmetic than geometric price indices. These aspects are disregarded in this relation. See Sarno and Taylor (2002) for further discussion.

that study mean reversion. Fama and French and Poterba and Summers use regression and the variance ratio, respectively. More recently, Balvers, Wu, and Gilliland (2000) study mean reversion using unit root tests. Their methods can be summarized as follows. Let $p_{i,t}$ denote the log of the total return index of the stock market in country i at the end of period t and assume that the evolution of $p_{i,t}$ is described by a mean-reverting process,

$$p_{i,t+1} - p_{i,t} = a_i + \lambda \left(p^*_{i,t+1} - p_{i,t} \right) + \varepsilon_{i,t+1}, \tag{1.4}$$

where $p^*_{i,t+1}$ is an unobserved fundamental value of the index, a_i is a positive constant, and $\varepsilon_{i,t+1}$ is a stationary disturbance with an unconditional mean of zero. Parameter λ is the speed of mean reversion and is assumed to be the same across countries. If $0 < \lambda < 1$, deviations of $p_{i,t}$ from its fundamental or trend value $p^*_{i,t+1}$ will be reversed over time. But if $\lambda = 0$, the log price follows a unit root process, and there is no mean reversion. Balvers, Wu, and Gilliland assume

$$p^*_{i,t} = p^*_{r,t} + z_i + \eta_{i,t}, \tag{1.5}$$

where r denotes a reference country, z_i is a constant, and $\eta_{i,t}$ is a stationary process with mean zero. Combining equations (1.4) and (1.5) eliminates $p^*_{i,t+1}$ and yields

$$r_{i,t+1} - r_{r,t+1} = \alpha_i - \lambda \left(p_{i,t} - p_{r,t} \right) + \omega_{i,t+1},$$

where $r_{i,t+1} = p_{i,t+1} - p_{i,t}$ is the log return on market i, $\alpha_i = a_i - a_r + \lambda z_i$, and $\omega_{i,t} = \varepsilon_{i,t} - \varepsilon_{r,t} + \lambda \eta_{i,t}$. Note that α_i is a constant and that $\omega_{i,t}$ is stationary with an unconditional mean of zero. In this formulation, no mean reversion (i.e., $\lambda = 0$) corresponds to the presence of a unit root in $\{p_{i,t} - p_{r,t}\}$. Thus, mean reversion can be tested using unit root tests. Balvers, Wu, and Gilliland report evidence of mean reversion in relative stock-index prices using stock-index data from 18 nations during the period 1969–1996.

1.3.6   Growth and Convergence

Economists have taken an interest in empirically investigating whether per capita outputs of nations converge to the same level, starting from the works of Baumol (1986) and DeLong (1988). Although these studies employ cross-sectional regressions, Quah (1994) and Bernard and Durlauf (1995) use a time series approach. In the latter works, two nations' per capita output converge if their difference is a stationary process with zero mean because this means that the difference is only transitory and fluctuates around zero. Thus, if there is a unit root in the difference, the convergence hypothesis is rejected. These works have generally rejected the convergence hypothesis.

1.3.7   Convergence of Real Interest Rates

Researchers in the field of international macroeconomics have been interested in testing for capital-market integration. One way of examining this issue is to study whether two nations' real interest rate differential follows a zero-mean stationary process. If it does, the two nations have essentially the same real interest rates, and their differences dissipate over time. Thus, the presence of a unit root in real interest rate differentials implies that the capital markets of the two nations are not fully integrated. This approach is taken, for example, in Herwartz and Roestel (2011).

1.3.8   Inflation Convergence

The issue of inflation convergence within European nations adopting the common currency euro has attracted much attention. This issue is important because it is related to whether the single monetary policy of the European Central Bank has succeeded in stabilizing the inflation rates of its member nations. Kocenda and Papell (1997) test this issue using panel unit root tests. Suppose that the i-th country's inflation rate, π_{it}, follows an AR(1) process:

$$\pi_{it} = \mu + \alpha \pi_{i,t-1} + u_{it}, (i = 1, \ldots, N). \tag{1.6}$$

The cross-sectional average of the inflation rates has the dynamics represented by

$$\overline{\pi}_{.t} = \mu + \alpha \overline{\pi}_{.t-1} + \overline{u}_{.t}, \tag{1.7}$$

where $z_{.t} = \frac{1}{N} \sum_{i=1}^{N} z_{it}$. Subtracting equation (1.7) from (1.6) yields

$$\pi_{it} - \overline{\pi}_{.t} = \alpha \left(\pi_{i,t-1} - \overline{\pi}_{.t-1} \right) + u_{it} - \overline{u}_{.t}.$$

If $|\alpha| < 1$, the difference between the i-th country's inflation rate and the average inflation rate is transitory; thus, it can be said that inflation rates converge. In contrast, if $\alpha = 1$, one can say that there is no inflation convergence. One can also use pairwise differences of inflation rates to examine inflation convergence as in the literature on growth convergence. In this case, the presence of a unit root implies divergence of the two nations' inflation rates. This approach is taken in Busetti, Forni, Harvey, and Venditti (2007).

1.3.9   Unemployment Hysteresis

Blanchard and Summers (1986, 1987) propose the concept of unemployment hysteresis, in which cyclical business fluctuations have permanent effects on the level of unemployment. If the unemployment-hysteresis hypothesis is accurate, high unemployment rates in an economy will persist unless government intervenes to correct them. That is, active government interventions in the labor market are supported by this hypothesis.

We discuss here how we can test the unemployment-hysteresis hypothesis following the framework of Brunello (1990) and Song and Wu (1997). To test this hypothesis, consider the Phillips curve,

$$P_t = E_{t-1}P_t - \beta(u_t - u_t^*) + \xi_t, \tag{1.8}$$

where P_t is the current inflation rate, $E_{t-1}P_t$ is the expected inflation rate of time t given information at time $t - 1$, β is a constant, u_t is the current unemployment rate, u_t^* is the natural unemployment rate, and ξ_t is an error term. Assume that the natural rate is a function of past unemployment rates, which can be expressed by

$$u_t^* = c + \alpha u_{t-1} + \zeta_t, \tag{1.9}$$

where c and α are constants and ζ_t is an error term. Substituting (1.9) into (1.8), we obtain

$$u_t = c + \alpha u_{t-1} + \varepsilon_t,$$

where $\varepsilon_t = (E_{t-1}P_t - P_t + \xi_t)/\beta + \zeta_t$. If $\alpha = 1$, the unemployment rate has no mean reversion and wanders around without being anchored to a particular point. Thus, the unemployment-hysteresis hypothesis can be tested by testing the null hypothesis of a unit root. Brunello reports some evidence supporting the unemployment-hysteresis hypothesis using Japanese data, whereas Song and Wu find evidence against it using panel data from the United States.

1.4   Other Branches of Social Science and Unit Roots

1.4.1   Political Science and Unit Roots

There is conspicuously less data analysis in political science than in economics, most likely due to the data limitations in the discipline. Still, researchers in political science have used unit root tests in their work. Some economic propositions can be probed by testing for a unit root as we have seen in the last section. In political science, however, because the presence or absence of a unit root seldom carries any structural implications (with the exception of macropartisanship, as discussed later), tests for a unit root have usually been used to decide whether to difference the time series for subsequent regressions and VARs. This subsection presents several works in political science that use unit root tests, without discussing their empirical results in full detail.

Chowdhury (1991) and Heo and Eger (2005), among others, study the relationship between economic growth and military spending. They find from applying the augmented Dickey-Fuller test (see Subsection 2.3.2) that some key variables such as defense spending and military share of GDP have a unit root, and they take the difference of these variables for subsequent regression and VAR analyses. Their empirical results suggest that the relationship between economic growth and military spending cannot be generalized across countries.

Clarke and Stewart (1994) and Price and Sanders (1993) study U.S. presidential approval ratings and UK government popularity, respectively, and relate these variables to some economic variables. In their studies, the null hypothesis of a unit root is not rejected for U.S. presidential approval ratings and UK government popularity. Subsequently, Clarke and Stewart use the error-correction model (see Engle and Granger, 1987), and Price and Sanders the AR regression with some exogenous variables. As expected, a strong economy increases U.S. presidential approval ratings and UK government popularity.

Blood and Phillips (1995) investigate the relationships among four variables: headlines referring to a recession from the *New York Times*, consumer sentiment, a composite measure of leading economic indicators, and presidential popularity. All these variables are found to have a unit root. The main conclusion from their cointegration analysis and Granger-causality test is that recession headlines significantly influence consumer sentiment.

Green, Palmquist, and Schickler (1998) and Box-Steffensmeier and Smith (1996) study macropartisanship—the aggregate distribution of party identification. They find some evidence for a unit root in some U.S. macropartisanship data, and Box-Steffensmeier and Smith argue that they are well modeled by nonstationary fractionally integrated processes. In addition, using macropartisanship data, Meffert, Norpoth, and Ruhil (2001) test for a unit root in the presence of possible structural changes, although it is not certain exactly what tests they used.

1.4.2 Sociology and Unit Roots

As in political science, sociologists usually use tests for a unit root to decide whether to difference the time series for subsequent analyses. This subsection introduces a few papers published in sociology journals that use unit root tests.

Jacobs and Helms (2001) study how the progressivity of the income tax is influenced by civil rights activities in the United States. They measure progressivity of the income tax by the logged marginal tax rates of different income groups. Explanatory variables are the number of civil rights actions, the number of riots, the percentage of nonwhites, median family income and dummy variables for a large number of crimes, and the presence of Republican presidents. They difference all these data except the dummy variables before running regressions, because unit root tests show that they have a unit root. They find that civil rights activities lead to redistributive tax codes, but that riots reduce tax progressivity.

Kristal (2010) studies the dynamics of labor's share of national income in 16 industrialized nations during the period 1960–1995. Labor's share of national income and other variables are differenced because there is evidence for a unit root in these variables. Using the error-correction model, Kristal reports that labor's share of national income is largely explained by indicators for working-class organizational power in economic and political spheres, working-class power in the global sphere, and working-class integration in the intraclass sphere.

Jacobs and Kent (2007) investigate what factors explain executions in the United States. The dependent variables in their regression study are the number of yearly executions from 1951–1998 and the percentage of respondents who support the death penalty in surveys. Both of them are found to have a unit root and are differenced in their regressions. According to Jacobs and Kent, economic inequality and Republican political strength in the states lead to both greater public support and increased executions, whereas civil rights protests reduce public support for capital punishment.

1.5   Technical Tools

This section briefly introduces some key technical tools that have been used in the literature on unit roots. No doubt, many other technical tools have been used, but discussing all of them is beyond the scope of this book. For more details, the reader is referred to such monographs as Davidson (1994) and Serfling (1980).

1.5.1   Brownian Motion

A continuous-time stochastic process, $\{W(r), 0 \leq r \leq 1\}$, is called Brownian motion or a Wiener process if it satisfies the following conditions.

(i) $W(0) = 0$, almost surely.
(ii) For $0 \leq t_0 \leq t_1 \leq \ldots \leq t_k$, $W(t_1) - W(t_0), \ldots, W(t_k) - W(t_{k-1})$ are independent.
(iii) $W(t) - W(s)$ $(t > s)$ follows $\mathbf{N}(0, t - s)$.

Brownian motion has been used to represent limiting distributions of estimators and test statistics in the literature on unit roots since Solo (1984), Phillips (1987a), and Chan and Wei (1988) started using it. White (1958) also used it to represent the limiting distribution of the OLS estimator of the AR coefficient for the AR(1) model with a unit root, but he did not provide a formal proof for the representation.

1.5.2 Functional Central Limit Theorem

Let $S_t = \sum_{i=1}^{t} u_i$, where $u_t \sim \text{iid}(0, \sigma_u^2)$. The functional central limit theorem (FCLT) or invariance principle of Donsker (1951) states that

$$X_T(r) = \frac{1}{\sqrt{T}\sigma_u} S_{[Tr]} \Rightarrow W(r) \, (0 \le r \le 1) \text{ as } T \to \infty,$$

where $[Tr]$ denotes the integer part of Tr and $\Rightarrow$ weak convergence. In the FCLT, $X_T(r)$ and its weak limits are functions of r unlike in the usual central limit theorem. When $r = 1$, this becomes the Lindeberg-Lévy central limit theorem.

There are many extensions of Donsker's FCLT. For example, Billingsley (1999) and Herrndorf (1984) extend Donsker's FCLT to the cases of stationary and ergodic innovations and of weakly dependent and heterogeneously distributed innovations, respectively. The latter type of innovation has often been used in the literature on unit roots since Phillips (1987a) introduced it to the econometrics literature.

1.5.3 Continuous-Mapping Theorem

Suppose that $X_T \Rightarrow X$ as $T \to \infty$, where X_T is a sequence of random vectors and X a random vector. The continuous mapping theorem states that $g(X_T) \Rightarrow g(X)$ as $T \to \infty$ where the function $g(\cdot)$ is continuous with probability one. This theorem has often been used to derive limiting distributions of estimators and test statistics in the literature on unit roots.

1.5.4 Stochastic Integrals

The stochastic, or Itô integral, of the form $\int_0^1 W(r) \, dW(r)$ appears often throughout this book. This integral does not allow for the use of the usual formula for the Riemann–Stieltjes integral and is not equal to $\left[\frac{1}{2} W^2(r)\right]_0^1 = \frac{1}{2} W^2(1)$. The reason for this is the excessive variability of $W(r)$. In other words, $W(r)$ is not of bounded variation so that the Riemann–Stieltjes integral does not exist with probability one. Stochastic integrals that include $\int_0^1 W(r) \, dW(r)$ as a special case are constructed using high-level probability theory as in, for example, Karatzas and Shreve (1991). To evaluate the stochastic integral $\int_0^1 W(r) \, dW(r)$, we need to use Itô's rule,

$$g(W(t)) - g(0) = \int_0^t g'(W(r)) \, dW(r) + \frac{1}{2} \int_0^t g''(W(r)) \, dr,$$

where $g : \mathbb{R} \to \mathbb{R}$ is twice continuously differentiable. For $g(W(r)) = W^2(r)$ and $t = 1$, this formula gives

$$\int_0^1 W(r)\,dW(r) = \frac{1}{2}(W^2(1) - 1) = \frac{1}{2}(\chi^2(1) - 1).$$

1.5.5   Other Integrals Involving $W(r)$

For a nonstochastic function $G : \mathbb{R} \to \mathbb{R}$ with the property $\int_0^t G^2(r)\,dr < \infty$, the integral $\int_0^t G(r)\,dW(r)$ is equal in distribution to $N(0, \int_0^t G^2(r)\,dr)$. The proof for this result can be found in Arnold (1974, p. 77). For $G(r) = r$ and $t = 1$, this gives $\int_0^1 r\,dW(r) = N(0, \frac{1}{3})$. Likewise, $\int_0^1 dW(r) = N(0, 1)$.

We also use integrals such as $\int_0^1 W(r)\,dr$, $\int_0^1 W^2(r)\,dr$, and $\int_0^1 rW(r)\,dr$. These are the usual Riemann–Stieltjes integrals for a fixed elementary event. Therefore, separate constructions of these integrals are not needed. Banerjee, Dolado, Galbraith, and Hendry (1993, p. 91) show that $\int_0^1 W(r)\,dr = N(0, \frac{1}{3})$ and that $\int_0^1 rW(r)\,dr = N(0, \frac{2}{15})$. The former result can also be proven using transformed Brownian motion as in Davidson (1994, p. 488).

1.6   Outline of Subsequent Chapters

This section outlines topics discussed in the subsequent chapters. Chapter 2 introduces basic methods for the inference on unit roots. It starts from the AR(1) model with a unit root or a near unit root and then introduces the AR and ARMA regression results with fractionally integrated errors. Dickey and Fuller's (1979) test for a unit root and its extensions are discussed next. Because Dickey and Fuller's (1979) test and its extensions are perceived to have low power, various attempts have been made to improve the power of unit root tests. Research results deriving from these efforts are introduced. Asymptotic theory for the AR models with negative and complex unit roots is also reported in this chapter.

Chapter 3 introduces inferential procedures for a unit root under model specifications that are different from the standard AR model. The topics of this chapter are unit root tests under structural changes in the nonstochastic regressors and the innovation variance, unit root tests with conditional heteroskedasticity, unit root tests in the presence of additive and innovational outliers, unit root distributions and testing under fat-tailed distributions, and unit root tests against nonlinear alternatives.

Chapter 4 introduces unit root tests against the alternatives of fractional integration, regression methods for the AR model that are robust to outliers, model-free tests for a unit root, bootstrapping methods, Bayesian inferential methods for a unit root, tests that take stationarity with or without structural changes as the null hypothesis, and tests for changing persistence.

Chapter 5 introduces a smorgasbord of topics that are relevant to unit roots, but are inappropriate to be included in the previous chapters. These include model selection, interval and point estimation for the AR model possibly with a unit root, improved estimation methods for the AR(1) model, distribution theory for the AR(1) model with unit roots, sampling frequency and tests for a unit root, and the effects of seasonal adjustments on unit root testing.

Chapter 6 is mostly about testing for seasonal unit roots, but it also discusses the periodic AR model, which is regarded as a viable alternative to the seasonal ARIMA model. The topics discussed in Chapter 6 include tests for seasonal unit roots, seasonal stationarity tests, seasonal unit root and stationarity tests under structural changes, periodic integration, and empirical evidence on seasonal unit roots.

Chapter 7 is about panel unit roots. It discusses methods of testing for unit roots and for stationarity using panel data. Topics discussed are unit root tests for independent panels, panel tests for the null of stationarity, unit root and stationarity tests under structural changes, unit root tests for cross-sectionally correlated panels, stationarity tests for cross-sectionally correlated panels, tests for seasonal panel unit roots, simulation studies, and miscellaneous related studies. Research results reported in Chapter 7 are newer than those in previous chapters, and the methods discussed there are being used extensively today.

In this book, unless otherwise stated, all the limits are taken under $T \to \infty$, with T denoting the number of time series observations. In Chapter 7, $N \to \infty$ is also used, where N is the number of cross-sectional observations.

2 Inference on Unit Roots: Basic Methods

2.1 Introduction

This chapter introduces basic methods for inference on unit roots. Naturally, it starts with the AR(1) model with a unit root or a near unit root, because this model is the cornerstone for research on unit roots. Studies in the AR(1) model were published as early as the 1940s (see, for example, Anderson, 1942; Koopmans, 1942; and Mann and Wald, 1943), but it was White (1958) who first studied the AR(1) model with a unit root. It is quite remarkable to observe how many papers on the AR(1) model have been published since then. Even today, it is easy to find papers on the AR(1) model in journals related to econometrics and statistics.

After discussing asymptotic results for the AR model, this chapter introduces Dickey and Fuller's (1979) test for a unit root and its extensions. Though there have been many unit root tests in the literature, Dickey and Fuller's test and some of its variants are still the most used in practice. However, because this test and its extensions are perceived to have low power, efforts have been made to develop unit root tests that have higher power. Research results of these efforts are introduced next. Because AR models may have other types of unit roots than unity, asymptotic theory for the AR models with negative and complex unit roots is also introduced in this chapter. It concludes with a summary and further remarks.

2.2 Asymptotic Distributions of the OLS Estimator for Nonstationary AR Models

This section presents basic asymptotic distribution theory of the OLS estimator for AR models with a positive unit root or roots near to one. Distribution theory for the AR(1) models with a unit root is discussed first, and then the discussion is extended to the AR(p) models. Then the section introduces asymptotic theory for the AR(1) models with roots near to one. Distribution theory for the AR(1) model with a unit root and fractionally integrated errors are presented last. Some of the results of this section are essential for the understanding of subsequent sections and will be used repeatedly throughout the book.

2.2.1 AR(1) Models with a Unit Root

We start from the AR(1) model:

$$y_t = \alpha y_{t-1} + u_t, (t = 2, \ldots, T) \tag{2.1}$$

$$\alpha = 1.$$

This AR model is said to have a (positive) unit root, because its characteristic equation $1 - z = 0$ has root one. The stochastic process $\{y_t\}$ is nonstationary because its variance grows over time with proper conditions on $\{u_t\}$.

White (1958) is the first paper that studied the distribution of the OLS estimator of α, $\hat{\alpha} = \left(\sum_{t=2}^{T} y_{t-1}^2 \right)^{-1} \sum_{t=2}^{T} y_t y_{t-1}$, for Model (2.1). He finds that the order of consistency of the OLS estimator for the case $\alpha = 1$ is $\frac{1}{T}$, rather than $\frac{1}{\sqrt{T}}$ as in a stationary case, and derives the limiting moment-generating function of $\hat{\alpha}$ assuming $u_t \sim \text{iid}\,N(0, \sigma_u^2)$ and $y_0 = 0$ (see Subsection 5.5.1 for the limiting moment-generating function).[1] He also writes at the end of the paper that an application of the FCLT of Donsker (1951) will give the asymptotic distribution of $T(\hat{\alpha} - 1)$ as

$$\left(\int_0^1 W^2(r)\,dr \right)^{-1} \int_0^1 W(r)\,dW(r), \tag{2.2}$$

regardless of the distribution of $\{u_t\}$. However, he does not provide a formal proof of this statement.

Fuller (1976, section 8.5) and Dickey and Fuller (1979) study Model (2.1) in greater depth than White (1958). Assuming $y_0 = 0$ and $u_t \sim \text{iid}\,N(0, \sigma_u^2)$, they derive the asymptotic distribution of the OLS estimator of α. They report that $T(\hat{\alpha} - 1)$ has the asymptotic distribution represented by

$$\frac{\left(\sum_{i=1}^{\infty} \sqrt{2}\gamma_i Z_i \right)^2 - 1}{2 \sum_{i=1}^{\infty} \gamma_i^2 Z_i^2}, \tag{2.3}$$

where $\gamma_i = 4/((2i - 1)\pi)^2$ and $Z_i \sim \text{iid}\,N(0, 1)$. The asymptotic distribution is not affected by the initial variable y_0 as long as it is $O_p(1)$. But the power of unit root tests is as is seen in Subsection 2.4.10.

---

[1] But the normalization constant for the case $\alpha = 1$ is written as $T/\sqrt{2}$, which is incorrect.

Using the series representation of Brownian motion,

$$W(r) = \sum_{i=0}^{\infty} \frac{2\sqrt{2}}{(2i+1)\pi} \sin\left(\left(i+\frac{1}{2}\right)\pi r\right) Z_i,$$

Chan and Wei (1988, corollary 3.1.3) show that random variable (2.3) is in fact equivalent in distribution to (2.2). Because Chan and Wei assume a martingale difference sequence for the errors, we find that the normality assumption made by Dickey and Fuller can be relaxed to the martingale difference errors without affecting the limiting distribution.

Dickey and Fuller (1979) also consider the AR(1) models with additional nonstochastic regressors:

$$y_t = \mu + \alpha y_{t-1} + u_t, \ (t = 2, \ldots, T) \tag{2.4}$$
$$\mu = 0, \ \alpha = 1$$

and

$$y_t = \mu + \beta t + \alpha y_{t-1} + u_t, \ (t = 2, \ldots, T) \tag{2.5}$$
$$\beta = 0, \ \alpha = 1.$$

Note that μ and β are restricted only in the DGP and that they are not restricted in estimation. Again it is assumed that $y_0 = 0$ and that $u_t \sim$ iid $N(0, \sigma_u^2)$. Dickey and Fuller derive the limiting distributions of the OLS estimators—$T \times$ (OLS estimator of $\alpha - 1$)—for Models (2.4) and (2.5) that are expressed via infinite series involving i.i.d. normal variables. But, as shown in Phillips and Perron (1988), these are equivalent to

$$\left(\int_0^1 \overline{W}^2(r)\,dr\right)^{-1} \int_0^1 \overline{W}(r)\,dW(r) \tag{2.6}$$

and

$$\left(\int_0^1 W^{*2}(r)\,dr\right)^{-1} \int_0^1 W^*(r)\,dW(r), \tag{2.7}$$

respectively, where

$$\overline{W}(r) = W(r) - \int_0^1 W(r)\,dr \tag{2.8}$$

and

$$W^*(r) = W(r) - 4 \left(\int_0^1 W(r)\,dr - \frac{3}{2} \int_0^1 r\,W(r)\,dr \right)$$

$$+ 6r \left(\int_0^1 W(r)\,dr - 2 \int_0^1 r\,W(r)\,dr \right). \quad (2.9)$$

$\overline{W}(r)$ is usually called the demeaned Brownian motion and $W^*(r)$ the demeaned and detrended Brownian motion. Restrictions on parameters μ and β in Models (2.4) and (2.5), respectively, are required to construct valid tests for a unit root, as is discussed in Subsection 2.3.1.

Quantiles of the cdfs of the random variables (2.2), (2.6), and (2.7) are tabulated in Fuller (1976, table 8.5.1). All the distributions are nonnormal, asymmetric, and skewed to the left. In addition, the distributions of the OLS estimators shift to the left as higher order time polynomials are added, making the OLS-based unit root tests less and less powerful. Section 5.5 discusses various approaches that have been used to evaluate the cdfs.

For Models (2.1) and (2.4), $\{y_t\}$ is expressed as

$$y_t = \sum_{i=1}^{t} u_i + y_0$$

and is called the integrated process. This process appears to have trends for certain segments of its realizations, but the trends do not show any regularity in terms of duration and direction. For this reason, the process is said to have stochastic trends. Financial variables such as stock prices, interest rates, and exchange rates mimic the integrated process when they are plotted. If $y_0 = 0$ and $\{u_t\}$ is i.i.d. with $E\,|u_t| < \infty$ for all t, $\{y_t\}$ is called the random walk process.

For Model (2.5), we have

$$y_t = \mu t + \sum_{i=1}^{t} u_i + y_0. \quad (2.10)$$

This process is called the integrated process with drift unless $\mu = 0$. Many aggregate macro variables mimic the integrated process with drift when plotted. Examples include the gross domestic product, consumer price index, and monetary aggregates.

Given representation (2.10), one may wonder if any restriction on μ is required for the asymptotic distribution (2.7). In fact, the OLS estimator of α for Model (2.5) is invariant to the value of μ under the restrictions $\beta = 0$ and

$\alpha = 1$. To verify this, write Model (2.5) in vector notation:

$$Y = \mu \mathbf{1} + \beta \Gamma + \alpha Y_- + u, \ \alpha = 1, \ \beta = 0,$$

where $\ Y = [y_2, \ldots, y_T]'$, $\quad \mathbf{1} = [1, \ldots, 1]'$, $\quad \Gamma = [2, \ldots, T]'$, $\quad Y_- = [y_1, \ldots, y_{T-1}]'$ and $\ U = [u_2, \ldots, u_T]'$. Because $\ y_t = \mu t + s_t + y_0 \ $ with $s_t = \sum_{i=1}^{t} u_i$, we may write Y_- as

$$Y_- = \mu \begin{bmatrix} 1 \\ \vdots \\ T-1 \end{bmatrix} + \begin{bmatrix} s_1 \\ \vdots \\ s_{T-1} \end{bmatrix} + y_0 \mathbf{1}$$

$$= \mu \Gamma - \mu \mathbf{1} + \begin{bmatrix} s_1 \\ \vdots \\ s_{T-1} \end{bmatrix} + y_0 \mathbf{1}$$

$$= \mu \Gamma + S + (y_0 - \mu)\mathbf{1},$$

where $S = [s_1, \ldots, s_{T-1}]'$. Letting $(\mathbf{1}, \Gamma) = Z$ and $P_z = Z(Z'Z)^{-1}Z'$, the OLS estimator of α for Model (2.5) is expressed as

$$\hat{\alpha} = \left[Y_-'(I - P_z)Y_- \right]^{-1} Y_-'(I - P_z)Y$$

$$= \left[S'(I - P_z)S \right]^{-1} S'(I - P_z)(\alpha S + U)$$

$$= \alpha + \left[S'(I - P_z)S \right]^{-1} S'(I - P_z)U.$$

This formula does not involve μ, showing that $\hat{\alpha}$ under the restrictions $\beta = 0$ and $\alpha = 1$ is invariant to μ. In other words, whether or not $\mu = 0$, $\hat{\alpha}$ has the same distribution. Thus, when we derive the asymptotic distribution of the OLS estimator of α for Model (2.5), we may assume $\mu = 0$ without any loss of generality.

Phillips (1987a) considerably relaxes the normal i.i.d. assumption made by Fuller (1976) and Dickey and Fuller (1979) and derives the asymptotic distribution of the OLS estimator of α for Model (2.1). To this end, he employs the FCLT. The use of the FCLT opened the floodgates for research on nonstationary time series, and it has become an essential tool in the related literature. At about the same time, Chan and Wei (1988) also began to employ the FCLT to study Model (2.1) and the AR models with complex and negative unit roots. In their work, $\{u_t\}$ is assumed to be a martingale difference sequence. Because the martingale difference sequence includes an i.i.d. sequence as a special case, their model is more general than that studied by Fuller (1976) and Dickey and Fuller (1979). However, because the martingale difference sequence is serially uncorrelated, their AR(1) model with a positive unit root is less general than that assumed in Phillips (1987a).

Phillips and Perron (1988) extend the distributional theory of Phillips (1987a) to Models (2.4) and (2.5). The main feature of the assumption on $\{u_t\}$ made by Phillips (1987a) and Phillips and Perron is that it is serially correlated but asymptotically independent. Asymptotic independence implies that u_t and u_{t-m} become independent as m goes to infinity for any t. But when m is small enough, they are correlated. Assumption 2.1 shows the details of their assumption.

Assumption 2.1 *(i)* $E(u_t) = 0$ *for all* t;
(ii) $\sup_t E |u_t|^{\beta+\varepsilon} < \infty$ *for some* $\beta > 2$ *and* $\varepsilon > 0$;
(iii) $\lim_{T\to\infty} E(\frac{1}{T}s_T^2) = \sigma_1^2$ *exists and* $\sigma_1^2 > 0$, *where* $s_T = u_1 + \cdots + u_T$;
(iv) $\{u_t\}$ *is strong mixing with mixing coefficients* α_m *that satisfy* $\sum_{m=1}^{\infty} \alpha_m^{1-\beta/2} < \infty$.

This assumption also allows $\{u_t\}$ to be heterogeneously distributed. If $\{u_t\}$ is weakly stationary with spectral density $f_u(\cdot)$, part (iii) of Assumption 2.1 is a consequence of parts (ii) and (iv). In this case,

$$\sigma_1^2 = 2\pi f_u(0) = E(u_1^2) + 2\sum_{k=1}^{\infty} E(u_1 u_k).$$

The quantity σ_1^2 is usually called the long-run variance of $\{u_t\}$, whereas $\sigma_u^2 = E(u_t^2)$ is the short-run variance of $\{u_t\}$.

Let $\overline{\alpha}$ and α^* denote the OLS estimators of α in Models (2.4) and (2.5), respectively. With Assumption 2.1 and stochastically bounded initial variable y_0,[2] Phillips (1987a) and Phillips and Perron (1988) report the following three results.

(1) For Model (2.1):

$$T(\hat{\alpha} - 1) \Rightarrow \left(\int_0^1 W^2(r)\, dr \right)^{-1} \left(\int_0^1 W(r)\, dW(r) + \lambda \right). \qquad (2.11)$$

(2) For Model (2.4):

$$T(\overline{\alpha} - 1) \Rightarrow \left(\int_0^1 \overline{W}^2(r)\, dr \right)^{-1} \left(\int_0^1 \overline{W}(r)\, dW(r) + \lambda \right). \qquad (2.12)$$

---

[2] If y_0 is a unit root process, we have an entirely different limiting theory. See Phillips and Magdalinos (2009) for details.

(3) For Model (2.5):

$$T(\alpha^* - 1) \Rightarrow \left(\int_0^1 W^{*2}(r)\, dr \right)^{-1} \left(\int_0^1 W^*(r)\, dW(r) + \lambda \right). \quad (2.13)$$

Here $\lambda = \frac{1}{2}\left(1 - \frac{\sigma_u^2}{\sigma_1^2}\right)$, $\sigma_u^2 = \lim_{T\to\infty} \frac{1}{T}\sum_{t=1}^T E(u_t^2)$, and $\overline{W}(r)$ and $W^*(r)$ are defined by relations (2.8) and (2.9), respectively. Remarkable aspects of these results are the nonnormality of the OLS estimators and their consistency in the presence of contemporaneous correlation between the regressor y_{t-1} and the error u_t. Because $\{y_{t-1}u_t\}$ and $\{y_{t-1}^2\}$ do not satisfy conditions for the central limit theorem (CLT) and the law of large numbers, respectively, we cannot apply either the CLT to $\sum_{t=1}^T y_{t-1}u_t$ or the law of large numbers to $\sum_{t=1}^T y_{t-1}^2$. The nonnormal distributions follow for this reason.

The consistency of the OLS estimators stems from the fact that the signal from the regressor is much stronger than that from the error term in the sense that $\text{Var}(y_{t-1}) = O(t)$, whereas $\text{Var}(u_t) = O(1)$. The consistency result must have been startling to researchers in econometrics and statistics at that time, because it had been well known that the regressor-error dependency results in inconsistent OLS estimators. For the first time, Phillips (1987a) discovered a case of regression in which the regressor-error dependency does not hamper the consistency of OLS estimators. Similar phenomena were later found in the literature on cointegration (for example, see Phillips and Durlauf, 1986).

By contrast, if $|\alpha| < 1$ and $u_t \sim \text{iid}(0, \sigma_u^2)$, applications of the CLT and the law of large numbers yield

$$\sqrt{T}(\hat{\alpha} - 1), \sqrt{T}(\overline{\alpha} - 1), \sqrt{T}(\alpha^* - 1) \Rightarrow N(0, 1 - \alpha^2).$$

Moreover, if $|\alpha| < 1$ and the errors are serially correlated as in Assumption 2.1, the OLS estimators would be inconsistent. In this case, both $\text{Var}(y_{t-1})$ and $\text{Var}(u_t)$ are $O(1)$ so that the signal from the regressor is not strong enough to overcome the contemporaneous correlation for consistency.

In addition, if there are no serial correlations in $\{u_t\}$, parameter λ becomes zero so that the distributions in relations (2.11), (2.12), and (2.13) reduce to those obtained by Fuller (1976) and Dickey and Fuller (1979).

West (1988) studies Model (2.4) when $\mu \neq 0$. He finds that

$$T^{3/2}(\overline{\alpha} - 1) \Rightarrow N\left(0, \frac{12\sigma_1^2}{\mu^2}\right),$$

unlike the limiting distribution in relation (2.12). This follows because $\mu(t - 1)$ dominates $\sum_{i=1}^{t-1} u_i + y_0$ in the limit, and therefore y_{t-1} behaves like $\mu(t - 1)$. But West's result cannot be used for unit root testing as is discussed in Subsection 2.3.1.

2.2.2   AR(p) Models with a Unit Root

This subsection considers the AR(p) process

$$y_t = \alpha_1 y_{t-1} + \cdots + \alpha_p y_{t-p} + u_t, \ (t = p+1, \ldots, T) \tag{2.14}$$

whose characteristic equation is written as

$$(1 - \alpha_1 z - \cdots - \alpha_p z^p) = (1 - z) \prod_{j=1}^{p-1}(1 - \gamma_j z) = 0 \tag{2.15}$$

with $|\gamma_j| < 1$ for all j. Because one of the roots of this equation is one and the rest are greater than one in modulus, the AR(p) process has one unit root and $p - 1$ stable roots. We assume that $u_t \sim$ iid($0, \sigma_u^2$) in this subsection, though this assumption can be relaxed to a martingale difference sequence.

Fuller (1976, Section 8.5) rewrites[3] Model (2.14) such that

$$y_t = \alpha y_{t-1} + \sum_{i=1}^{p-1} \rho_i \Delta y_{t-i} + u_t \tag{2.16}$$

$$= \alpha y_{t-1} + \rho' x_t + u_t,$$

where $\alpha = 1$, $\rho_i = -\sum_{k=i+1}^{p} \alpha_i$, $\rho = [\rho_1, \ldots, \rho_{p-1}]'$, and $x_t = [\Delta y_{t-1}, \ldots, \Delta y_{t-p+1}]'$. In this model, the regressor $\{y_{t-1}\}$ is a nonstationary process, whereas $\{x_t\}$ is a weakly stationary process. The purpose of rewriting Model (2.14) is to isolate a unit root into the first regressor of Model (2.16).

The OLS estimators of α and ρ, $\hat\alpha$ and $\hat\rho$, have the following asymptotic distributions if y_0 is a stochastically bounded random variable:

$$T(\hat\alpha - 1) \Rightarrow \frac{\sigma_u}{\sigma_{l\Delta y}} \left(\int_0^1 W(r)^2 \, dr \right)^{-1} \int_0^1 W(r) \, dW(r), \tag{2.17}$$

where $\sigma_{l\Delta y}^2 = \sum_{h=-\infty}^{\infty} \mathrm{Cov}(\Delta y_t, \Delta y_{t+h})$ and

$$\sqrt{T}(\hat\rho - \rho) \Rightarrow \mathrm{N}(0, \sigma_u^2 \Lambda^{-1}), \ \text{where } \Lambda = plim_{T\to\infty} T^{-1} \sum_{t=p+1}^{T} x_t x_t'.$$

These results show that $T(\hat\alpha - 1)$ has a nonstandard distribution and that standard asymptotic normality theory holds for $\hat\rho$. When an intercept term is

---

[3] This is similar to and, in fact, turns out to be an application of Beveridge and Nelson's (1981) decomposition (cf. Phillips and Solo, 1992). This decomposition refers to an algebraic relation $\Omega(z) = \sum_{j=0}^{\infty} w_j z^j = \Omega(1) - (1 - z)\Omega^*(z)$, where $\Omega^*(z) = \sum_{j=0}^{\infty} w_j^* z^j$ and $w_j^* = \sum_{k=j+1}^{\infty} w_k$. This relation can be used to rewrite Model (2.14) as Model (2.16) with $\Omega(z) = 1 - \alpha_1 z - \cdots - \alpha_p z^p$.

included in Model (2.16), $\left(\int_0^1 W(r)^2 \, dr \right)^{-1} \int_0^1 W(r) \, dW(r)$ should be replaced by $\left(\int_0^1 \overline{W}^2(r) \, dr \right)^{-1} \int_0^1 \overline{W}(r) \, dW(r)$. Likewise, when an intercept and a linear time trend are included in Model (2.16), it should be replaced by $\left(\int_0^1 W^{*2}(r) \, dr \right)^{-1} \int_0^1 W^*(r) \, dW(r)$. The inclusion of the nonstochastic terms does not bring any changes to the limiting distribution of $\hat{\rho}$.

Suppose that Model (2.14) has at least one stable root (i.e., at least one γ_j in (2.15) is nonzero). If we run OLS on Model (2.14) without the transformation, we have

$$\sqrt{T} \begin{pmatrix} \hat{\alpha}_1 - \alpha_1 \\ \vdots \\ \hat{\alpha}_p - \alpha_p \end{pmatrix} \Rightarrow N(0, \sigma_u^2 A \Lambda^{-1} A') \text{ where } A = \begin{bmatrix} 1 & & 0 \\ -1 & \ddots & \\ \vdots & \ddots & 1 \\ 0 & & -1 \end{bmatrix}$$

as shown in Choi (1993).[4] The covariance $A \Lambda^{-1} A'$, however, does not have full rank because $\text{rank}(A \Lambda^{-1} A') = p - 1$. Still, individual t-ratios on the coefficients $\alpha_1, \ldots, \alpha_p$ have a standard normal distribution in the limit.

2.2.3   AR(1) Models with Roots Near to One

This subsection introduces research results on the AR(1) model with a coefficient near one. As is shown in this subsection, there are various ways to model the AR(1) coefficient, and different asymptotic results follow depending on how it is modeled.

The OLS coefficient estimator for the AR(1) model has a nonnormal distribution in the limit when there is a unit root, whereas it has a normal distribution when the root is stable. However, when the root is close to one, the OLS estimator appears to have a nonnormal distribution in the limit. Chan and Wei (1987) and Phillips (1987b)[5] provide the first asymptotic theory that can explain this phenomenon. Chan and Wei develop their theory using the assumption of a martingale difference sequence for the errors, and Phillips employs the more general assumption given in Subsection 2.2.1. Here, I follow Phillips's exposition.

Consider the AR(1) model

$$y_t = \alpha_T y_{t-1} + u_t, \ (t = 2, \ldots, T) \tag{2.18}$$

$$\alpha_T = \exp\left(\frac{c}{T}\right) \ (-\infty < c < \infty),$$

---

[4] Choi (1993) considers a transformed AR model with m unit roots and at least one stable root.
[5] See also Bobkoski's (1983) unpublished PhD thesis.

where $\{u_t\}$ satisfies Assumption 2.1 in Subsection 2.2.1 and the initial variable y_0 is an $O_p(1)$ random variable. Because $\alpha_T = 1 + \frac{c}{T} + O(T^{-2})$, α is near to one. In the literature, $\{y_t\}$ is called the nearly integrated process. For his asymptotic theory, Phillips (1987b) uses the stochastic process

$$J_c(r) = \int_0^r e^{(r-s)c} \, dW(s). \tag{2.19}$$

This is the Ornstein-Uhlenbeck process generated by the stochastic differential equation

$$dJ_c(r) = cJ_c(r) \, dr + dW(r)$$

with initial condition $J_c(0) = 0$. $J_c(r)$ can also be represented by

$$J_c(r) = W(r) + c \int_0^r e^{(r-s)c} W(s) \, ds.$$

When $c = 0$, we have $dJ_c(r) = dW(r)$ and $J_c(r) = W(r)$.

Phillips (1987b) shows for the OLS estimator $\hat{\alpha}_T$ of α_T that

$$T(\hat{\alpha}_T - \alpha_T) \Rightarrow \left(\int_0^1 J_c^2(r) \, dr \right)^{-1} \left(\int_0^1 J_c(r) \, dW(r) + \lambda \right), \tag{2.20}$$

where $\lambda = \frac{1}{2}\left(1 - \frac{\sigma_u^2}{\sigma_1^2}\right)$. He obtains similar results for the AR(1) model with an intercept and with an intercept and a linear time trend. These explain why we observe nonnormal distributions for the OLS estimators of the AR(1) coefficient when it is close to but not exactly equal to one. The results obtained by Phillips and Chan and Wei (1987) have been used profitably for constructing power functions of unit root tests and for interval estimation of the largest AR root. These methods are discussed in Subsections 2.4.4 and 5.3.1, respectively.

Cox and Llatas (1991) study the M-estimator for Chan and Wei's (1987) AR(1) model with a near unit root (i.e., $\alpha_T = 1 - \frac{c}{T}$). The M-estimator of α_T is obtained by minimizing $\sum_{t=2}^T \rho(y_t - \alpha y_{t-1})$ with respect to α for some criterion function $\rho(\cdot)$. They derive the limiting distribution of the M-estimator assuming that the error variance is known. They find that the M-estimator is $O_p(T^{-1})$ and that the limiting distribution involves the first derivative of the criterion function $\rho(\cdot)$. The M-estimator is known to be robust to outliers when the criterion function is properly chosen, but Cox and Llatas do not deal with the issue of estimator robustness.

Cox (1991) studies the model

$$y_t - \mu_T = \alpha_T(y_{t-1} - \mu_T) + u_t, \, (t = 2, \ldots, T),$$

where $\mu_T = \sqrt{T}\nu$, ν is a constant, $\alpha_T = 1 - \frac{c}{T}$ ($c > 0$), and $u_t \sim$ iid($0, \sigma_u^2$). He derives the joint limiting distributions of the MLE and conditional MLE of μ_T, α_T and σ_u^2.

Andrews and Guggenberger (2008) show that the assumption $y_0 = O_p(1)$ plays an important role for the limiting result (2.20). They demonstrate that relation (2.20) changes when $y_0 = \sum_{j=0}^{\infty} \alpha_T^j u_{-j}$ because the initial variable is no longer asymptotically negligible. Assuming i.i.d. errors for Model (2.18), Andrews and Guggenberger report for $c < 0$ that

$$T(\hat{\alpha}_T - \alpha_T) \Rightarrow \left(\int_0^1 \tilde{J}_c^2(r)\,dr \right)^{-1} \int_0^1 \tilde{J}_c(r)\,dW(r)$$

where $\tilde{J}_c(r) = J_c(r) + (-2c)^{-1/2} \exp(cr)Z$ and Z is an independent standard normal variate. This distribution is certainly different from the distribution derived by Phillips (1987b) and Chan and Wei (1987).

The near unit root considered by Phillips (1987b) and Chan and Wei (1987) satisfies $T(1 - \alpha_T) \to c$, where c is a constant. Phillips and Magdalinos (2007)[6] consider the case where the root is farther away from unity than in Phillips and Chan and Wei. Namely, they let $\alpha_T = 1 + \frac{c}{k_T}$ with $k_T = o(T)$, which implies $T(1 - \alpha_T) \to \pm\infty$. Assuming an i.i.d. sequence for the errors and $y_0 = o_p(\sqrt{k_T})$, Phillips and Magdalinos derive the following asymptotic results:

$$\sqrt{Tk_T}(\hat{\alpha}_T - \alpha_T) \Rightarrow N(0, -2c) \text{ for } c < 0;$$

$$\frac{k_T \alpha_T^T}{2c}(\hat{\alpha}_T - \alpha_T) \Rightarrow C \text{ for } c > 0,$$

where C denotes a standard Cauchy variate.[7] The case $c < 0$ corresponds to near-stationarity and $c > 0$ to near-explosiveness. These results are similar to the asymptotics for stationary and explosive cases in the sense that asymptotic normality follows for the near-stationary case and the Cauchy distribution is obtained for the near-explosive case; these results reflect the fact that the root is far away from unity, and therefore, the effect of a unit root is much more mitigated than in the near-unit root case of Phillips (1987b) and Chan and Wei. The initial variable y_0 does not affect the asymptotic results under the given condition.

[6] Aue and Horváth (2007) obtain an analogous result for the case $T(1 - \alpha_T) \to \infty$. In this work, the innovation sequence is assumed to consist of i.i.d. random variables in the domain of attraction of a strictly α-stable law. See Section 3.5 for related discussions.

[7] Magdalinos (2012) reports similar result for the mildly explosive AR(1) model (i.e., $c > 0$), assuming a long-memory process for the error terms.

Aue (2008) studies the random coefficient AR(1) model

$$y_t = (\alpha_T + b_t(T)) y_{t-1} + u_t, \; (t = 2, \ldots, T),$$

where $b_t(T) = \omega_T \gamma_t$, $y_0 = 0$ and $\{(\gamma_t, u_t)\}$ is an i.i.d. sequence with $E(\gamma_1) = E(u_1) = 0$, $E(\gamma_1^2) = E(u_1^2) = 1$, and $E(\gamma_1 u_1) = 0$. In this model, $b_t(T)$ introduces randomness for the AR(1) coefficient. Letting $\tilde{\alpha}_T = \alpha_T - 1$, Aue assumes $T |\tilde{\alpha}_T| \to \infty$, $\sqrt{T} |\tilde{\alpha}_T| \to 0$, and $\sqrt{T} \omega_T \to 0$. Under these assumptions, he shows

$$\sqrt{\frac{T}{2 |\tilde{\alpha}_T|}} (\hat{\alpha}_T - \alpha_T) \Rightarrow \mathrm{N}(0, 1) \text{ for } \tilde{\alpha}_T < 0;$$

$$\frac{e^{T \tilde{\alpha}_T}}{2 \tilde{\alpha}_T} (\hat{\alpha}_T - \alpha_T) \Rightarrow C \text{ for } \tilde{\alpha}_T > 0,$$

where $\hat{\alpha}_T$ is the OLS estimator of the AR(1) coefficient as before. Because $T \tilde{\alpha}_T = T(\alpha_T - 1) \simeq \log(\alpha_T^T)$, Aue's result for the mildly explosive case is qualitatively no different from that of Phillips and Magdalinos (2007). The same can be said about the mildly stationary case.

In contrast to Phillips and Magdalinos (2007) and Aue (2008), Andrews and Guggenberger (2008) study the case of a near unit root very close to unity. They assume $\alpha_T = 1 - \frac{h_T}{T}$ where $|\alpha_T| < 1$, h_T is positive and $h_T \to 0$. In this setup, the root is very close to unity because $T(1 - \alpha_T) \to 0$. Assuming $y_0 = \sum_{j=0}^{\infty} \alpha_T^j u_{-j}$, they obtain[8]

$$\sqrt{\frac{1}{2h_T}} T(\hat{\alpha}_T - \alpha_T) \Rightarrow C.$$

This result shows that the OLS estimator converges to the true AR parameter arbitrarily quickly. This phenomenon is due to the signal from $\{y_{t-1}\}$, which can be arbitrarily strong depending on the rate at which α_T approaches unity. In contrast to the result by Phillips and Magdalinos, the initial variable y_0 is almost a unit root process and plays an important role for Andrews and Guggenberger's result because it dominates the behavior of $\{y_t\}$.

2.2.4 AR Models with Fractionally Integrated Errors

This subsection introduces the AR regression with fractionally integrated errors. Before doing that, it is necessary to introduce basic concepts of fractionally integrated processes. A time series $\{u_t\}$ follows a fractionally integrated

---

[8] See Phillips and Magdalinos (2009) for a related result.

process if

$$(1 - B)^d u_t = \varepsilon_t, \tag{2.21}$$

where $\{\varepsilon_t\}$ is an I(0) process with a bounded spectral density function $f_\varepsilon(\cdot)$. The time series $\{u_t\}$ is stationary when $-\frac{1}{2} < d < \frac{1}{2}$, and it is nonstationary when $d \geq \frac{1}{2}$. The spectral density of $\{u_t\}$ is

$$f_u(\lambda) = \frac{f_\varepsilon(\lambda)}{\left|1 - e^{i\lambda}\right|^{2d}}, \quad -\pi \leq \lambda < \pi.$$

Because $1 - e^{i\lambda} = 2 \sin \frac{\lambda}{2}$ and $\lim_{\lambda \to 0} \lambda^{-1} 2 \sin \frac{\lambda}{2} = 1$,

$$f_u(\lambda) \sim \frac{f_\varepsilon(0)}{\lambda^{2d}} \text{ as } \lambda \to 0, \tag{2.22}$$

where "$a \sim b$" implies that $\frac{a}{b} \to 1$. This shows that the spectral density $f_u(\lambda)$ has a pole at frequency zero when $d > 0$, a property similar to that of I(1) processes (see Section 1.2). Thus, when $0 < d < \frac{1}{2}$, $\{u_t\}$ is a stationary process and, at the same time, has a strong long-run component. It is commonly said that a time series has long memory when its spectral density has a pole at frequency zero. In addition, if relation (2.22) holds for $0 < d < \frac{1}{2}$, the autocorrelation function of $\{u_t\}$, $\rho_u(\cdot)$, has the following property for a constant c:

$$\rho_u(k) \sim c k^{2d-1} \text{ as } k \to \infty, \tag{2.23}$$

which implies that the autocorrelation function decays slowly as k grows and that $\sum_{k=-\infty}^{\infty} |\rho_u(k)| = \infty$. In fact, relations (2.22) and (2.23) are equivalent (see Beran, 1994, p. 43). The reader is referred to Baillie (1996), Beran (1994), Granger and Joyeux (1980), Hosking (1981), Marinucci and Robinson (1999), and Tanaka (1999) for additional references related to the fractionally integrated process.

Sowell (1990) studies the AR(1) model (2.1) that has errors $\{u_t\}$ generated by (2.21) with $-\frac{1}{2} < d < \frac{1}{2}$. It is further assumed that $y_0 = 0$ and that $\{\varepsilon_t\}$ is an i.i.d. process.[9] According to Marinucci and Robinson (1999), Sowell erroneously uses "Type II" rather than "Type I" fractional Brownian motion in his representation of the limiting distributions of the OLS estimator. When corrections are made properly, Sowell's results for the OLS estimator of α are

---

[9] Tanaka (1999) extends Sowell's (1990) results to the case of linear processes.

written as follows:

$$T(\hat{\alpha} - 1) \Rightarrow \frac{1}{2} \left(\int_0^1 B_d^2(r) \, dr \right)^{-1} [B_d(1)]^2, \ d > 0;$$

$$T(\hat{\alpha} - 1) \Rightarrow \left(\int_0^1 W(r)^2 \, dr \right)^{-1} \int_0^1 W(r) \, dW(r), \ d = 0;$$

$$T^{1+2d}(\hat{\alpha} - 1) \Rightarrow - \left(\int_0^1 B_d^2(r) \, dr \right)^{-1} \left(\frac{1}{2} + d \right) \frac{\Gamma(1+d)}{\Gamma(1-d)}, \ d < 0,$$

where $B_d(r)$ is "Type I" fractional Brownian motion[10] and $\Gamma(\cdot)$ is the gamma function. When $d > 0$, the limiting distribution has nonnegative support, whereas the support is negative when $d < 0$. It is remarkable that the limiting distribution undergoes abrupt changes depending on the value of d. Sowell also reports that the t-ratio for the null hypothesis of a unit root ($\hat{\tau}$ defined in relation (2.27)) has the following properties:

$$\hat{\tau} \xrightarrow{p} \infty, \ d > 0;$$

$$\hat{\tau} \xrightarrow{p} -\infty, \ d < 0.$$

Thus, the t-ratio has degenerate distributions in the limit when $d \neq 0$ and cannot be used for unit root testing.

Chan and Terrin (1995) study the AR(p) model with fractionally integrated error terms. The error terms are modeled to be a Gaussian process with regularly varying spectral density

$$f(\lambda) = |\lambda|^{-2d} L(|\lambda|^{-1}),$$

where $0 < d < \frac{1}{2}$ and $L(\cdot)$ is slowly varying at ∞ in the sense that $\frac{L(ta)}{L(t)} \to 1$ as $t \to \infty$ for any $a > 0$. The error terms include the Gaussian ARIMA(0,d,0) process as a special case. Chan and Terrin derive the limiting distributions of the OLS estimators in the presence of positive, negative, and complex unit roots. But their results do not cover the case $-\frac{1}{2} < d < 0$.

Ling and Li (2001) study the model where $\{(1 - B)^d y_t\}$ follows the ARMA(p, q) model with positive, negative, and complex unit roots. The difference between Chan and Terrin (1995) and Ling and Li is that the order of fractional integration d is estimated along with other parameters in the latter,

---

[10] "Type I" Brownian motion is defined as $B_d(r) = \frac{1}{A(d)} \int_{-\infty}^{\infty} [\{(r - s)_+\}^d - \{(-s)_+\}^d]$ $dW(s)$ ($r \in R$), where $(t)_+ = \max(t, o)$, $A(d) = \sqrt{\frac{1}{2d+1} + D(d)}$ and $D(d) = \int_0^{\infty} \{(1 + s)^d - s^d\}^2 ds$. When $d = 0$, it becomes Brownian motion, $W(r)$. Its mean and variance are, respectively, 0 and $|r|^{2d+1}$. Moreover, the increment $B_d(j + 1) - B_d(j)$, for integer j, has zero mean, unit variance, and autocovariance $\gamma(j)$ that satisfies the relation $\gamma(j) \sim cj^{2d-1}$ as $j \to \infty$ for a constant c. See Marinucci and Robinson (1999) for further details.

whereas it is a given parameter for the error terms in the former. Ling and Li report asymptotic results similar to those of Chan and Wei (1988) and show that the nonlinear least squares estimator of d has a normal distribution in the limit.

2.3   The Dickey-Fuller Test and Its Extensions

Fuller (1976) and Dickey and Fuller (1979) first proposed methods for testing the null hypothesis of a unit root for AR models. Their test, now commonly known as the Dickey-Fuller test, became the cornerstone for many subsequent unit root tests. This section introduces the Dickey-Fuller test and its extensions. The main feature of these extensions is that they adopt more general error structures than the Dickey-Fuller test. Although they enjoy the same asymptotic distributions and asymptotic local power as the Dickey-Fuller test, their finite-sample properties are all different.

2.3.1   Dickey-Fuller Test

The Dickey-Fuller unit root test employs the AR(1) models (2.1), (2.4), and (2.5) of the previous section with $y_0 = 0$ and $u_t \sim \text{iid}\,\mathbf{N}(0, \sigma_u^2)$. The null hypothesis of the Dickey-Fuller test is

$$H_0 : \alpha = 1, \tag{2.24}$$

and the alternative hypothesis of stationarity is

$$H_1 : |\alpha| < 1. \tag{2.25}$$

Model (2.1) is seldom used for unit root testing because most time series are believed to have nonzero means when they are stationary. For the AR(1) model with an intercept, Model (2.4), the intercept term is assumed to be zero under the null. Under this restriction, $y_t = y_0 + s_t$ ($s_t = \sum_{i=1}^{t} u_i$) under the null, but $y_t = \frac{\mu}{1-\alpha} + \sum_{i=0}^{\infty} \alpha^i u_{t-i}$ with $|\alpha| < 1$ under the alternative. Thus, when Model (2.4) is used, we are testing the null of a unit root process against the alternative of a stationary process with a nonzero mean. The stochastic process under the alternative is called the level-stationary process in the literature.

For the AR(1) model with an intercept and a linear time trend, Model (2.5), we assume that the coefficient for the linear trend term is zero ($\beta = 0$) under the null, which gives $y_t = y_0 + \mu t + s_t$. Thus, when Model (2.5) is employed, the null of a unit root process with drift is tested against the alternative of a stationary process with a nonzero mean and a linear trend. The latter is called the trend-stationary process.[11]

---

[11]   See Bierens (1997) for a unit root test against the alternative of stationarity with nonlinear trends.

Using Model (2.1) to test the null of a unit root against the alternative of level stationarity results in the loss of finite-sample power according to some simulation results that I have obtained. Using Model (2.4) to test the null of a unit root with drift against the alternative of trend stationarity is more problematic because it results in test inconsistency. To show this, suppose that the true DGP is trend stationary (i.e., $y_t = \mu' + \beta' t + \sum_{i=0}^{\infty} \alpha^i u_{t-i}$ with $|\alpha| < 1$) and that Model (2.4) is estimated by OLS,

$$y_t = \overline{\mu} + \overline{\alpha} y_{t-1} + \overline{u}_t,$$

where $\overline{\mu}$ and $\overline{\alpha}$ are OLS estimators and $\{\overline{u}_t\}$ denotes OLS residuals. Then, letting $\overline{y}_- = \frac{1}{T-1} \sum_{t=2}^{T} y_{t-1}$ and $\overline{y} = \frac{1}{T-1} \sum_{t=2}^{T} y_t$, it follows that

$$\overline{\alpha} = \frac{\sum_{t=2}^{T} (y_{t-1} - \overline{y}_-)(y_t - \overline{y})}{\sum_{t=2}^{T} (y_{t-1} - \overline{y}_-)^2}$$

$$= \frac{\sum_{t=2}^{T} \left((t-1) - \frac{T}{2}\right)\left(t - \frac{(T+2)}{2}\right)}{\sum_{t=2}^{T} \left((t-1) - \frac{T}{2}\right)^2} + o_p(1) \xrightarrow{p} 1.$$

This indicates that the AR(1) coefficient estimator converges to one in probability even under the alternative. Thus, unit root tests using $\overline{\alpha}$ are bound to be inconsistent. By contrast, using Model (2.5) to test the null of a unit root with drift against the alternative of trend stationarity does not suffer from this problem.

Dickey and Fuller (1979) consider using the test statistics

$$T(\hat{\alpha} - 1), \ T(\overline{\alpha} - 1), \ \text{and} \ T(\alpha^* - 1) \tag{2.26}$$

for Models (2.1), (2.4), and (2.5), respectively. These are called the coefficient test statistics for a unit root. As shown in the last section, the asymptotic distributions of the coefficient test statistics—see relations (2.2), (2.6), and (2.7)—are free of nuisance parameters.

Additionally, they consider using the t-ratios

$$\hat{\tau} = \frac{\hat{\alpha} - 1}{\sqrt{\hat{\sigma}_u^2 \left(\sum_{t=2}^{T} y_{t-1}^2\right)^{-1}}}, \ \overline{\tau} = \frac{\overline{\alpha} - 1}{\sqrt{\overline{\sigma}_u^2 \left(\sum_{t=2}^{T} \overline{y}_{t-1}^2\right)^{-1}}}, \ \text{and} \ \tau^* = \frac{\alpha^* - 1}{\sqrt{\sigma_u^{*2} \left(\sum_{t=2}^{T} y_{t-1}^{*2}\right)^{-1}}}$$

$$\tag{2.27}$$

for Models (2.1), (2.4), and (2.5), respectively. Here $\{\overline{y}_{t-1}\}$ denotes the OLS regression residuals obtained by regressing $\{y_{t-1}\}$ on $\{1\}$, and $\{y_{t-1}^*\}$ the OLS regression residuals obtained by regressing $\{y_{t-1}\}$ on $\{1, t\}$. For Model (2.1), $\hat{\sigma}_u^2 = \frac{1}{T-1} \sum_{t=2}^{T} (y_t - \hat{\alpha} y_{t-1})^2$ and $\overline{\sigma}_u^2$ and σ_u^{*2} are defined similarly. Because the OLS estimators are consistent, so are $\hat{\sigma}_u^2$, $\overline{\sigma}_u^2$, and σ_u^{*2}. The asymptotic

Table 2.1. *Asymptotic critical values of the Dickey-Fuller test*

	Significance level		
Test statistic	1%	5%	10%
$T(\hat{a} - 1)$	−13.8	−8.1	−5.7
$T(\overline{a} - 1)$	−20.7	−14.1	−11.3
$T(a^* - 1)$	−29.5	−21.8	−18.3
$\hat{\tau}$	−2.58	−1.95	−1.62
$\overline{\tau}$	−3.43	−2.86	−2.57
τ^*	−3.96	−3.41	−3.12

Note: These critical values are taken from tables 8.5.1 and 8.5.2 of Fuller (1976). If the computed value of the test statistic is less than its critical value at a chosen significance level, reject the null of a unit root.

distributions of these test statistics are given by

$$\hat{\tau} \Rightarrow \frac{\int_0^1 W(r)\,\mathrm{d}W(r)}{\sqrt{\int_0^1 W^2(r)\,\mathrm{d}r}}, \tag{2.28}$$

$$\overline{\tau} \Rightarrow \frac{\int_0^1 \overline{W}(r)\,\mathrm{d}W(r)}{\sqrt{\int_0^1 \overline{W}^2(r)\,\mathrm{d}r}}, \tag{2.29}$$

$$\tau^* \Rightarrow \frac{\int_0^1 W^*(r)\,\mathrm{d}W(r)}{\sqrt{\int_0^1 W^{*2}(r)\,\mathrm{d}r}}. \tag{2.30}$$

Empirical quantiles of the Dickey-Fuller test statistics are tabulated in Fuller (1976, tables 8.5.1 and 8.5.2) and those only for $T = \infty$ are reported in Table 2.1.

Because $\sqrt{T}(\hat{a} - \alpha) \Rightarrow N(0, 1 - \alpha^2)$ under the alternative hypothesis, we have

$$T(\hat{a} - 1) = T(\hat{a} - \alpha) + T(\alpha - 1) = O_p(T)$$

and

$$\hat{\tau} = \frac{\sqrt{T}(\hat{a} - \alpha)}{\sqrt{\hat{\sigma}^2 \left(T^{-1} \sum_{t=2}^{T} y_{t-1}^2\right)^{-1}}} + \frac{\sqrt{T}(\alpha - 1)}{\sqrt{\hat{\sigma}^2 \left(T^{-1} \sum_{t=2}^{T} y_{t-1}^2\right)^{-1}}}$$

$$= O_p(1) + O_p(\sqrt{T})$$

$$= O_p\left(\sqrt{T}\right).$$

These relations show that the Dickey-Fuller test statistics $T(\hat{\alpha} - 1)$ and $\hat{\tau}$ diverge to $-\infty$ in probability under alternative hypothesis (2.25). Thus, we reject null hypothesis (2.24) if the computed values of $T(\hat{\alpha} - 1)$ and $\hat{\tau}$ are less than their corresponding critical values. The same is true of the other test statistics.

According to Dickey and Fuller (1979), the coefficient statistic tends to yield a more powerful test than the corresponding t-ratio statistic. Moreover, the empirical power of the Dickey-Fuller test decreases as higher order time polynomials are included in the model. This happens because the null distributions shift leftward as higher order time polynomials are added.

Dickey and Fuller (1981) study the LR test of the joint null hypotheses $(\mu, \alpha) = (0, 1)$ and $(\beta, \alpha) = (0, 1)$ for Models (2.4) and (2.5), respectively. However, the LR test does not improve on the Dickey-Fuller test in terms of empirical power as their simulation results show.

The Dickey-Fuller test is based on the AR(1) model, which has limited use in practice. Various testing procedures have been developed to overcome this shortcoming as discussed in the rest of this section.

2.3.2 Augmented Dickey-Fuller Test

Said and Dickey (1984) extend the Dickey-Fuller test to the ARMA model using Berk's (1974) method. However, instead of estimating the ARMA model, they use the long autoregression model that does not require the nonlinear optimization used for the ARMA model estimation. This feature of Said and Dickey's test makes it very convenient in practice. Said and Dickey's test is often called the augmented Dickey-Fuller (ADF) test. It is one of the most often used unit root tests in the literature.

Said and Dickey (1984) consider the ARMA model described by[12]

$$y_t = \alpha y_{t-1} + z_t, \tag{2.31}$$

$$\phi(B)z_t = \theta(B)u_t,$$

where $u_t \sim \text{iid}(0, \sigma_u^2)$, $\phi(z) = 1 + \phi_1 z + \cdots + \phi_p z^p$, and $\theta(z) = 1 + \theta_1 z + \cdots + \theta_q z^q$. It is assumed that all the roots of the equations $\phi(z) = 0$ and $\theta(z) = 0$ lie outside the unit circle; that is, $\{z_t\}$ is a weakly stationary and invertible ARMA(p, q) process. Thus, the null hypothesis of a unit root and the alternative of stationarity are equivalent to $H_0 : \alpha = 1$ and $H_1 : |\alpha| < 1$, respectively.

---

[12] Chang and Park (2002) consider the case where $\{z_t\}$ follows a linear process and derive the same asymptotic distribution of the ADF test statistic as in Said and Dickey (1984).

Write $\theta(z)^{-1} = 1 - \Pi(z)$ and let $(1 - \alpha z)\phi(z) = 1 - \Gamma(z)$. Then, inverting the MA part yields

$$\theta(B)^{-1}(1 - \alpha B)\phi(B)y_t = (1 - \Pi(B))(1 - \Gamma(B))y_t \qquad (2.32)$$

$$= y_t - B^{-1}(\Pi(B) + \Gamma(B) - \Pi(B)\Gamma(B))y_{t-1}$$

$$= y_t - \Omega(B)y_{t-1}$$

$$= u_t.$$

Applying the Beveridge–Nelson decomposition, we obtain

$$\Omega(z) = \sum_{j=0}^{\infty} w_j z^j = \Omega(1) - (1 - z)\tilde{\Omega}(z), \qquad (2.33)$$

where $\tilde{\Omega}(z) = \sum_{j=0}^{\infty} \tilde{w}_j z^j$ and $\tilde{w}_j = \sum_{k=j+1}^{\infty} w_k$. Using the decomposition (2.33) for equation (2.32), Model (2.31) can be written as an AR model of infinite order

$$\Delta y_t = (\Omega(1) - 1)y_{t-1} + \sum_{j=0}^{\infty} \tilde{w}_j \Delta y_{t-1-j} + u_t \qquad (2.34)$$

$$= \rho y_{t-1} + \sum_{j=0}^{\infty} \tilde{w}_j \Delta y_{t-1-j} + u_t.$$

Under the null hypothesis of a unit root, $\Omega(1) = 1$ because $\Gamma(1) = 1$. Under the alternative hypothesis $H_1 : |\alpha| < 1$,

$$\Omega(1) = \Pi(1) + \Gamma(1) - \Pi(1)\Gamma(1)$$

$$= 1 - (1 - \Pi(1))(1 - \Gamma(1)) < 1,$$

because $1 - \Pi(1) > 0$ and $1 - \Gamma(1) > 0$ by the invertibility and stationarity conditions. Therefore, the null hypothesis of a unit root can be written as $H_0 : \rho = 0$ and the alternative as $H_0 : \rho < 0$.

Model (2.34) contains an infinite number of regressors and is inadequate for estimation. Thus, Said and Dickey (1984) use the truncated version

$$\Delta y_t = \rho y_{t-1} + \sum_{j=0}^{k} \tilde{w}_j \Delta y_{t-1-j} + u_{kt}, \; (t = k+3, \ldots, T). \qquad (2.35)$$

Note that $\{u_{kt}\}$ is no longer an i.i.d. process because of the truncation error.

Regarding the truncation parameter k, Said and Dickey (1984) assume the following:

Assumption 2.2 *(i)* $k \to \infty$ *and* $k^3/T \to 0$ *as* $T \to \infty$ *and*
(ii) there exists $c > 0$ *and* $r > 0$ *such that* $ck > T^{1/r}$.

Under this assumption, Said and Dickey (1984) show that the ADF test statistic has the same asymptotic distribution as the Dickey-Fuller t-ratio for Model (2.1), which was given earlier as (2.28). Models with an intercept and with an intercept and a linear time trend can be considered in the same manner. The ADF test statistics for these models have the same asymptotic distributions as the corresponding Dickey-Fuller t-ratios, (2.29) and (2.30).

Assumption 2.2 (i) states that k should grow to infinity as T does, but at a slower rate than T. If the latter part of Assumption 2.2 (i) were not satisfied, there would be too many regressors that induce excessive variability of the estimators. Assumption 2.2 (ii) requires that k should be large enough for the truncated model to provide a decent approximation to the true model of infinite dimension. Ng and Perron (1995) show that the asymptotic distributions of the ADF statistics can be obtained without Assumption 2.2 (ii) and that Assumption 2.2 (ii) is required only for the $\sqrt{T}$-consistency of the OLS estimators of $\tilde{w}_j$.

The ADF test is sensitive to the choice of k. If k is too large, the test tends to have good empirical size, but poor power. By contrast, if it is too small, it has poor empirical size and high power ensues. Thus, in practice, the choice of k is important. Unfortunately, Assumption 2.2 cannot provide practical guidance regarding that choice. Ng and Perron (1995)[13] recommend a sequential, general-to-specific test for the choice of k, which has the following three steps.

Step 1: Set k_{max}.
Step 2: Calculate the t-ratio for the coefficient $\tilde{w}_{k_{max}}$.
Step 3: If the t-ratio is significant, use k_{max}. Otherwise, repeat Steps 1 and 2 starting from $k_{max} - 1$.

In Step 1, the larger k_{max} is, the higher the probability of choosing a larger k becomes. Thus, a larger k_{max} induces good empirical size at the expense of power losses.

Ng and Perron (1995) report that the sequential test makes the ADF test have better size properties than such information criterion as Akaike's (1973). However, the better size property does not come freely. Agiakloglou and Newbold

---

[13] Hall (1994) also considers the lag-selection problem for the ADF test, but his model is ARIMA(p, 1, 0) so that the autoregressive lag length does not grow with the sample size. The model is obviously more specialized than the ARIMA(p, 1, q) model being considered here.

(1996) report simulation results showing that the general-to-specific test results in lower empirical power than Akaike's (1973) and Schwarz's (1978) information criteria. These works indicate that the tradeoff between size and power should be considered when making the choice between the general-to-specific test and information criteria.

Ng and Perron (2001) propose modified information criteria that alleviate the size problem of the conventional information criteria, as discussed in Section 5.2.

2.3.3   Phillips-Perron Test

Phillips' (1987a) and Phillips and Perron's (1988) test, now commonly called the Phillips-Perron test, assumes that $\{u_t\}$ satisfies the mixing conditions given in Assumption 2.1. Their test's main feature is that it does not assume a parametric structure for the serial correlation of $\{u_t\}$.

As relations (2.11), (2.12), and (2.13) show, the asymptotic distributions of the AR(1) coefficient estimators contain the nuisance parameter $\lambda = \frac{1}{2}\left(1 - \frac{\sigma_u^2}{\sigma_1^2}\right)$. But if $\{u_t\}$ is weakly stationary, σ_u^2 can be estimated consistently using OLS residuals. For Model (2.1), these are estimated by $\hat{\sigma}_u^2 = \frac{1}{n}\sum_{t=1}^{n}\hat{u}_t^2$ where $\{\hat{u}_t\}$ denotes the OLS residuals. The long-run variance, σ_1^2, is estimated by

$$\hat{\sigma}_1^2 = n^{-1}\sum_{t=1}^{n}\hat{u}_t^2 + 2n^{-1}\sum_{s=1}^{l}w_{sl}\sum_{t=s+1}^{n}\hat{u}_t\hat{u}_{t-s}, \tag{2.36}$$

where w_{sl} denotes a lag window and the parameter l is the truncation point, which is usually called the lag length. For Models (2.4) and (2.5), the long-run variances are similarly defined by using OLS residuals. Because $\sigma_1^2 = 2\pi f_u(0)$, with $f_u(\lambda)$ denoting the spectral density of $\{u_t\}$ at frequency λ, σ_1^2 is the spectral density estimator at the zero frequency. Consistency of spectral density estimators and optimal choices of the lag window and the lag length have been studied in the time series literature for decades (cf. Priestley, 1981). It is well known that the choice of the lag length is more important for the efficiency of the spectral density estimation than the lag window. In the econometrics literature, Newey and West (1987, 1994) and Andrews (1991) study the long-run variance estimation in detail. Using $\hat{\sigma}_u^2$ and $\hat{\sigma}_1^2$, λ can be estimated consistently.

Phillips (1987a) and Phillips and Perron (1988) suggest test statistics that eliminate λ asymptotically, allowing the Dickey-Fuller distributions to be used. The Phillips-Perron coefficient test statistics for Models (2.1), (2.4), and (2.5) are, respectively,

$$Z(\hat{\alpha}) = T(\hat{\alpha} - 1) - \left(T^{-2} \sum_{t=1}^{T} y_t^2 \right)^{-1} \hat{\delta}$$

$$Z(\overline{\alpha}) = T(\overline{\alpha} - 1) - \left(T^{-2} \sum_{t=1}^{T} \overline{y}_t^2 \right)^{-1} \overline{\delta}$$

and

$$Z(\alpha^*) = T(\alpha^* - 1) - \left(T^{-2} \sum_{t=1}^{T} y_t^{*2} \right)^{-1} \delta^*,$$

where $\hat{\delta} = \frac{1}{2}(\hat{\sigma}_1^2 - \hat{\sigma}_u^2)$, $\overline{\delta}$ and δ^* are defined similarly to $\hat{\delta}$, $\{\overline{y}_{t-1}\}$ denotes the OLS regression residuals obtained by regressing $\{y_{t-1}\}$ on $\{1\}$, and $\{y_{t-1}^*\}$ denotes the OLS regression residuals obtained by regressing $\{y_{t-1}\}$ on $\{1, t\}$. The asymptotic distributions of the $Z(\hat{\alpha})$ test statistics are the same as the Dickey-Fuller coefficient test statistics whose asymptotic quantiles are reported in Table 2.1. Phillips (1987a) and Phillips and Perron (1988) also suggest using corrected t-ratios that have the same asymptotic distributions as the Dickey-Fuller t-ratios. These statistics are not introduced here because their experimental results favor the coefficient test.

2.3.4 Empirical Size and Power Properties of the ADF and Phillips-Perron Tests

Various experimental studies report size distortions of the ADF and Phillips-Perron tests. Using the ARIMA(0, 1, 1) model, Phillips and Perron (1988) report that the ADF and Phillips-Perron tests show serious size distortions when there are negative correlations in the errors, though the problem is less severe for the ADF test. Using the same data-generating scheme, Schwert (1989) shows extensive simulation results illustrating these tests' size distortion problem. He concludes that the Phillips-Perron test has a more serious size distortion problem than the ADF test. By contrast, Agiakloglou and Newbold (1992) illustrate how severe the size distortions of the ADF test can be when the true DGP is unknown and involves a large MA component.

Leybourne and Newbold (1999) perform simulations for the Phillips-Perron test using true values of the short- and long-run variances. They still find size distortions for the Phillips-Perron test and conclude that the main source of the size distortion problem of the Phillips-Perron test is not the sampling errors obtained from estimating those parameters. However, compared to other simulation results, the size distortions become less severe when the true values of the short- and long-run variances are used (see table I, column C of Leybourne and Newbold, 1999). This finding suggests that more efficient estimators of the nuisance parameters can improve the Phillips-Perron test's size-distortion problem. Relatedly, Perron and Ng (1996, 1998) devise methods to estimate the nuisance parameters of the Phillips-Perron test more efficiently under the null hypothesis of a unit root. These methods are discussed in the next subsection.

There are some analytical studies of the ADF and Phillips-Perron tests' size properties. Pantula (1991) assumes the ARIMA(0, 1, 1) model with the MA component represented by $e_t - \theta_T e_{t-1}$, $\theta_T = 1 - T^{-\delta}$, $\delta > 0$, and $e_t \sim$ iid$(0, \sigma_e^2)$. Because $\theta_T \to 1$, this framework can study the effect of negative values of the MA coefficient on the asymptotic size of the unit root test. He reports that the ADF test statistic diverges to negative infinity for $\delta > 0.25$ under the null hypothesis of a unit root, as do the Phillips-Perron coefficient test statistic and t-ratio for $\delta > 0.1875$—thereby explaining size distortions of the ADF and Phillips-Perron tests under negative values of the MA coefficient. He also reports that the Phillips-Perron coefficient test statistic diverges faster than the ADF test statistic, explaining why it rejects the null hypothesis more often than the ADF test.

Galbraith and Zinde-Walsh (1999) derive the asymptotic distribution of the ADF test statistic at a fixed lag length, reporting that the distribution depends on the values of the MA coefficients. Especially when the coefficient of an MA(1) process takes negative values, the Dickey-Fuller distribution does not provide valid approximations to the true limiting distribution at a fixed lag length, thereby explaining the ADF test's size-distortion problem with a negative MA coefficient and a small lag length.

Phillips and Perron (1988) report that the Phillips-Perron coefficient test is more powerful than the ADF test when there are positive correlations in the MA(1) errors. Choi (1992b) also shows that the Phillips-Perron coefficient test has much higher finite-sample power than the ADF tests for aggregate data. However, it is generally perceived that the ADF and Phillips-Perron tests have low power in finite samples, especially when the alternative hypothesis is trend stationarity—a view reinforced[14] by DeJong, Nankervis, Savin, and Whiteman (1992a, 1992b). This finding motivated subsequent studies on new tests that outperform the ADF and Phillips-Perron tests in terms of finite-sample power.

---

[14] However, the yardstick for the perceived low power of the ADF and Phillips-Perron tests remains unclear. Gonzalo and Lee (1996) consider the empirical power of the t-ratio for the two cases $H_0 : \alpha = 1$ vs. $H_1 : \alpha = 0.9$ and $H_0 : \alpha = 0.5$ vs. $H_1 : \alpha = 0.4$. They find by using various data-generation schemes that the t-ratio for the former case tends to have higher power than that for the latter.

2.3.5 Other Extensions

Many other testing procedures have been proposed that use the same asymptotic distributions as the Dickey-Fuller test statistics. These extensions of the Dickey-Fuller test have been proposed by Said and Dickey (1985), Hall (1989), Choi and Phillips (1993), Perron and Ng (1996, 1998), and Xiao and Phillips (1998). Said and Dickey (1985) estimates the ARIMA(p, 1, q) model by the nonlinear least squares method and devise a t-ratio for the unit root null hypothesis. Hall (1989)[15] estimates the AR(1) model with MA errors by the instrumental variables method and proposes Dickey-Fuller-type test statistics. Choi and Phillips (1993) use the frequency domain regression of Hannan (1963) to devise Dickey-Fuller-type test statistics. Perron and Ng (1996, 1998) suggest a modified Phillips-Perron test with improved size properties. When the short-run variance is estimated using differenced time series, the Phillips-Perron coefficient test statistic becomes $\left(2T^{-2}\sum_{t=2}^{T}y_{t-1}^2\right)^{-1}\left(T^{-1}y_T^2 - \hat{\sigma}_1^2\right)$. Because this can be written as

$$Z(\hat{\alpha}) - \frac{2}{T}(\hat{\alpha} - 1)^2,$$

it is called the modified Phillips-Perron coefficient test statistic.[16] Obviously, it has the same limiting distribution as the Phillips-Perron coefficient test statistic. In addition, Perron and Ng recommend estimating the long-run variance using the ADF regression to improve the test's finite-sample size properties. Finally, Xiao and Phillips (1998) use the ADF regression and propose a modified Dickey-Fuller coefficient test based on it. Because the Dickey-Fuller coefficient test statistic for the ADF regression has a limiting distribution that depends on a nuisance parameter, modifying it as in Xiao and Phillips is required to eliminate the nuisance parameter dependency.

2.4 Unit Root Tests with Improved Power

This section introduces various unit root tests that attempt to improve on the Dickey-Fuller test in relation to power. In addition, effects of the initial variable (i.e., the first observation) on the power of unit root tests are discussed. All the tests of this section use asymptotic distributions different from those for the Dickey-Fuller test.

---

[15] There are some works related to Hall (1989). Pantula and Hall (1991) extend Hall's tests to general ARMA time series. A. Hall (1992) considers the model-selection problem for his IV unit root tests. Li (1995) modifies Hall's t-test to overcome its possible negative standard error problem. Hall and Lee (1996) study the asymptotic distributions of Hall's test statistics when the chosen AR and MA orders are too large.

[16] This test statistics was first proposed by Stock (1999), the working paper version of which was written in 1990.

2.4.1   Score-Based Test

Schmidt and Phillips (1992; SP hereafter)[17] use the DGP

$$y_t = \mu + \beta t + x_t, \ x_t = \alpha x_{t-1} + u_t, \ u_t \sim \text{iid} \, \text{N}(0, \sigma_u^2), \ (t = 1, \ldots, T)$$
(2.37)

for the observations $\{y_t\}$ and propose unit root tests based on scores. DGP (2.37) allows for the presence of a linear time trend under both the null of a unit root and the alternative of trend stationarity. Thus, restrictions on the coefficients of the nonstochastic terms, as in the Dickey-Fuller test, are not required. Moreover, parameters μ and β are not related to the true value of α, unlike in the Dickey-Fuller regression. Under the null hypothesis $H_0 : \alpha = 1$, the MLEs of β and $\mu_x = \mu + x_0$ are, respectively, $\tilde{\beta} = (T - 1)^{-1} (y_T - y_1)$ and $\tilde{\mu}_x = y_1 - \tilde{\beta}$. The estimates of x_t using these estimators are $\tilde{x}_t = y_t - \tilde{\mu}_x - \tilde{\beta} t$. Using $\tilde{x}_t$, SP consider the OLS regression

$$\Delta y_t = intercept + \phi \tilde{x}_{t-1} + error.$$

Because $\Delta y_t = \beta + \Delta x_t$ and $\tilde{x}_{t-1} \simeq x_{t-1}$ under the null, this regression is similar to the Dickey-Fuller regression in spirit except that it uses the restricted MLEs of the coefficients of nonstochastic terms. Letting $\tilde{\phi}$ be the OLS estimator of ϕ, SP propose using $\tilde{\rho} = T \tilde{\phi}$ and the usual t-ratio for $\phi = 0$ (denoted as $\tilde{\tau}$) as unit root test statistics. The numerator of $\tilde{\phi}$ is proportional to $\sum_{t=2}^{T}(\Delta y_t - \tilde{\beta})\tilde{x}_{t-1}$, the score vector evaluated at the restricted MLEs. Thus, the Schmidt-Phillips test statistics can be said to be based on the scores. But they are not an exact score test statistic. The exact score test statistic is the t-ratio for ϕ in the regression $\Delta y_t = \phi \tilde{x}_{t-1} + error$ and is studied in Schmidt and Lee (1991). They find that the Schmidt-Phillips test statistics perform better in finite samples than the exact score test statistic.

Using Assumption 2.1 for $\{u_t\}$, SP find

$$\tilde{\rho} \Rightarrow - \left(2 \int_0^1 \overline{V}^2(r) \, dr \right)^{-1} \omega^2;$$

$$\tilde{\tau} \Rightarrow -\frac{1}{2} \left(\int_0^1 \overline{V}^2(r) \, dr \right)^{-\frac{1}{2}} \omega,$$

where $\omega^2 = \sigma_u^2/\sigma_1^2$, $\overline{V}(r) = V(r) - \int_0^1 V(r) \, dr$, and $V(r) = W(r) - r W(1)$ is a Brownian bridge. Because ω^2 can be estimated consistently as discussed

---

[17] Sargan and Bhargava's (1983) test statistic for the random walk hypothesis is similar to that of Schmidt and Phillips. However, Schmidt and Phillips's method to handle a linear trend term, which is essential for their test, is not considered in Sargan and Bhargava. Moreover, Sargan and Bhargava do not provide proper asymptotic analysis of their test statistics, which makes it hard to use their test for the unit root hypothesis.

Table 2.2. *Asymptotic critical values of the Schmidt-Phillips test*

Test statistic	Significance level		
	1%	5%	10%
$\tilde{\omega}^{-2}\tilde{\rho}$	−25.2	−18.1	−15.0
$\tilde{\omega}^{-1}\tilde{\tau}$	−3.56	−3.02	−2.75

Note: If the computed value of the test statistic is less than its critical value at a chosen significance level, reject the null of a unit root.

earlier, the corrected test statistics $\tilde{\omega}^{-2}\tilde{\rho}$ and $\tilde{\omega}^{-1}\tilde{\tau}$ can be used in practice where $\tilde{\omega}^2$ is a consistent estimator of ω^2. Quantiles of the asymptotic distributions of the corrected test statistics are reported in table 1A of SP and reproduced in Table 2.2. The lower tails of these distributions should be used in practice. The distributions of the Schmidt-Phillips test statistics shift less to the left than the Dickey-Fuller distributions of Table 2.1 with the inclusion of a linear time trend in the model. SP report a finite-sample power gain of $\tilde{\omega}^{-2}\tilde{\rho}$ over the Dickey-Fuller coefficient test when the alternative is trend stationarity. This result can partly be explained by the aforementioned shape of the Schmidt-Phillips null distribution.

There are some works related to the SP test statistics. Ahn (1993) assumes the ARMA process for x_t and devises the score test for a unit root. Following Hall (1989), Lee and Schmidt (1994) use the IV method for the regression $\Delta\tilde{x}_t = \phi\tilde{x}_{t-1} + error$ and propose unit root tests. Oya and Toda (1998) modify the Schmidt-Phillips test using an ADF-type regression for $\tilde{x}_t$ and report simulation result comparing the Dickey-Fuller and Schmidt-Phillips tests. Their simulation results are mixed: the Dickey-Fuller test is more powerful than the Schmidt-Phillips test in some cases and less powerful in others.

2.4.2 Durbin-Hausman Test

Choi (1992a) uses the Durbin-Hausman principle to devise a unit root test. For Model (2.5), $\{1, t, y_t\}$ is used as an instrument, and the resulting estimator of the coefficient α, α_{IV}^*, is used to formulate a test statistic. More specifically, the Durbin-Hausman test statistic is defined as

$$DHS = \frac{(\alpha_{IV}^* - \alpha^*)^2}{\sigma_u^{*2}\left(\sum_{t=2}^{T} y_{t-1}^{*2}\right)^{-1}},$$

Table 2.3. *Asymptotic critical values of the Durbin-Hausman test*

	Significance level		
Test statistic	1%	5%	10%
Model (2.1)	29.70	17.97	13.16
Model (2.4)	41.34	27.69	21.97
Model (2.5)	58.95	43.41	36.39

Note: If the computed value of the test statistic is greater than its critical value at a chosen significance level, reject the null of a unit root.

where α^* is the OLS estimator of α and σ_u^{*2} and y_{t-1}^* are the same as those for the Dickey-Fuller test of Subsection 2.3.1. Test statistics for Models (2.1) and (2.4) are similarly defined. Under the null of a unit root, both the estimators are consistent for α. Because $\alpha_{IV}^* \xrightarrow{p} \frac{1}{\alpha}$ and $\alpha^* \xrightarrow{p} \alpha$ under the alternative of stationarity, the test statistic diverges to ∞ in probability. The Durbin-Hausman test's discriminating power originates from the distance $\left|\frac{1}{\alpha} - \alpha\right|$, which is larger than $|1 - \alpha|$, the Dickey-Fuller test's source of power. Thus, the Durbin-Hausman test may exhibit higher power in finite samples than the Dickey-Fuller test. Indeed, simulation results in Choi (1992a) show that there is a nonnegligible power gain over the Dickey-Fuller coefficient test.

For serially correlated errors as in Phillips (1987a) and Phillips and Perron (1988), the Durbin-Hausman test statistic can be modified as

$$DHS^M = \frac{(\alpha_{IV}^* - \alpha^*)^2}{\omega^* \sigma_u^{*2} \left(\sum_{t=2}^{T} y_{t-1}^{*2} \right)^{-1}},$$

where ω^* is a consistent estimator of $\frac{\sigma_u^2}{\sigma_1^2}$. The asymptotic distribution of this test statistic is given as

$$\left(\int_0^1 W^{*2}(r)\, dr \right)^{-1},$$

where $W^*(r)$ is defined by relation (2.9). Quantiles for this and other related distributions are reported by Choi (1992a) and reproduced in Table 2.3. Upper tails of the distributions should be used in practice for unit root testing.

2.4.3 MAX Test

Leybourne (1995) considers using a reverse regression to devise a unit root test. Instead of observations $y_1, \ldots, y_T$, he uses the reversed time series y_T,

Table 2.4. *Asymptotic critical values of the MAX test*

Test statistic	Significance level		
	1%	5%	10%
Model (2.4)	−3.04	−2.43	−2.13
Model (2.5)	−3.70	−3.09	−2.82

Note: If the computed value of the test statistic is less than its critical value at a chosen significance level, reject the null of a unit root.

$y_{T-1}, \ldots, y_1$ to calculate the ADF test statistic. His test employs the maximum of this and the usual ADF test statistic and is called the MAX test. The asymptotic distribution of the MAX test statistic for the null of a unit root with drift against trend stationarity is given as

$$
\max\left\{ \left(\int_0^1 W^{*2}(r)\,dr \right)^{-1} \int_0^1 W^{*2}(r)\,dW(r), \right.
$$

$$
\left. -\left(\int_0^1 W^{*2}(r)\,dr \right)^{-1} \int_0^1 W^{*2}(r)\,dW(r) \right\},
$$

and similarly for the null of level stationarity. Leybourne reports simulated critical values of his test statistics, which are reproduced in Table 2.4.

Leybourne (1995) shows that the MAX test is more powerful than the Dickey-Fuller test in finite samples. Leybourne and Taylor (2003) explain that the higher power of the MAX test is due to the shifted critical values: "A test based on their pairwise maximum value must have limiting critical values that are closer to the origin, or right-shifted, relative to those of the standard DF distribution" (p. 442). Leybourne, Kim and Newbold (2005) study the asymptotic local power and the finite-sample power of the MAX test, reporting that it is more powerful than the Dickey-Fuller and Dickey-Fuller-GLS tests (see Subsection 2.4.4).

2.4.4 Dickey-Fuller-GLS Test

Elliott, Rothenberg, and Stock (1996; ERS hereafter) employ the unobserved components model,

$$
y_t = d_t + x_t,\ x_t = \alpha x_{t-1} + u_t,\ (t = 1, \ldots, T), \tag{2.38}
$$

where $d_t = \beta_0 + \beta_1 t + \cdots + \beta_p t^p$, x_1 has a distribution with bounded second moment, and u_t is a stationary and ergodic process with zero mean. ERS derive the Gaussian power envelopes (locus of maximum power attainable based on a normal likelihood) for unit root testing against the local alternatives $H_1 : 1 - T^{-1}c$ using Dufour and King's (1991) methods. This is a meaningful exercise because it can show if there is room for power improvement in existing tests and it can be used to evaluate the existing tests.

For the cases $d_t = \beta_0$ and $d_t = \beta_0 + \beta_1 t$, the power of Dickey and Fuller's (1979) test statistics does not reach the corresponding power envelope, implying that it may be possible to increase the power of the Dickey-Fuller test. However, there are some caveats in interpreting ERS's power envelope. First, it depends on the initial variable x_1, as does the power of any unit root test. In ERS, it is assumed that $x_1 = 0$. Müller and Elliott (2003) extend ERS's power envelopes to various initial values and show that the power envelopes are sensitive to them. This is discussed in more detail in Subsection 2.4.10. Second, ERS's power envelopes depend on the assumption of normality. Rothenberg and Stock (1997) and Jansson (2008)[18] derive the power envelopes for unit root testing assuming nonnormal distributions for the errors. The shapes of these power envelopes are shown to be quite sensitive to the extent of nonnormality. Therefore, if the true distribution of the errors is nonnormal, ERS's power envelopes are less useful.

If $\{x_t\}$ is stationary, it is well known that the OLS and GLS estimators of the coefficients $\beta_0, \beta_1, \ldots, \beta_p$ are asymptotically equivalent (see Grenander and Rosenblatt, 1957). Using OLS for the trend coefficients, therefore, does not entail any loss of efficiency. However, the equivalence of OLS and GLS does not extend to the case where $\{x_t\}$ is nonstationary or nearly nonstationary. Using this observation, ERS propose what they call the Dickey-Fuller-GLS test. To calculate the Dickey-Fuller-GLS test statistic, let

$$a = 1 - \bar{c}/T \qquad (2.39)$$

and introduce transformations of the observations

$$y_a = (y_1, y_2 - ay_1, \ldots, y_T - ay_{T-1})',$$

$$W_a = (w_1, w_2 - aw_1, \ldots, w_T - aw_{T-1})',$$

where $w_t = (1, t, \ldots, t^p)'$. Then, assuming that the constant $\bar{c}$ in equation (2.39) is known, run the OLS regression

$$y_a = W_a \hat{\beta} + \hat{f}_a.$$

Estimator $\hat{\beta}$ is the GLS estimator of the coefficient vector $\beta = (\beta_0, \ldots, \beta_p)'$ under specification (2.39). It is perceived to be more efficient than the OLS estimator using untransformed data, although Burridge and Taylor (2000) claim

---

[18] Jansson (2008) derives the power envelopes using the limits of experiments approach (see, for example, van der Vaart (1991)), whereas Rothenberg and Stock (1997) use the Neyman-Pearson framework.

an opposite view as discussed later. Next, formulate the detrended series $y_{at}^d = y_t - \hat{\beta}' w_t$ and run the augmented Dickey-Fuller regression

$$\Delta y_{at}^d = \hat{\gamma}_0 y_{a(t-1)}^d + \hat{\gamma}_1 \Delta y_{a(t-1)}^d + \cdots + \hat{\gamma}_p \Delta y_{a(t-p)}^d + \hat{g}_t.$$

The Dickey-Fuller-GLS test statistics (Dickey-Fuller-GLS$^\mu$ and Dickey-Fuller-GLS$^\tau$) are the t-ratios for the null hypothesis $\gamma_0 = 0$ using $w_t = 1$ and $w_t = (1, t)'$, respectively. ERS suggest using $\bar{c} = -7$ and $\bar{c} = -13.5$ for $d_t = \beta_0$ and $d_t = \beta_0 + \beta_1 t$, respectively, because the power envelopes reach 0.5 at these points and because these values make the power of the test almost identical to the maximum asymptotic local power attainable. In addition to the Dickey-Fuller-GLS test, ERS also propose a feasible point-optimal test. This test, however, does not have good size properties and has been less popular than the Dickey-Fuller-GLS test for this reason. Asymptotic efficiency of this test is established in Müller (2011) which shows—in a general context that includes unit root testing as a specialized case—that efficient tests in the original problem are simply given by efficient tests in the limiting problem (i.e., only the limiting random element is observed) evaluated at sample analogs.

The limiting distributions of the Dickey-Fuller-GLS$^\mu$ and Dickey-Fuller-GLS$^\tau$ test statistics are, respectively,

$$\frac{\int_0^1 W(r)\,dW(r)}{\sqrt{\int_0^1 W^2(r)\,dr}}$$

and

$$\frac{\int_0^1 V(r)\,dW(r)}{\sqrt{\int_0^1 V^2(r)\,dr}},$$

where $V(r, \bar{c}) = W(r) - r\left(\rho W(1) + 3(1 - \rho) \int_0^1 r W(r)\,dr\right)$ with $\rho = (1 - \bar{c})/(1 - \bar{c} + \frac{\bar{c}^2}{3})$. Notably, the asymptotic distribution of the Dickey-Fuller-GLS$^\mu$ test statistic is the same as that of the Dickey-Fuller t-ratio for Model (2.1). So the critical values of $\hat{\tau}$ in Table 2.1 can be used. Quantiles of the Dickey-Fuller-GLS$^\tau$ test statistic using $\bar{c} = -13.5$ are reported in ERS (cf. Table 1) and reproduced in Table 2.5. ERS report that the Dickey-Fuller-GLS test has higher asymptotic local power and is more powerful in finite samples than the Dickey-Fuller test. As will be discusses in Subsection 2.4.10, however, this finding depends on ERS's assumption on the initial variable. With a different assumption, the Dickey-Fuller-GLS test can be less powerful than the Dickey-Fuller test.

It is commonly believed the source of the power improvement in the Dickey-Fuller-GLS test is its greater efficiency in estimating the deterministic component. However, Burridge and Taylor (2000) provide contrarian simulation

Table 2.5. *Asymptotic critical values of the Dickey-Fuller-GLS test*

Test statistic	Significance level		
	1%	5%	10%
Dickey-Fuller-GLS$^\tau$	−3.48	−2.89	−2.57

Note: If the computed value of the test statistic is less than its critical value at a chosen significance level, reject the null of a unit root.

results for the case $d_t = \beta_0$, showing that the GLS estimator of β_0 is sometimes less efficient that the OLS estimator, whereas the GLS-based test is always more powerful than the OLS-based test. Thus, the common intuition for the power improvement of the Dickey-Fuller-GLS test seems to be unwarranted. Regarding the source of the power improvement of the Dickey-Fuller-GLS test, Burridge and Taylor write, "The extra power of the GLS-type tests over the conventional DF tests comes from the fact their null distributions are shifted toward the origin, relative to that of the DF test, to a greater extent than is the distribution under the alternative" (p. 644). However, the literature has yet to answer the question of why the null distributions shift toward the origin to a greater extent. The systematic power gain of the Dickey-Fuller-GLS test still needs to be explained.

The idea of GLS detrending can be used to modify existing tests. Ng and Perron (2001) apply GLS detrending to their modified Phillips-Perron test (cf. Perron and Ng, 1996), and Xiao and Phillips (1998) use it to devise a coefficient test for a unit root framed in the ADF regression.

Elliott (1999) extends ERS's test to the case of an initial variable drawn from its unconditional distribution under the fixed alternative. He assumes that the initial variable x_1 has zero mean and variance $\sigma_u^2/(1-\alpha^2)$ and develops theory for the point-optimal and Dickey-Fuller-GLS tests as in ERS. The resulting limiting distributions are different from those of ERS, demonstrating the sensitivity of the ERS procedure to the assumed initial variable.

2.4.5   Covariate Augmented Dickey-Fuller Test

Hansen (1995) proposes a test using covariates that increases the power of the Dickey-Fuller test. For simplicity, his test is introduced using the simplest possible model. Consider the AR(1) model

$$\Delta y_t = \rho y_{t-1} + u_t, \tag{2.40}$$

where $u_t \sim \text{iid}(0, \sigma_u^2)$. Assume that there exists an additional variable $\{x_t\}$ such that $\begin{pmatrix} \Delta x_t \\ u_t \end{pmatrix} \sim \text{iid}\left(0, \begin{bmatrix} \sigma_x^2 & \sigma_{xu} \\ \sigma_{xu} & \sigma_u^2 \end{bmatrix}\right)$, and let $e_t = u_t - b\Delta x_t$ with $b = \sigma_{xu}/\sigma_x^2$.

Then the AR(1) model can be rewritten as

$$\Delta y_t = \rho y_{t-1} + b \Delta x_t + e_t. \tag{2.41}$$

Because $\{y_{t-1}\}$ and $\{\Delta x_t\}$ are uncorrelated and the variance of $\{e_t\}$ is smaller than or equal to that of $\{u_t\}$ by construction, the OLS estimator of ρ using Model (2.41) is asymptotically more efficient than that using Model (2.40). This will lead to higher power for unit root testing. The t-ratio for coefficient ρ in Model (2.41) is the covariate augmented Dickey-Fuller test. Hansen (1995) shows that it has higher empirical power than the Dickey-Fuller test unless $\{e_t\}$ and $\{u_t\}$ are perfectly uncorrelated. Using Model (2.41) along with a Gaussian likelihood, Hansen also derives power envelopes for unit root testing against the local alternatives. These envelopes show that the Dickey-Fuller test does not reach the maximum power attainable. The covariate augmented Dickey-Fuller test can also be defined for higher order AR processes straightforwardly, as shown in Hansen (1995).

Although the idea of using covariates for unit root testing is intriguing and new, the covariate augmented Dickey-Fuller test is inconvenient to use in practice. First, its asymptotic distribution depends on the correlation between $\{e_t\}$ and $\{u_t\}$. This implies that it is necessary to find critical values for each value of the correlation coefficient between $\{e_t\}$ and $\{u_t\}$, which is cumbersome. Calculating p-values is even more difficult. Second, it is necessary to identify covariates for unit root testing, which may be difficult in practice.

There are several papers related to Hansen (1995). Caporale and Pittis (1999) explain analytically why the covariate augmented Dickey-Fuller test has higher power than the Dickey-Fuller test. Elliott and Jansson (2003) develop a feasible, point-optimal unit root test that uses covariates. Last, Juhl and Xiao (2003) derive the power function and envelope of the covariate augmented Dickey-Fuller test.

2.4.6 Unit Root Test Using the Weighted Symmetric Estimator

When $u_t \sim \text{iid} \, N(0, \sigma_u^2)$, Park and Fuller (1995) observe[19] that a normal stationary process $\{y_t\}$ satisfying[20] $y_t = \mu(1 - \alpha) + \alpha y_{t-1} + u_t$ can also be written as $y_t = \mu(1 - \alpha) + \alpha y_{t+1} + u_t$. This observation led them to consider an estimator of α minimizing

$$Q(\alpha) = \sum_{t=2}^{T} w_t (Y_t - \alpha Y_{t-1})^2 + \sum_{t=1}^{T-1} (1 - w_{t+1})(Y_t - \alpha Y_{t+1})^2,$$

---

[19] Their idea originates from Dickey, Hasza, and Fuller (1984).
[20] This comes from an unobserved components model $y_t = \mu + x_t, x_t = \alpha x_{t-1} + u_t$.

where $w_t = T^{-1}(t-1)$ are weights and $Y_t = y_t - \check{y}$ with $\check{y} = T^{-1}\sum_{t=1}^{T} y_t$. The resulting estimator,

$$\hat{\alpha}_{ws} = \frac{\sum_{t=2}^{T} Y_t Y_{t-1}}{\sum_{t=2}^{T-1} Y_t^2 + T^{-1}\sum_{t=1}^{T} Y_t^2},$$

is called the weighted symmetric estimator.

For unit root testing, they propose using the coefficient test statistic,

$$T(\hat{\alpha}_{ws} - 1), \tag{2.42}$$

and the t-ratio

$$\hat{\tau}_{ws} = (\hat{\alpha}_{ws} - 1)\left(\sum_{t=2}^{T-1} Y_t^2 + T^{-1}\sum_{t=1}^{T} Y_t^2\right)^{1/2} \hat{\sigma}_{ws}^{-1}, \tag{2.43}$$

where $\hat{\sigma}_{ws}^2 = (T-2)^{-1} Q(\hat{\alpha}_{ws})$. Test statistics (2.42) and (2.43) have asymptotic distributions represented by

$$\left(\int_0^1 \overline{W}^2(r)\,dr\right)^{-1}\left(\int_0^1 \overline{W}(r)\,dW(r) - \int_0^1 W^2(r)\,dr + 2\left(\int_0^1 W(r)\,dr\right)^2\right)$$

and

$$\left(\int_0^1 \overline{W}^2(r)\,dr\right)^{-1/2}\left(\int_0^1 \overline{W}(r)\,dW(r) - \int_0^1 W^2(r)\,dr + 2\left(\int_0^1 W(r)\,dr\right)^2\right),$$

respectively. The empirical 5% critical values of these statistics are -13.07 and -2.50, respectively, as reported in Pantula, Gonzalez-Farias, and Fuller (1994, table 2). These test statistics are also extended to higher order AR processes using the ADF regression. Only $\hat{\tau}_{ws}$ can be used in this case, and it has the same asymptotic distribution as in the AR(1) case. The test is also extended to the case of a linear time trend. Relevant test statistics are defined in the same way by replacing Y_t with $y_t - \hat{a} - \hat{b}t$ where $\hat{a}$ and $\hat{b}$ are the OLS estimators obtained by regressing y_t on $\{1, t\}$.

When the alternative is a level-stationary process with its initial observation satisfying $y_1 \sim N(\mu, (1-\alpha^2)^{-1}\sigma_u^2)$, the test using the weighted symmetric estimator tends to have higher empirical power than the Dickey-Fuller and Dickey-Fuller-GLS tests. Pantula, Gonzalez-Farias, and Fuller (1994) also consider a test statistic using the unconditional maximum likelihood estimator, with its initial observation satisfying $y_1 \sim N(\mu, (1-\alpha^2)^{-1}\sigma_u^2)$. Compared to those based on the weighted symmetric estimator, this requires much more complicated calculations, but shows a similar performance.

Table 2.6. *Asymptotic critical values of the recursive mean-adjustment unit root test*

Test statistic	Significance level		
	1%	5%	10%
Coefficient test statistic	-15.8	-9.69	-7.07
t-ratio	-2.53	-1.88	-1.54

Note: If the computed value of the test statistic is less than its critical value at a chosen significance level, reject the null of a unit root.

2.4.7 Recursive Mean Adjustment for Unit Root Testing

Shin and So (2001) propose an alternative method of demeaning to construct unit root tests. For the unobserved components model

$$y_t = \mu + x_t, \ x_t = \alpha x_{t-1} + u_t, \ u_t \sim \text{iid}(0, \sigma_u^2), \tag{2.44}$$

they consider estimating the mean recursively and suggest using the mean-adjusted observations

$$\tilde{y}_t = y_t - \tilde{\mu}_{t-1} \text{ and } \tilde{y}_{t-1} = y_{t-1} - \tilde{\mu}_{t-1},$$

where $\tilde{\mu}_{t-1} = (t-1)^{-1} \sum_{j=1}^{t-1} y_j$. Note that $\tilde{\mu}_{t-1}$ is used both for $\tilde{y}_t$ and $\tilde{y}_{t-1}$. Because

$$\tilde{y}_t = \alpha \tilde{y}_{t-1} + (1-\alpha)(\mu - \tilde{\mu}_{t-1}) + u_t,$$

the Dickey-Fuller coefficient test statistic and t-ratio can be devised by regressing $\{\tilde{y}_t\}$ on $\{\tilde{y}_{t-1}\}$ under $\alpha = 1$. The asymptotic distributions of these statistics are

$$\left(\int_0^1 \left(W(r) - \tilde{W}(r) \right)^2 \, dr \right)^{-1} \int_0^1 \left(W(r) - \tilde{W}(r) \right)^2 \, dW(r),$$

and

$$\left(\int_0^1 \left(W(r) - \tilde{W}(r) \right)^2 \, dr \right)^{-1/2} \int_0^1 \left(W(r) - \tilde{W}(r) \right)^2 \, dW(r),$$

respectively, where $\tilde{W}(r) = r^{-1} \int_0^r W(s) \, ds$. Shin and So report its simulated asymptotic quantiles, which are reproduced in Table 2.6. The t-ratio is extended to higher order AR processes using the ADF regression. Shin and So also consider the Phillips-Perron test using the recursive mean adjustment.

Because $\{\tilde{y}_{t-1}\}$ is uncorrelated with $\{u_t\}$ under the null, the AR regression using $\{\tilde{y}_{t-1}\}$ avoids the well-known bias problem of the OLS estimator. Under the alternative hypothesis, the finite-sample AR bias is reduced as analyzed in

Sul, Phillips, and Choi (2005). This leads to finite-sample power higher than that of the Dickey-Fuller test as reported in Shin and So (2001).

When a linear time trend term βt is added to Model (2.44), one may extend the mean-adjustment transformation (2.45) and consider using

$$\tilde{y}_t = y_t - \tilde{\mu}_{t-1} - \tilde{\beta}_{t-1}(t-1) \text{ and } \tilde{y}_{t-1} = y_{t-1} - \tilde{\mu}_{t-1} - \tilde{\beta}_{t-1}(t-1), \quad (2.45)$$

where $(\tilde{\mu}_{t-1}, \tilde{\beta}_{t-1})$ are obtained by regressing $\{y_{t-1}\}$ on $\{1, t-1\}$. However, as shown by Sul, Phillips, and Choi (2005) and Rodrigues (2006), the transformation does not fully detrend the data. Thus, the Dickey-Fuller test using the transformations in (2.45) will have an asymptotic distribution that depends on the unknown value of β, making the test unusable for empirical applications. Alternatively, Taylor (2002) considers using $\breve{y}_t = y_t - \breve{\mu}_t - \breve{\beta}_t t$ and $\breve{y}_{t-1} = y_{t-1} - \breve{\mu}_{t-1} - \breve{\beta}_{t-1}(t-1)$, where $(\breve{\mu}_t, \breve{\beta}_t)$ are obtained by regressing $\{y_t\}$ on $\{1, t\}$. He shows that these transformations effectively detrend the data and suggests using them for seasonal and nonseasonal unit root testing. See Subsection 6.2.2 for a related discussion.

2.4.8   Variance Ratio Test Using Wavelets

Fan and Gençay (2010) propose a variance ratio test that uses wavelets. The reader is referred to Percival and Walden (2000) and Tanaka (2008) for the wavelet analysis of time series. The discrete wavelet transformation of a time series can separate out their high- and low-frequency components. When the unit-scale Haar discrete wavelet transformation is used for Model (2.1) with even T, the short- and long-run components (or wavelet and scaling coefficients in the terminology of the wavelet analysis) are written, respectively, as

$$W_{t,1} = \frac{1}{\sqrt{2}}(y_{2t} - y_{2t-1}), \quad \left(t = 1, \ldots, \frac{T}{2}\right);$$

$$V_{t,1} = \frac{1}{\sqrt{2}}(y_{2t} + y_{2t-1}), \quad \left(t = 1, \ldots, \frac{T}{2}\right).$$

Under the null hypothesis of a unit root, $\sum_{t=1}^{T/2} V_{t,1}^2$ dominates $\sum_{t=1}^{T/2} W_{t,1}^2$ because the former is $O_p(T^2)$ whereas the latter is $O_p(T)$. Thus, Fan and Gençay's variance ratio statistic is constructed as

$$\hat{S}_T = \frac{\sum_{t=1}^{T/2} V_{t,1}^2}{\sum_{t=1}^{T/2} V_{t,1}^2 + \sum_{t=1}^{T/2} W_{t,1}^2}.$$

When Assumption (2.1) holds, $T(\hat{S}_T - 1) \Rightarrow -\omega^2 \left(\int_0^1 W^2(r)\,dr\right)^{-1}$ ($\omega^2 = \frac{\sigma_u^2}{\sigma_1^2}$) under the null hypothesis of a unit root. Thus, if $\hat{\omega}^2$ is a consistent estimator of ω^2, $T(\hat{S}_T - 1)/\hat{\omega}^2$ can be used as a test statistic that is distributed as $-\left(\int_0^1 W^2(r)\,dr\right)^{-1}$ in the limit. Interestingly, this limiting distribution is the same as that of the Durbin-Hausman test statistic with a sign change (see Subsection 2.4.2). Fan and Gençay extend their test to models with nonstochastic terms and illustrate the use of their variance ratio test that employs more general types of wavelet filters. When the errors are negatively correlated, the test used by Fan and Gençay shows higher empirical power than the Dickey-Fuller-GLS test of ERS.

2.4.9 Nearly Efficient Likelihood Ratio Test

Jansson and Nielsen (2012a) employ Model (2.38) with $\alpha = 1 - \frac{c}{T}$ and derive an LR test statistic for the unit root hypothesis. For simplicity, we assume $u_t \sim \text{iid} \, N(0, \sigma_u^2)$, although Jansson and Nielsen (2012a) allow AR dynamics for the error terms. Their quasi-LR[21] test statistic is written as

$$LR_T = \max_{\bar{\alpha} \leq 1} \mathcal{L}(\bar{\alpha}, \hat{\sigma}_u^2) - \mathcal{L}(1, \hat{\sigma}_u^2),$$

where $\mathcal{L}(\alpha, \sigma_u^2) = -\frac{T}{2}\log(\sigma_u^2) - \frac{1}{2\sigma_u^2}Y_\alpha' Y_\alpha + \frac{1}{2\sigma_u^2}Y_\alpha' D_\alpha(D_\alpha' D_\alpha)^{-1}D_\alpha' Y_\alpha$, Y_α and D_α are matrices with row $t = 2, \ldots, T$ given by $(1 - \alpha B)y_t$ and $(1 - \alpha B)d_t$, respectively, and $\hat{\sigma}_u^2$ is an estimator of σ_u^2 obtained from the differenced null model $\Delta y_t = \Delta d_t + u_t$ in the usual manner. Note that $\hat{\sigma}_u^2$ is consistent under the local alternatives $\alpha = 1 - \frac{c}{T}$. The limiting distributions of the quasi-LR test statistics under the local alternatives $\alpha = 1 - \frac{c}{T}$ are

$$LR_T \Rightarrow \max_{\bar{c} \leq 0} \Lambda_c(\bar{c}) \text{ for } d_t = 1;$$

$$LR_T \Rightarrow \max_{\bar{c} \leq 0} \Lambda_c^\tau(\bar{c}) \text{ for } d_t = (1, t)',$$

where $\Lambda_c(\bar{c}) = \bar{c}\left(\int_0^1 J_c(r)\,dJ_c(r)\right) - \frac{1}{2}\bar{c}^2 \int_0^1 J_c^2(r)\,dr$, $\Lambda_c^\tau(\bar{c}) = \Lambda_c(\bar{c}) + \frac{1}{2} \times \left((1 - \bar{c})J_c(1) + \bar{c}^2 \int_0^1 r J_c(r)\,dr\right)^2 / \left(1 - \bar{c} + \bar{c}^2/3\right) - \frac{1}{2}J_c^2(1)$ and $J_c(r)$ is defined by equation (2.19). The asymptotic critical values of the quasi-LR test statistics are given in Table 2.7.

---

[21] The estimator of σ_u^2 that Jansson and Nielsen (2012a) use is the MLE only when $\alpha = 1$. Thus, strictly speaking, their test statistic is not the LR.

Table 2.7. *Asymptotic critical values of Jansson and Nielsen's (2012a) test*

	Significance level		
Test statistic	1%	5%	10%
Mean case	3.29	1.88	1.31
Linear trend case	5.82	4.05	3.26

Note: If the computed value of the test statistic is greater than its critical value at a chosen significance level, reject the null of a unit root.

Jansson and Nielsen (2012a) show that their test is nearly efficient in the sense that its asymptotic local power curves reach ERS's Gaussian power envelope curves. But, similar to ERS, this optimal property depends on the assumption of nearly negligible initial variable. Further studies are needed to investigate how their test performs under a more general assumption on the initial variable. In addition, Jansson and Nielsen's (2012a) result rests on the assumption of Gaussianity. The property of the test when it does not hold remains unresolved. Jansson and Nielsen (2012b) show that their test is sometimes more powerful than ERS's test in finite samples, which is an important achievement.

2.4.10   Initial Variables and the Power of Unit Root Tests

This chapter has described various tests that improve on the Dickey-Fuller test in terms of power. However, it is difficult to conclude which test should be most preferred because no single test is uniformly most powerful. In particular, the initial variable x_1 in equation (2.38) significantly affects the power of unit root tests, which makes it difficult to compare different tests. To study the impact of the initial variable on unit root tests, Müller and Elliott (2003) employ Model (2.38) to consider a point-optimal test for the alternative hypothesis $\alpha = \alpha^0 < 1$. More specifically, they assume a Gaussian linear process structure for the innovation process $\{u_t\}$ and let

$$x_1 \sim \mathbf{N}\left(0, k \times \mathrm{Var}\left(\sum_{j=0}^{\infty} \alpha^{0j} u_{-j}\right)\right), \tag{2.46}$$

where k is a constant that controls the magnitude of the initial variable. Under this specification, they derive a point-optimal test statistic that maximizes a weighted power criterion with respect to the initial variable. Obviously, the test statistic depends on the values of α^0 and k. Müller and Elliott develop asymptotic theory for the test statistic under the local alternatives (i.e., $\alpha^0 = 1 - T^{-1}\bar{c}$) and use it to derive Gaussian power envelopes that relate the power of the test to the magnitude of the initial variable under $k = 0, 1, \infty$. They show that the power envelopes display quite different characteristics depending on the value of k.

The point-optimal test is found to be related to existing tests. Müller and Elliott (2003) show that the Dickey-Fuller t-ratio corresponds to the point-optimal test with a large value of k and the Dickey-Fuller-GLS t-ratio with a small value of k. This finding has two implications: (i) if the initial variable takes relatively small values, the Dickey-Fuller-GLS test is approximately optimal, and (ii) if the initial variable takes relatively large values, the Dickey-Fuller test is optimal.

Based on Müller and Elliott's (2003) conclusions, Harvey and Leybourne (2005) consider combining the Dickey-Fuller t-ratio and the Dickey-Fuller-GLS test statistic with weights depending on the estimate of the initial variable. More specifically, using Model (2.38) and letting σ_u^2 be the variance of u_t, Harvey and Leybourne assume $x_1 = \omega\sigma$, where $\sigma^2 = \frac{\sigma_u^2}{1-\alpha^2}$ and

$$\omega \sim \mathbf{N}\left(\mu_\omega \mathbf{1}\left\{\sigma_\omega^2 = 0\right\}, \sigma_\omega^2\right).$$

Depending on the values of σ_ω^2, there are three specifications for x_1: (i) $\sigma_\omega^2 > 0$; $\sigma_\omega^2 \neq 1$; $x_1 \sim \mathbf{N}(0, \sigma^2\sigma_\omega^2)$, (ii) $\sigma_\omega^2 = 1$; $x_1 \sim \mathbf{N}(0, \sigma^2)$, and (iii) $\sigma_\omega^2 = 0$; $x_1 = \mu_\omega\sigma$. In Case (i), we have an initial variable similar to (2.46) considered by Müller and Elliott. Case (ii) is the usual assumption used for the unconditional maximum likelihood estimation. Case (iii) is the condition for the conditional maximum likelihood estimation. Thus, Harvey and Leybourne's specification of the initial variable can handle various cases considered in the literature regarding the initial variable. Using their framework, Harvey and Leybourne simulate the power envelopes of the Dickey-Fuller and the Dickey-Fuller-GLS test statistics, which show their dependence on σ_ω and μ_ω.

Harvey and Leybourne (2005) estimate $|\omega|$ using the relation

$$\omega = \frac{y_1 - d_1}{\sigma}$$

and the estimators of d_1 and σ. Then, they combine the ADF and Dickey-Fuller-GLS test statistics with weights $1 - \exp(-0.4\,|\hat{\omega}|)$ and $\exp(-0.4\,|\hat{\omega}|)$, respectively. Thus, if $|\hat{\omega}|$ is large, less weight is given to the Dickey-Fuller-GLS test statistic, and vice versa. They find their test to be less sensitive to the initial variable than the Dickey-Fuller and Dickey-Fuller-GLS tests.

If a unit root test produces inferential results that depend heavily on the initial variable's magnitude, such results can vary considerably with sampling periods. This is certainly undesirable. To tackle this issue, Elliott and Müller (2006) develop tests whose power does not vary much with the magnitude of the initial variable; these tests are based on the theory of Müller and

Elliott (2003) and Dufour and King (1991). Their main idea is to choose k in Müller and Elliott's test statistic such that the initial variable does not affect the local power of the test. Simulation results show that their test has stable power over a wide range of initial variables. However, the power stability comes at a price: Elliott and Müller's test is less powerful than the Dickey-Fuller test when the initial variable takes large values.

Similar to Harvey and Leybourne (2005), Harvey and Leybourne (2006) consider combining Elliott and Müller's (2006) point-optimal test statistic and the Dickey-Fuller t-ratio. They report that their combination test tends to have higher power than Elliott and Müller's point-optimal test in finite samples.

Harvey, Leybourne, and Taylor (2009) suggest using a simple decision rule according to which the unit root null hypothesis is rejected if either the Dickey-Fuller-GLS or Dickey-Fuller test rejects. Their test statistic is written for the mean case as

$$\text{Dickey-Fuller-GLS}^\mu \mathbf{1}\{\text{Dickey-Fuller-GLS}^\mu < \tau_\gamma cv_\gamma^\mu\}$$

$$+\text{ADF}^\mu \mathbf{1}\{\text{Dickey-Fuller-GLS}^\mu \geq \tau_\gamma cv_\gamma^\mu\},$$

where ADF^μ denotes the ADF test statistic for the mean case, cv_γ^μ is the critical value of the Dickey-Fuller-GLS$^\mu$ at an asymptotic size of γ, and τ_γ is a scaling constant that keeps the overall asymptotic size of the test at γ. If Dickey-Fuller-GLS$^\mu < \tau_\gamma cv_\gamma^\mu$, this test statistic is equivalent to Dickey-Fuller-GLS$^\mu$. Otherwise, it is the same as ADF^μ. For $\gamma = 0.1$, 0.05, and 0.01, $\tau_\gamma = 1.126$, 1.095, and 1.065, respectively. For the model with an intercept and a linear time trend, the test statistic is similarly defined with $\tau_\gamma = 1.070$, 1.058, and 1.043 for $\gamma = 0.1$, 0.05, and 0.01, respectively. Harvey, Leybourne, and Taylor's procedure is shown to perform better than Harvey and Leybourne's (2005, 2006).

2.4.11   Uncertainty over the Trend

In practice, it is uncertain whether a linear time trend should be included in the model for unit root testing. When it is included unnecessarily, the power of unit root tests is decreased. However, when the alternative hypothesis of trend stationarity holds and the trend term is omitted, unit root tests become inconsistent (see Subsection 2.3.1 for related discussions). Harris, Harvey, Leybourne, and Taylor (2009)[22] deal with this practically important problem. They recommend a simple decision rule whereby the unit root null hypothesis

---

[22] To deal with the uncertainty over both the trend and initial condition, Harvey, Leybourne, and Taylor (2012b) suggest decision rules based on the union of rejections of four standard unit root tests—Dickey-Fuller-GLS and Dickey-Fuller tests with either mean or mean and trend. See Smeekes and Taylor (2012) for their bootstrapped versions.

is rejected when either Dickey-Fuller-GLS$^\mu$ and Dickey-Fuller-GLS$^\tau$ yields a rejection. This simple union of a rejections-based decision rule can bring noticeable power gain in finite samples.

To be more specific, their test statistic takes the form

$$\text{Dickey-Fuller-GLS}^\mu \mathbf{1}\{\text{Dickey-Fuller-GLS}^\mu < \tau_y cv_y^\mu\}$$

$$+\text{Dickey-Fuller-GLS}^\tau \mathbf{1}\{\text{Dickey-Fuller-GLS}^\tau \geq \tau_y cv_y^\tau\},$$

where cv_y^μ and cv_y^τ are the critical values of the Dickey-Fuller-GLS$^\mu$ and Dickey-Fuller-GLS$^\tau$ at an asymptotic size of y, respectively, and τ_y is a scaling constant that keeps the overall asymptotic size of the test at y. For $y = 0.1$, 0.05, and 0.01, $\tau_y = 1.123$, 1.095, and 1.064, respectively. Harvey, Leybourne, and Taylor (2009) also consider the strategy of pretesting for the presence of a trend and choosing a unit root test statistic. But they conclude that this strategy is inferior to the union of rejections-based rule.

2.5 Asymptotic Theory for Complex and Negative Unit Roots

The discussion so far has focused on a positive unit root, but there can be complex and negative unit roots in the AR process. This section introduces asymptotic theory for the AR model with either complex unit roots or a negative one.

We consider theory for the AR(1) model with a negative unit root first because this is simpler. When the observations $\{y_t\}$ follow the AR(1) model

$$y_t = \alpha y_{t-1} + u_t, \ (t = 2, \ldots, T)$$

$$\alpha = -1,$$

$\{y_t\}$ has a negative unit root. The asymptotic distribution of the OLS estimator of α, derived by Chan and Wei (1988) under the assumption of martingale difference errors,[23] is represented by

$$T(\hat{\alpha} + 1) \Rightarrow -\left(\int_0^1 W^2(r)\,dr\right)^{-1} \int_0^1 W(r)\,dW(r),$$

which shows that the distribution is the mirror image of that for a positive unit root (see Subsection 2.2.1 for the distribution under a positive unit root). If one is interested in testing for a negative unit root, the tables in Fuller (1976) can be used.

When the observations $\{y_t\}$ are generated by the model

$$y_t = \alpha_1 y_{t-1} + \alpha_2 y_{t-2} + u_t,$$

---

[23] See also Fuller (1976).

the characteristic equation of which has roots $\exp(i\theta)$ and $\exp(-i\theta)$ with $\theta \in (0, \pi)$, $\{y_t\}$ has complex unit roots.[24] When there are complex unit roots, we have

$$|\alpha_1| = 2\cos(\theta) \text{ and } \alpha_2 = -1.$$

The limiting distribution of the OLS estimator of α_2, $\hat{\alpha}_2$, is derived by Ahtola and Tiao (1987), Chan and Wei (1988), and Tanaka (1998). Ahtola and Tiao use the method of Dickey and Fuller (1979), and the latter two use the FCLT. Chan and Wei's result, obtained under the assumption of martingale difference errors, is represented as

$$T(\hat{\alpha}_2 + 1) \Rightarrow \left(\int_0^1 \left(W_1^2(r) + W_2^2(r) \right) dr \right)^{-1} \left(2 - W_1^2(1) - W_2^2(1) \right),$$

(2.47)

where $W_1(\cdot)$ and $W_2(\cdot)$ are independent Brownian motions. Because this distribution does not depend on θ, it can be used to test for complex unit roots following the same methods as in Dickey and Fuller. Asymptotic quantiles of $T(\hat{\alpha}_2 + 1)$ are reported in Ahtola and Tiao. In addition, Ahtola and Tiao report the limiting distribution of the OLS estimator of α_1, which depends on θ. Tanaka extends the results of Chan and Wei and Ahtola and Tiao to the case of serially correlated errors. Interestingly, he reports that the limiting distribution of $\hat{\alpha}_2$ depends on θ when the error terms are serially correlated.

Although the test using $\hat{\alpha}_2$ and its limiting distribution (2.47) is for the case of white noise errors, Bierens (2001) and Gregoir (2006) propose tests for complex unit roots for the case of serially correlated errors. Bierens constructs his test statistic using periodograms and applies it to U.S. unemployment data. He argues that the U.S. business cycles are well described by the presence of complex unit roots. Gregoir devises various test statistics using OLS and ERS's procedures. He recommends using ERS's GLS-based test statistic.

2.6   Summary and Further Remarks

This chapter introduced basic asymptotic theory for the AR model with unit roots or roots near to unity. Furthermore, it introduced the most important test in the literature on unit roots—the Dickey-Fuller test—and its variants. Tests that show higher power than the Dickey-Fuller test were also discussed.

This chapter alone introduced more than 10 tests for a unit root. After reading it, the reader may pose a legitimate question: "What test should I use

---

[24] Note that $|\exp(i\theta)| = |\exp(-i\theta)| = \sqrt{\sin^2(\theta) + \cos^2(\theta)} = 1$.

in practice? If I use tests programmed in commercial software such as the ADF and Phillips-Perron tests, am I losing something?" My answer to this question is a debatable "Not much," because tests that outperform the ADF and Phillips-Perron tests do not tend to do so significantly at moderate sample sizes.

However, if sample sizes are small and the power of unit root tests is a real concern, it is advisable to try other tests that outperform the ADF and Phillips-Perron tests. They may provide test results different from those of the ADF and Phillips-Perron tests. It is difficult to tell which one should be preferred among the more powerful tests, because no test seems to be dominant. Moreover, performance of these tests depend on the initial variable and the trend coefficient, which makes comparisons more complex. The best practical strategy is to try as many unit root tests as possible and see whether there are any differences, although doing so requires a lot of efforts. It is hoped that commercial computational software will incorporates more of the unit root tests of this chapter in the future so that researchers can have easier access to them.

3 Unit Root Tests under Various Model Specifications

3.1 Introduction

Chapter 2 used the standard AR model for the inference on unit roots. However, one may contemplate testing for a unit root using different model specifications, and doing so might result in different inferential results. This chapter introduces inferential procedures for a unit root that use model specifications that depart from the standard AR model.

The first section of this chapter addresses unit root tests under structural changes in the nonstochastic regressors added to the AR model. This research area, initiated by Perron (1989), received much attention because the presence of structural changes in the parameters of nonstochastic regressors sometimes yields different inferential results. It also provided further challenges for econometric theorists and resulted in various new inferential procedures. The second section examines unit root tests with conditional heteroskedasticity. Because conditional heteroskedasticity is known to be prevalent in high-frequency financial time series, it is natural to consider unit root testing in its presence. As is discussed, the presence of conditional heteroskedasticity brings some complications in devising unit root tests. This chapter then addresses unit root tests in the presence of additive and innovational outliers. It is well-known that outliers can affect inferential results in a significant manner. This section discusses the effects of outliers on unit root testing and the methods of unit root testing in the presence of outliers. The fourth topic of this chapter encompasses unit root distributions and tests under fat-tailed distributions. This discussion show that fat-tailed distributions introduce nuisance parameters in the limiting distributions of Dickey and Fuller's (1979) and Phillips and Perron's (1988) test statistics. The last topic of this chapter is unit root tests against nonlinear alternatives. This discussion considers threshold AR and smooth-transition AR models, which are representative nonlinear models in time series analysis. In addition, it introduces inference methods using random-coefficient AR models. A summary and further remarks conclude the chapter.

3.2 Unit Root Tests under Structural Changes

In econometrics and statistics, the terms "structural changes" or "breaks" refer to a circumstance in which parameters undergo changes in their values. The presence of structural changes significantly affects inference on a unit root. This section discusses effects of structural changes on unit root testing and introduces methods of unit root testing under structural changes. The literature considers two categories of structural changes in relation to unit root testing—changes in level and trend and changes in innovation variances. These two categories are discussed separately in this section. Perron's (2006), Aue and Horváth's (2013), and Jandhyala, Fotopoulos, MacNeill, and Liu's (2013) survey papers contain discussions on structural changes not necessarily related to unit roots and are recommended for further reading.

3.2.1 Structural Changes in Level and Trend

This subsection first discusses how conventional unit root tests behave when there are structural changes in the nonstochastic parts of the observations. Then, it discusses methods of unit root testing in the presence of structural changes.

Effects of Structural Changes on Unit Root Testing
Interest in structural changes in relation to unit root testing originated with Perron (1989).[1] He considers a stationary process with a level shift and a linear time trend as in

$$y_t = \mu_1 + (\mu_2 - \mu_1)\mathbf{1}\{t > T_B\} + \beta t + x_t, \tag{3.1}$$

where $\mathbf{1}\{\cdot\}$ is an indicator function and $\{x_t\}$ is a mixing process (cf. Assumption 2.1). In this DGP, $(\mu_2 - \mu_1)\mathbf{1}\{t > T_B\}$ signifies a level shift from μ_1 to μ_2 occurring at date T_B. Letting $T_B = \lambda T$ for all T ($0 < \lambda < 1$), he reports that the OLS estimator of the AR(1) coefficient in the AR(1) regression with a constant and a linear time trend (cf. Model (2.5)), denoted here as α^*, has the following property.

$$\alpha^* \xrightarrow{p} \frac{(\mu_1 - \mu_2)^2 A + \gamma}{(\mu_1 - \mu_2)^2 A + \sigma_x^2}, \tag{3.2}$$

where $A = \lambda - 4\lambda^2 + 6\lambda^3 - 3\lambda^4$, $\sigma_x^2 = \lim_{T\to\infty} T^{-1} \sum_{t=1}^{T} E(x_t^2)$, and $\gamma = \lim_{T\to\infty} T^{-1} \sum_{t=1}^{T} E(x_t x_{t-1})$.

---

[1] Rappoport and Reichlin (1989) also consider the problem of unit root testing under a structural change in the trend component of the observations.

The probability limit of relation (3.2) can be written as

$$\frac{\gamma}{\sigma_x^2} + \frac{(\mu_1 - \mu_2)^2 A(\sigma_x^2 - \gamma)}{\sigma_x^2 \left[(\mu_1 - \mu_2)^2 A + \sigma_x^2\right]}. \tag{3.3}$$

Because $A, \sigma_x^2 - \gamma > 0$, the second term in (3.3) is positive, implying that the probability limit is greater than the true AR(1) coefficient of $\{x_t\}$, $\frac{\gamma}{\sigma_x^2}$. In other words, α^* is asymptotically biased toward one. Thus, unit root tests using α^* are bound to have low finite-sample power, though they are still consistent.[2]

Perron (1989) also considers a stationary processes with a trend shift:

$$y_t = \mu + \beta_1 t + (\beta_2 - \beta_1)(t - T_B)\mathbf{1}\{t > T_B\} + x_t; \tag{3.4}$$

$$y_t = \mu_1 + \beta_1 t + (\mu_2 - \mu_1)\mathbf{1}\{t > T_B\}$$

$$+ (\beta_2 - \beta_1)(t - T_B)\mathbf{1}\{t > T_B\} + x_t. \tag{3.5}$$

The trend component of process (3.4) is $\beta_1 t$ when $t \leq T_B$, whereas it is $\beta_2 t$ when $t > T_B$. Process (3.5) has a level shift in addition. Perron reports for these processes that

$$\alpha^* \xrightarrow{p} 1, \tag{3.6}$$

which implies that unit root tests using α^* are inconsistent.[3] In other words, if a stationary processes has a breaking trend, it cannot be distinguished from a unit root process with drift.

In contrast to Perron's (1989) results, spurious rejections of a unit root can occur along with structural changes in level and trend. Leybourne, Mills, and Newbold (1998) and Leybourne and Newbold (2000) study properties of the Dickey-Fuller test when the true DGP is a unit root process under structural changes. They report that the Dickey-Fuller t-test tends to lead to spurious rejections of a unit root when the structural change occurs early in the series. Psaradakis (2001b)[4] reports a similar result using the DGP $y_t = \mu_0 + (\mu_1 - \mu_0)s_t + x_t$ where $\{s_t\}$ is a time-homogeneous, first-order Markov chain with state space $\{1, 0\}$ and $\{x_t\}$ is a unit root process.

Methods of Unit Root Testing in the Presence of Structural Changes
This subsubsection discusses various methods for unit root testing in the presence of structural changes in the nonstochastic parts of the observations.

---

[2] Perron (1990) considers a stationary process with a level shift only (i.e., $y_t = \mu_1 + (\mu_2 - \mu_1)\mathbf{1}\{t > T_B\} + x_t$) and reaches the same conclusion.
[3] Montañés and Reyes (1998) study the same issue in more detail. Sen (2001) reports that Dickey and Fuller's (1981) F-test is consistent when the alternative process is stationary with a trend shift, whereas it is inconsistent when the alternative process is stationary with both level and trend shifts.
[4] See also Psaradakis (2002) for a related result.

Perron (1989) first considered the problem of unit root testing in the presence of structural changes. The structural changes are allowed to be present both under the null and alternative hypotheses. Assuming that the date of structural change (T_B) is known, he devises Dickey-Fuller t-ratios as follows. First, $\{y_t\}$ is regressed on $\{1, 1\{t > T_B\}, t\}$, $\{1, t, (t - T_B)1\{t > T_B\}\}$, and $\{1, t, 1\{t > T_B\}, (t - T_B)1\{t > T_B\}\}$ for Models (3.1), (3.4) and (3.5), respectively. Next, the residuals from these regressions are used to formulate the Phillips-Perron and ADF test statistics. The limiting distributions of these test statistics depend on λ ($= \frac{T_B}{T}$), and their percentiles are tabulated for some selected values of λ. Choosing the date of structural change as the 1929 stock market crash and the alternative hypothesis as trend stationarity with a level shift, Model (3.1), Perron's testing procedure rejects the null of a unit root for 11 of the 14 series studied by Nelson and Plosser (1982). These are surprising empirical results, given that most studies cannot refute Nelson and Plosser's statistical conclusion. In addition, the null of a unit root is rejected for the U.S. postwar quarterly real GNP series when the oil-price shock of 1973 is assumed to bring a structural change in the trend component of the data.

As first pointed out by Christiano (1992), Perron's (1989) testing strategy and empirical results may be inadequate because he assumes that the date of structural change is known. Several studies try to overcome the perceived shortcoming of Perron's approach. Zivot and Andrews (1992) consider testing the null of a unit root against the alternative of trend stationarity under structural changes. To this end, for each T_B, Zivot and Andrews consider running ADF-type regressions with the following three models:

$$\Delta y_t = \mu_1 + \mu_2 1\{t > T_B\} + \beta t + \rho y_{t-1} + \sum_{j=0}^{k} c_j \Delta y_{t-1-j} + u_t, \qquad (3.7)$$

$$\Delta y_t = \mu_1 + \beta t + \gamma (t - T_B)1\{t > T_B\} + \rho y_{t-1} + \sum_{j=0}^{k} c_j \Delta y_{t-1-j} + u_t, \qquad (3.8)$$

$$\Delta y_t = \mu_1 + \mu_2 1\{t > T_B\} + \beta t + \gamma (t - T_B)1\{t > T_B\}$$
$$+ \rho y_{t-1} + \sum_{j=0}^{k} c_j \Delta y_{t-1-j} + u_t, \qquad (3.9)$$

and employ the minimum of each ADF t-ratio over T_B as their test statistics. These regressions belong to the class of sequential statistics in the literature on structural change because the date of the hypothetical structural change is incremented sequentially to compute them. The alternative hypotheses for

Table 3.1. *Asymptotic critical values of the Zivot-Andrews test for a unit root*

	Significance level			
Alternative model	1%	2.5%	5%	10%
Trend stationarity under a level shift	−5.34	−5.02	−4.80	−4.58
Trend stationarity under a trend shift	−4.93	−4.67	−4.42	−4.11
Trend stationarity under level and trend shifts	−5.57	−5.30	−5.08	−4.82

Note: If the computed value of the Zivot-Andrews test statistic is less than its critical value at a chosen significance level, reject the null of a unit root with drift against the relevant alternative model.

regression Models (3.7), (3.8), and (3.9) are, respectively, stationarity with a level shift, a trend shift, and level and trend shifts.

In calculating the limiting null distributions of their test statistics, Zivot and Andrews (1992) employ restrictions $\mu_2 = \beta = \rho = 0$, $\beta = \gamma = \rho = 0$, and $\mu_2 = \beta = \gamma = \rho = 0$ for Models (3.7), (3.8), and (3.9), respectively, obviously because these correspond to the null of a unit root with drift. The limiting null distributions do not depend on any nuisance parameters. Simulated asymptotic critical values of the test statistics for Models (3.1), (3.4), and (3.5) are reported in Table 3.1. Because these critical values are smaller than those under fixed λ, using percentiles given in Perron will invite bias toward rejecting the null of a unit root. For the Nelson-Plosser dataset, Zivot and Andrews find more favorable evidence for the null of a unit root with drift than Perron does.

The null hypothesis of the Zivot-Andrews test is a unit root with drift. That is, we assume $\mu_2 = \beta = \gamma = \rho = 0$ for the Zivot-Andrews test based on the regression models (3.7), (3.8), and (3.9). One may also consider testing the null hypothesis of a unit root with changing drift. For example, if $\mu_2 \neq 0$ and $\beta = \rho = 0$ for Model (3.7), $\{y_t\}$ is a unit root process with changing drift. Vogelsang and Perron (1998) provide asymptotic analysis of the ADF test statistic for this case. Nunes, Newbold, and Kuan (1997) also extend the Zivot-Andrews test to DGPs with structural changes under the null of a unit root by using bootstrap methods and apply their test to the Nelson-Plosser data. For most of the series, they fail to reject the null hypothesis of a unit root.

The Zivot-Andrews test discussed so far assumes one structural change of each type. In practice, there might be more than one structural change. Extensions of the Zivot-Andrews test to the case of two structural changes are made in Lumsdaine and Papell (1997). Using the Nelson-Plosser dataset, they find more evidence against the unit root hypothesis than Zivot and Andrews (1992), but less than Perron (1989). Lee and Strazicich (2003) also consider testing for a unit root in the presence of two structural changes of unknown dates under both the null and alternative hypotheses. They employ the minimum of the Schmidt-Phillips test statistic for this purpose and report that their test rejects less often for the Nelson-Plosser dataset than does the Lumsdaine-Papell test. Kapetanios (2005) further generalizes Lumsdaine and Papell's test by considering more than two structural changes of unknown dates.

For Models (3.7)–(3.9), it is possible to estimate T_B consistently. Vogelsang and Perron (1998)[5] estimate T_B using the maximum of the absolute values of the t-ratio for the term related to structural change—e.g., μ_2 in Model (3.7)— and test for a unit root using the estimate of T_B as if it were the true value. The report an asymptotic analysis of the ADF test using the estimated change point.

Banerjee, Lumsdaine, and Stock (1992; BLS hereafter) investigate the inference on a unit root possibly under structural changes, suggesting broad classes of tests. They consider three classes of test statistics: recursive, rolling, and sequential. According to their simulations, the most promising recursive and rolling tests are those based on the minimum of the ADF test statistics. To compute their recursive test statistics using the ADF regression, $\{\Delta y_t\}_{t=k+2,\ldots,[T\delta]}$ are regressed on $\{1, t, y_{t-1}, \Delta y_{t-1}, \ldots, \Delta y_{t-k}\}_{t=k+2,\ldots,[T\delta]}$ for each δ, $0 < \delta_o \leq \delta \leq 1$. In other words, data points up to $[T\delta]$ are used for this regression. Note that δ_0 should be chosen by the researcher, and BLS choose $\delta_0 = 0.25$ in their simulation.

BLS define their rolling test similarly with $\{\Delta y_t\}_{t=[T(\delta-\delta_o)]+1,\ldots,[T\delta]}$ regressed on $\{1, t, y_{t-1}, \Delta y_{t-1}, \ldots, \Delta y_{t-k}\}_{t=[T(\delta-\delta_o)]+1,\ldots,[T\delta]}$ for each δ, $0 < \delta_o \leq \delta \leq 1$. That is, data points from $[T(\delta - \delta_o)] + 1$ to $[T\delta]$ are used for this regression. Again, δ_0 should be chosen by the researcher, and BLS choose $\delta_0 = \frac{1}{3}$ in their simulation.

The maximum and minimum of the recursive (rolling) ADF test statistic over δ and their difference are BLS's recursive (rolling) test statistics. Among these, the minimum of the recursive ADF test statistic and that of the rolling ADF test statistic seem to be most promising according to BLS's simulation results. Asymptotic critical values of BLS's recursive and rolling test statistics are reported in Table 3.2. When the null hypothesis is not rejected, we may interpret that the observations follow a unit root process with or without drift. But when the null is rejected, it may imply structural changes for either or both of the nonstochastic and stochastic parts of the observations. Functional forms of the structural changes cannot be known in this case. Therefore, further studies are required to obtain more detailed information on the structural changes. In addition, BLS report that the recursive and rolling tests tend to have low finite-sample power within their simulation design. Note that BLS's recursive and rolling tests can also be used for the case of multiple structural changes.

---

[5] See also Perron and Vogelsang (1992) for the model with only a level shift. Perron and Vogelsang (1992) and Vogelsang and Perron (1998) also consider the additive outlier model, which is an unobserved components model with structural changes in the nonstochastic component.

Table 3.2. *Asymptotic critical values of the recursive and rolling unit root tests*

		Significance level		
		2.5%	5%	10%
Recursive test	$t_{\text{ADF}}^{\min}$	−4.42	−4.18	−3.88
Rolling test	$t_{\text{ADF}}^{\min}$	−5.00	−4.79	−4.55

Note: If the computed value of the Banerjee-Lumsdaine-Stock test statistic is less than its critical value at a chosen significance level, reject the null of a unit root with drift against the alternative of unspecified structural changes.

In addition to the recursive and rolling test statistics, BLS consider some sequential test statistics that Zivot and Andrews (1992) do not. The most promising one among these is Quandt's (1960) LR test statistic according to their simulation results. For this, consider the ADF regressions

$$\Delta y_t = \mu_1 + \beta_1 t + \rho_1 y_{t-1} + \sum_{j=0}^{k} c_j \Delta y_{t-1-j} + u_t, (t = k+3, \ldots, T_\text{B}),$$

$$\Delta y_t = \mu_2 + \beta_2 t + \rho_2 y_{t-1} + \sum_{j=0}^{k} c_j \Delta y_{t-1-j} + u_t, (t = T_\text{B}+1, \ldots, T).$$

The Quandt LR statistic tests the null hypothesis that there are no structural changes for any parameters under the restriction $\beta_1 = \beta_2 = \rho_1 = \rho_2 = 0$; it is defined as the maximum of the LR test statistic over T_B. Its functional form is

$$Q_{LR}(k) = \max_{T_0 \leq T_\text{B} \leq T - T_0} (-2 \log \lambda(T_\text{B}, k)),$$

for some chosen value of T_0, where

$$\lambda(T_\text{B}, k) = \frac{\overline{\sigma}_{k+3,T_\text{B}}^{T_\text{B}-k-2} \overline{\sigma}_{T_\text{B}+1,T}^{T-T_\text{B}}}{\overline{\sigma}_{k+3,T}^{T-k-2}}$$

and $\overline{\sigma}_{t_1,t_2}^2$ is the Gaussian MLE of the regression error variance using observations from t_1 to t_2. For simulation, BLS choose $T_0 = [0.15 \times T]$. Asymptotic critical values of BLS's Quandt test are reported in Table 3.3. Note that they depend on the number of differenced variables k. When the null hypothesis is not rejected by the Quandt test, it implies a unit root process with or without drift. When the null is rejected, it implies structural changes for either or both of the nonstochastic and stochastic parts of the observations. The Quandt LR test tends to have higher finite-sample power than the recursive and rolling

Table 3.3. *Asymptotic critical values of the Quandt test for a unit root*

	Significance level		
	2.5%	5%	10%
$Q_{LR}(0)$	30.42	27.80	25.19
$Q_{LR}(4)$	37.00	34.00	30.72
$Q_{LR}(8)$	43.00	39.95	36.84

Note: If the computed value of the Quandt test statistic is greater than its critical value at a chosen significance level, reject the null of a unit root with drift against the alternative of unspecified structural changes. The numbers in parentheses are those of the differenced dependent variables on the right-hand-side of the ADF regression.

tests according to BLS's simulation results, but it does not allow for multiple structural changes.

Perron and Rodríguez (2003) apply ERS's GLS-detrending to propose tests for a unit root in the presence of a structural change. They apply the detrending to an unobserved components model under structural changes

$$y_t = d_t + x_t, \quad x_t = \alpha x_{t-1} + u_t, \tag{3.10}$$

where $d_t = \psi' z_t$ with $z_t = [1, t, (t - T_B)\mathbf{1}\{t > T_B\}]'$ or $z_t = [1, \mathbf{1}\{t > T_B\}, t, (t - T_B)\mathbf{1}\{t > T_B\}]'$; they then devise modified Phillips-Perron coefficient test statistics and some other statistics. Maximums of these test statistics over possible structural change dates are the final test statistics that can be used for an unknown structural change date. Note that a structural change may occur under both the null and alternative hypotheses in Perron and Rodríguez, unlike in previous works such as Zivot and Andrews (1992) and BLS. Liu and Rodríguez (2006) study the same problem as Perron and Rodríguez, but assume that the initial variable is drawn from its unconditional distribution.

Harris, Harvey, Leybourne, and Taylor[6] (2009) and Harvey, Leybourne, and Taylor (2012a) extend Perron and Rodríguez's test to the case where the presence of a trend change is uncertain. These papers employ auxiliary test statistics to detect the presence of a trend change and use the outcome to decide whether to employ Model (3.10) or that without a trend change. Harvey, Leybourne, and Taylor (2013) propose a unit root test for the case in which partial information on the change date is available. The test is based on the idea

---

[6] Cavaliere, Harvey, Leybourne, and Taylor (2011) study Harris et al.'s (2009) inferential problem under the nonstationary volatility of Cavaliere and Taylor (2007) and suggest using the wild bootstrap.

of using a union of rejections strategy, as in Harvey, Leybourne, and Taylor (2009) (see Subsection 2.4.11).

Kim and Perron (2009) consider a model that is slightly more general than Model (3.10) in the sense that it allows the case of a level shift only. They show that the ADF test statistic using a consistent estimator (at a rate faster than $\frac{1}{\sqrt{T}}$) of the change fraction $\left[\frac{T_B}{T}\right]$ has the same limiting distribution as that using the true change fraction. Carrion-i-Silvestre, Kim, and Perron (2009) extend Kim and Perron (2009) to the case of multiple changes in level and trend and use Stock's (1999) test statistics along with the GLS-detrending. Rodrigues (2013) employs the recursive adjustment method of Subsection 2.4.7 to test the null hypothesis of a unit root without structural changes and suggests the minimum of the Dickey-Fuller t-ratio over the possible change fraction $\left[\frac{T_B}{T}\right]$ and the Dickey-Fuller t-ratio using the estimated change fraction. But he reports that the recursive adjustment method does not yield uniformly higher finite-sample power than OLS and GLS (in the sense of ERS). Fossati (2013) combines the ideas of Hansen (1995) (see Subsection 2.4.5), ERS, and Perron and Rodríguez (2003) to suggest a unit root test under structural changes. His test has a power gain over Perron and Rodríguez's, but the limiting distributions of his test statistics depend on nuisance parameters as does Hansen's test.

Saikkonen and Lütkepohl (2002)[7] study how to test for a unit root in the presence of a level shift under both the null and alternative hypotheses. The change date is assumed to be unknown in this study. Saikkonen and Lütkepohl consider the model[8]

$$y_t = \mu + \beta t + \gamma' f_{tT_B}(\theta) + x_t,$$

where $f_{tT_B}(\theta)$ is a vector of deterministic sequences that introduces structural changes and $\{x_t\}$ is an AR process. Examples of $f_{tT_B}(\theta)$ are

$$f_{tT_B}(\theta) = \mathbf{1}\{t > T_B\};$$

$$f_{tT_B}(\theta) = \frac{1}{1 + \exp\{-\theta(t - T_B)\}}, \ \theta > 0.$$

The first example is the often used dummy variable, and the second is a logistic function that displays a slow transition from zero to one. The speed of transition depends on the magnitude of parameter θ. Note that $f_{tT_B}(\theta)$ does not allow a changing trend, which was a matter of interest in previous studies. In contrast to those studies, Saikkonen and Lütkepohl estimate the deterministic part of

---

[7] See also Lanne, Lütkepohl, and Saikkonen (2003). This study and Saikkonen and Lütkepohl (2002) can be considered as extensions of Lanne, Lütkepohl, and Saikkonen (2002) that assume a known break date.

[8] Saikkonen and Lütkepohl (2002) also consider a model in which lagged dependent variables appear on the right-hand side of the equation. I omit this model from the discussion for brevity.

the process[9] after differencing observations along the lines of ERS and apply the Dickey-Fuller test to the residuals. Interestingly, the limiting distribution for their unit root test does not depend on the estimator of the change date and is the same as that of ERS's GLS-based test for a model with an intercept and a linear time trend. An intuition for this result is that the level shift of the type considered by Saikkonen and Lütkepohl is not conspicuous enough to bring changes to the limiting distribution for their unit root test.

Leybourne, Newbold, and Vougas (1998) and Sollis, Leybourne, and Newbold (1999) consider testing the null hypothesis of a unit root against the alternative hypothesis of stationarity around a function that permits a smooth transition from one linear time trend to another. In their approach, the nonlinear function is estimated by the least squares method in the first step. Then the resulting residuals are used to formulate the Dickey-Fuller test statistic.

Using Saikkonen and Lütkepohl's (2002) idea, Cavaliere and Georgiev (2007) consider testing for a unit root in a model with multiple level shifts represented by $\mu_t = \sum_{s=1}^{t} \delta_s \theta_s$ where $\{\delta_t\}$ is an unobservable sequence of binary random variables and $\{\theta_t\}$ is the sequence of shift sizes. They propose a method to estimate μ_t consistently and formulate "de-jumped" time series using that estimate. The ADF test statistic applied to this time series has the same distribution as the usual one.

Extending Becker, Enders, and Lee (2006; see Subsection 4.8.1), Enders and Lee (2012a) propose a unit root test that can be used when the change dates, the precise form of changes, and/or the exact form of the changes are unknown. They consider the AR(1) model with an unknown deterministic term d_t,

$$y_t = d_t + \beta t + \alpha y_{t-1} + u_t, \tag{3.11}$$

and approximate d_t using the Fourier expansion

$$\alpha_0 + \sum_{j=1}^{n} a_k \sin\left(\frac{2\pi kt}{T}\right) + \sum_{j=1}^{n} b_k \cos\left(\frac{2\pi kt}{T}\right), \; n < \frac{T}{2}, \tag{3.12}$$

where n is the number of frequencies and k represents a particular frequency. In Model (3.11), the nonstochastic term d_t is a nonlinear function of t that may be subject to structural changes of an unknown form. Choosing a single frequency for (3.12), Enders and Lee rewrite model (3.11) as

$$y_t = \alpha_0 + a_k \sin\left(\frac{2\pi kt}{T}\right) + b_k \cos\left(\frac{2\pi kt}{T}\right) + \beta t + \alpha y_{t-1} + u_t$$

and devise a score-based test statistic as in Schmidt and Phillips (1992; see Subsection 2.4.1).[10] The limiting distribution of the score-based test statistic

---

[9] Some of these estimators are inconsistent without posing problems for unit root tests.

[10] See Enders and Lee (2012b) for an extension to the Dickey-Fuller test.

depends on the chosen frequency k, and the critical values of the test statistic are tabulated for $k = 1, 2, 3, 4, 5$. Because the value of k is unknown in practice, Enders and Lee suggest estimating the frequency k with the least squares method and using the estimator for the score-based test. Enders and Lee also consider using several frequencies cumulatively. According to their simulation results, this does not have noticeable effects on the size of the test, but power decreases rapidly when the number of included frequencies increases. Thus, in practice, it is advised to use a small number of frequencies (i.e., $n = 1$ or $n = 2$ in the Fourier expansion (3.12)).

Rodrigues and Taylor (2012) apply the method of Becker, Enders, and Lee (2006) and Enders and Lee (2012a, 2012b) to ERS (see Subsection 2.4.4). According to their simulation results, their test tends to be slightly more powerful than Enders and Lee's.

Many procedures that are designed to test for a unit root in the presence of structural changes have been discussed so far in this subsection. The procedure most often used in practice appears to be Zivot and Andrews (1992). It is useful when the null hypothesis is a unit root with drift. If one wishes to include structural changes under the null hypothesis too, then Perron and Rodríguez (2003) and Kim and Perron (2009) are recommended for applications.

3.2.2   Structural Changes in Innovation Variances

Hamori and Tokihisa (1997) find that the limiting distributions of the Dickey-Fuller test statistics are not invariant to structural changes in the innovation variance and tend to overreject the null of a unit root under upward shifts in the variance. They consider a unit root process with a structural change in the innovation variance,

$$y_t = y_{t-1} + u_t, \quad u_t = e_t + \mathbf{1}\{t > T_B\}\eta_t, \quad e_t \sim \text{iid}(0, \sigma_e^2), \quad \eta_t \sim \text{iid}(0, \sigma_\eta^2),$$

and report that the limiting distributions of the Dickey-Fuller test statistics depend on the nuisance parameters σ_e^2, σ_η^2, and $\lambda = \frac{T_B}{T}$.

Kim, Leybourne, and Newbold (2002) report similar results based on a more general model:

$$y_t = \mu + x_t, \quad x_t = \alpha x_{t-1} + \sum_{j=1}^{p} \phi_j \Delta x_{t-j} + u_t, \quad u_t = \sigma_t \eta_t,$$

$$\sigma_t^2 = \sigma_1^2 \mathbf{1}\{t \leq \lambda T\} + \sigma_2^2 \mathbf{1}\{t > \lambda T\}, \quad \text{Var}(\eta_t) = 1.$$

In this model, the variance of the innovations $\{u_t\}$ changes from σ_1^2 to σ_2^2.

Without giving a structure to σ_t^2 as in Kim, Leybourne, and Newbold (2002), Cavaliere (2004) also reports dependency of the limiting distributions of the

Dickey-Fuller and Phillips-Perron test statistics on the nuisance parameter $\lim_{T\to\infty} T^{-1} \sum_{t=1}^{T} \sigma_t^2$.

Kim, Leybourne, and Newbold (2002) consider how to estimate parameter λ and test for a unit root in the presence of a structural change in the innovation variance. To estimate λ, they consider the quasi-MLE and least squares methods. The quasi-MLE estimator of λ is obtained by minimizing the objective function

$$Q(\lambda) = \lambda \log \sigma_1^2(\lambda) + (1 - \lambda) \log \sigma_2^2(\lambda),$$

where $\sigma_1^2(\lambda) = (\lambda T)^{-1} \sum_{t=1}^{\lambda T} e_t^2$, $\sigma_2^2(\lambda) = ((1 - \lambda) T)^{-1} \sum_{t=\lambda T+1}^{T} e_t^2$, and $\{e_t\}$ represents regression residuals from the ADF regression with an intercept that uses $\{y_t\}$. The least squares estimator of λ follows from minimizing the objective function[11]

$$V(\lambda) = \lambda(1 - \lambda) \left(\sigma_2^2(\lambda) - \sigma_1^2(\lambda)\right)^2.$$

Both estimators are consistent when there is a structural change in the innovation variance and perform similarly in finite samples according to Kim, Leybourne, and Newbold. Using an estimator of λ, $\hat{\lambda}$, they consider a transformed regression model,

$$y_t(\hat{\lambda}) = \mu_0 + \mu_1 \mathbf{1}\{t > \hat{\lambda}T\}$$

$$+ \mu_2 \mathbf{1}\{t = \hat{\lambda}T + 1\} + \sum_{j=1}^{p} \theta_j \mathbf{1}\{t - j = \hat{\lambda}T + 1\}$$

$$+ \alpha y_{t-1}(\hat{\lambda}) + \sum_{j=1}^{p} \phi_j \Delta y_{t-j}(\hat{\lambda}) + \eta_t,$$

where $y_{t-j}(\hat{\lambda}) = \hat{\sigma}_1^{-1} y_{t-j} \mathbf{1}\{t \leq \hat{\lambda}T\} + \hat{\sigma}_2^{-1} y_{t-j} \mathbf{1}\{t > \hat{\lambda}T\}(j = 0, \ldots, p)$ and $\hat{\sigma}_i^2 = \sigma_i^2(\hat{\lambda}) (i = 1, 2)$. The GLS transformation of $\{y_{t-j}\}$ makes the innovation process have an unchanging variance in the limit. The level shift represented by μ_1 occurs due to the GLS transformation. The one-time dummy variables $\mathbf{1}\{t - j = \hat{\lambda}T + 1\}$ $(j = 0, \ldots, p)$ are included in the regression to free the t-statistic for a unit root of the nuisance parameters σ_1 and σ_2. The t-ratio for the null hypothesis $\alpha = 1$ has a limiting distribution that depends only on λ. The limiting distribution is the same as that for Perron's (1990) unit root test and is tabulated in that paper.

Sen (2007) employs the same model as Kim, Leybourne, and Newbold (2002) and tests the joint null hypothesis $\mu_0 = \mu_1 = 0$, $\alpha = 1$. Finally, Cavaliere and Taylor (2007) derive asymptotic distributions of some unit root test

---

[11] This objective function is equivalent to $S_T(\lambda) = \sum_{t=1}^{\lambda T}(e_t^2 - \sigma_1^2(\lambda)) + \sum_{t=\lambda T+1}^{T}(e_t^2 - \sigma_2^2(\lambda))$.

statistics using the specification $\sigma_{[sT]} = \omega(s)$ for all $s \in [0, 1]$ where $\omega(\cdot)$ is nonstochastic and strictly positive. Because the distributions depend on $\omega(\cdot)$, they propose using parametric bootstrapping methods for the inference on a unit root.

3.3   Unit Root Tests with Conditional Heteroskedasticity

ARCH and GARCH effects have often been observed in high-frequency financial data. A natural question about unit root tests in relation to ARCH and GARCH is whether their asymptotic distributions hold in the presence of ARCH and GARCH errors. Another question is whether we can improve unit root tests by incorporating the information on conditional heteroskedasticity. This section introduces some research results related to these questions.

3.3.1   Simulation Study

Although the limiting distributions of the Dickey-Fuller test statistics were obtained using the assumption of i.i.d. normal errors, the same distributions will result if the errors are a martingale difference sequence satisfying the conditions of the martingale functional central limit theorem (cf. Hall and Heyde, 1980). However, if the martingale difference errors do not satisfy those conditions, there is no assurance that the same asymptotic distributions will follow for the Dickey-Fuller test statistics. Kim and Schmidt (1993) conduct a simulation study regarding the finite-sample size of the Dickey-Fuller test that confirms this intuition. They generate the unit root AR(1) process with the errors having the conditional (on information up to time $t - 1$) variance h_t that is modeled by the GARCH(1, 1) process,

$$h_t = \phi_0 + \phi_1 u_{t-1}^2 + \gamma_1 h_{t-1}. \tag{3.13}$$

If $\phi_0 > 0$ and $\phi_1 + \gamma_1 < 1$, the unconditional variance of $\{u_t\}$ exists and is equal to $\frac{\phi_0}{1-\phi_1-\gamma_1}$. In this case, the martingale functional central limit theorem works for $\{u_t\}$, and the Dickey-Fuller test statistics have the same limiting distributions as for i.i.d. errors (see Wang, 2006, for details). Indeed, Kim and Schmidt report that the Dickey-Fuller coefficient and t-test statistics are well sized in this case. However, either when $\phi_0 = 0$ and $\phi_1 + \gamma_1 \leq 1$ or when $\phi_0 > 0$ and $\phi_1 + \gamma_1 = 1$, they report serious finite-sample size distortions. In the former case, the GARCH process converges to zero; in the latter, the unconditional variance of $\{u_t\}$ is infinite. In both the cases, the martingale functional central limit theorem would not work, which is the main cause of the failure of the Dickey-Fuller test.

3.3.2 Maximum Likelihood Estimation and Related Tests under GARCH Errors

Several papers study the maximum likelihood estimation of the ARMA model with GARCH errors. Ling and Li (1998) provide quite general theory for the maximum likelihood estimation of the nonstationary ARMA process with GARCH errors. They consider the ARMA model

$$\alpha(B)y_t = \psi(B)u_t$$

with GARCH errors

$$u_t = \eta_t \sqrt{h_t}, \quad h_t = \phi_0 + \sum_{i=1}^{r} \phi_i u_{t-i}^2 + \sum_{j=1}^{s} \gamma_i h_{t-i},$$

where the polynomial equation $\alpha(z) = 0$ has roots on or outside the unit circle, $\psi(z) = 0$ has roots only outside the unit circle, and $\eta_t \sim \text{iid}(0, 1)$ with a symmetric distribution. For the GARCH coefficients, they assume

$$\sum_{i=1}^{r} \phi_i + \sum_{j=1}^{s} \gamma_i < 1,$$

excluding integrated GARCH processes. The MLE (or quasi-MLE if a normality assumption does not hold for $\{\eta_t\}$) is obtained by maximizing

$$L(\lambda) = \sum_{t=1}^{T} l_t(\lambda) \text{ and } l_t = -\frac{1}{2} \log h_t - \frac{1}{2} \frac{u_t^2}{h_t}$$

with respect to λ (the vector of all parameters in the model) conditional on the starting values for $\{y_t\}$. For the AR(1) model with a unit root and GARCH(1, 1) errors, the MLE[12] of the AR(1) coefficient α, $\hat{\alpha}_{\text{ML}}$ has a limiting distribution represented by

$$T(\hat{\alpha}_{\text{ML}} - 1) \Rightarrow \frac{\int_0^1 B_1(r) \, dB_2(r)}{K \int_0^1 B_1(r)^2 \, dr}, \tag{3.14}$$

where $(B_1(r), B_2(r))'$ is bivariate Brownian motion having the covariance matrix

$$r \begin{bmatrix} \sigma^2 & 1 \\ 1 & K \end{bmatrix}$$

with $\sigma^2 = E(\frac{1}{h_t})$ and $K = E(\frac{1}{h_t}) + 2\phi_1^2 \sum_{i=1}^{\infty} \gamma_1^{2(i-1)} E(\frac{u_{t-i}^2}{h_t^2})$. Notice that the limiting distribution (3.14) contains a nuisance parameter related to the coefficients of the GARCH process. Independently, Seo (1999) reports similar

---

[12] Ling and Li (2003) study the one-step local quasi-MLE for the same model. The resulting limiting distribution is the same as (3.14).

results for the AR(p) model with a unit root under a slightly different set of assumptions. He also considers the AR(p) models with an intercept and with an intercept and a linear time trend.

Some MLE-based, t-ratio type test statistics for a unit root in the presence of GARCH errors are suggested in Seo (1999) and Ling, Li, and McAleer (2003). Their simulation results favor the MLE-based tests over those using the OLS estimator in terms of finite-sample power. However, their test statistics contain nuisance parameters in their limiting distributions. Thus, critical values should be simulated at each nuisance parameter value, which can be inconvenient in practice.

Ling and McAleer (2003) study adaptive maximum likelihood estimation of the ARIMA(p, 1, q) model with GARCH errors and suggest a unit root test that uses their adaptive MLE. But the limiting distribution of their test statistic depends on nuisance parameters, such as those introduced earlier. This is inconvenient for practical applications and obviously a downside of their test. Adaptive maximum likelihood estimation uses an estimator of the unknown density to construct a Newton-Raphson style estimator and is asymptotically equivalent to the MLE based on the true density. See Kreiss (1987), Koul and Schick (1996), Linton (1993), and Shin and So (1999b), for example, for time series applications of the adaptive estimation method.

Li and Li (2009) study the least absolute deviation estimator for the nonstationary AR(p) process with GARCH errors and propose some test statistics for a unit based on it. Their simulation results demonstrate that their test statistics perform well when the errors are heavy-tailed.

All the tests discussed so far exclude the case of integrated GARCH (i.e., $\phi_1 + \gamma_1 = 1$), which is one of the motivations for Kim and Schmidt's (1993) earlier simulation study. For the case of errors following an integrated GARCH(1,1) process driven by i.i.d. normal random variables, Kourogenis and Pittis (2008) suggest a new test that shows stable size in finite samples (see Section 3.5 for details). In addition, they show via simulation that Breitung's (2002) variance ratio test (see Subsection 4.4.3) also performs well under the integrated GARCH(1,1) errors.

3.4   Unit Root Tests in the Presence of Additive and Innovational Outliers

Time series data sometimes have observations that are quite different from the rest; they are called outliers. For example, interest rates of various Asian nations at the peak of the Asian currency crisis look quite different from those in other periods. In the literature on unit roots, various papers have studied the outliers' effects on unit root inferences. This section introduces some of the major results in this research area.

A convenient way to model outliers for a univariate time series is to assume that they appear as shocks to the observations in an additive manner. That is, observations $\{y_t\}$ are assumed to be generated by the model

$$y_t = x_t + w_t, \tag{3.15}$$

where $\{x_t\}$ follows an ARMA process and $\{w_t\}$ is a sequence of contaminating random variables that cause the occurrences of outliers. Equation (3.15) signifies a typical model for additive outliers.

To study how the presence of additive outliers affects the distributions of the Dickey-Fuller test statistics, Franses and Haldrup (1994) model $\{x_t\}$ in (3.15) as an AR(1) process with white noise innovations $\{u_t\}$ and let $w_t = \theta \delta_t$ where δ_t is a Bernoulli random variable that takes the value 1 or -1 with a given probability π and is zero otherwise. If $|\theta|$ is large and π is small, this model will generate infrequent outliers with large magnitudes, which is the case for many economic time series. Franses and Haldrup find that the limiting distributions of the Dickey-Fuller coefficient and t-statistics are, respectively,

$$\left(\int_0^1 W^2(r)\,dr \right)^{-1} \left(\int_0^1 W(r)\,dW(r) - \frac{\pi\theta^2}{\sigma_u^2} \right)$$

and

$$\frac{\int_0^1 W(r)\,dW(r) - \frac{\pi\theta^2}{\sigma_u^2}}{\sqrt{\left(1 + \frac{2\pi\theta^2}{\sigma_u^2}\right) \int_0^1 W^2(r)\,dr}},$$

where σ_u^2 is the variance of u_t. These results show that the distributions shift leftward with the presence of the additive outliers (more so as the magnitude of the outliers, θ^2, becomes large), implying that the use of Dickey-Fuller distributions will result in overrejection under the null hypothesis of a unit root.

Shin, Sarkar, and Lee (1996) study the same problem, assuming $w_t = \sum_{k=1}^m \theta_k I_t(T_k)$ where $\{\theta_k\}$ are a sequence of either constants or random variables with zero mean and $I_t(T_k) = 1$ if $t = T_k$ and $I_t(T_k) = 0$ otherwise. The outliers of Shin, Sarkar and Lee are fixed at given time points, whereas those of Franses and Haldrup are generated in a systematic manner by a Bernoulli random variable. Shin, Sarkar, and Lee report that the limiting distributions of the Dickey-Fuller test statistic depend on the parameter κ, which is the probability limit of $T^{-1} \sum_{k=1}^m \theta_k^2$. This implies that the number of fixed outliers should increase at the same rate as the sample size for the outliers to affect the limiting distributions of the Dickey-Fuller test statistics. If the number increases at a slower rate than the sample size, the outliers have no impact on the limiting distributions. In practice, it is not obvious how we can perform unit root testing if the number of outliers increases at the same rate as the sample size and if the outliers' positions in time are unknown.[13]

Recognizing the importance of additive outliers for inference on a unit root, Vogelsang (1999) considers how to test for a unit root in their presence. He observes that outliers of the type considered by Franses and Haldrup introduce an MA component in the model under the null hypothesis of a unit root. To understand this, take a difference of $\{y_t\}$ in (3.15). Then, we obtain $\Delta y_t = u_t + \theta\,(\delta_t - \delta_{t-1})$. Because the covariance structure of Δy_t is equivalent to that of an invertible MA(1) process, Δy_t can be parametrized as an MA(1) process. Thus, Vogelsang recommends using such unit root tests as Perron and Ng (1996, 1998), which show good finite-sample properties with an MA component in the errors. A single outlier of the form $\delta_t = I_t(T_{ao})$, where $I_t(T_{ao}) = 1$ if $t = T_{ao}$ and zero otherwise, is also considered in Vogelsang. However, the single outlier does not affect the limiting distributions of the Dickey-Fuller test statistics as discovered by Shin, Sarkar and Lee.[14] This is also confirmed by Vogelsang's Table III. Therefore, no action is needed for a single outlier at least in large samples.

Vogelsang (1999) also considers how to detect multiple outliers and proposes a sequential testing procedure that can find the number and locations of outliers. But Perron and Rodríguez (2003) show that Vogelsang's testing procedure has serious size distortions when there are multiple outliers. As an alternative, they propose a test using the first differences of the data. But the limiting distribution of their test depends on the true distribution of the errors, which is certainly undesirable.

Because it seems nontrivial to find the number and locations of outliers, it is advisable for practitioners to use unit root tests that are robust to the presence of MA(1) errors as suggested by Vogelsang. Or one may use the bootstrap version of Perron and Rodríguez's test as suggested in Astill, Harvey, and Taylor (2013).

A different class of outliers is the innovational outlier defined by the model

$$\phi(B)y_t = \theta(B)(u_t + w_t),$$

where $\phi(z)$ and $\theta(z)$ are polynomials in z and $\{w_t\}$ is the source of the outlying behavior of the observations $\{y_t\}$. Note that the outliers $\{w_t\}$ are part of the

---

[13] Perron and Rodríguez's (2003) outlier detection procedure is inapplicable since they assume a finite number of outliers.
[14] See also Amsler and Lee (1995), who study the effect of a single outlier on the Schmidt-Phillips test.

innovation process in this model. Shin, Sarkar, and Lee (1996) consider the AR(1) model with innovation outliers

$$y_t - \alpha y_{t-1} = u_t + \sum_{k=1}^{m} \theta_k I_t(T_k),$$

where θ_k are iid $(0, \sigma_\theta^2)$ and independent of $\{u_t\}$, $I_t(T_k) = 1$ if $t = T_k$ and $I_t(T_k) = 0$ otherwise. The innovation outliers of the type they consider do not affect the limiting null distributions of the Dickey-Fuller test statistics because the sum of $\{u_t\}$ and the outliers satisfy the functional central limit theorem.

3.5 Unit Root Distributions and Tests under Fat-Tailed Distributions

There has been on going interest in distributions with infinite variance in relation to financial time series. Some empirical examples are Akgiray and Booth (1988) and Lau, Lau, and Wingender (1990) for stock prices and Akgiray, Booth, and Seifert (1988), Falk and Wang (2003), and Koedijk and Kool (1992) for exchange rates. This section introduces research results for the AR(1) regression with a unit root under the distribution with infinite variance.

Chan and Tran (1989)[15] and Phillips (1990) consider the AR(1) model with a unit root, the errors of which have an infinite variance. Because Phillips assumes a more general error structure, I focus on Phillip's result here. In Phillips, the error process $\{u_t\}$ follows a linear process,

$$u_t = \sum_{j=0}^{\infty} d_j \varepsilon_{t-j}, \ d_0 = 1, \ \sum_{j=0}^{\infty} d_j \neq 0,$$

where $\{\varepsilon_t\}$ are i.i.d. and symmetrically distributed around the origin and ε_1 belongs to the domain of normal attraction (DNA) of a stable law with index $\boldsymbol{\alpha}$.[16,17] This is equivalent to assuming that $\frac{1}{T^{1/\alpha}} \sum_{t=1}^{T} \varepsilon_t$ converges in law to a

---

[15] They assume that $\{u_t\}$ belong to the domain of attraction of a stable law with index $\boldsymbol{\alpha}$. See also Chan (1990), which extends the results of Chan and Tran (1989) to the case of the nearly integrated (in the sense of Chan and Wei, 1987) AR(1) model and finds that the limiting distribution of the OLS estimator is similar to that of Chan and Wei except that the Lévy process is used instead of Brownian motion.

[16] In this book, the AR(1) coefficient is denoted as α. Still, I use the same symbol bold faced, $\boldsymbol{\alpha}$, for the stable law because it is a standard notation in the literature; in fact, no one uses a different notation.

[17] The stable law is a family of distributions with finite and infinite variances. For example, the stable law with $\boldsymbol{\alpha} = 2$ is a normal distribution, whereas that with $\boldsymbol{\alpha} = 1$ is a Cauchy distribution given further restrictions on the distribution's other parameters. More information on the stable law can be found in Ibragimov and Linnik (1971), Samorodnitsky and Taqqu (1994), and John P. Nolan's website (http://academic2.american.edu/~jpnolan/stable/stable.html).

symmetric, stable distribution with index α. See Ibragimov and Linnik (1971, pp. 92–93) for the DNA. The tail probabilities of ε_1 when $0 < \alpha < 2$ are given as

$$P[\varepsilon_1 < z] = \frac{c_1 a^\alpha}{|z|}(1 + o(1)), \ z < 0;$$

$$P[\varepsilon_1 > z] = \frac{c_2 a^\alpha}{|z|}(1 + o(1)), \ z > 0,$$

as $|z| \to \infty$, where a, c_1, and c_2 are constants with $c_1, c_2 \geq 0$, and $c_1 + c_2 = 1$. These relations show that the pdf of ε_1 has fat-tails.

Phillips (1990) shows that

$$T(\hat{a} - 1) \Rightarrow \frac{\int_0^1 U_\alpha^-(r)\, dU_\alpha(r) + \frac{1}{2}\left(1 - \frac{\sigma^2}{\omega^2}\right)\int_0^1 (dU_\alpha(r))^2\, dr}{\int_0^1 U_\alpha(r)^2\, dr},$$

where $U_\alpha(r)$ is a symmetric, stable process with unit scale coefficient, $U_\alpha^-(r)$ is its left limit, $\omega = \sum_{j=0}^\infty d_j$, and $\sigma^2 = \sum_{j=0}^\infty d_j^2$. The symmetric stable process is a special case of the Lévy process and does not have the Brownian motion component in its Itô representation (cf. Resnick, 1986, p. 72). It looks more like a jump process as α takes smaller values, as the figures in Phillips show. Phillips also studies the limiting distributions of the Phillips-Perron test statistics and finds that they are expressed as functions of the symmetric stable process and depend on the unknown parameter α. This indicates that the conventional critical values for these test statistics cannot be used when the AR(1) errors have an infinite variance.

Extensions of Chan and Tran (1989) and Phillips (1990) to the AR(1) model with an intercept and with an intercept and a linear time trend are made in Ahn, Fotopoulos, and He (2001) and Callegari, Cappuccio, and Lubian (2003). Results similar to the case of finite variance are reported in these papers, except that they use the Lévy process instead of Brownian motion. Chan and Zhang (2012) consider the AR(p) model with real and complex unit roots and with the errors of infinite variance. They derive the limiting distribution of the OLS estimator using the method similar to that of Chan and Wei (1988).

Knight (1989)[18] estimates the AR(1) model with a unit root and i.i.d. errors that belong to the domain of attraction (DA) of a stable law with index α using the M- and least absolute deviation (LAD) estimators. We say that u_1 is in the domain of attraction of a stable law with index α if there exist constants $a_T > 0$ and b_T such that $a_T^{-1}\left[\sum_{t=1}^T (u_t - b_T)\right]$ converges in distribution to a stable random variable with index α. It follows that $a_T = T^{1/\alpha}L(T)$, where $L(T)$ denotes a slowly varying function defined by the relation $\lim_{t\to\infty} \frac{L(tx)}{L(t)} = 1$

---

[18] Knight (1991) extends Knight (1989) to the case of the mixing errors represented by a linear process.

for $x > 0$. Because Knight assumes that $E(u_1) = 0$ for $1 < \alpha < 2$ and that u_1 is symmetrically distributed around zero for $0 < \alpha \leq 1$, $b_T = 0$ in Knight. Because infinite variance implies the presence of a multitude of outliers, it is natural to consider the M- and LAD estimators for the AR(1) model with fat-tailed errors. As discussed in detail in Section 4.3, the M-estimator of the coefficient α is derived by solving the equation

$$\sum_{t=2}^{T} y_{t-1} \psi(y_t - \hat{\alpha}_M y_{t-1}) = 0 \qquad (3.16)$$

for some function $\psi(\cdot)$. Knight finds that the rate of convergence for the M- and LAD estimators is $\frac{1}{a_T \sqrt{T}}$ where $a_T = T^{1/\alpha} L(T)$. Thus, smaller α implies faster convergence of the M- and LAD estimators. In other words, more outliers or fatter tails imply the faster convergence of the estimators. The limiting distributions derived by Knight are more complex than those of Chan and Tran (1989) and Phillips (1990) and depend on $\psi(\cdot)$ and $\psi'(\cdot)$ in the case of the M-estimator and the pdf of the errors in the case of the LAD estimator. To overcome the parameter dependency of the limiting distributions, Moreno and Romo (2012) use bootstrapping and show that it works well in finite samples. The bootstrap sample size, $m(T)$, in their work should satisfy the conditions $m(T) \to \infty$ and $m(T)/T \to 0$ as $T \to \infty$ for the bootstrap to be consistent.

Shin and So (1999a) also consider the M-estimation as in Knight (1989), but they replace y_{t-1} in equation (3.16) with sign(y_{t-1}), which takes value 1 when $y_{t-1} \geq 0$ and -1 otherwise. The resulting estimator has the same rate of convergence as those in Knight.

Zhang and Chan (2012) consider the nearly integrated AR(1) model of Chan and Wei (1987) with i.i.d. α-stable errors[19] and jointly estimate the AR(1) coefficient and the parameters originating from the characteristic function of the errors by MLE. The rate of convergence of the MLE of the AR(1) coefficient is shown to depend on the parameter α and the mean of the errors. They also find that MLE is more efficient than OLS in finite samples, particularly in the case $\alpha < 1$.

Chan and Tran (1989) and Phillips (1990) assume the DA and DNA of a stable law for the errors, respectively, whereas Phillips (1987a) studies the DNA of a normal law (i.e., partial sum of the errors divided by $\hat{\sigma}_1 \sqrt{T}$ weakly converges to Brownian motion). The case of the DA of a normal law is studied by Kourogenis and Pittis (2008). To be more precise, they assume $\{u_t\}$ is a strictly stationary sequence with $E|u_1|^{\delta} < \infty$ for every $0 \leq \delta < 2$. When the latter condition holds, $\{u_t\}$ is said to have just barely infinite variance (see

---

[19] See Samorodnitsky and Taqqu (1994) for the characteristic function of the α-stable distribution.

Bradley, 1988), and there exists a sequence $a_T = L(T)\sqrt{T}$ such that

$$\frac{1}{a_T} S_{[Tr]} \Rightarrow W(r) \ (0 \leq r \leq 1),$$

where $S_t = \sum_{i=1}^{t} u_i$. Kourogenis and Pittis show that Phillips' (1987a) and Phillips and Perron's (1988) test statistics continue to have corresponding Dickey-Fuller distributions in the limit if and only if $\frac{a_T}{\hat{\sigma}_1\sqrt{T}} \xrightarrow{p} 1$. Because it is difficult to check the latter condition in practice, Kourogenis and Pittis suggest a new test statistic $A_\alpha = T\left(\hat{\alpha} - 1 + \frac{\sum_{t=2}^{T}\hat{u}_t^2}{2\sum_{t=2}^{T-1} y_t^2}\right)$, which has the limiting distribution

$$\left(2\int_0^1 W^2(r)\,dr\right)^{-1} W^2(1).$$

Because an integrated GARCH(1,1) process (see Subsection 3.3.2 for related discussions) driven by i.i.d. normal random variables has just barely infinite variance, this test statistic can be used for unit root testing when the errors follow integrated GARCH(1,1) processes. But Kourogenis and Pittis report critical values of their test just for the AR(1) model without nonstochastic terms, which hinders its use in practice. They report via simulation that their test keeps nominal size reasonably well for the errors following integrated GARCH processes.

3.6   Unit Root Tests against Nonlinear Alternatives

Various nonlinear models have been studied in time series analysis (see Tong, 1993, for a survey of nonlinear time series models). Inference on a unit root can also be embedded in nonlinear models, and many related approaches have been devised in the literature. This section introduces a variety of tests for the null hypothesis of a unit root against the alternative of a nonlinear process.

However, before those tests are introduced, it seems appropriate for the reader to be aware of a few caveats about them. First, rejecting the unit root null hypothesis does not necessarily imply stationarity of the observed time series because a nonlinear process can be nonstationary even when the null is rejected. Second, the rejection of the unit root null hypothesis using a particular nonlinear model should not be interpreted as a signal that the nonlinear model is appropriate for the observed time series. Selection of the true model usually requires more effort. In summary, it is hard to arrive at any conclusions about the stochastic properties of the observed time series when the null hypothesis of a unit root is rejected.

3.6.1   Threshold AR Processes

Tong's (1983) threshold autoregressive (TAR) model has often been used to model asymmetric adjustment paths. Enders and Granger (1998)[20] employ it to introduce a test for a unit root. The simplest models they consider are

$$\Delta y_t = \rho_1 y_{t-1} \mathbf{1}\{y_{t-1} \geq 0\} + \rho_2 y_{t-1} \mathbf{1}\{y_{t-1} < 0\} + u_t; \qquad (3.17)$$

$$\Delta y_t = \rho_1 y_{t-1} \mathbf{1}\{\Delta y_{t-1} \geq 0\} + \rho_2 y_{t-1} \mathbf{1}\{\Delta y_{t-1} < 0\} + u_t. \qquad (3.18)$$

The latter model is called the momentum threshold autoregressive (M-TAR) model. In these models, if y_{t-1} (or Δy_{t-1}) is above its long-run equilibrium level, which is zero, the adjustment is made by $\rho_1 y_{t-1}$; if y_{t-1} (or Δy_{t-1}) is below its long-run equilibrium level, the adjustment is made by $\rho_2 y_{t-1}$. Thus, these models can capture the asymmetric adjustment paths of $\{y_t\}$ toward its long-run equilibrium. The null hypothesis of a unit root for these models is $H_0 : \rho_1 = \rho_2 = 0$. Enders and Granger (1998) propose using an F-test for this null hypothesis.

Models (3.17) and (3.18) are extended in two ways to incorporate a nonzero long-run equilibrium point:

$$\Delta y_t = \rho_1 y_{t-1}^* \mathbf{1}\{y_{t-1} \geq \alpha\} + \rho_2 y_{t-1}^* \mathbf{1}\{y_{t-1} < \alpha\} + u_t; \qquad (3.19)$$

$$\Delta y_t = \rho_1 y_{t-1}^* \mathbf{1}\{\Delta y_{t-1} \geq \alpha\} + \rho_2 y_{t-1}^* \mathbf{1}\{\Delta y_{t-1} < \alpha\} + u_t \qquad (3.20)$$

and

$$\Delta y_t = \rho_1 y_{t-1}^{**} \mathbf{1}\{y_{t-1} \geq \alpha + \beta(t-1)\}$$
$$+ \rho y_{t-1}^{**} \mathbf{1}\{y_{t-1} < \alpha + \beta(t-1)\} + u_t; \qquad (3.21)$$

$$\Delta y_t = \rho_1 y_{t-1}^{**} \mathbf{1}\{\Delta y_{t-1} \geq \alpha + \beta(t-1)\}$$
$$+ \rho_2 y_{t-1}^{**} \mathbf{1}\{\Delta y_{t-1} < \alpha + \beta(t-1)\} + u_t, \qquad (3.22)$$

where $y_{t-1}^* = y_{t-1} - \alpha$ and $y_{t-1}^{**} = y_{t-1} - \alpha - \beta(t-1)$. In practice, parameters α and β are estimated by OLS, and their estimates are plugged into the models. Critical values of the F-test are simulated in Enders and Granger (1998) and reported in Table 3.4. Enders and Granger show via simulation that their test is more powerful than the Dickey-Fuller test in the presence of asymmetry in the DGPs. Cook (2003) provides more simulation results for the Enders-Granger test. He reports that it tends to be more powerful than other unit root tests when the extent of the asymmetry is extreme.

---

[20] Gao, Tjostheim, and Yin (2013) study the TAR model with known thresholds that is slightly more general than that studied by Enders and Granger (1998). In their model, one of the coefficients takes value one, whereas the other takes value less than one in absolute value. They develop asymptotic theory for this model.

Table 3.4. *Critical values of the Enders-Granger test for a unit root*

	Significance level				Significance level		
Model	1%	5%	10%	Model	1%	5%	10%
(3.17)	5.36	3.75	3.04	(3.18)	4.85	3.21	2.51
(3.19)	6.41	4.56	3.74	(3.20)	6.91	4.95	4.05
(3.21)	8.12	6.08	5.15	(3.22	8.74	6.57	5.60

Note: If the computed value of the Enders-Granger test statistic is greater than its critical value at a chosen significance level, reject the null of a unit root.

Caner and Hansen (2001) consider a type of M-TAR model where the threshold effect is introduced via $y_t - y_{t-m}$ $(m > 0)$. An essential case of their model[21] is

$$\Delta y_t = (\mu_1 + \rho_1 y_{t-1})\mathbf{1}\{y_t - y_{t-m} \geq \lambda\}$$
$$+ (\mu_2 + \rho_2 y_{t-1})\mathbf{1}\{y_t - y_{t-m} < \lambda\} + u_t, \quad (3.23)$$

where λ is an unknown threshold parameter. Unlike in Enders and Granger (1998), the threshold parameter should be estimated by the nonlinear least squares method. For the unit root null hypothesis, $H_0 : \rho_1 = \rho_2 = 0$, Caner and Hansen suggest using test statistics

$$R_{1T} = t_1^2 \mathbf{1}\{\hat{\rho}_1 < 0\} + t_2^2 \mathbf{1}\{\hat{\rho}_2 < 0\};$$

$$R_{2T} = t_1^2 + t_2^2,$$

where $\hat{\rho}_1$ and $\hat{\rho}_2$ are nonlinear least squares estimators of ρ_1 and ρ_2, respectively, and t_1 and t_2 are corresponding t-ratios. They derive asymptotic distributions of these test statistics for the cases[22] $\mu_1 = \mu_2$ and $\mu_1 \neq \mu_2$ and report that these depend on nuisance parameters. Caner and Hansen propose using bound testing and bootstrapping as remedies for this situation, and their simulation results favor bootstrapping. Shin and Lee (2003) consider using So and Shin's (1999) instrumental variables estimation (see Subsection 5.3.5) for Model (3.23), but the limiting distributions of their test statistics also depend on nuisance parameters.

Bec, Guay, and Guerre (2008; BGG hereafter)[23] and Kapetanios and Shin (2006) study testing for a unit root using three-regime TAR models. BGG

---

[21] More complex models include the lagged dependent variables as regressors.
[22] When $\mu_1 = \mu_2$, the threshold parameter λ is not identified because the model becomes linear. But when $\mu_1 \neq \mu_2$, λ can be identified under the null of a unit root.
[23] See also Bec, Ben Salem, and Carrasco (2004) for related results.

Table 3.5. *Critical values of the BGG test for a unit root*

	Significance level		
	1%	5%	10%
BGG's Test	18.28	14.20	12.28

Note: If the computed value of the BGG test statistic is greater than its critical value at a chosen significance level, reject the null of a unit root.

employ the symmetric mirroring three-regime TAR model

$$\Delta y_t = u_t + \begin{cases} \mu_1 + \rho_1 y_{t-1} & \text{if } y_{t-1} \in (-\infty, -\lambda] \\ \mu_2 + \rho_2 y_{t-1} & \text{if } y_{t-1} \in [-\lambda, \lambda] \\ -\mu_1 + \rho_1 y_{t-1} & \text{if } y_{t-1} \in (\lambda, +\infty] \end{cases}$$

and test the null hypothesis $H_0 : \rho_1 = \rho_2 = 0$. Rewriting this model using indicator functions as earlier and assuming that λ is known, BGG consider using the Wald test for this null hypothesis. For the case of unknown λ, BGG suggest using the maximum of the Wald statistic over $\lambda \in \Lambda$. The choice of the interval Λ is important for the consistency of the sup-Wald test. Based on their simulation results, BGG recommend

$$\Lambda = [\lambda_L, \lambda_U] \text{ with } \lambda_L = |y|_2 + \frac{\hat{\sigma}_u}{\delta |DF|} \text{ and } \lambda_U = \lambda_L + \delta \hat{\sigma}_u |DF|$$

where $|y|_2$ is the second smallest value of the series $\{y_t\}$, $\hat{\sigma}_u^2$ is the usual estimator of the regression error variance using the AR(1) model with an intercept, DF is the Dickey-Fuller t-ratio using the same model, and δ is a positive constant of the econometrician's choice. Under the null hypothesis, the interval Λ is bounded. But when the null is violated, it is unbounded because $|DF|$ diverges in probability to plus infinity. BGG claim that the sup-Wald test gains power because the chosen interval becomes unbounded under the alternative, which is ascertained by their simulation results. When the interval is chosen as earlier, the sup-Wald test is consistent and has a limiting distribution free of nuisance parameters. Critical values of the sup-Wald test are reported in Table 3.5. BGG also extend their test to the TAR model of order p.

Kapetanios and Shin (2006) consider a three-regime TAR model

$$\Delta y_t = u_t + \tag{3.24}$$

$$\begin{cases} \rho_1 y_{t-1} & \text{if } y_{t-1} \in (-\infty, \lambda_1] \\ \rho y_{t-1} & \text{if } y_{t-1} \in [\lambda_1, \lambda_2] \\ \rho_2 y_{t-1} & \text{if } y_{t-1} \in (\lambda_2, +\infty] \end{cases}$$

with a restriction $\rho = 0$ and test for the null hypothesis $H_0 : \rho_1 = \rho_2 = 0$. Unlike in BGG, the rejection of a null still implies a nonstationary process. Kapetanios and Shin report that the limiting distribution of the Wald-type test for the null hypothesis under known λ_1 and λ_2 is the same as that under a restriction $\lambda_1 = \lambda_2 = 0$. There is a simple explanation for this finding: because $y_{t-1} = O_p(\sqrt{T})$ even under the null, we would have $1\{y_{t-1} \geq \lambda_1\} = 1\{y_{t-1}/\sqrt{T} \geq \lambda_1/\sqrt{T}\} \simeq 1\{y_{t-1}/\sqrt{T} \geq 0\}$ as long as λ_1 and λ_2 are finite. Thus, the values of λ_1 and λ_2 become essentially zero for their asymptotic results. For unknown threshold values, they employ the supremum, average, and exponential average of the Wald statistic, assuming finite width of the middle regime. A caution when using Kapetanios and Shin's (2006) approach is that the rejection of the null still implies nonstationarity of the observed time series. In this sense, test results using their approach are difficult to interpret.

Seo (2008) studies a two-regime TAR model (i.e., Model (3.24) without the middle regime) and proposes to use sup-Wald test as in previous works. He assumes serially correlated errors and suggests using the residual-based bloc bootstrap because the limiting distribution of the sup-Wald test depends on nuisance parameters originating from the serial correlated errors.

3.6.2 Smooth-Transition AR Processes

Kapetanios, Shin, and Snell (2003) consider an exponential smooth-transition AR model[24]:

$$\Delta y_t = \rho y_{t-1} + \gamma y_{t-1}[1 - \exp(-\theta y_{t-d}^2)] + u_t, \ (\theta \geq 0). \qquad (3.25)$$

In this model, as y_{t-d}^2 increases, the coefficient of y_{t-1} changes from ρ to $\rho + \gamma$ because $0 \leq 1 - \exp(-\theta y_{t-d}^2) \leq 1$. Under the unit root null hypothesis, $\rho = \theta = 0$. Imposing $\rho = 0$ and using a Taylor expansion,[25] they estimate the model

$$\Delta y_t = \delta y_{t-1}^3 + error$$

and test the null hypothesis using the t-ratio for δ. The asymptotic distribution for this t-test is reported and tabulated via simulation. When the process has nonzero mean and a linear time trend, the usual detrending can be used before implementing the test. Critical values of Kapetanios, Shin, and Snell's t-ratio are reported in Table 3.6. They report that their test works reasonably well in finite samples.

---

[24]   The reader is referred to Granger and Teräsvirta (1993) for discussions on the smooth-transition autoregressive model.
[25]   This strategy originates from Luukkonen, Saikkonen, and Teräsvirta (1988).

Table 3.6. *Asymptotic critical values of the Kapetanios, Shin, and Snell (2003) test for a unit root*

	Significance level		
	1%	5%	10%
Raw	−2.82	−2.22	−1.92
Demeaned	−3.48	−2.93	−2.66
Demeaned and detrended	−3.93	−3.40	−3.13

Note: If the computed value of the t-ratio is less than its critical value at a chosen significance level, reject the null of a unit root.

Demetrescu and Kruse (2013) study the asymptotic local power of Kapetanios, Shin, and Snell's t-ratio. They find that its asymptotic local power (i.e., asymptotic power under $\gamma = -\frac{c}{T}$, $\theta = \frac{g}{T}$, $c > 0$, $g > 0$) for Model (3.25) without the first term on the right-hand side is higher than the Dickey-Fuller test when the GLS detrending method is used.

He and Sandberg (2006) consider a more general model than Kapetanios, Shin, and Snell (2003) and propose a unit root test using the model

$$y_t = x_t'\pi_1 + x_t'\pi_2 F(t, \gamma, c) + u_t,$$

where $x_t = (1, t, y_{t-1}, \ldots, y_{t-p})'$, π_1 and π_2 are parameter vectors, and $F(t, \gamma, c)$ is a transition function defined by

$$F(t, \gamma, c) = \frac{1}{1 + \exp\{-\gamma(t - c)\}} - \frac{1}{2}.$$

As t grows from $-\infty$ to ∞, the transition function smoothly changes from $-\frac{1}{2}$ to $\frac{1}{2}$ and takes value zero when $t = c$. Parameter c can be considered as a focal point of a gradual structural change. In addition, parameter γ determines the speed of transition. In their model, both the nonstochastic and stochastic parts involve nonlinearity. He and Sandberg's testing strategy is to linearize the model by using a third-order Taylor expansion of $F(t, \gamma, c)$ given by

$$\frac{\gamma(t - c)}{4} + \frac{\gamma^3(t - c)^3}{48} + r(\gamma),$$

where $r(\gamma)$ is a remainder term; they then and perform a unit root test using this linearized model. For the simple case of $x_t = (1, y_{t-1})'$, the linearized model becomes

$$y_t = s_t'\mu + y_{t-1}s_t'\varphi + u_t^*,$$

where $s_t = (1, t, t^2, t^3)'$, $\mu = (\mu_0, \mu_1, \mu_2, \mu_3)'$, and $\varphi = (\varphi_0, \varphi_1, \varphi_2, \varphi_3)$. The null hypothesis of a unit root is written as $\mu_0 = \mu_1 = \mu_2 = \mu_3 = 0$,

Table 3.7. *Asymptotic critical values of the He and Sandberg (2006) t-test for a unit root*

	Significance level		
	1%	5%	10%
Raw	−3.76	−3.04	−2.65
Demeaned	−3.65	−2.94	−2.56
Demeaned and detrended	−5.07	−4.52	−4.25

Note: If the computed value of the *t*-ratio is less than its critical value at a chosen significance level, reject the null of a unit root.

$\varphi_0 = 1$, and $\varphi_1 = \varphi_2 = \varphi_3 = 0$. He and Sandberg suggest using the Dickey-Fuller coefficient and *t*-test statistics for the restriction $\varphi_0 = 1$ and derive their limiting distributions. Their test is also extended to the case of multiple lagged variables. The asymptotic critical values of He and Sandberg's *t*-test statistic are reported in Table 3.7.

3.6.3   Random-Coefficient AR Processes

Random-coefficient AR processes are the AR processes whose coefficients are random variables. They introduce more flexibility than the conventional, fixed-coefficient AR processes and thereby can be more useful for forecasting. In relation to unit root testing, Leybourne, McCabe, and Tremayne (1996; LMT hereafter) test the null of a fixed-coefficient unit root against the alternative of a random unit root. LMT use employ the model

$$y_t - \lambda_t - \sum_{i=1}^{p} \alpha_i y_{t-i} = \rho_t \left(y_{t-1} - \lambda_{t-1} - \sum_{i=1}^{p} \alpha_i y_{t-1-i} \right) + u_t,$$

where $\rho_t \sim \text{iid}(1, \omega^2)$, $u_t \sim \text{iid}(0, \sigma_u^2)$, and $\lambda_t = a + bt + ct(t + 1)/2$. When $\omega^2 = 0$, $\{\Delta y_t\}$ is either level stationary ($c = 0$) or trend stationary ($c \neq 0$) as long as the roots of the equation $1 - \sum_{i=1}^{p} \alpha_i z^i = 0$ lie outside the unit circle, because Δy_t can be represented by

$$\Delta y_t = b + ct + \sum_{i=1}^{p} \alpha_i \Delta y_{t-1-i} + u_t. \tag{3.26}$$

When $\omega^2 > 0$, $\{y_t\}$ has a random unit root or is heteroskedastically integrated.

Table 3.8. *Critical values of the LMT test for a unit root*

	Significance level		
	1%	5%	10%
LMT test	0.261	0.149	0.104

Note: If the computed value of the LMT test statistic is greater than its critical value at a chosen significance level, reject the null of a random unit root.

For the null hypothesis $H_0 : \omega^2 = 0$, LMT derive the LM test statistic,

$$H_T = T^{-3/2} \sigma_u^{-2} \kappa^{-1} \sum_{t=p+3}^{T} \left(\sum_{j=p+2}^{t-1} \hat{u}_j \right)^2 \left(\hat{u}_t^2 - \hat{\sigma}_u^2 \right),$$

where κ is the variance of $\{u_t^2\}$, $\{\hat{u}_t\}$ is the regression residual from Model (3.26), and $\hat{\sigma}_u^2 = \frac{1}{T-p-2} \sum_{t=p+3}^{T} \hat{u}_t^2$. However, its limiting distribution depends on the correlation between $\{u_t\}$ and $\{u_t^2\}$. As a remedy, LMT consider using a modified test statistic,

$$H_T^* = \left(1 - \hat{\psi}^2 \right)^{-1/2} \hat{H}_T - \hat{\psi} \left(1 - \hat{\psi}^2 \right)^{-3/2} \hat{H}_T^+,$$

where $\hat{\psi} = \sum_{i=p+1}^{T} \hat{u}_t (\hat{u}_t^2 - \hat{\sigma}_u^2) / \sqrt{\sum_{i=p+1}^{T} \hat{u}_t^2 \sum_{i=p+1}^{T} (\hat{u}_t^2 - \hat{\sigma}_u^2)}$, $\hat{H}_T$ is the same as H_T except that consistent estimators of σ_u^2 and κ are used ($\hat{\kappa} = \frac{1}{T-p-2} \sum_{t=p+3}^{T} (\hat{u}_t^2 - \hat{\sigma}_u^2)$), and

$$\hat{H}_T^+ = T^{-3/2} \hat{\sigma}_u^{-3} \sum_{t=p+3}^{T} \left(\sum_{j=p+2}^{t-1} \hat{u}_j \right)^2 \hat{u}_t^2.$$

H_T^* has a limiting distribution that is the same as that of H_T with zero correlation between $\{u_t\}$ and $\{u_t^2\}$. Thus, it is free of nuisance parameters. Critical values for the LMT test are reported in Table 3.8.

Granger and Swanson (1997) study a random-coefficient AR(1) model,[26]

$$y_t = \rho_t y_{t-1} + u_t,$$

where

$$\rho_t = \exp(\gamma_t), \quad \gamma_t = \mu + \delta \gamma_{t-1} + \eta_t, \quad |\delta| < 1.$$

---

[26] They call it an AR(1) model with a stochastic unit root. Yoon (2006) reports some properties of the stochastic unit root process.

They show that LMT's LM test has power against their random-coefficient AR(1) process. In addition, using the random-coefficient AR(1) model with its coefficient $\rho_t \sim \text{iid}(\rho, \omega^2)$, Distaso (2008) studies the LM test for the unit root null hypothesis $H_0 : \rho = 1, \omega^2 = 0$.

3.7   Summary and Further Remarks

This chapter discussed how to perform inference on a unit root in the presence of structural changes in the parameters of nonstochastic regressors or the innovation variance, conditional heteroskedasticity in the errors, outliers in the data, or errors with fat-tailed distributions. It showed that existing methods should be adapted to accommodate each specification. In addition, it considered unit root tests against nonlinear alternatives. Again, new procedures are required to cope with these new alternatives.

The methods introduced in this chapter are useful under specific circumstances. If one has good reason to suspect that the standard AR model is not appropriate for a given dataset, it will be worthwhile to consider using the procedures discussed in this chapter. Structural changes in the parameters of nonstochastic regressors or the innovation variance are likely when a dataset covering a long sampling period is used. It is hard to believe that the same DGP will generate data for many years. Methods for structural changes should be considered seriously when using data collected over a long period.

Because ARCH and GARCH effects are prevalent in high-frequency financial data, it is natural to consider unit root tests that accommodate them. However, the MLE-based and adaptive t-ratios' limiting distributions depend on nuisance parameters in the limit, which makes it inconvenient, if not impossible, to use them in practice. Using conventional unit root tests does not result in serious problems unless the errors follow an integrated GARCH process. But the power of the conventional test is inferior to that of the MLE-based and adaptive t-tests. Thus, further efforts are needed to make the MLE-based or adaptive t-tests user-friendly. Bootstrapping is a way to do so, but it has not yet been explored in the literature.

Outliers are often observed in financial time series. Thus, it is worthwhile to consider using unit root tests that can deal with the outlier problem. In practice, using unit root tests that are relatively robust to the presence of MA(1) errors or the bootstrap version of Perron and Rodríguez's (2003) test seems appropriate.

Fat-tailed errors are of concern when dealing with financial time series, although the case of infinite variance seems to be rare. It has been found that the unit root distributions undergo changes with the fat-tailed errors. But there has been little research on how to do inference on a unit root under the fat-tailed errors. The only methods suggested in the literature are the modified bootstrapping proposed by Moreno and Romo (2012) and Kourogenis and Pittis's (2008) test that can be used in the case of the DA of a normal law. Moreover, the latter method should be extended to the case involving nonstochastic regressors to make it more practical. It is hoped that more methods for unit root testing will be developed to deal with the fat-tailed errors.

When regime-swiching behavior of a time series is expected, it is better to embed unit root tests in the nonlinear models discussed in this chapter. Which model to choose in practice will depend on each circumstance. But one needs to exercise caution when the null of a unit root is rejected, because the rejection can be interpreted in various ways. Selection of the best dynamic model for a given time series requires more than unit root testing.

4 Alternative Approaches to Inference on Unit Roots

4.1 Introduction

Inferential procedures in the previous chapters use mostly OLS or MLE along with asymptotic critical values, take the alternative hypothesis as stationary AR processes, and have a unit root as their null hypothesis. They also belong to the class of classical statistical procedures that treat parameters as unknown constants. But there are many other approaches to inference on a unit root that do not necessarily share these features. This chapter introduces those alternative approaches to inference on a unit root.

This chapter deals with the following topics. First, unit root tests that take the alternative hypothesis as fractionally integrated processes are introduced. Unlike most unit root tests in this book that embed their null and alternative hypotheses in the AR model, these tests use fractionally integrated models. They also have standard distributions in the limit unlike other types of unit root tests. Second, this chapter introduces regression methods for the AR model that are robust to outliers. These methods are based on different asymptotic theory from OLS and are technically more involved than OLS. Third, model-free tests for a unit root are introduced. These tests are less model dependent, and some are robust to outliers and useful in this sense. Fourth, bootstrapping methods are discussed in relation to the inference on a unit root. Bootstrapping methods are known to be useful to find finite-sample critical values for hypothesis testing and to construct more accurate confidence intervals. How bootstrapping works for the AR model with a unit root is explained. Fifth, Bayesian inferential methods for a unit root are surveyed. These methods sometimes yield empirical results different from those using the classical approach and hence have attracted much attention. They have also evoked vigorous and stimulating methodological debates among Bayesians and non-Bayesians. Sixth, tests that take stationarity with or without structural changes as the null hypothesis are introduced. Some of these tests are used quite often in practice to complement unit root test results.

Last, tests for changing persistence are discussed. The chapter concludes with a summary and further remarks.

4.2 Unit Root Tests against the Alternatives of Fractional Integration

This section introduces unit root tests that take the alternative hypothesis as fractionally integrated processes. See Subsection 2.2.4 for a brief introduction to fractionally integrated processes. Diebold and Rudebusch (1991) and Hassler and Wolters (1994) report that the Dickey-Fuller-type tests have quite low empirical power against the alternative hypothesis of fractional integration, although Krämer (1998) shows that the augmented Dickey-Fuller test is consistent if the order of autoregression does not tend to infinity too quickly. The low power of the Dickey-Fuller-type test necessitates unit tests against the alternative hypothesis of fractional integration. Broadly speaking, there are three kinds of unit tests under this category: LM, LR, and Wald tests. Their asymptotic local power properties are equivalent, but the ways to implement them make the tests look quite different.

4.2.1 LM Tests

Robinson (1994) studies LM tests for fractionally integrated models. A special case of his model[1] relevant to this section is

$$(1 - B)^{1+\theta} y_t = u_t, \ (t = 1, \ldots, T) \tag{4.1}$$

$$y_t = 0, \ t \leq 0.$$

Assuming an i.i.d. normal distribution for $\{u_t\}$, Robinson derives an LM test statistic for the null hypothesis $H_0 : \theta = 0$ against the alternative $H_1 : \theta \neq 0$. Under the null hypothesis, $\{y_t\}$ is an I(1) process, but it becomes a fractionally integrated process under the alternative. In particular, if $\theta < -\frac{1}{2}$, $\{y_t\}$ is a stationary process. The LM test statistic takes the form

$$R = \frac{T}{\bar{\sigma}^4} \bar{a}' \bar{A}^{-1} \bar{a},$$

where $\bar{a} = \sum_{l=1}^{T-1} \frac{1}{l} \frac{1}{T-l} \sum_{t=1}^{T-l} \Delta y_t \Delta y_{t+l}$, $\bar{A} = \sum_{l=1}^{T-1} \frac{1}{l^2}(1 - \frac{l}{T})$, and $\bar{\sigma}^2 = \frac{1}{T} \sum_{t=1}^{T-l} (\Delta y_t)^2$. Robinson devises a frequency version of the test statistic R and claims that it is more convenient to use in practice. He reports that the test statistic has a chi-square distribution with one degree of freedom in the limit. This

---

[1] Robinson's (1994) model enables us to test the nulls of double unit roots, complex unit roots, seasonal unit roots, $1/f$ noise, and MA unit roots against the alternatives of fractional integration. His model also allows the presence of nonstochastic variables in the time series $\{y_t\}$.

asymptotic result requires only that $\{u_t\}$ be a martingale difference sequence. The normality assumption made for the derivation of the LM test statistic is not needed for the asymptotic result. Robinson extends his LM test to the unobserved components model (cf. equation (2.38)) that includes nonstochastic trend variables. Still, the LM test has a chi-square distribution in the limit.

Robinson (1994) also considers the case of autocorrelated errors that have spectral density of the form

$$\frac{\sigma^2}{2\pi} g(\lambda; \tau), \quad -\pi < \lambda \leq \pi,$$

where $g(\cdot)$ is a known function of the frequency λ and the unknown parameter vector τ. Robinson's frequency domain test statistic requires a specification of the function $g(\cdot)$, and he recommends the use of Bloomfield's (1973) exponential spectrum model:

$$g(\lambda; \tau) = \exp\left(2\sum_{j=1}^{q} \tau_j \cos(\lambda_j)\right).$$

Simulation results in Robinson indicate that his test performs better than the Dickey-Fuller and SP's tests for the alternatives of fractional integration, and vice versa for the AR alternatives.

Remarkably, Robinson's (1994) test statistics have a standard distribution – chi-square—in the limit with or without nonstochastic trend variables, a feature not shared by most of the unit root tests discussed in this book. His test is useful when the alternatives are fractionally integrated processes. But if the alternatives are stationary AR processes, it is better to use conventional unit root tests. Because the DGP under the alternative hypothesis is unknown, it is worthwhile to try Robinson's test in practice.

Gil-Alana and Robinson (1997) apply Robinson's (1994) LM test statistic and its variant to an extended version of Nelson and Plosser's (1982) dataset. They report that the null of a unit root is not rejected for most series. When Bloomfield's exponential spectrum model is used, most series find evidence favoring $\theta = 0$ or $\theta = -0.25$.

Tanaka (1999) studies the problem of testing the null hypothesis $H_0 : \theta = 0$ against the alternatives $H_1 : \theta > 0$ and $H_2 : \theta < 0$ for Model (4.1) in the time domain.[2] The LM test statistic for the null hypothesis is derived as[3]

$$S_{T1} = T \sum_{k=1}^{T-1} \frac{1}{k} \hat{\rho}_k,$$

---

[2] Tanaka's (1999) model includes deterministic trend variables. I omit them here for simplicity. Hassler, Rodrigues, and Rubia (2009) extend Tanaka's (1999) LM test to Robinson's (1994) model that includes various fractional alternatives.

[3] See also Agiakloglou and Newbold (1994).

where $\hat{\rho}_k = \sum_{t=k+1}^{T} \Delta y_{t-k} \Delta y_t / \sum_{t=2}^{T} \Delta y_t^2$. Tanaka derives the null distribution of the LM test statistic as follows:

$$S'_{T1} = \frac{1}{\sqrt{T\pi^2/6}} S_{T1} \Rightarrow N(0, 1).$$

When S'_T is larger than a critical value, reject H_0 against $H_1 : \theta > 0$; when it is smaller than a critical value, reject it against $H_2 : \theta < 0$. Tanaka also extends his test to serially correlated ARMA errors. The variance of the limiting normal distribution in this case depends on the ARMA parameters in a complicated manner. In principle, Tanaka's test is no different from Robinson's (1994) except that it takes a time domain approach. But he shows that the LM test is asymptotically uniformly most powerful invariant (UMPI) in the sense that its power attains the highest power of all the invariant tests as $T \to \infty$ under the local alternatives $\theta = \frac{\delta}{\sqrt{T}}$ (δ is a constant). This is the difference from the LM test for an AR unit root that is not UMPI.

Demetrescu, Kuzin, and Hassler (2008) devise a regression-based LM test. They recognize that the LM test statistic can be written as

$$\tau = \frac{1}{\sqrt{T}} \sum_{t=2}^{T} \Delta y_t x^*_{t-1} \text{ with } x^*_{t-1} = \sum_{k=1}^{t-1} \frac{\Delta y_{t-k}}{k}.$$

Assuming that $\{\Delta y_t\}$ is a linear process driven by a martingale difference sequence, they consider the OLS regression[4]

$$\Delta y_t = \hat{\phi} x^*_{t-1} + \hat{a}_1 \Delta y_{t-1} + \cdots + \hat{a}_p \Delta y_{t-p} + \hat{\varepsilon}_t$$

and show that the t-ratio for x^*_{t-1} has a standard normal distribution in the limit under the null hypothesis of a unit root when the AR order p grows to infinity at a slower rate than the sample size T. For the AR order, they suggest using $p = [4(T/100)^{1/4}]$ as in Schwert (1989). According to the simulation results of Demetrescu, Kuzin, and Hassler, their test's finite-sample performance is similar to that of Dolado, Gonzalo, and Mayoral's (2002) Wald test (see Subsection 4.2.2). Demetrescu, Kuzin, and Hassler's test deals with the serial correlation in $\{u_t\}$ conveniently and effectively, and hence it deserves much attention in empirical applications.

4.2.2   Wald Tests

Tanaka (1999) studies estimation of the order of fractional integration by MLE. For the model

$$(1 - B)^d y_t = u_t, \ (t = 1, \ldots, T) \tag{4.2}$$

$$y_t = 0, \ t \leq 0$$

---

[4] See also Agiakloglou and Newbold (1994) for a similar approach.

with $u_t \sim \text{iid} N(0, \sigma^2)$, he considers the MLE of d that maximizes the log-likelihood function

$$l(d) = -\frac{T}{2} \log(2\pi \sigma^2) - \frac{T}{2} \log \left[\sum_{t=1}^{T} \left((1 - B)^d y_t\right)^2 / \sigma^2 \right].$$

He reports that the MLE, $\hat{d}$, has the asymptotic distribution

$$\sqrt{T}(\hat{d} - d) \Rightarrow N\left(0, \frac{6}{\pi^2}\right).$$

Thus, the null hypothesis $H_0 : d = 1$ can be tested by the Wald test statistic:

$$W = \frac{\sqrt{T}(\hat{d} - 1)}{\sqrt{\frac{6}{\pi^2}}}.$$

The limiting local power of the Wald test is the same as that of the LM test. Tanaka also extends the Wald test to serially correlated ARMA errors.

In addition to the MLE, there are many estimators of d (e.g., log-periodogram, local-Whittle, and averaged periodogram estimators) that work under less restrictive model specifications than the MLE as reviewed by Robinson (2003) and Velasco (2006).[5] In theory, these estimators can be used to construct Wald tests for a unit root. But because these estimators converge to unity at a slower rate than $\frac{1}{\sqrt{T}}$, it has been conjectured that the Wald tests do not have high power, although formal experimental studies have yet to be done. If this conjecture is correct, Wald tests that are introduced here should be preferred in empirical practice.

Dolado, Gonzalo, and Mayoral (2002; DGM hereafter) consider the generalized Dickey-Fuller regression model

$$\Delta y_t = \rho \Delta^{d_1} y_t + u_t, \tag{4.3}$$

where $u_t \sim \text{iid}(0, \sigma^2)$. It boils down to the Dickey-Fuller regression model for $d_1 = 0$. When $\rho = 0$, it follows that $y_t = I(1)$. But when $\rho < 0$, Model (4.3) can be written as

$$(\Delta^{1-d_1} - \rho B)\Delta^{d_1} y_t = u_t.$$

Because all the roots of the polynomial equation $\Pi(z) = (1 - z)^{1-d_1} - \rho z = 0$ are outside the unit circle when $-2^{1-d_1} < \rho < 0$, we have $y_t = I(d_1)$ under the given restriction on ρ. Thus, the null hypothesis $H_0 : y_t = I(1)$ can be tested against the alternative $H_1 : y_t = I(d_1)$ by testing $H_0 : \rho = 0$ against $H_1 : \rho < 0$.

---

[5] See Phillips and Shimotsu (2004) and Phillips (2007) for the unit root case.

Let the OLS estimator of ρ in Model (4.3) be denoted as $\hat{\rho}$. When $u_t \sim$ iid$(0, \sigma^2)$, it follows under $H_0 : y_t = I(1)$ that

$$T^{1-d_1}\hat{\rho} \Rightarrow \frac{\int_0^1 W_{-d_1}(r)\,\mathrm{d}W(r)}{\int_0^1 W_{-d_1}^2(r)\,\mathrm{d}r}, \ 0 \leq d_1 < 0.5;$$

$$(T \log T)^{1/2}\,\hat{\rho} \Rightarrow \mathbf{N}(0, \pi), \ d_1 = 0.5;$$

$$T^{1/2}\hat{\rho} \Rightarrow \mathbf{N}\left(0, \frac{\Gamma^2(d_1)}{\Gamma(2d_1 - 1)}\right), \ 0.5 < d_1 < 1,$$

where $W_d(r)$ is the Type II fractional Brownian motion.[6] When $d_1 = 0$, the usual Dickey-Fuller distribution is restored because $W_0(r)$ is Brownian motion. Moreover, the t-ratio using $\hat{\rho}$, $t_{\hat{\rho}}$, has the asymptotic distribution

$$t_{\hat{\rho}} \Rightarrow \frac{\int_0^1 W_{-d_1}(r)\,\mathrm{d}W(r)}{\left(\int_0^1 W_{-d_1}^2(r)\,\mathrm{d}r\right)^{1/2}}, \ 0 \leq d_1 < 0.5;$$

$$t_{\hat{\rho}} \Rightarrow N(0, 1), \ 0.5 \leq d_1 < 1.$$

According to these results, the t-ratio has a standard normal distribution when the alternative is close to the null, but it has a nonstandard one when the alternative is away from the null. The t-ratio is shown to be consistent for any value of $d_1 \in [0, 1)$ if the DGP under the alternative hypothesis is given by $\Delta^{d_1} y_t = u_t \mathbf{1}\{t > 0\}$.

A practical difficulty encountered when using DGM's test is the unknown value of d_1. To resolve this issue, they recommend using an estimator of d_1— $\hat{d}_1$— that originates from the trimming rule

$$\hat{d}_1 = \begin{cases} \hat{d}_T, & \text{if } \hat{d}_T < 1 - c \\ 1 - c, & \text{if } \hat{d}_T \geq 1 - c \end{cases}, \ 0 < c < \frac{1}{2},$$

where $\hat{d}_T$ is any $\sqrt{T}$-consistent estimator of d_1. When $\hat{d}_T$ is used, the t-ratio has a standard normal distribution in the limit. DGM also extend their test to the case of AR errors using an augmented Dickey-Fuller-type regression model.

Lobato and Velasco (2006) study how to choose d_1 for DGM's test. In a fixed alternative framework with white noise errors, they suggest using the rule

$$d_1^* = -0.31 + 0.719\tilde{d}_T,$$

---

[6] "Type II" Brownian motion is defined as $W_d(r) = \sqrt{2d+1} \int_0^r (r-s)^d dW(s)$, $r \geq 0$ and $W_d(r) = -\sqrt{2d+1} \int_r^0 (s-r)^d dW(s)$, $r < 0$. Its mean and variance are the same as those of Type I Brownian motion, but their covariances are different. Additionally, the increments of $W_d(r)$ are nonstationary unlike those of Type I Brownian motion. See Marinucci and Robinson (1999) for further details.

where $T^\tau(\tilde{d}_T - d) = o_p(1)$ for some $\tau > 0$ and $|\tilde{d}_T| \leq K$ for some $K < \infty$. This rule comes from maximizing the squared correlation between $\{\Delta y_t\}$ and $\{\Delta^{d_1} y_t\}$. For serially correlated errors, the rule becomes more complicated because it depends on the short-run dynamics of the error terms. Lobato and Velasco suggest a sequential method to choose d_1 in this case, which performs quite well according to their experimental results.

Lobato and Velasco (2007) test the null hypothesis $H_0 : d = 1$ against the alternative $H_1 : d < 1$ for Model (4.2) with $u_t \sim$ iid$(0, \sigma^2)$. They rewrite Model (4.2) as

$$\Delta y_t = (\Delta - \Delta^d)y_t + u_t = (1 - \Delta^{d-1})\Delta y_t + u_t. \tag{4.4}$$

When d is set to be d_2, Model (4.4) is written as

$$\Delta y_t = \varphi(\Delta^{d_2-1} - 1)\Delta y_t + u_t,$$

where $\varphi = 0$ under the null and $\varphi = -1$ under the alternative. To make the regressor continuous at $d_2 = 1$, Lobato and Velasco employ the rescaled regression model

$$\Delta y_t = \phi z_{t-1}(d_2) + u_t,$$

where $z_{t-1}(d_2) = \frac{\Delta^{d_2-1}-1}{1-d_2}\Delta y_t$. They suggest testing the null hypothesis by testing the significance of the coefficient ϕ with $d_2 > \frac{1}{2}$ by means of a left-sided t-test. In practice, d_2 can be chosen to be an estimator of d (e.g., Velasco and Robinson, 2000) that is greater than $\frac{1}{2}$. Lobato and Velasco report that their test has higher empirical power than that of DGM. They also extend their test to an ARIMA(p,d,0) model.

Kew and Harris (2009) define a class of fractional unit root tests within the regression framework making use of White's (1980) heteroskedasticity-robust standard error, which includes DGM, Lobato and Velasco's (2007), and Demetrescu, Kuzin, and Hassler's (2008) tests. They show that these tests are asymptotically valid in the presence of both conditional and unconditional heteroskedasticity.

Gao and Robinson (2013) consider testing for a unit root in the presence of an unknown, smooth, nonparametric function of deterministic trend. A special case of their model is

$$(1 - B)^d y_t = g\left(\frac{t}{T}\right) + u_t, \ (t = 1, \dots, T). \tag{4.5}$$

Gao and Robinson employ a kernel-type estimator of the trend function $g(\cdot)$ to obtain an estimate of u_t and then estimate the parameter d by minimizing the sum of squared residuals. The estimator of d is used to formulate the Wald test statistic. Gao and Robinson's model allows for short-memory dynamics in $\{y_t\}$

as well. Their test is useful when it is uncertain how to choose the deterministic function in unit root testing. It can also be used when there might be structural changes in the deterministic part of the observations, because those structural changes can be approximated by a continuous function as in Becker, Enders, and Lee (2006; see Subsection 4.8.1).

4.2.3 LR Test

Nielsen (2004a) considers the LR test[7] for the null hypothesis $H_0 : d = 1$ for Model (4.2).[8] The LR test statistic is defined as $T \log(\tilde{\sigma}^2/\hat{\sigma}^2)$, where $\tilde{\sigma}^2$ and $\hat{\sigma}^2$ are restricted (i.e., $d = 1$) and unrestricted MLEs of σ^2, respectively. He shows that the Wald, LR, and LM tests have the same limiting distribution under a sequence of local alternatives, but claims that the LR test performs best in finite samples and is easier to compute for ARMA errors.

Gao and Robinson (2013) devise a pseudo-log LR test for a unit root using the ratio of the restricted and unrestricted sum of squared residuals from Model (4.5). Its distribution is chi-square in the limit. They show that the test works reasonably well in finite samples.

4.2.4 Further Remarks

Comparing the tests discussed so far, the LM tests of Robinson (1994), Tanaka (1999), and Demetrescu, Kuzin, and Hassler (2008) do not need to estimate the order of fractional integration, whereas the LR and Wald-type tests do so. In this sense, the LM tests are easier to implement in practice. Moreover, for the LR and Wald-type tests to work well in finite samples, a good estimator of the order of fractional integration is needed. But given the well-known difficulties in estimating the order of fractional integration in finite samples, it is difficult to expect that these tests would have better finite-sample size properties than the LM test, although large scale simulation studies are needed to confirm this conjecture. In relation to the power of the Wald, LR, and LM tests, Lobato and Velasco (2008) establish the well-known inequality among those tests. However, this inequality should not be interpreted as the order of power of these tests because it holds under both the null and alternative hypotheses.

As we have seen in Subsection 2.4.10, initial observations can have an enormous impact on the finite-sample power of unit root tests. Moreover, ways to estimate deterministic components affect the power of unit root tests. But the literature on fractional integration has been silent on these issues, which invites further study.

---

[7] See Nielsen (2004b, 2005) for multivariate extensions.
[8] Note that Model (4.2) is a special case of his model.

4.3   Robust Regressions in the Presence of a Unit Root

When the data are contaminated by outliers, one may use estimation methods that are robust to outliers. The often-used estimators are the M-, LAD, and quantile regression estimators. This section discusses the AR regression using the M-, LAD, and quantile regression estimators.

Lucas (1995b)[9] considers estimating the AR(1) model with mixing errors by using the M-estimator. For the AR(1) model with an intercept and a linear time trend, the M-estimators of μ, β, and α are derived by solving

$$\sum_{t=2}^{T} \begin{pmatrix} 1 \\ t \\ y_{t-1} \end{pmatrix} \psi(y_t - \hat{\mu}_M - \hat{\beta}_M t - \hat{\alpha}_M y_{t-1}) = 0$$

for some function $\psi(\cdot)$. The equation can be considered as the first-order condition for the problem of minimizing

$$\sum_{t=2}^{T} \rho(y_t - \mu - \beta t - \alpha y_{t-1})$$

with respect to μ, β, and α, once we regard $\psi(\cdot)$ as the first derivative of $\rho(\cdot)$. The M-estimator was devised as a robust alternative to the OLS estimator in the presence of outliers in the data (cf. Huber, 1967). Lucas reports the limiting distributions of $\hat{\alpha}_M$ and the related t-ratio for the case $\alpha = 1$. They depend on nuisance parameters and are different from those of OLS. Lucas corrects the estimator and t-ratio along the line of Phillips (1987a) and shows that they are free of nuisance parameters in the limit. For $\psi(\cdot)$, he considers $\psi(x) = \frac{4x}{3+x^2}$ and $\psi(x) = \min(1.345, \max(-1.345, x))$. The former is motivated by the maximum likelihood estimation for t-distributed observations, and the latter is often used in the literature on robust statistics (cf. Huber, 1981). Simulation results in Lucas show that his modified test statistics tend to enjoy higher empirical power than the Phillips-Perron test statistics when there are many outliers. However, they also tend to have size distortions when the errors are serially correlated.

Herce (1996) estimates the AR(1) model (2.1) with stationary errors using the LAD estimator, which is defined as

$$\arg\min_{\alpha \in R} \sum_{t=2}^{T} |y_t - \alpha y_{t-1}|. \tag{4.6}$$

He also considers the AR(1) model with an intercept. The limiting distributions of the LAD estimator are derived for the case $\alpha = 1$. They are different from

---

[9]   See also Lucas (1995a) for related discussion.

those of OLS and are represented as the sum of the weak limit of the OLS estimator and a mixture normal random variable. Because the limiting distributions involve nuisance parameters, the LAD estimator and related t-ratio are modified to eliminate them. The resulting test statistics are shown to have higher power than the Phillips-Perron test statistics when the data have many outliers but to have serious size distortions for the MA(1) errors.

Koenker and Bassett's (1978) quantile regression can also be used for robust inference. The quantile regression approach enables the researcher to study a range of conditional quantile functions, which allow various forms of conditional heterogeneity. See Koenker (2005) for a detailed introduction to quantile regression. Koenker and Xiao (2004) apply the quantile regression methods to the AR(1) model with a unit root. For the AR(1) model without nonstochastic terms (i.e., Model (2.1)), let $Q_u(\tau)$ denote the τ-th quantile of u_t and let $Q_{y_t}(\tau \mid y_{t-1})$ denote the τ-th conditional quantile of y_t given y_{t-1}. Then,

$$Q_{y_t}(\tau \mid y_{t-1}) = Q_u(\tau) + \alpha y_{t-1} = \alpha_0(\tau) + \alpha_1(\tau)y_{t-1}.$$

The quantile regression solves the problem

$$\min_{\alpha_0(\tau),\alpha_1(\tau)} \sum_{t=1}^{T} \rho_\tau(y_t - \alpha_0(\tau) - \alpha_1(\tau)y_{t-1}), \tag{4.7}$$

where $\rho_\tau(u) = u(\tau - 1\{u < 0\})$. When $\tau = 0.5$, the objective function becomes

$$\min_{\alpha_0(0.5),\alpha_1(0.5)} \frac{1}{2} \sum_{t=1}^{T} |y_t - \alpha_0(0.5) - \alpha_1(0.5)y_{t-1}|,$$

which is similar to but not exactly the same as the objective function (4.6). Note that the quantile AR regression introduces an intercept term that is not present in the original AR(1) model. Koenker and Xiao derive the limiting distributions of the estimators from the optimization problem (4.7) for the unit root case $\alpha = 1$. The limiting distributions involve the demeaned Brownian motion due to the presence of the term $\alpha_0(\tau)$. The limiting distribution of the estimator of $\alpha_1(0.5)$ is different from that of Herce (1996) for the same reason. The t-ratio for a unit root based on the quantile regression has a limiting distribution that depends on nuisance parameters. Koenker and Xiao recommend the use of bootstrapping to deal with the nuisance parameters. When bootstrapping is used and when the error terms follow Student's t-distribution, Koenker and Xiao's t-test with $\tau = 0.5$ tends to show higher power than the Dickey-Fuller test. But it is not certain why $\tau = 0.5$ should be used in Koenker and Xiao's t-test. Moreover, their t-test is expected to have lower power than Herce's because the former's limiting distribution involves the demeaned Brownian motion rather than a standard one, based on a similar phenomenon for the Dickey-Fuller test (see Subsection 2.3.1).

4.4 Model-Free Tests for a Unit Root

This section introduces various tests for a unit root that do not assume any particular parametric models. Thus, they are less model dependent than those in the previous chapters, but they tend to have lower power than the Dickey-Fuller test.

4.4.1 Rank-Based Tests

Granger and Hallman (1991) consider the following question: if $\{y_t\}$ is a unit root process, is $\{h(y_t)\}$—a monotonic transformation of $\{y_t\}$—a unit root process too? Because time series observations are often transformed (e.g., logarithmic transformation) before unit root tests are applied, Granger and Hallman claim that this is an empirically relevant question if one wants to know properties of the transformed time series. No doubt, a straightforward answer to Granger and Hallman's question can be obtained by applying unit root tests to $\{h(y_t)\}$. However, Granger and Hallman suggest using rank-based tests for which subsequent researchers have found other virtues such as robustness to fat-tailed distributions and to structural changes (cf. Breitung and Gouriéroux, 1997). More precisely, Granger and Hallman's question can be stated as the following null hypothesis:

$$H_0 : h(y_t) = h(y_{t-1}) + \varepsilon_t, \ \{\varepsilon_t\} \text{ is an i.i.d. process.}$$

Granger and Hallman suggest applying the Dickey-Fuller test to the rank of y_t among the observations $y_1, \ldots, y_T$, denoted here as $R_{T,t}$. It is not intuitively evident why $\{R_{T,t}\}$ should be a random walk process when $\{y_t\}$ is. However, Granger and Hallman show by simulation that the rank-based Dickey-Fuller test has discriminating power in finite samples. When the null hypothesis is rejected, we may say that both $\{y_t\}$ and $\{h(y_t)\}$ do not follow a random walk process.

Subsequently, Fotopoulos and Ahn (2003) derive the limiting distributions of the rank-based Dickey-Fuller test statistics. Additionally, they show via simulation that the rank-based Dickey-Fuller test has lower power than the Dickey-Fuller test, even when the innovation process is subject to nonnormality, and that the rank-based Dickey-Fuller t-test has an anomalous power profile in the vicinity of the null hypothesis.

Instead of using $R_{T,t}$, Breitung and Gouriéroux (1997) consider using the rank of Δy_t among $\Delta y_2, \ldots, \Delta y_T$, denoted as $r_{T,t}$, and apply SP's score-type test to $\{r_{T,t}\}$. Their null hypothesis is a random walk with drift and the alternative trend stationarity. Because differences of the observations are used, the presence of drift under the null does not pose any problem. The finite-sample power of Breitung and Gouriéroux's test tends not to be high compared to the Dickey-Fuller and Granger and Hallman's (1991) tests according to Breitung and Gouriéroux's and Fotopoulos and Ahn's (2003) simulation results.

Hallin, Van den Akker, and Werker (2011) propose a class of tests using $r_{T,t}$. Their test statistics are derived by using the asymptotic theory of statistical experiments and have some optimal features when the reference pdf, needed to construct test statistics, is the same as the true pdf of the errors. Their tests are shown via simulation to be more robust to fat-tailed error distributions than conventional unit root tests.

Hasan and Koenker (1997) propose a unit root test that uses the regression rank scores from Gutenbrunner and Jurěcková (1992) and Gutenbrunner, Jurěcková, Koenker, and Portnoy (1993). The regression rank scores stem from the dual solution for Koenker and Bassett's (1978) regression quantiles. Because Hasan and Koenker's test is based on the complex theory of quantile regression and rank test, it is difficult to present it in a limited space. We, therefore, refer the reader to their original papers for the test. We do note, however, that the test has good power when the innovation process has heavy tails.[10]

Note that the rank-based tests discussed so far require an i.i.d. assumption on the errors, which may not be appropriate in some applications. More investigations are needed to determine now the rank-based tests deal with the case of serially correlated and heteroskedastic errors.

4.4.2 Tests Using the Number of Level Crossings

It is well known that the expected waiting time between returns to the origin of a random walk process is infinite, whereas that for a stationary process is finite. Burridge and Guerre (1996) use this observation to propose a unit root test. Let the normalized number of crossings of the level 0 be

$$K_T(0) = \frac{1}{\sqrt{T}} \sum_{t=1}^{T} [\mathbf{1}\{y_{t-1} \leq 0, y_t > 0\} + \mathbf{1}\{y_{t-1} > 0, y_t \leq 0\}]$$

where $y_t = y_{t-1} + u_t$ and $\{u_t\}$ is an i.i.d. process with zero mean and finite variance σ_u^2. Then, $\sqrt{T} K_T(0)$ measures how many times $\{y_t\}$ crosses the level 0 during the sampling period. Burridge and Guerre find that

$$K_T(0) \Rightarrow \frac{E |u_1|}{\sigma_u} \times |N(0, 1)|.$$

---

[10] Hasan (2001) extends Hasan and Koenker (1997) to the case of infinite variance innovations.

Thus, their unit root test takes the functional form

$$K_T^*(0) = \frac{\hat{\sigma}_u}{\sum_{t=1}^{T} |\Delta x_t| / T} K_T(0),$$

where $\hat{\sigma}_u = \sqrt{\sum_{t=1}^{T} (\Delta x_t)^2 / T}$, which has a limiting distribution free of nuisance parameters. García and Sansó (2006) extend Burridge and Guerre's test to the case of serially correlated errors. Though the test using the number of level crossings is interesting, its finite-sample power is inferior to that of the Dickey-Fuller test according to Burridge and Guerre.

4.4.3   Variance Ratio Test

Breitung (2002) suggests a variance ratio test[11] that is model-free and does not require estimating the long-run variance. His test statistic is defined as

$$B_T = \frac{T^{-2} \sum_{t=1}^{T} S_t^2}{\sum_{t=1}^{T} y_t^2},$$

where $S_t = \sum_{i=1}^{t} y_i$. When $\{y_t\}$ is a unit root process,

$$B_T \Rightarrow \int_0^1 \left(\int_0^a W(r) \, dr \right)^2 da / \int W(r)^2 \, dr.$$

But when $\{y_t\}$ is stationary, $B_T \xrightarrow{p} 0$, making the test consistent. Breitung extends the test statistic to the case where $\{y_t\}$ has a deterministic trend. The test statistic has reasonably good finite-sample size and power properties. In addition, it is known to work well under integrated GARCH errors (see Subsection 3.3.2).

Nielsen (2009) considers a variance ratio test statistic

$$\rho(d) = T^{2d} \frac{\sum_{t=1}^{T} y_t^2}{\sum_{t=1}^{T} \tilde{y}_t^2},$$

where $\tilde{y}_t = (1 - B)^{-d} y_t$ and d is a constant that needs to be chosen. If $d = 1$, $\rho(d) = \frac{1}{B_T}$. He derives the limiting distribution of the variance ratio test statistic under the null hypothesis that $\{y_t\}$ is a unit root process. He reports that the variance ratio test with $d = 0.1$ and the GLS-detrending has higher empirical power than the Dickey-Fuller-GLS test. The case where $\{y_t\}$ has a deterministic trend is also dealt with in Nielsen.

---

[11] See also Bierens (1997) for a similar idea. The asymptotic local power of Breitung's (2002) variance ratio test is derived in Hosseinkouchack (2013).

4.4.4 Range-Based Test

Cavaliere (2001) employs a range statistic for unit root testing. For the AR(1) model (2.1) with mixing errors, his range statistic is defined as

$$\hat{r} = \frac{\max_{t=0,\ldots,T}\{y_t\} - \min_{t=0,\ldots,T}\{y_t\}}{\hat{\sigma}_1\sqrt{T}},$$

where $\hat{\sigma}_1^2$ is the long-run variance estimator defined in (2.36). If the true DGP is I(1), $\hat{r}$ has a nondegenerate asymptotic distribution. But if the DGP is I(0), $\hat{r}$ converges to zero in probability as the sample size grows. Thus, the range statistic can distinguish I(1) from I(0). By contrast, if the true DGP is I(2), the range statistic is shown to diverge in probability to plus infinity. Extensions to the AR(1) model with deterministic trends are also made in Cavaliere. The asymptotic local power of the range test is comparable to that of the Dickey-Fuller test.

4.5 Bootstrapping for Unit Root Testing

Bootstrapping is used for hypothesis testing either when the distributions of test statistics depend on unknown parameters or when using asymptotic distributions is deemed to be unsuitable at a given sample size. Davison and Hinkley (1997), Efron and Tibshirani (1993), Hall (1992), and Shao and Tu (1995), among others, provide an excellent introduction to bootstrap methods. This section discusses several bootstrap methods for the inference on a unit root.

4.5.1 Bootstrap Failure in the Presence of a Unit Root

Basawa, Mallik, McCormick, Reeves, and Taylor (1991b; BMMRTb hereafter) consider the AR(1) process

$$y_t = \alpha y_{t-1} + u_t, \ (t = 1, \ldots, T), \tag{4.8}$$

$$\alpha = 1, \ y_0 = 0, \ u_t \sim \text{iid } N(0, 1),$$

and study how bootstrapping behaves for this nonstationary process. They construct the bootstrap[12] sample, $\{y_t^*\}_{t=1}^T$, using the data-generating scheme

$$y_t^* = \hat{\alpha}y_{t-1}^* + u_t^*, \ y_0^* = 0, \ u_t^* \sim \text{iid } N(0, 1), \tag{4.9}$$

where $\hat{\alpha}$ is an OLS estimator of α based on $\{y_t\}_{t=1}^T$. BMMRTb derive the limiting distribution (conditional on the sample $\{y_t\}_{t=1}^T$) of the bootstrap estimator of

---

[12] Their bootstrap is different from the standard bootstrap, which uses sampling with replacements from the pool of residuals. The latter scheme is often called the nonparametric bootstrap, whereas that of BMMRTb is the parametric bootstrap (cf. Davison and Hinkley, 1997).

α,—i.e., $\left(\sum_{t=2}^{T} y_{t-1}^{*2}\right)^{-1} \sum_{t=2}^{T} y_t^* y_{t-1}^*$—and report that it is different from that using the original data $\{y_t\}_{t=1}^{T}$. Thus, the bootstrap employing BMMRTb's data-generating scheme should not be used for the inference on a unit root. Because the bootstrap method is known to work for the stationary and explosive cases (cf. Bose, 1988, and Basawa, Mallik, McCormick, and Taylor, 1989), BMMRTb's result has been recorded as an interesting case of bootstrap failure[13] and has aroused much interest in bootstrapping unit root processes since then.

4.5.2   Using Bootstrapping for the Inference on a Unit Root

To overcome BMMRTb's bootstrap failure, Basawa, Mallik, McCormick, Reeves, and Taylor (1991a)[14] and Ferretti and Romo (1996) introduce a resampling scheme using the OLS residuals $\hat{u}_t = y_t - \hat{\alpha} y_{t-1}$ with the restriction $\alpha = 1$. That is, they generate bootstrap data according to

$$y_t^* = y_{t-1}^* + u_t^*, \; y_0^* = 0,$$

where u_t^* is sampled with replacements from $\{\hat{u}_1 - \bar{u}, \ldots, \hat{u}_T - \bar{u}\}$ with $\bar{u} = \frac{1}{T}\sum_{t=1}^{T} \hat{u}_t$. The key difference from BMMRTb is that the restriction $\alpha = 1$ is imposed at the stage of resampling so that $\{y_t^*\}_{t=1}^{T}$ follows an exact unit root process. Basawa et al. (1991a) and Ferretti and Romo (1996) show that the OLS estimator using $\{y_t^*\}_{t=1}^{T}$ has the conventional unit root distribution in the limit conditional on the observations $\{y_t\}_{t=1}^{T}$. This indicates that the critical values obtained from both of their bootstrap methods can be used for the inference on a unit root. Ferretti and Romo also consider the case of errors having the AR(1) structure and show that the OLS estimator using $\{y_t^*\}_{t=1}^{T}$ has the same limiting distribution as that given in Phillips (1987a).

Though Basawa et al. (1991a) and Ferretti and Romo (1996) overcome the bootstrap failure for a unit root process, the errors of their model have a restrictive structure. There have been various attempts to extend Basawa et al. (1991a) and Ferretti and Romo's (1996) results to more general error processes. In the case of stationary time series, block bootstrapping (cf. Künsch, 1989, and Liu and Singh, 1992) has been used to generate resampled data that retain the serial correlation structure of the original series. Block bootstrapping divides the sample (or residuals) into nonoverlapping blocks and constructs bootstrap

---

[13] Heimann and Kreiss (1996) provide a remedy for BMMRTb's bootstrap. They show that the OLS estimator using BMMRTb's bootstrap sample has the same limiting distribution as that using the original sample if the bootstrap sample size, $m(T)$, satisfies the conditions $m(T) \rightarrow \infty$ and $m(T)/T \rightarrow 0$ as $T \rightarrow \infty$.

[14] Basawa, Mallik, McCormick, Reeves, and Taylor (1991a) also introduce a sequential bootstrap following the idea of Lai and Siegmund (1983). But because it is likely to use part of the full sample, percentiles from it may not approximate well those of the true finite-sample distribution.

samples by sampling from the set of blocks with replacements. Paparoditis and Politis (2003) apply the idea of block bootstrapping to unit root testing by considering the null DGP

$$y_t = \mu + \alpha y_{t-1} + u_t, \ \alpha = 1,$$ (4.10)

where $\{u_t\}$ is either a stationary linear process or a strong mixing process. Paparoditis and Politis's block bootstrap is composed of four steps:

Step 1: Calculate the centered residuals

$$\tilde{u}_t = (y_t - \hat{\alpha} y_{t-1}) - \frac{1}{T-1} \sum_{j=2}^{T} (y_j - \hat{\alpha} y_{j-1}), \ (t = 2, \ldots, T),$$

where $\hat{\alpha}$ is a consistent estimator of α using $\{y_t\}$.

Step 2: Choose a block-size parameter b ($< T$) and let $i_0, \ldots, i_{k-1}$ be drawn randomly from the set $\{1, 2, \ldots, T - b\}$ (take $k = [(T - 1)/b]$). Construct the bootstrap series $\{y_t^*\}_{t=1}^{l}$ ($l = kb + 1$) with

$$y_1^* = y_1, \ y_t^* = \hat{\mu} + y_{t-1}^* + \tilde{u}_{i_m+s}, \ (t = 2, \ldots, l),$$

where $m = [(t - 2)/b], s = t - mb - 1$, and $\hat{\mu}$ is a $\sqrt{T}$-consistent estimator of μ.

Step 3: Compute a unit root test statistic γ^* using $\{y_t^*\}_{t=1}^{l}$.

Step 4: Repeat Steps 2 and 3 B times to formulate the empirical distribution of γ^*. The α-quantile of this distribution is a consistent approximation of that of the null distribution of the unit root test statistic.

In Step 1, $\hat{\alpha}$ should satisfy $\hat{\alpha} = \alpha + O_p(T^{-(2+\delta(\mu))/2})$ where $\delta(\mu) = 1$ if $\mu \neq 0$ and $\delta(\mu) = 0$ if $\mu = 0$. The OLS estimator of α using Model (4.10) satisfies the requirement. In Step 2, $\hat{\mu}$ can be obtained by running OLS using $\{\Delta y_t\}$, or it can be set at zero if this is deemed to be appropriate. The block size b should be chosen in Step 2. Paparoditis and Politis (2003) discuss various methods for choosing b. Note that the null restriction is imposed in generating the bootstrap series $\{y_t^*\}_{t=1}^{l}$ in Step 3 as in Basawa, Mallik, McCormick, Reeves, and Taylor (1991a) and Ferretti and Romo (1996). In Step 3, we may use, for example, the Phillips-Perron coefficient test statistic. Paparoditis and Politis also discuss how to bootstrap the ADF test, though it seems that the standard bootstrap can be used for the ADF test.

Additionally, Paparoditis and Politis argue against the use of centered differences $(y_t - y_{t-1}) - \frac{1}{T-1} \sum_{j=2}^{T} (y_j - y_{j-1})$ for block bootstrap because it brings a loss of power, confirmed both theoretically and via simulation. However, Paparoditis and Politis's simulation results show that the size-distortion problems of the ADF and Phillips-Perron tests (see Subsection 2.3.3) are not resolved by the block and sieve (introduced later) bootstraps. This casts some doubt on the usefulness of the bootstrap procedures for unit root testing.

Another bootstrap method that has been used for stationary time series is Bühlmann's (1997) sieve bootstrap. The sieve bootstrap assumes a linear process structure for the sample (or unobserved error process) and approximates the linear process by an AR model the order of which increases as the sample size increases. This idea is applied to unit root testing by Psaradakis (2001a), Chang and Park (2003), and Swensen (2003). Because they all use differences of the data for the sieve bootstrap, their findings are subject to the criticism of Paparoditis and Politis (2003) mentioned earlier. Palm, Smeekes, and Urbain (2008) introduce modified sieve bootstrap procedures that use residuals. They also report via simulation that the residual-based bootstraps bring higher power in finite samples than the difference-based bootstraps, a conclusion consistent with Paparoditis and Politis.

Swensen (2003) and Parker, Paparoditis, and Politis (2006)[15] apply Politis and Romano's (1994) stationary bootstrap to unit root testing. The stationary bootstrap generates stationary bootstrap samples using blocks with random starting points and lengths. Its main advantage is that no model needs to be specified for the bootstrap data generation. However, Palm, Smeekes, and Urbain (2008) show that the stationary bootstrap performs worse than the block and sieve bootstraps discussed earlier.

Other applications of bootstrap for unit root testing include Moreno and Romo (2000, 2012), Cavaliere and Taylor (2008), Cavaliere, Harvey, Leybourne, and Taylor (2011) and Smeekes and Taylor (2012). Moreno and Romo bootstrap the M- and least absolute deviation estimators. The rest apply bootstrap to unit root testing under permanent changes in the innovation variance because the limiting distributions of their test statistics depend on nuisance parameters.

Park (2003) provides a theory for the asymptotic refinement of bootstrap unit root tests that is in accordance with the well-known fact that bootstrapping helps compute critical values accurately in finite samples (cf. Hall 1992). He studies the Dickey-Fuller t-ratio (2.27) and coefficient test statistic (2.26) and shows that the test statistics using the bootstrap critical values have rejection probabilities closer to their nominal ones than those using asymptotic ones. His simulation results based on the AR(2) model with i.i.d. errors show that the bootstrap critical values perform better than asymptotic ones at sample sizes as small as 25. But if sample sizes are larger (50 or 100), the advantage of bootstrapping virtually disappears.

---

[15] Swensen (2003) uses the first differences of observations, and Parker, Paparoditis, and Politis (2006) employ regression residuals.

4.6 Bayesian Inference on a Unit Root

Most of the studies of unit roots are based on the classical approach that regards parameters as fixed constants. In contrast, this section introduces the unit root literature that takes the Bayesian stance. Zellner (1971) is still a valuable reference for those who wish to study Bayesian econometrics, though there are more recent monographs such as Berger (1985), Bernardo and Smith (1994), Koop, Poirier, and Tobias (2007), and West and Harrison (1989), among many others.

4.6.1 Sims' (1988) Criticism

When there is a unit root in the AR process, the classical approach yields a nonstandard asymptotic theory that also makes the inference on a unit root nonstandard. Sims (1988) makes important and interesting comments on the classical approach. First, he points out that constructing confidence intervals for the coefficient of the AR(1) model is problematic when the classical asymptotic theory is used because the t-ratio has different distributions depending on the location of the characteristic root. That is, the asymptotic confidence intervals depend on which distribution (normal or unit root) is being used to construct them. Second, he argues that using the Bayesian approach provides a sounder basis for the inference on a unit root because the posterior distribution of the coefficient of the AR(1) model under a flat prior is unaffected by the presence of a unit root.

Sims' (1988) second point is further elaborated by Sims and Uhlig (1991). They generate the AR(1) model

$$y_t = \alpha y_{t-1} + u_t, \ u_t \sim \text{iid} \, N(0, 1), \ y_0 = 0, \ (t = 1, \ldots, 100),$$

with $\alpha \sim U[0.8, 1.10]$,[16] and they plot the joint distribution of α and its OLS estimator, $\hat{\alpha}$, assuming that the variance of $\{u_t\}$ is known to be one. For a given value α, the plot provides the classical distribution of $\hat{\alpha}$. The distribution of $\hat{\alpha}$, given $\alpha = 1$, is asymmetric, a well-known fact in the literature. For a given value of $\hat{\alpha}$, the plot gives the posterior distribution of α. The posterior distribution of α is symmetric around $\hat{\alpha}$ regardless of the value of α.

Factually, Sims and Uhlig's (1991) simulation result illustrates a special case of the Bayesian analysis of the AR(1) model given in Zellner (1971, pp. 186–190). Using a flat prior, $\text{pdf}(\alpha, \sigma) \propto \frac{1}{\sigma}$, Zellner shows that $(\alpha - \hat{\alpha})/\sqrt{\hat{\sigma}_u^2 \left(\sum_{t=2}^{n} y_{t-1}^2 \right)^{-1}}$, where $\hat{\sigma}_u^2 = \frac{1}{T-1} \sum_{t=2}^{T} (y_t - \hat{\alpha} y_{t-1})^2$ follows a Student t-distribution regardless of the value of α. Because the Bayesian highest posterior density (HPD) interval for α can be constructed using this distribution

---

[16] $U[a, b]$ denotes a uniform distribution over the interval $[a, b]$.

alone, one can argue that the Bayesian approach is free of the problem posted by the classical confidence interval for the AR(1) model possibly with a unit root. However, as is shown shortly, if a different prior is used, posteriors can be bimodal, which may yield disconnected HPD intervals.

The problem of the classical confidence interval indicated by Sims has been addressed by several papers, including Stock (1991), Andrews (1993), Choi (1993), Hansen (1999), Romano and Wolf (2001), So and Shin (1999), Phillips and Han (2008), Chen and Kuo (2013), and Gorodnichenko, Mikusheva, and Ng (2012). See Section 5.3 for details. Sims' second argument that using the Bayesian approach provides a sounder basis for the inference on a unit root has stimulated much related research and controversy, as discussed next, and was refuted mainly by Phillips (1991).[17]

4.6.2   Priors and Posteriors in the Presence of a Unit Root

DeJong and Whiteman (1991c) is representative of studies on Nelson and Plosser's (1982) data using the Bayesian approach with a flat prior. They consider the AR(3) model with an intercept and a linear time trend,

$$y_t = \mu + \beta t + \sum_{i=1}^{3} \alpha_i y_{t-i} + u_t, \ u_t \sim \text{iid} \, \text{N}(0, \sigma^2),$$

and focus on the posterior probability of the largest root, Λ, of the characteristic equation $1 - \alpha_1 z - \alpha_2 z^2 - \alpha_3 z^3 = 0$. Using the two priors $\beta = 0$, $\Lambda \in [0.65, 1.155)$ and $(\beta, \Lambda) \in \{[0, 0.016) \times [0.55, 1.055]\}$, they report the posterior mean of Λ and the probability of the event $\Lambda \geq 0.975$. The results using the second prior (which seem more relevant to the Nelson-Plosser dataset) show that the probability is less than 0.1 for most of the series except the consumer price index, velocity, and bond yields. They conclude from these results that the evidence for a unit root weakens[18] when their Bayesian approach is used.

Although DeJong and Whiteman's (1991c) results are new and interesting, Sowell (1991) criticizes them, claiming that: they depend on the chosen prior and the AR(3) model, and the particular rule $\Lambda \geq 0.975$ is subjective. In response to Sowell's criticism, DeJong and Whiteman (1991b) provide results of the robustness check of their empirical finding in DeJong and Whiteman (1991c), concluding that their previous results are robust to different specifications of the prior.

---

[17] Chris Sims and Harold Uhlig did not provide any response to Phillips's (1991) criticism of Sims (1988) and Sims and Uhlig (1991).

[18] Nelson and Plosser (1982) cannot reject the null of a unit root for 13 of 14 time series they study.

The Bayesian approaches introduced so far are based on flat priors. Phillips (1991) argues that flat priors ignore the way information is gathered via the value of the AR(1) coefficient and adopts Jeffreys' (1961) prior instead. (Jeffreys' prior is also called the ignorance prior.) The main point he makes is that Bayesian results are sensitive to the chosen prior. More specifically, for the AR(1) model with the coefficient α and the innovation variance σ_u^2, he assumes that the joint prior of $\theta = (\alpha, \sigma_u)$, denoted by $\pi(\theta)$, is

$$\pi(\theta) \propto \sqrt{\det(I_{\theta\theta}(\alpha, \sigma_u))}, \tag{4.11}$$

where $I_{\theta\theta}(\alpha, \sigma_u)$ is the information matrix. The main advantage of the Jeffreys prior is that it is invariant to the 1:1 transformation of the parameter space. Conditional on the initial variable y_0,[19] the Jeffreys' prior (4.11) boils down to[20]

$$\pi(\theta) \propto \frac{1}{\sigma_u} \sqrt{I_{\alpha\alpha}},$$

where

$$I_{\alpha\alpha} = \begin{cases} \frac{T}{1-\alpha^2} + \frac{1}{1-\alpha^2}\frac{1-\alpha^{2T}}{1-\alpha^2} + \left(\frac{y_0}{\sigma_u}\right)^2 \frac{1-\alpha^{2T}}{1-\alpha^2}, & \alpha \neq 1 \\ \frac{T(T-1)}{2} + T\left(\frac{y_0}{\sigma_u}\right)^2, & \alpha = 1. \end{cases}$$

This prior is certainly different from the flat priors introduced so far: it depends on T and y_0, and increases with α. The latter aspect implies that this prior gives more weight to the coefficient values greater than or equal to one than those less than one. Kim and Maddala (1991), in their Monte Carlo study on the AR(1) model, show that this feature results in a bias of the posterior mean and mode of the AR coefficient toward one when its true value is actually less than one.

Using Jeffreys' prior and assuming $y_0 = 0$, Phillips (1991) derives the posterior for α

$$p(\alpha \mid y) \propto \sqrt{I_{\alpha\alpha}} \left[m(\hat{u}) + (\alpha - \hat{\alpha})^2 m(y)\right]^{-T/2}, \tag{4.12}$$

where $m(\hat{u}) = \sum_{t=2}^{T} \hat{u}_t^2$, $\{\hat{u}_t\}$ is the OLS-based AR(1) regression residuals, and $m(y) = \sum_{t=2}^{T} y_{t-1}^2$. Unlike in the case of flat priors, this posterior is not symmetric about $\hat{\alpha}$ and may have two modes depending on the values of $m(\hat{u})$ and $m(y)$. When they have two modes, the HPD intervals can be disconnected, which one may find problematic. Phillips also reports extensions of his posterior analysis to a model with nonstochastic trend variables and lagged differences.

---

[19] Otherwise, we need to know the mean value of y_0 to calculate the prior (cf. Berger and Yang, 1994, p. 462).

[20] This is based on an approximation of the determinant of the information matrix. Uhlig (1994) derives Jeffreys' prior using the exact likelihood. The differences between Phillips's and Uhlig's priors seem quite minor.

The Jeffreys' prior of the coefficient α for the model with trends depends on the trends' parameters—an aspect of his approach that may be discomforting. However, Phillips argues that its shapes are essentially no different from the case of no trends. This is a controversial point that has invited further research as discussed later.

Phillips (1991) shows that the evidence for stationarity slightly weakens compared to DeJong and Whiteman (1991c) when his approach is used for the Nelson-Plosser dataset, but his results tend to favor trend stationarity compared to those using the classical approach. In addition, the results are quite sensitive to the chosen number of lagged differences: Using AR(3) rather than AR(1) provides stronger evidence for stationarity. See also DeJong and Whiteman (1991a), which criticizes Phillips's approach.

Schotman and van Dijk (1991b), in their comment on Phillips (1991), employ the unobserved components model

$$y_t = \mu + \beta t + x_t, \ (t = 1, \ldots, T);$$ (4.13)

$$x_t = \alpha x_{t-1} + u_t, \ y_0 = \mu, u_t \sim \text{iid} \, \text{N}(0, \sigma_u^2),$$

and show that it can bring noticeable changes in the behavior of priors and posteriors. They report that the joint Jeffreys' prior for Model (4.13) becomes

$$\pi(\mu, \beta, \alpha, \sigma_u) \propto \frac{(1 - \alpha)^2}{\sigma_u^3} \sqrt{\frac{1}{1 - \alpha^2} \left(T + \frac{1 - \alpha^{2T}}{1 - \alpha^2} \right)},$$ (4.14)

the main features of which are (i) it is independent of the nuisance parameters μ and β and (ii) it goes down to zero as α approaches one from below and increases upward as α becomes larger beyond one in the presence of non-stochastic trend variables. The first feature makes it more straightforward to study properties of the marginal prior of α, which is certainly an advantage of using the unobserved components model (4.13). The second feature is in sharp contrast to the properties of the Jeffreys' priors reported in Phillips. The marginal prior of α in Phillips increases steadily with α, at least for the values of the coefficients of nonstochastic trend variables used there. This implies that the Jeffreys' prior can show strikingly different behavior depending on the model chosen: The Jeffreys' prior used for the AR(1) model with nonstochastic trend variables puts more weight on the values of α greater than or equal to one than those less than one, whereas the prior used for the unobserved components model gives zero weight to the unit root.

Furthermore, Schotman and van Dijk (1991b) show that a flat prior,

$$\pi(\mu, \beta, \alpha, \sigma_u) \propto \frac{1}{\sigma_u},$$

for the unobserved components model (4.13) gives posterior probability of one to the unit root. This is in contrast to DeJong and Whiteman (1991c), which report posteriors supportive of stationarity for most of the Nelson-Plosser data. I find from these contrasting claims that flat priors can also display starkly different behavior depending on the model chosen.

Zivot (1994) rewrites the unobserved components model (4.20), discussed later, as

$$y_1 = \mu + \alpha x_0 + u_1;$$

$$y_t = \mu(1 - \alpha) + \alpha y_{t-1} + u_t, \quad (t = 2, \dots, T) \tag{4.15}$$

and studies the Jeffreys' prior. Setting $x_0 = 0$, Zivot derives the joint Jeffreys' prior as

$$\pi(\mu, \alpha, \sigma_u) \propto \frac{1}{\sigma_u} \sqrt{\phi_1(\alpha)\phi_0(\alpha)}, \tag{4.16}$$

where

$$\phi_1(\alpha) = \begin{cases} \left[T + \left(1 - \alpha^{2T}\right) / \left(1 - \alpha^2\right)\right] / \left(1 - \alpha^2\right), & \alpha \neq 1 \\ T(T-1)/2, & \alpha = 1 \end{cases}$$

and $\phi_0(\alpha) = 1 + (T - 1)(1 - \alpha)^2$. This does not depend on parameter μ as does the Jeffreys' prior for Model (4.20). However, its value at $\alpha = 1$ is $\frac{1}{\sigma_u}\sqrt{T(T-1)/2}$, which is the same as for the Jeffreys' prior derived by Phillips (1991) for the AR(1) model without nonstochastic trend variables. Moreover, the marginal prior of α increases with α, giving more weight to the region $\{\alpha \mid \alpha \geq 1\}$ than to $\{\alpha \mid \alpha < 1\}$. This is certainly different from the prior derived by Schotman and van Dijk (1991b). This difference arises due to the different treatments of the initial variable and indicates that the initial observation can also play an important role in characterizing the Jeffreys' prior.

Another important finding from Zivot (1994) is that misspecifying the initial value, x_0, can have important consequences for the posteriors. An unusually large initial value in a stationary model can produce posteriors that lead to incorrect inferences. In relation to this, we have already seen that the power of classical unit root tests depends strongly on the initial value. It is interesting to observe that the initial value also plays a major role in the Bayesian analysis. To overcome the uncertainty related to the initial value, Zivot assumes that the data started at some time $t = -S$ and suggests using the prior

$$x_0 \sim \mathbf{N}(0, v(\alpha, S)),$$

where

$$v(\alpha, S) = \begin{cases} \left(1 - \alpha^{2T}\right) / \left(1 - \alpha^2\right), & \alpha \neq 1 \\ S, & \alpha = 1. \end{cases}$$

In implementing this scheme, however, the researcher should determine the value of S, which seems difficult in practice.

Some other works also use priors. Lubrano (1995) uses

$$\pi(\alpha) \propto \frac{1}{\sqrt{1 + v} - \alpha}$$

with $v = 0.5$ and the initial variable $y_0 \sim \mathbf{N}(\mu, \sigma_u^2/(1 - \alpha^2))$ for the unobserved components model (4.13) and analyzes the extended Nelson-Plosser data. His results are less favorable to the unit root hypothesis than those using Phillips's (1991) method.

Berger and Yang (1994) study the AR(1) model without nonstochastic terms and suggest the following noninformative prior (called the symmetrized asymptotic prior):

$$\pi(\alpha) \propto \begin{cases} 1 \big/ \left[2\pi \sqrt{1 - \alpha^2}\right], & |\alpha| < 1 \\ 1 \big/ \left[2\pi |\alpha| \sqrt{1 - \alpha^2}\right], & |\alpha| > 1. \end{cases} \tag{4.17}$$

The main principle that generates this prior is to minimize the expected distance between the prior and posterior. The Kullback-Leibler divergence is used as a distance measure. Prior (4.17) is proper and assigns the same probability to the regions $\{\alpha \mid |\alpha| > 1\}$ and $\{\alpha \mid |\alpha| < 1\}$, unlike the Jeffreys prior. Technically, the derivation of the symmetrized asymptotic prior involves solving a complicated, implicit equation, which is not easy to extend to more complex models. In spite of this difficulty, Berger and Yang claim that the information-based criteria they used for prior (4.17) have by far the best track record in suggesting noninformative priors that turn out to have nice operational properties. Such nice operational properties are also demonstrated via simulation for the AR(1) model in Berger and Yang.

4.6.3 Bayesian Testing for a Unit Root

This subsection introduces Bayesian testing methods for a unit root. Before discussing the related literature, a short digression[21] on the posterior odds ratio is now in order. Suppose that the parameter of interest is θ and the null and alternative hypotheses are written as, respectively, $H_0 : \theta = \theta^0$ and $H_1 : \theta \in I$ where I is an interval that does not contain θ^0. The posterior odds

---

[21]   See chapter X of Zellner (1971) for an introductory account on posterior odds.

ratio compares the posterior probability of the null hypothesis with that of the alternative hypothesis and is written, in its simplest form, as

$$\frac{P(\theta = \theta^0 \mid y)}{P(\theta \in I \mid y)} = \frac{P(\theta = \theta^0)}{P(\theta \in I)} \frac{P(y \mid \theta = \theta^0)}{P(y \mid \theta \in I)}.$$

Thus, if we assume that the prior probabilities of the null and alternative hypotheses are the same, the Bayesian hypothesis testing procedure accepts H_0 if $\frac{P(y \mid \theta = \theta^0)}{P(y \mid \theta \in I)} > 1$.

Now, we apply the basic principle to Model (4.13) for the null hypothesis of a unit root against the alternative of stationarity. Then, letting $\phi = (\mu, \beta)$, the posterior pdf of the unit root null hypothesis for Model (4.13) is written as

$$
\begin{aligned}
p(\alpha = 1, \phi \mid y) &= \frac{p(\alpha = 1, \phi, y)}{p(y)} \\
&= \frac{p(\alpha = 1, \phi)p(y \mid \alpha = 1, \phi)}{p(y)} \\
&= \frac{p(\alpha = 1)p(\phi \mid \alpha = 1)p(y \mid \alpha = 1, \phi)}{p(y)}.
\end{aligned}
$$

Thus, assuming that the pdf of α at $\alpha = 1$ is the probability of the event $\{\alpha = 1\}$, we have

$$P(\alpha = 1 \mid y) = \frac{P(\alpha = 1) \int_\Phi p(\phi \mid \alpha = 1)p(y \mid \alpha = 1, \phi) \, d\phi}{p(y)}, \quad (4.18)$$

where Φ denotes the parameter space of ϕ. Likewise, if the alternative hypothesis is written as $\alpha = \alpha^* \in S$, where S is a parameter space of α under the alternative hypothesis of stationarity,

$$P(\alpha = \alpha^* \mid y) = \frac{p(\alpha = \alpha^*) \int_\Phi p(\phi \mid \alpha = \alpha^*)p(y \mid \alpha = \alpha^*, \phi) \, d\phi}{p(y)},$$

which gives

$$P(\alpha \in S \mid y) = \frac{P(\alpha \in S) \int_S \int_\Phi p(\phi)p(y \mid \alpha \in S, \phi) \, d\phi \, d\alpha}{p(y)}. \quad (4.19)$$

Relations (4.18) and (4.19) give the posterior odds ratio as

$$\frac{P(\alpha = 1 \mid y)}{P(\alpha \in S \mid y)} = \frac{P(\alpha = 1)}{P(\alpha \in S)} \frac{\int_\Phi p(\phi \mid \alpha = 1)p(y \mid \alpha = 1, \phi) \, d\phi}{\int_S \int_\Phi p(\phi)p(y \mid \alpha \in S, \phi) \, d\phi \, d\alpha}.$$

If the null and alternative are assumed to have equal probability—i.e., $P(\alpha = 1) = P(\alpha \in S)$—the posterior odds ratio is equal to the ratio of the averaged likelihoods. Using this representation, Schotman and van Dijk (1991b) study the Bayesian posterior odds ratio for the null of a unit root against the alternative of stationarity. They report that the posterior odds ratio using the Jeffreys' prior diverges to infinity, mainly because the priors on nuisance parameters are improper. This implies probability one for the unit root. From this, Schotman and van Dijk conclude that the Jeffreys' prior is ill suited for the Bayesian test of the unit root hypothesis.

Schotman and van Dijk (1991a) further study the Bayesian posterior odds ratio for the null hypothesis of a unit root against the alternative of stationarity. They employ the unobserved components model

$$y_t = \mu + x_t, \; x_t = \alpha x_{t-1} + u_t, \; u_t \sim \text{iid} \, N(0, \sigma_u^2), \; (t = 1, \ldots, T), \quad (4.20)$$

where x_0 is a known constant. Assuming $\alpha \in S \cup \{1\}$, $S = \{\alpha \mid -1 < a \le \alpha < 1\}$, and using the priors

$$\pi(\alpha \mid \alpha \in S) = \frac{1}{1-a}, \; \pi(\sigma_u) = \frac{1}{\sigma_u}, \; \text{and} \; \pi(\mu \mid \alpha, \sigma_u, y_0) \sim N\left(y_0, \frac{\sigma_u^2}{1-\alpha^2}\right),$$

Schotman and van Dijk derive the Bayes factor $\frac{P(y|\alpha=1)}{P(y|\alpha\in S)}$. Note that flat priors are used for α and σ_u, but not for μ. A flat prior for μ will give rise to an anomalous result, as is discussed shortly. The Bayes factor requires specifying the value of a, for which Schotman and van Dijk (1991a) propose a data-dependent rule.

Schotman and van Dijk (1991a) assume equally likely null and alternative hypotheses and apply their Bayesian posterior odds ratio to some real exchange-rate series. The results show that the random walk hypothesis for the series is a posteriori as probable as a stationary AR(1) process for four out of the eight series they investigate.

In addition, Schotman and van Dijk (1991a) show that the posterior odds ratio diverges to infinity (i.e., the null of a unit root is accepted) if the prior on the parameter μ is set to be $\pi(\mu \mid \alpha, \sigma_u, y_0) \sim U[-\frac{M}{2}, \frac{M}{2}]$ and if $M \to \infty$. Because $P(y \mid \alpha \in S, \mu, \sigma_u, y_0)$ is basically a likelihood averaged over the space of parameters, the averaged likelihood shrinks as the parameter space domain widens. Thus, the Bayes factor increases with the size of the parameter space.[22] This is the intuition behind the diverging posterior odds ratio. The diverging posterior odds ratio implies that the null of a unit root will be accepted if M is large under the given prior. This is certainly a troubling aspect of Bayesian analysis: its result depends even on the chosen prior for the nuisance parameter μ.

Using the same prior as in Schotman and van Dijk (1991a), Hasegawa, Chaturvedi, and van Hoa (2000) devise the Bayesian posterior odds ratio for the nonnormal errors that follow an Edgeworth series distribution (cf. Davis,

---

[22] This is also related to Lindley's (1957) paradox, where a posterior odds ratio using a nondiffuse prior gives rise to strong evidence for a null hypothesis, while the null is rejected by the frequentist approach.

1976) with finite first four cumulants and negligible higher order cumulants. Applications of the Bayesian posterior odds ratio to the real-exchange-rate series used by Schotman and van Dijk (1991a) reveal very different results from those of Schotman and van Dijk (1991a), which indicates the sensitivity of their results to the type of errors.

Koop (1992) considers the Bayesian posterior odds ratio test using Zellner and Siow's (1980) and Zellner's (1986) priors and reports empirical results for the Nelson-Plosser dataset that are more favorable to trend-stationarity than previous reports using the classical approach.

The posterior odds ratio discussed thus far compares the posterior probabilities of parameters under the null and alternative hypotheses. Its shortcoming when used for a point null and a composite alternative has already been observed (recall the diverging posterior odds ratio of Schotman and van Dijk, 1991a). Phillips and Ploberger (1994)[23] suggest an alternative way to perform hypothesis tests using a weighted LR. In the sense that the weights are coming from a given prior density, their approach is Bayesian. However, because they assume a known error variance and use its classical estimator in the end, it is a hybrid of the Bayesian and classical approaches.

For the AR(1) model

$$\Delta y_t = \alpha y_{t-1} + u_t, \quad u_t \sim \text{iid N}(0, \sigma_u^2) \tag{4.21}$$

with a prior density $\pi(\alpha) = \alpha_0$ (a constant), Phillips and Ploberger's (1994) pseudo-Bayesian LR test statistic for a unit root becomes

$$PBLR = \left(\frac{\sum_{t=2}^{T} y_{t-1}^2}{\hat{\sigma}_u^2} \right)^{-1/2} \exp \left(\frac{\hat{\alpha} \sum_{t=2}^{T} y_{t-1}^2}{2\hat{\sigma}_u^2} \right), \tag{4.22}$$

where $\hat{\sigma}_u^2$ is the usual estimator of σ_u^2 using Model (4.21). The null of a unit root is accepted when $PBLR < 1$, and vice versa. The test statistic $PBLR$ converges to zero in probability under the null hypothesis of a unit root, whereas it diverges to plus infinity in probability under the alternative $|\alpha| < 1$. Thus, both Type I and Type II errors become zero in the limit. When there are nonstochastic trends and lagged differences of $\{y_t\}$ in the model, y_{t-1} in equation (4.22) is replaced by the residual obtained by regressing $\{y_{t-1}\}$ on those added variables. Phillips and Ploberger's simulation results show that the test has reasonable power in finite samples when the usual classical experimental format is used. However, it tends to overreject under the null hypothesis compared to the conventional unit root tests such as Said and Dickey's (1984).

---

[23] See Phillips and Ploberger (1996) for more abstract and general treatment of the ideas in Phillips and Ploberger (1994).

Several aspects of the *PBLR* test are worthy of our attention. First, the *PBLR* test uses a diffuse prior, and Phillips and Ploberger show that any continuous prior will bring the same test asymptotically. However, the finite-sample properties of the *PBLR* test may change when a different prior is used. Second, the *PBLR* test does not suffer from the problem of the posterior odds ratio that occurs for a point null and a composite alternative because it uses a weighted LR rather than the ratio of weighted likelihoods as in the posterior odds ratio. This is certainly an advantage of the *PBLR* test. Third, the *PBLR* test results will differ when σ_u^2 is treated in a Bayesian manner. How it will behave when a prior is given to σ_u^2 is not yet known.

4.6.4   Bayesian Inference on a Unit Root under a Structural Change

The Bayesian approach is also used for models possibly under a structural change. Zivot and Phillips (1994), using the AR(1) model with nonstochastic trend variables, extend Phillips's (1991) method to the model under a structural change in the nonstochastic trend variables. When the date of structural change is unknown, they assume a flat prior for it that is independent of other parameters. Other parameters are treated by using Phillips's methods.

Koop and Steel (1994) study the AR(p) model having an intercept and linear time trend that are possibly under structural changes, and they assume elliptical densities for the observations, which are more general than the normal densities used elsewhere. Their likelihood function is a mixture of the likelihood functions of several models classified by the presence of structural changes and the differences in the variance–covariance matrices of the observations. Using a flat prior for the unit root parameter, they derive a proper posterior, which can be used to assess evidence for the presence of structural changes and an MA component in the model. The prior can also be used to find posterior probabilities of the regions related to the unit root parameter. In addition, they propose a decision-theoretic approach that can help us determine the "right" model for the observations. Their approach may lead us to choose, for example, the AR model with a unit root and an MA component that has a structural change in the intercept. Koop and Steel's decision-theoretic approach seems to be more convenient than the posterior odds ratio, which can only reveal the odds between the two models compared. However, their approach requires a loss function because a decision should be made such that the expected loss is minimized. The choice of the loss function is naturally subjective. Koop and Steel devise a loss function based on the predictive variances and illustrate how it can be used for empirical data. Their empirical analysis of the Nelson-Plosser data using the decision-theoretic approach produces results that are somewhat different from those of other Bayesian works: they are much more supportive of a unit root than the others.

Marriott and Newbold (2000) consider four models—ARIMA(p, 1, q), stationary ARMA($p + 1, q$), ARIMA(p, 1, q) plus a constant term under a structural change, and stationary ARMA($p + 1, q$) plus a constant term under a structural change—and devise posterior model probabilities assuming that these four model are equally likely a priori. These probabilities can be used to assess evidence for these models. They use uniform priors for the ARMA coefficients.

4.6.5 Asymptotics for Posteriors

The Bayesian analyses discussed so far assume a finite sample size. What would happen to posteriors when $T \rightarrow \infty$? This question is studied by Kim (1998), who provides a set of conditions for the asymptotic normality of posteriors for possibly nonstationary processes. One condition is finiteness of priors, which is satisfied by the flat prior of Sims (1988) but violated by Phillips's (1991) Jeffreys' prior, and Berger and Yang's (1994) symmetrized asymptotic prior. Intuitively, when the prior is finite, the likelihood function dominates the prior and therefore invokes the asymptotic normality of the posterior.

4.6.6 Summary

Five major lessons we have learned so far from the Bayesian analysis of a unit can be stated as follows.

(i) It seems almost impossible to choose an objective prior for the unit root inference. Every prior considered so far has a good reason for researchers to trust or distrust it.

(ii) The same prior can lead to priors of totally different functional forms for the unit root parameter, depending on the model used and the treatment of the initial variable.

(iii) Nuisance parameters can have enormous impacts on the priors of the unit root parameter.

(iv) Empirical results using the Bayesian approach are sensitive to the chosen priors, model specification, and the treatment of the initial variable. Regarding the model specification, the number of lagged variables in the AR specification and the choice of a reduced- or unobserved components model can have significant impacts on empirical results.

(v) The Bayesian posterior odds ratio for the null hypothesis of a unit root against the alternative of stationarity also depends on the priors of the parameter of interest and nuisance parameters. If the priors of the nuisance parameters are chosen inappropriately, the Bayesian posterior odds ratio test is highly likely to support the unit root hypothesis.

Arnold Zellner, an eminent Bayesian, once said in a conference that a Nobel Peace Prize should be given to someone who can get Bayesian and classical statisticians to reconcile their views on statistics. According to what we have observed from the Bayesian literature on a unit root, it seems that a Nobel Peace Prize should also be given to someone who can get Bayesians to agree on their priors. Depending on the chosen priors, it has been shown that significantly different results may occur—a point emphatically made by Phillips (1991). Although the controversy about the Bayesian methodology may make the reader a bit confused, it makes literature more interesting to read. Research in econometrics will benefit from controversies of this sort, and it is hoped that they be kept well alive.

4.7 Stationarity Tests

Tests for the null of stationarity or stationarity tests have been developed to be used in conjunction with unit root tests. In addition, because stationarity is more often what economic theory predicts, minimizing the risk of rejecting the null of stationarity by taking it as a null hypothesis is a natural strategy of hypothesis testing. This section reports research developments in this area.

4.7.1 Locally Best Tests for an MA Unit Root

Let

$$y_t = \mu + \alpha y_{t-1} + u_t, \ (t = 2, \ldots, T),$$

where $\{u_t\}$ is a weakly stationary, linear process without an MA unit root. If $\alpha = 1$, $\Delta y_t = u_t$ has no MA unit root. But if $|\alpha| < 1$, $\Delta y_t = (1 - \alpha B)^{-1}(1 - B)u_t$ has an MA unit root. Therefore, the null of level stationarity is equivalent to the presence of an MA unit root in Δy_t. In the same manner, the trend-stationary process

$$y_t = \mu + \beta t + \alpha y_{t-1} + u_t, \ (t = 2, \ldots, T),$$

$$\beta \neq 0, \ |\alpha| < 1,$$

has an MA unit root when differenced once because $\Delta y_t = \beta' + (1 - \alpha B)^{-1}(1 - B)u_t$ ($\beta' \neq 0$). This is the main idea underlying many tests introduced in this section.

To devise a test for an MA unit root, consider the MA(1) model

$$x_t = e_t - \theta e_{t-1}, \ e_t \sim \text{iid} \, \mathbf{N}(0, \sigma^2) \, (t = 1, \ldots, T). \tag{4.23}$$

Table 4.1. *Asymptotic critical values of Tanaka's test*

	Significance level			
	1%	2.5%	5%	10%
Critical values	0.744	0.581	0.461	0.347

Note: If the computed S' is greater than the critical value, reject the null of level stationarity against the unit root alternative.

Then, as shown in Tanaka (1990), the locally best invariant test statistic[24] for $\theta = 1$ is given as

$$S = \frac{1}{T} \frac{\sum\limits_{t=1}^{T} s_t^2 - \frac{1}{T+1} \left(\sum\limits_{t=1}^{T} s_t \right)^2}{\sum\limits_{t=1}^{T} e_t^2}, \tag{4.24}$$

where $s_t = \sum\limits_{i=1}^{T} e_i$. It is straightforward to show that

$$S \Rightarrow \int_0^1 \overline{W}(r)^2 \, dr, \tag{4.25}$$

where $\overline{W}(r)$ is the demeaned Brownian motion defined in Subsection 2.2.1. If $\{e_t\}$ is a linear process with the long-run variance σ_1^2 and $\mathrm{Var}(e_t) = \sigma_e^2$, $S \Rightarrow \frac{\sigma_1^2}{\sigma_e^2} \int_0^1 \overline{W}(r)^2 \, dr$. If $\hat{\sigma}_1^2$ and $\hat{\sigma}_e^2$ are consistent estimators of σ_1^2 and σ_e^2, respectively, the test statistic $S' = \frac{\hat{\sigma}_e^2}{\hat{\sigma}_1^2} S_T$ has the same limiting distribution as S given in (4.25). This is the test statistic proposed by Tanaka (1990). The limiting distribution of S is tabulated in Anderson and Darling (1952) and MacNeill (1978, table 2), and its percentiles are reported in Table 4.1.

Saikkonen and Luukkonen (1993b) assume that $\{e_t\}$ is a stationary and invertible ARMA process of known order and devise a test using Tanaka's (1990) principle of the locally best invariant test. The main difference between their test and Tanaka's is the treatment of serial correlation in the data. Saikkonen and Luukkonen (1996) extend Saikkonen and Luukkonen's (1993b) test to the model with exogenous $I(0)$ and $I(1)$ variables.

4.7.2 LM Tests for an MA Unit Root

The MA(1) model (4.23) does not admit Wald, LR, or LM tests because the score takes value zero at $\theta = 1$ irrespective of the true value of θ. But if e_0 is

---

[24] See Ferguson (1967) or Casella and Berger (1990) for the locally best invariant test.

a constant in Model (4.23), Choi (1994) observes that the LM test statistic for $H_0 : \theta = 1$ is derived as[25]

$$LM = \left[\frac{\sum\limits_{t=2}^{T} s_{t-1} e_t}{\sum\limits_{t=1}^{T} e_t^2} \right]^2 , \qquad (4.26)$$

where $s_t = \sum_{i=1}^{T} e_i$.

To extend test statistic (4.26) to the level- and trend-stationary models,

$$y_t = \mu + e_t, \ (t = 1, \ldots, T);$$

$$y_t = \mu + \beta t + e_t, \ (t = 1, \ldots, T),$$

where $\{e_t\}$ is a linear process without an MA unit root, run the OLS regressions[26]

$$c_t = \hat{\mu} t + \hat{s}_t;$$

$$c_t = \tilde{\mu} t + \tilde{\beta} \frac{t(t+1)}{2} + \tilde{s}_t,$$

where $c_t = \sum_{i=1}^{t} y_i$, and estimate $\{s_t\}$ and $\{e_t\}$ using the regression residuals and their differences. Using the residuals $\{\hat{s}_t\}$, an analog of the LM test statistic (4.26) is formulated as

$$LM' = \left[\frac{\sum\limits_{t=2}^{T} \hat{s}_{t-1} \Delta \hat{s}_t}{\hat{\sigma}_1^2} - \frac{1}{2}\left(1 - \frac{\hat{\sigma}_e^2}{\hat{\sigma}_1^2} \right) \right]^2 ,$$

where $\hat{\sigma}_e^2 = \frac{1}{T-1} \sum_{t=2}^{T} (\Delta \hat{s}_t)^2$ and $\hat{\sigma}_1^2$ is the estimator of the long-run variance σ_1^2 using $\Delta \hat{s}_t$. This test statistic can be used for the null of level stationarity and has $(\int \overline{W} \, d\overline{W})^2$ as its limiting distribution. A similar test statistic for the null of trend stationarity is formulated using $\Delta \tilde{s}_t$, and its limiting distribution is $(\int W^* \, dW^*)^2$. Recall that $W^*(r)$ denotes the demeaned and detrended Brownian motion defined in Subsection 2.2.1. These limiting distributions are tabulated in Choi (1994) and reproduced in Table 4.2.

---

[25] See Choi and Ahn (1999) for multivariate extensions of this and other test statistics.

[26] Running the OLS regressions $y_t = \hat{\mu} + \hat{e}_t$ and $y_t = \tilde{\mu} + \tilde{\beta} t + \tilde{e}_t$ results in degenerate distributions of the Lagrange multiplier test statistics presented later.

Table 4.2. *Asymptotic critical values of Choi's test*

	Significance level		
	1%	5%	10%
Level stationarity	0.2500	0.2496	0.2485
Trend stationarity	0.2500	0.2498	0.2492

Note: If the computed value of the LM test statistic is greater than the critical value, reject the null of stationarity against the alternative of a unit root.

4.7.3 Point-Optimal Tests for an MA Unit Root

Saikkonen and Luukkonen (1993a; SL hereafter) apply the point-optimal test (see King and Hillier, 1985, and King, 1987, for discussions on the point-optimal test) to the problem of testing for an MA unit root. They consider the DGP

$$y_1 = \mu + u_1; \tag{4.27}$$
$$\Delta y_t = u_t - \theta u_{t-1}, \ (t = 2, \ldots, T),$$

where $\{u_t\}$ is the Gaussian, stationary, and invertible ARMA process represented by

$$\phi(B)u_t = \psi(B)e_t, \ e_t \sim \text{iid} \, N(0, \sigma_e^2). \tag{4.28}$$

The null hypothesis of interest is $H_0 : \theta = 1$.

In vector notation, Model (4.27) can be written as

$$B(1)y = \mu e_{(1)} + B(\theta)u,$$

where $e_{(1)} = [1, 0, \ldots, 0]'$ and $B(\theta) = I_T - \theta L_T$, with L_T being a $T \times T$ matrix with ones in the diagonal immediately below the main diagonal and zeros elsewhere. The covariance matrix of u is denoted as $\sigma_e^2 \Sigma$, which depends on the parameters of the ARMA process (4.28). Because $B(1)^{-1} = I_T + L_T + \cdots + L_T^{T-1}$, we have

$$y \sim N\big(\mu e, \sigma_e^2 \Omega(\theta)\big),$$

where $e = [1, \ldots, 1]'$ and $\Omega(\theta) = B(1)^{-1}B(\theta)\Sigma B(\theta)'B(1)^{-1'}$. The most powerful invariant test rejects the null of an MA unit root for small values of the test statistic

$$S(\theta) = \frac{\hat{u}(\theta)'\Omega(\theta)^{-1}\hat{u}(\theta)}{\hat{u}(1)'\Omega(1)^{-1}\hat{u}(1)},$$

Table 4.3. *Asymptotic critical values of SL's test*

	Significance level		
δ_1	1%	5%	10%
7	1.399	−0.953	−1.955
10	1.030	−1.686	−2.877
14	0.175	−2.885	−4.263

Note: If the computed value of SL's test statistic is greater than the corresponding critical value, reject the null of level stationarity against the alternative of a unit root.

where $\hat{u}(\theta) = y - \hat{\mu}(\theta)e$ and $\hat{\mu}(\theta) = (e'\Omega(\theta)^{-1}e)^{-1}e'\Omega(\theta)^{-1}y$. Now, suppose that the alternative hypothesis is $H_1 : \theta = \theta_1$. Then the test statistic for the point-optimal test under the given alternative is $S(\theta_1)$, and this test is the most powerful for the alternative $H_1 : \theta = \theta_1$. Assuming for simplicity $u_t = e_t$ (i.e., no serial correlation in $\{u_t\}$) and letting $\theta_1 = 1 - \frac{\delta_1}{T}$, SL report the finite-sample power of their point-optimal test for $\delta_1 = 7, 10, 14$ and compare it to the maximum power attainable (i.e., the power of $S(\theta)$ when the true value θ is used). They find that the power difference is not quite noticeable whatever value δ_1 takes.

When $\{u_t\}$ is an ARMA process, asymptotic theory is needed because nuisance parameters related to the serial correlation structure of $\{u_t\}$ should be estimated. Asymptotic theory requires standardizing the test statistic $S(\theta_1)$ such that

$$R(\theta_1) = T(1 - S(\theta_1)).$$

This statistic depends on the parameters of the ARMA process, as does Σ. SL suggest fitting the ARMA model

$$\phi(B)\Delta y_t = (1 - \theta B)\psi(B)e_t$$

to estimate the ARMA coefficients and using them to construct an estimator of Σ. An explicit formula connecting the ARMA coefficients and Σ can be found, for example, in Dent (1977). Note that fitting the ARMA model $\phi(B)y_t = \psi(B)e_t$ to estimate Σ results in an inconsistent test. Selecting $\theta_1 = 1 - \frac{\delta_1}{T}$ ($0 \leq \delta_1 < \infty$), SL report the limiting quantiles of $R(\theta_1)$ for $\delta_1 = 7, 10, 14$, which are reproduced in Table 4.3. A practical problem for the SL test is the choice of δ_1. This could be handled as in ERS, but doing so requires further computation.

Jansson (2004) devises a point-optimal test for an MA unit root in the presence of stationary covariates following the original idea of Hansen (1995) discussed in Subsection 2.4.5. For the DGP[27]

$$y_t = x_t, \ (t = 1, \ldots, T);$$

$$\Delta x_t = u_t - \theta u_{t-1},$$

he supposes that a stationary process correlated with $\{u_t\}$, denoted as $\{z_t\}$, is available and that $\begin{pmatrix} u_t \\ z_t \end{pmatrix} \sim \text{iid } N(0, \Omega)$ with $\Omega = \begin{bmatrix} \sigma_{uu} & \sigma'_{zu} \\ \sigma_{zu} & \Omega_{zz} \end{bmatrix}$. Then, using the representation

$$y_t = (1 - \theta) \sum_{i=1}^{t-1} u_i + u_t, \tag{4.29}$$

he obtains

$$y_t - \sigma'_{zu} \Omega_{zz}^{-1} z_t = (1 - \theta) \sum_{i=1}^{t-1} u_i + u_t^*, \tag{4.30}$$

where $u_t^* = u_t - \sigma'_{zu} \Omega_{zz}^{-1} z_t$. Because $\text{Var}(u_t^*) = (1 - \rho^2) \text{Var}(u_t)$ with $\rho^2 = \sigma'_{zu} \Omega_{zz}^{-1} \sigma_{zu} / \sigma_{uu}$ ($0 \le \rho^2 \le 1$), the transitory component in relation (4.30) is "weaker" than that in (4.29). Thus, using the stationary covariates as in relation (4.30) makes it easier to detect the permanent component of $\{y_t\}$. As in SL, Jansson lets $\theta = 1 - \frac{\delta}{T}$ ($0 \le \delta < \infty$) and considers the point-optimal test for an MA unit root. The resulting power envelope shows that using the presence of stationary covariates expands the maximum power attainable, confirming the intuition explained earlier. Jansson also extends the point-optimal test to serially correlated time series. Like Hansen's test, however, Jansson's point-optimal test statistic has a limiting distribution that depends on the parameter ρ. This aspect makes his test inconvenient to use in practice, though it is based on an interesting idea.

4.7.4 Tests for Parameter Constancy

Kwiatkowski, Phillips, Schmidt, and Shin (1992; KPSS hereafter) consider the local-level model (see Harvey, 1989, Chapter 2)

$$y_t = \xi t + r_t + e_t, \ (t = 1, \ldots, T); \tag{4.31}$$

$$r_t = r_{t-1} + u_t,$$

where $u_t \sim \text{iid}(0, \sigma_u^2)$. The initial value r_0 is fixed and serves the role of an intercept. If $\{e_t\}$ is a stationary process, the null of trend stationarity is equivalent

---

[27] Jansson assumes the presence of a deterministic component, but this is omitted for the sake of brevity.

Table 4.4. *Asymptotic critical values of the KPSS test*

	Significance level			
	1%	2.5%	5%	10%
KPSS test	0.218	0.177	0.148	0.119

Note: If the computed value of the η_τ test statistic is greater than the critical value, reject the null of trend stationarity against the alternative of a unit root.

to

$$H_0 : \sigma_u^2 = 0. \tag{4.32}$$

Let $\{\hat{e}_t\}$ be the residuals from the regression of $\{y_t\}$ on an intercept and a linear time trend. When $e_t \sim \text{iid} \, N(0, \sigma_e^2)$, the LM test statistic[28] for the null hypothesis is $\frac{1}{\hat{\sigma}_e^2} \sum_{t=1}^T \hat{s}_t^2$, where $\hat{s}_t = \sum_{i=1}^t \hat{e}_i$ and $\hat{\sigma}_e^2 = \frac{1}{T} \sum_{t=1}^T \hat{e}_t^2$.

When $\{e_t\}$ is serially correlated, the long-run variance estimator of $\{e_t\}$ can be used instead of $\hat{\sigma}_e^2$. Thus, KPSS's test statistic is defined by

$$\eta_\tau = \frac{1}{\hat{\sigma}_1^2} \sum_{t=1}^T \hat{s}_t^2, \tag{4.33}$$

where $\hat{\sigma}_1^2$ is the long-run variance estimator using $\{\hat{e}_t\}$. The limiting distribution of this test statistic is

$$\int_0^1 V_2(r)^2 \, dr, \tag{4.34}$$

where $V_2(r) = W(r) + (2r - 3r^2)W(1) + (-6r + 6r^2) \int_0^1 W(s) \, ds$. KPSS call $V_2(r)$ the second-level Brownian bridge. Quantiles of the limiting distribution (from MacNeill, 1978, table 2) are reported in Table 4.4.

To test the null of level stationarity, regress $\{y_t\}$ on an intercept and use the residuals to formulate the test. The limiting distribution of the resulting test statistic, η_μ, is

$$\int_0^1 V_1(r)^2 \, dr,$$

where $V_1(r) = W(r) - r W(1)$ is a Brownian bridge. The limiting distribution of η_μ is the same as Tanaka's (1990) test reported in Table 4.1.

Phillips and Jin (2002) extend the KPSS test, replacing ξt in equation (4.31) with deterministic seasonal dummies. They show that the limiting distribution

---

[28] Nyblom's (1989) locally best test statistic for parameter constancy has the same functional form.

of the KPSS statistic is the same as that for η_τ. de Jong, Amsler, and Schmidt (2007) and Pelagatti and Sen (2013) extend the KPSS test using indicators and ranks, respectively. Their motivation is to make the KPSS test robust to fat-tailed distributions, but it is not obvious that their tests are more robust than the KPSS test according to their simulation results.

Leybourne and McCabe (1994)[29] also use a local-level model as in KPSS to derive their test statistic, but adopt a parametric approach to handle serial correlation in the data. More specifically, they assume the DGP

$$\phi(B)y_t = \xi t + r_t + e_t; \tag{4.35}$$

$$r_t = r_{t-1} + u_t,$$

where $\phi(z) = 1 + \sum_{i=1}^{p} \phi_i z^i$ and the roots of the equation $\phi(z) = 0$ are outside the unit circle, and they test the null hypothesis (4.32). Assuming $\{e_t\}$ and $\{u_t\}$ are independent and that r_0, ξ, and ϕ_i are known, Leybourne and McCabe report that their locally best test statistic is proportional to $\varepsilon'V\varepsilon$, where $\varepsilon = [\varepsilon_1, \ldots, \varepsilon_T]'$ with

$$\varepsilon_t = y_t - r_0 - \xi t - \sum_{i=1}^{p} \phi_i y_{t-i}$$

and V is a matrix whose (i, j)-th element is equal to the minimum of i and j. Regressing $\{y_t\}$ on $\{1, t, y_{t-1}, \ldots, y_{t-p}\}$ to estimate $\{\varepsilon_t\}$ is deemed to be natural, but Leybourne and McCabe show that it produces an inconsistent test. This is because the resulting residuals do not contain a unit root even under the alternative hypothesis. To understand why this occurs, note that Model (4.35) is second-order equivalent in moments to the ARMA model

$$\phi(B)(1 - B)y_t = \xi + (1 - \theta B)\zeta_t,$$

where $\zeta_t \sim \text{iid}(0, \sigma_\zeta^2)$ with $\sigma_\zeta^2 = \frac{\sigma_e^2}{\theta}$, $\theta = \frac{1}{2}(r + 2 - \sqrt{r^2 + 2r})$ and $r = \frac{\sigma_u^2}{\sigma_e^2}$. Under the null hypothesis (4.32), this is a trend-stationary AR(p) model because $\theta = 1$. But it is an ARIMA(p, 1, 1) model with an invertible MA component under the alternative. Thus, if we regress $\{y_t\}$ on $\{1, t, y_{t-1}, \ldots, y_{t-p}\}$ under the alternative, the resulting residuals do not have a unit root, thereby making the test inconsistent. For example, when $p = 1$, Δy_t is a stationary and invertible process. Thus, regressing $\{y_t\}$ on $\{y_{t-1}\}$ yields residuals without a unit root.

Leybourne and McCabe (1994) suggest the following steps for the construction of a consistent test statistic:

---

[29] A simple modification of their test that enhances the divergence rate under the alternative is given in Leybourne and McCabe (1999).

Step 1: Estimate the ARMA(p, 1) model

$$\Delta y_t = \xi + \sum_{i=1}^{p} \phi_i \Delta y_{t-i} + \zeta_t - \theta \zeta_{t-1}$$

and obtain the estimators $\{\phi_i^*\}$.
Step 2: Construct $y_t^* = y_t - \sum_{i=1}^{p} \phi_i^* y_{t-i}$.
Step 3: Regress $\{y_t^*\}$ on $\{1, t\}$ and let the residuals be the estimators of $\{\varepsilon_t\}$.

Using the residuals from Step 3 as $\{\varepsilon_t^*\}$, Leybourne and McCabe's (1994) test statistic is defined as

$$\frac{\varepsilon^{*\prime} V \varepsilon^*}{\hat{\sigma}_\varepsilon^2 T^2},$$

where $\varepsilon^* = [\varepsilon_1^*, \ldots, \varepsilon_T^*]'$ and $\hat{\sigma}_\varepsilon^2 = \frac{\varepsilon^{*\prime} \varepsilon^*}{T}$. Its limiting distribution is the same as (4.34). Under the alternative hypothesis, note that $\{y_t^*\}$ constructed in Step 2 contains a unit root unlike the residuals obtained by regressing $\{y_t\}$ on $\{1, t, y_{t-1}, \ldots, y_{t-p}\}$.

4.7.5 Tests for an AR Unit Root

Letting $\Delta y_t = x_t$, Tsay (1993) considers the ARMA process

$$\phi(B)x_t = (1 - \theta B)\theta^*(B)e_t,$$

where all the roots of the equations $\phi(z) = 0$ and $\theta^*(z) = 0$ are outside the unit circle. The null hypothesis is $H_0 : \theta = 1$, and the alternative $H_1: |\theta| < 1$. Letting $b_t = \frac{\theta^*(B)}{\phi(B)} e_t$, we have

$$x_t = b_t - \theta b_{t-1}.$$

Now, consider the derived process $d_t = \frac{\partial b_t}{\partial \theta}$, which satisfies the relation

$$d_t = \theta d_{t-1} + b_{t-1}.$$

This shows that we need to test for an AR unit root in order to test the null of stationarity.[30] One remaining problem is that $\{d_t\}$ are not observed. Using the relation $b_t = (1 - \theta B)^{-1} x_t$, however, we obtain a recursive relation

$$(1 - \theta B)^2 d_t = x_t,$$

---

[30] Arellano and Pantula's (1995) test also uses the unit root distributions of Dickey and Fuller (1979), though it is different from Tsay's. Tsay reports that his test is more powerful than Arellano and Pantula's in finite samples.

Table 4.5. *Asymptotic critical values of Xiao's test*

	Significance level		
	1%	5%	10%
Level stationarity	1.63	1.36	1.22
Trend stationarity	1.04	0.90	0.83

Note: If the computed value of Xiao's test statistic is greater than the critical value, reject the null of stationarity against the alternative of a unit root.

which gives, under the restriction $\theta = 1$ and the assumption $d_t = 0$ for $t \leq 0$,

$$d_t = \begin{cases} 0, & t \leq 0 \\ x_1, & t = 1 \\ 2d_{t-1} - d_{t-2} + x_t, & t \geq 2. \end{cases}$$

This recursive relation provides $\{d_t\}$ for unit root testing. Therefore, we can employ various unit root tests using $\{d_t\}$ to test the null of level stationarity against the alternative of a unit root. Under the alternative, the generated $\{d_t\}$ is a stationary and invertible ARMA process and, therefore, Tsay's test is consistent. Simulation results in Tsay show that Tsay's test, which is the Dickey-Fuller test applied to $\{d_t\}$, is slightly less powerful than Tanaka's (1990) test.

4.7.6 Fluctuation Tests

Observing that a stationary time series fluctuates much less than a nonstationary one, Xiao (2001) proposes a fluctuation test (see Sen, 1980) for the null of stationarity. For a time series $\{y_t\}$ represented by

$$y_t = \mu + x_t, \ (t = 1, \ldots, T), \tag{4.36}$$

where $\{x_t\}$ is a linear process, the fluctuation test statistic is defined as

$$F_T = \max_{t=1,\ldots,T} \frac{k}{\hat{\sigma}_1^2 \sqrt{T}} \left| \frac{1}{k} \sum_{t=1}^{k} \hat{y}_t - \frac{1}{T} \sum_{t=1}^{T} \hat{y}_t \right|,$$

where $\hat{\sigma}_1^2$ is an estimator of the long-run variance of $\{x_t\}$, $\hat{y}_t = y_t - \bar{y}$, and $\bar{y} = \frac{1}{T} \sum_{t=1}^{T} y_t$. Its limiting distribution is $\sup_{0 \leq r \leq 1} |V_1(r)|$, where $V_1(r) = W(r) - rW(1)$ is a Brownian bridge. In testing for trend stationarity, a linear time trend should be added to equation (4.36) and the residuals should be adjusted accordingly. See Table 4.5 for critical values of Xiao's tests.

4.7.7 *Lag-Length Selection and Stationarity Tests*

The aforementioned stationarity tests using the nonparametric method of serial correlation correction are quite sensitive to the choice of lag length for the long-run variance estimation. To handle this problem, one may consider using an estimator of the lag length l, denoted here as $\hat{l}$, with Andrews' (1993) methods. But this makes the tests inconsistent because $\hat{l} = O_p(T)$ under the alternative.[31]

A method to circumvent this difficulty is proposed in Choi and Ahn (1999). Their idea is to use the estimator $\hat{l}$ if it is not too large. But if $\hat{l} > T^\varepsilon$, where $\frac{1}{2} < \varepsilon < 1$, put $\hat{l} = c$ (an appropriately chosen constant). In the limit, the estimated value will eventually be used because $\hat{l} = O_p(T^\delta)$ $(0 < \delta < \frac{1}{2})$ under the null. However, under the alternative, eventually $\hat{l}$ will be chosen as a constant. This trick makes the tests consistent under the alternative and provides better empirical size than the fixed lag lengths when ε and c are properly chosen. Choi and Ahn show that this scheme stabilizes the sizes of some stationarity tests and enhances their powers as well in finite samples.

4.7.8 *Stationarity Test against the Alternative of Long Memory*

Harris, McCabe, and Leybourne (2008) consider the model[32]

$$(1 - B)^d y_t = u_t,$$

and propose a test for the null hypothesis $H_0 : d = 0$ against the alternative $H_1 : d > 0$. Because they assume a stationary linear process for $\{u_t\}$, $\{y_t\}$ is I(0) under the null, whereas it is a long-memory process under the alternative (see Subsection 2.2.4 and Section 4.2 for related discussions).

Their test statistic is a modified version of Robinson's (1994) (see also Tanaka, 1999), and is defined as

$$S_k = \frac{N_k}{\omega_l},$$

where $N_k = \sqrt{T - k} \sum_{j=k}^{T-1} \frac{\gamma_j}{j-k+1}$, $\gamma_j = T^{-1} \sum_{t=j+1}^{T} y_t y_{t-j}$, $\omega_l^2 = \sum_{j=-l}^{l} h_j \sum_{i=-l}^{l} \gamma_i \gamma_{i+j}$, $h_0 = \frac{\pi^2}{6}$ and $h_j = \sum_{i=1}^{|j|} \frac{1}{i}/|j|$. Notice that this test statistic uses only higher order autocovariances, which is reasonable because the power of the test comes from them. The limiting distribution of S_k is a standard normal when $k = c\sqrt{T}$ for a positive constant c. The test is also shown to be consistent. Their simulation results show that choosing $c = 1$

---

[31] In accordance with this property, Lee (1996) reports low finite-sample power of KPSS's test using optimal lag-selection methods.
[32] I omit nonstochastic terms for simplicity.

makes the test work well in finite samples and that their test has superior empirical size and power properties to KPSS against the alternative of I(1).

4.7.9   Size and Power of Stationarity Tests

In the vicinity of a unit root, stationarity tests tend to show serious size distortions to the extent that the test results cannot be trusted at all. Caner and Kilian (2001) emphasize this point with their simulation results. There are several attempts to overcome this difficulty. Lanne and Saikkonen (2003) modify Leybourne and McCabe's (1994) Step 2 to devise a better sized test. Psaradakis (2003, 2006) uses the sieve- and block-bootstrap methods, respectively, to improve the size properties of Tanaka's (1990) and KPSS's stationarity tests. Choi (2009) applies an idea of sample splitting to improve the finite sample size of the KPSS test. Sul, Phillips, and Choi (2005) introduce a new long-run variance estimator using AR-regression-based prewhitening along with a restriction rule on the prewhitening estimates. They report that the KPSS test's size performance improves with the new estimator. Kurozumi and Tanaka (2010) improve the size performance of the KPSS test with a bias correction along with Sul, Phillips, and Choi's long-run variance estimator.

Müller (2005) provides an analytic framework that illustrates the size distortion problem of KPSS-type tests for stationarity. He assumes a near unit root process of Phillips (1987b) and Chan and Wei (1987) and shows that the KPSS test rejects with probability one when the usual estimator of the long-run variance is used. This means that the test will reject too often even when the null is quite apart from the alternative, which reaffirms the results of previous simulation studies. As Müller also acknowledges, his analytic result as well as previous simulation studies cannot provide a compelling argument against the use of stationarity tests because no tests can discriminate the null from the alternative perfectly. However, Müller's paper other studies are a meaningful reminder that stationarity test results should be taken with caution, especially when they reject the null hypothesis.

Cappuccio and Lubian (2006) report size-adjusted finite-sample powers of various stationarity tests. However, because the size adjustment cannot be made for the stationarity tests in practice and because most of these tests entail enormous size distortions in the vicinity of a unit root, the information given in Cappuccio and Lubian cannot alone provide guidance in evaluating the usefulness of the tests. Deciding which test is best to use in practice is difficult pending more investigation.

The effects of sampling frequency on the power of unit root tests have been studied by several authors as we see later in Section 5.6. Relatively few researchers have studied the effects of the sampling frequency on the power of stationarity tests. Busetti and Taylor (2005) is the only work related to the subject. They consider a continuous-time local-level model and find that the asymptotic local power of the KPSS test increases with the sampling frequency in the case of stock data, but not in the case of flow data. Intuitively, the former result is in accordance with the fact that the root of an AR(1) process converges to one as the sampling frequency for stock data increases—see equation (5.15) in Subsection 5.6.1 and the discussions that follow. For a fixed time span, they show that the KPSS test for stock data is consistent as the sampling frequency tends to infinity, whereas that for flow data is not. Results similar to the latter are reported in Chambers (2004) as we see in Subsection 5.6.2.

Amsler and Schmidt (2012) perform simulation that studies robustness of stationarity tests for fat tails. They find that Choi's (1994) LM test has excellent robustness properties, but is not generally as powerful as the KPSS test. As an analytical framework for fat tails, they suggest local-to-finite-variance asymptotics that represent the innovation process as a weighted sum of a finite-variance process and an infinite-variance process. The weights depend on sample size and a constant. The innovation process has an infinite variance at every sample size, but the partial sum of them converges to a random process on standardization. They claim that the sensitivity of the asymptotic distribution of a test statistic to the weighting constant is a good indicator of its robustness to fat tails.

4.8   Stationarity Tests under Structural Changes

Stationarity tests are as significantly influenced by the presence of structural changes as are unit root tests. This section introduces research results on stationarity tests under structural changes.

4.8.1   Structural Changes in Level and Trend

Discussions on the stationarity tests under structural changes revolve around the null models,

Model 1: $y_t = \mu + \delta \mathbf{1}\{t > T_B\} + u_t$;

Model 2: $y_t = \mu + \delta \mathbf{1}\{t > T_B\} + \beta t + \gamma (t - T_B)\mathbf{1}\{t > T_B\} + u_t$;

Model 3: $y_t = \mu + \delta \mathbf{1}\{t > T_B\} + \beta t + u_t$;

Model 4: $y_t = \mu + \beta t + \gamma (t - T_B)\mathbf{1}\{t > T_B\} + u_t$,

where $\{u_t\}$ is a stationary process. Model 1 has a structural change only in level, and Model 2 has one in both level and slope. Models 3 and 4 have a structural change in level only and slope only, respectively. Extensions of these models to those of multiple structural changes are straightforward.

Lee, Huang, and Shin (1997) show that the KPSS test rejects the null hypothesis with probability tending to one under the null models 1 and 2. Thus, using the KPSS test without regard to structural changes can make the Type I error close to one.

Various approaches have been proposed to fix the problem raised by Lee, Huang, and Shin (1997). Lee (1999) considers testing the null of stationarity in the presence of multiple structural changes. Lee's null DGPs are stationary processes with multiple structural changes in level, and in level and a linear time trend (i.e., Model 1 and Model 2 extended to the case of multiple changes). Assuming that the number of structural changes and the dates of changes are known, Lee derives the limiting distributions of the KPSS test statistics and tabulates the distributions for a few selected cases. The distributions depend on the number of structural changes and the dates of changes. He then uses the Bayesian information criteria (BIC) to estimate the number of structural changes and the dates of changes and suggests using these estimators to construct the KPSS test statistics, assuming that these estimators are consistent for true values.

Lee and Strazicich (2001) develop the KPSS test along the same line as in Lee (1999), but estimate the unknown change dates by minimizing the KPSS test statistic with respect to them. An inconvenient aspect of the approach of estimating the change dates in these studies is that the resulting test statistics have limiting distributions that depend on the true change dates.

Busetti and Harvey (2001) study the KPSS test under weak structural changes. That is, they assume $\delta = O(T^{-\frac{1}{2}})$ and $\gamma = O(T^{-\frac{3}{2}})$. Denoting the KPSS test statistic for Model i as η_i $(i = 1, 2, 3, 4)$, they show that the test statistics $\inf_{\lambda \in \Lambda} \eta_i$, where $\lambda = \frac{T_B}{T}$ and Λ is a subset of an interval $[0, 1]$, have limiting distributions free of nuisance parameters. Quantiles of their tests statistics using the interval $\Lambda = [0, 1]$ are reported in Table 4.6. Harvey and Mills (2004) report quantiles of the same test statistics using the interval $\Lambda = [0.2, 0.8]$. They are slightly different, which may cause problems in applications. In addition, the assumption of weak structural changes is difficult to confirm in practice. If this assumption is not met, Busetti and Harvey's test loses its grounding. As remedy to this, Busetti and Harvey (2003a) suggest estimating change dates for the KPSS test as in Lee and Strazicich (2001) and using them for inference without the assumption of weak structural changes. The only difference between Busetti and Harvey (2003a) and Lee and Strazicich is that the former estimate structural change dates by the least squares method, whereas the latter do so by minimizing the KPSS statistic with respect to unknown change dates. Kurozumi (2002b)[33] also suggests the same idea as in Busetti and Harvey (2003a).

All the tests discussed so far have assumed abrupt structural changes. In contrast, Harvey and Mills (2004) consider testing for gradual structural changes

---

[33] Kurozumi also derives the characteristic function of the KPSS test statistic under the local alternative using the Fredholm determinant approach.

Table 4.6. *Asymptotic critical values of Busetti and Harvey's test*

	Significance level		
	1%	5%	10%
Model 1	0.134	0.087	0.071
Model 2	0.054	0.041	0.033
Model 3	0.125	0.089	0.071
Model 4	0.084	0.060	0.050

Note: If the computed value of Busetti and Harvey's test statistic is greater than the critical value, reject the null of stationarity against the alternative of a unit root.

using Granger and Teräsvirta's (1993) smooth-transition model. To be more precise, they assume under the null

Model 1: $y_t = \delta S_t + u_t$;

Model 2: $y_t = \delta S_t + \beta t + \gamma S_t + u_t$;

Model 3: $y_t = \beta t + \gamma S_t + u_t$,

where $\{u_t\}$ is a stationary process,

$$S_t = \frac{1}{1 + \exp(-\pi (t - T_B)/\hat{\sigma}(t))}$$

and $\hat{\sigma}(t)$ is the standard deviation of the transition variable t. The presence of $\hat{\sigma}(t)$ allows one to interpret π as transition speeds for different sample sizes independent of T. Because S_t changes gradually from 0 to 1 with the transition midpoint T_B, it can capture changes in parameters. A higher value of π brings more rapid change. When $\pi = \infty$, S_t reduces to the indicator function $\mathbf{1}\{t > T_B\}$. Harvey and Mills suggest estimating all the parameters in these models and to use them to construct the KPSS test statistic. However, they fail to derive relevant limiting distributions analytically, so they report critical values of their test statistics via simulation.

Becker, Enders, and Lee (2006) suggest approximating structural changes using a Fourier expansion and then testing the null of stationarity. This approach is sensible because any absolutely integrable function can be approximated by a Fourier series to any desired level of accuracy. They consider the null DGP

$$y_t = d_t + \xi' Z_t + u_t,$$

where $\{d_t\}$ is a deterministic component, $Z_t = \left[\sin\left(\frac{2\pi kt}{T}\right), \cos\left(\frac{2\pi kt}{T}\right)\right]'$, and $\{u_t\}$ is a stationary process. They choose this form for Z_t because any function $\alpha(t)$ with an unknown number of structural changes of unknown form can be approximated by

$$\alpha_0 + \sum_{k=1}^{n} a_k \sin\left(\frac{2\pi kt}{T}\right) + \sum_{k=1}^{n} b_k \cos\left(\frac{2\pi kt}{T}\right), \ n < \frac{T}{2},$$

where n is the number of frequencies and k represents a particular frequency. For simplicity, Becker, Enders, and Lee choose a single frequency, which results in Z_t. For a given k, they construct the KPSS test statistic and derive its limiting distribution, which depends on the frequency k. Because this is inconvenient in practice, they suggest estimating the frequency k by the least squares method and using the estimator for the KPSS test as if it were the true parameter. The limiting distributions derived by Becker, Enders, and Lee can be used for this feasible version of their test.

4.8.2 Structural Changes in Innovations

Busetti and Taylor (2003b) consider the model

$$y_t = d_t + u_t, \ (t = 1, \ldots, T),$$

where $\{d_t\}$ is a deterministic component, and the variance of $\{u_t\}$ changes at a date T_B. To test for the stationarity of $\{u_t\}$, they construct a modified KPSS test under the circumstance of changing variance. In the simplest case, $d_t = 0$, the test statistic is the sum of two KPSS test statistics that use the data $\{y_t\}_{t=1,\ldots,T_B}$ and $\{y_t\}_{t=T_B+1,\ldots,T}$. The limiting distribution of this test statistic depends on the ratio $\lambda = \frac{T_B}{T}$, which can be estimated as in the previous subsection. Busetti and Taylor also consider more complex cases where the deterministic component, $\{d_t\}$, undergoes structural changes.

4.9 Tests for Changing Persistence

In empirical applications, the stochastic behavior of time series may change over the sampling period. Kim (2000) gives some examples involving inflation rates and budget deficits. This section introduces tests that take the null as either a unit root or stationarity and the alternative as a process with a changing stochastic behavior.

4.9.1 The Null Hypothesis of a Unit Root

Leybourne, Kim, Smith, and Newbold (2003) consider the unobserved components model

$$y_t = d_t + x_t, \ \Delta x_t = \rho x_{t-1} + \phi(B)\Delta x_{t-1} + u_t, \ (t = 2, \ldots, T),$$

where $\{d_t\}$ is a deterministic component, $\phi(B)$ is a lag polynomial of known order $p - 1$, and the roots of $1 - \phi(z) = 0$ lie outside the unit circle. The null hypothesis is $H_0 : \rho = 0$, and the alternatives are

$$H_1 : \rho < 0 \text{ for } t \leq \lambda T \text{ and } \rho = 0 \text{ for } t > \lambda T$$

and

$$H_1' : \rho = 0 \text{ for } t \leq \lambda T \text{ and } \rho < 0 \text{ for } t > \lambda T,$$

where λ is an unknown constant belonging in the interval $(0, 1)$. In case of the alternative hypothesis H_1, Leybourne et al. compute ERS's t-ratio (see Subsection 2.4.4) using the data up to $[\lambda T]$ and $\bar{c} = 25$, denoted here as $DF_G(\lambda)$, assuming for the moment that λ is known. Because λ is unknown in practice, Leybourne et al. suggest using $\inf_{\lambda \in (0,1)} DF_G(\lambda)$. For the alternative hypothesis H_1', the same procedure is repeated for the t-ratio that uses the data from $[\lambda T] + 1$ to T. When the alternative is not specified, Leybourne et al. propose using the minimum of the infimum statistics.

Kurozumi (2005) considers the same model and hypotheses as in Leybourne, Kim, Smith, and Newbold (2003) for $d_t = \beta_0$ and $d_t = \beta_0 + \beta_1 t$. He devises LM test statistics for a known change point and proposes using the exponential average of the statistics. For the case $d_t = \beta_0 + \beta_1 t$, the LM test statistic is found to be equivalent to the sum of the t-ratios for the coefficients ρ_1 and ρ_2 in the regression

$$\Delta \tilde{x}_t = \rho_1 D_{1t} \tilde{x}_{t-1} + \rho_2 D_{2t} \tilde{x}_{t-1} + \phi(B) \Delta \tilde{x}_{t-1} + w_t,$$

where $\tilde{x}_t = y_t - y_0 - \tilde{\beta}_1 t$, $\tilde{\beta}_1 = T^{-1} \sum_{t=1}^{T} \Delta y_t$, $D_{1t} = 1$ for $t \leq \lambda T$ and zero otherwise, and $D_{2t} = 1 - D_{1t}$. Because the limiting distribution of the LM test statistic depends on the unknown parameter λ, Kurozumi proposes using the exponential average of the test statistic[34] and shows via simulation that this performs better than the other options he considers. The case $d_t = \beta_0$ is simpler to analyze, and the LM test can be devised in exactly the same manner.

Leybourne, Taylor, and Kim (2007) propose a ratio of standardized cumulative sums (CUSUMs) to test the null hypothesis of a unit root against the alternatives H_1 and H_1' given earlier. Their test statistic for an unknown change point is defined for a parameter set Λ as

$$R = \frac{\inf_{\lambda \in \Lambda} K^f(\lambda)}{\inf_{\lambda \in \Lambda} K^r(\lambda)}.$$

Here, $K^f(\lambda) = [\lambda T]^{-2} \sum_{t=1}^{[\lambda T]} \hat{x}_{t,\lambda}^2 / \hat{\sigma}_1^f$, $\hat{x}_{t,\lambda}$ is the OLS residual obtained by regressing $\{y_t\}$ on $\{d_t\}$ using data up to point $[\lambda T]$, and $\hat{\sigma}_1^{f2}$ is the usual

---

[34] The exponential average of $LM(\lambda)$ is defined as $\log \int_{\lambda \in \Lambda} \exp(LM(\lambda)) \, d\lambda$, where Λ is a subset of the interval $(0, 1)$. See Andrews and Ploberger (1994) for further details.

long-run variance estimator using data up to $[\lambda T]$. Similarly, $K^r(\lambda) = (T - [\lambda T])^{-2} \sum_{t=1}^{T-[\lambda T]} \tilde{x}_{t,\lambda}^2 / \hat{\sigma}_1^r$, where $\tilde{x}_{t,\lambda}^2$ is the OLS residual obtained by regressing $\{y_{T-t+1}\}$ on $\{d_t\}$ using data from $t = 1$ to $t = [\lambda T]$, and $\hat{\sigma}_1^{r2}$ is the long-run variance estimator using data $\{y_{T-t+1}\}_{t=1,\ldots,[\lambda T]}$. Under the null hypothesis, the test statistic converges in distribution to a random variable. However, under H_1, it converges to zero in probability, whereas it diverges to ∞ in probability under H_1'. Thus, when R takes a large absolute value, the null hypothesis is rejected. A convenient feature of Leybourne, Taylor, and Kim's test is that the direction of change need not be specified. Sibbertsen and Kruse (2009) extend Leybourne, Taylor, and Kim's test to long-memory processes. Their null hypothesis is a constant memory parameter (d in Subsection 2.2.4), and the alternative is a changing memory parameter.

Kejriwal, Perron, and Zhou (2013) devise sup-Wald tests of the null hypothesis that the process is I(1) against the alternative hypothesis that the process alternates between I(1) and I(0) multiple times. Their alternative hypothesis generalizes that of Leybourne, Kim, Smith, and Newbold (2003). Their Wald test statistics are constructed by using the difference of the unrestricted and restricted sum of squared residuals as usual. Assuming a known number of structural changes and unknown change dates, they construct the sup-Wald test statistics and derive their limiting distributions. The limiting distributions depend on the number of structural changes.

Phillips, Wu, and Yu (2011) define the bubble of a financial market as an explosive AR behavior, according to which AR models can be used to test for the presence of bubbles. Using the ADF regression with an intercept (see Subsection 2.3.1), they test the null of a unit root against the alternative

$$H_1 : \rho = 0 \text{ for } t \leq \lambda T \text{ and } \rho > 0 \text{ for } t > \lambda T,$$

where λ is an unknown constant belonging in the interval $(0, 1)$. Under this alternative, the data show explosive or bubble behavior when $t > \lambda T$. For the null and alternative hypotheses, Phillips, Wu, and Yu suggest using the test statistic $\sup_{\lambda^o \leq \lambda \leq 1} \bar{\tau}(\lambda)$ where $\bar{\tau}(\lambda)$ is the ADF statistic using data from the origin to $[\lambda T]$ and λ^o is some fraction of the total sample. In their empirical application to the NASDAQ stock price index in the 1990s, they use $\lambda^o = 0.1$.

Homm and Breitung (2012) propose several test statistics that serve the same purpose as Phillips, Wu, and Yu's test statistic (2011). Among these, the most promising one is the t-ratio for parameter δ in the model

$$\Delta y_t = \delta(y_{t-1} \mathbf{1}\{t > [\lambda T]\}) + u_t.$$

The null and alternative hypotheses are $H_0 : \delta = 0$ and $H_1 : \delta > 0$, respectively. Because the parameter λ is unknown, they suggest using the supremum of the t-ratio over λ belonging to the interval $[0, 1 - \lambda_0]$, with λ_0 being a chosen constant. They report that their test has higher finite-sample power than Phillips, Wu, and Yu's. They also suggest a variant of Busetti and Taylor's (2004) test statistic that also performs well in finite samples.

4.9.2   The Null Hypothesis of Stationarity

Kim (2000)[35] tests the null of stationarity against the alternative of changing persistence. Kim's null model is

$$y_t = \mu + u_t, \ (t = 1, \ldots, T),$$

where $\{u_t\}$ is a stationary process, and the alternatives are

$$y_t = \mu + u_t \text{ for } t \le \lambda T \text{ and } y_t = \mu + z_t \text{ for } t > \lambda T; \qquad (4.37)$$

$$y_t = \mu + z_t \text{ for } t \le \lambda T \text{ and } y_t = \mu + u_t \text{ for } t > \lambda T, \qquad (4.38)$$

where $\{z_t\}$ is a unit root process. Let the KPSS test statistic (see Subsection 4.7.4) using the data up to $[\lambda T]$ be $\eta_\tau(\lambda)$ and that using the data from $[\lambda T] + 1$ to T be $\eta_\tau(1 - \lambda)$. The long-run variance estimators of these test statistics are set to be one.[36] Then, Kim's proposed test statistic are

$$\max_{\lambda \in \Lambda} \frac{\eta_\tau(1 - \lambda)}{\eta_\tau(\lambda)}, \ \int_{\lambda \in \Lambda} \frac{\eta_\tau(1 - \lambda)}{\eta_\tau(\lambda)} d\lambda, \ \log \int_{\lambda \in \Lambda} \exp\left(\frac{\eta_\tau(1 - \lambda)}{\eta_\tau(\lambda)}\right) d\lambda, \ (4.39)$$

where Λ is a subset of the interval $(0, 1)$. Kim derives the limiting distributions of these test statistics and shows that his test is consistent against the alternatives (4.37) and (4.38). Among the three, the mean score test statistic (the second one in (4.39)) shows the best size performance in finite samples. Kim also proposes an estimator of the change point λ. But Halunga and Osborn (2012) show that his estimator is inconsistent unless $\mu = 0$.

Busetti and Taylor (2004) consider the same problem as Kim (2000) and additionally propose a locally best invariant test using the framework of King and Hillier (1983) and King (1987). It is basically the KPSS test using the data from $[\lambda T] + 1$ to T for the alternative (4.37) and the data up to $[\lambda T]$ for the alternative (4.38). They demonstrate via simulation that their locally best invariant test delivers higher power than Kim's ratio test.

---

[35]   See Kim, Belaire-Franch, and Amador (2002) for a related corrigendum regarding the limiting distributions of Kim's (2000) test statistics.

[36]   Leybourne and Taylor (2004) consider the ratio of the KPSS test statistics without setting the long-run variance estimators at one. They report that this modified test statistic shows better size performance in finite samples.

4.10   Summary and Further Remarks

This chapter introduced unit root tests against the alternatives of fractional integration, robust regression methods, model-free tests for a unit root, bootstrapping methods, Bayesian inferential methods for a unit root, tests that take stationarity with or without structural changes as the null hypothesis, and tests for changing persistence.

Unit root tests against the alternatives of fractional integration should be employed if data were generated by the ARIMA(p, d, q) model, with d not necessarily being an integer. Because there are many variables from economics and political science (e.g., macropartisanship time series studied by Box-Steffensmeier and Smith, 1996) that seem to be well represented by fractionally integrated processes, they deserve serious considerations in applications. In particular, because the LM tests of Robinson (1994), Tanaka (1999), and Demetrescu, Kuzin, and Hassler (2008) are easy to implement and have good power properties, they are recommended in practice.

Robust regression methods should be given close attention when outliers are expected to be present. Lucas's (1995b) and Herce's (1996) unit tests seem be quite useful in this regard, although the latter test needs to be extended to the AR(1) model with a liner time trend. Because both of the tests use only Phillips's (1987a) approach, developing Dickey-Fuller-type tests may be worthwhile from a practical viewpoint.

Among the model-free tests of this chapter, the rank-based tests and Burridge and Guerre's (1996) test require an i.i.d. assumption and tend to have low power, although an advantage of these tests is their robustness to outliers. The users of these tests should be aware of these pros and cons in practice. The variance ratio test of Breitung (2002) is model-free and does not require estimating the long-run variance. Moreover, it works well in finite samples. When outliers and/or integrated GARCH errors are suspected, this test is worth consideration.

Bootstrapping methods are relatively new and interesting, but unfortunately they do not yield correct size in the case of MA(1) errors with a negative coefficient—the most important case in the literature that illustrates deteriorating finite-sample size of unit root tests. But in the case of positive serial correlations in the errors, bootstrapping methods can deliver better finite-sample size. Paparoditis and Politis's (2003) block bootstrapping and Palm, Smeekes, and Urbain's (2008) sieve bootstrapping are recommended for use. In addition, when the limiting distribution of a unit root test statistic depends on nuisance parameters (e.g., unit root testing under permanent changes in variance), bootstrapping methods can provide valid critical values.

Empirical results using the Bayesian approach have been found to be quite sensitive to the chosen priors, model specification, and the treatment of the initial variable. Thus, it is hard to decide which Bayesian approach should be used in practice. The Bayesian posterior odds ratio for the null hypothesis of a unit root against the alternative of stationarity depends on the priors of the parameter of interest and onuisance parameters as well. For this reason, again, it is difficult to interpret results of the Bayesian posterior odds ratio. When using Bayesian methods for empirical problems, one needs to exercise maximum caution in selecting the method and in interpreting empirical results. Furthermore, a robustness check that investigates effects of the chosen priors and model specifications is much needed in the Bayesian inference.

Stationarity tests are quite often used in practice, and some are programmed into commercial packages: the most popular one is the KPSS test, although other tests are as good as it. In practice, stationarity test results should be taken with caution when they reject the null hypothesis, because they are subject to size distortions in the vicinity of the alternative hypothesis of a unit root.

In reality, changes in the dynamic structure of data may occur due to economic crises, changes in economic institutions, and so on. Tests for changing persistence are useful in detecting such changes. When testing the null hypothesis that the process is I(1) against the alternative that the process alternates between I(1) and I(0), one can use procedures by Leybourne, Kim, Smith, and Newbold (2003), Kurozumi (2005), Leybourne, Taylor, and Kim (2007), and Kejriwal, Perron and Zhou (2013). Relative merits of these procedures need to be studied further. When the alternative hypothesis is an explosive process, Phillips, Wu, and Yu's (2011) and Homm and Breitung's (2012) methods can be employed. These two procedures are useful for detecting bubble behaviors in financial markets. To test the null of stationarity against the alternative of changing persistence, Kim's (2000) and Busetti and Taylor's (2004) test should be considered. Busetti and Taylor argue that their test has higher power than Kim's test.

5 Other Issues Related to Unit Roots

5.1 Introduction

This chapter introduces a smorgasbord of topics that are relevant to unit roots, but are inappropriate for the previous chapters: model selection, interval and point estimation for the AR model possibly with a unit root, distribution theory for the AR(1) model with a unit root, sampling frequency and tests for a unit root, and effects of seasonal adjustments on unit root testing.

Model selection is certainly an important topic in time series analysis. This chapter shows that most model selection methods are applicable to the AR model possibly with a unit root. In addition to hypothesis tests for a unit root, this chapter introduces methods for interval and point estimation for the AR model possibly with a unit root. The presence of a unit root makes it difficult to construct confidence intervals, but a few clever methods can be used to overcome these difficulties, as shown in this chapter. Median-unbiased estimation of the AR coefficient is also covered. Distribution theory for the AR(1) model with a unit root was a starting point of research on unit roots (cf. White, 1958). This chapter summarizes a few methods that have been proposed to calculate distributions of estimators and tests for the AR(1) model with a unit root. Sampling frequency can affect the power of unit root tests. This finding has been studied in a few works, which are surveyed in this chapter. Most data are seasonally adjusted before publication, and one might wish to know how this adjustment affects unit root tests. The research results from studies of this issue are presented in this chapter.

5.2 Model Selection for Nonstationary Time Series

Order selection for the ARMA model has been an important research theme in time series analysis. This section introduces research results on model selection in relation to nonstationary time series. The reader is referred to Burnham and Anderson (2002), Hannan and Deistler (1988), Rao and Wu (2001), and references therein for the literature on model selection.

Tsay (1984) studies the properties of Akaike's (1973), Schwarz's (1978), and Hannan and Quinn's (1979) model selection criteria for the AR process, possibly with real and complex unit roots. Letting k denote the AR order used for model fitting, the three model selection criteria are written as a function of k, respectively, as

$$AIC(k) = \log\left(\hat{\sigma}_u^2(k)\right) + 2k/T,$$

$$BIC(k) = \log\left(\hat{\sigma}_u^2(k)\right) + k\log(T)/T,$$

$$\phi(k) = \log\left(\hat{\sigma}_u^2(k)\right) + ck\log\log(T)/T, \ c > 2,$$

where $\hat{\sigma}_u^2(k)$ is the usual estimator of error variance using k lagged variables. Setting the maximum AR order at P, the AR order for each criterion is selected by minimizing the relevant function of k over $0 \leq k \leq P$. Properties of these criteria for stationary time series are well known. Shibata (1976) derives the asymptotic distribution of $AIC(k)$, showing that the probability of underfitting is zero and that the probability of overfitting[1] is positive in the limit. If we assume that the true model is an AR model with a given order less than or equal to P,[2] the order estimator from $AIC(k)$ is not consistent for the true order. Hannan and Quinn show that $BIC(k)$ and $\phi(k)$ select the true model, if it is an AR model with an order less than or equal to P, with probability one as the sample size goes to infinity (i.e., they are strongly consistent for the true model). Adding to these well-known results, Tsay shows that the presence of unit roots does not essentially bring any changes. The limiting probabilities of $AIC(k)$ remain the same, and the probability of choosing the true model converges to one as the sample size increases when $BIC(k)$ and $\phi(k)$ are used (i.e., they are weakly consistent for the true model). An implication of these results is that we need not pay attention to the presence of unit roots when these information criteria are used.

Pötscher (1989) derives general conditions for the strong consistency of model selection criteria for possibly nonstationary linear models. The model selection criteria he considers for the AR model with unit roots are

$$\log\left(\hat{\sigma}_u^2(k)\right) + kC(T)/T \text{ and } \hat{\sigma}_u^2(k) + kC(T)/T.$$

He shows that the estimates of the true AR order obtained by minimizing these criteria over k are strongly consistent if $C(T)/T \to 0$ and $C(T)/\log(T) \to \infty$

---

[1] It is a function of $k - p$ and $P - k$ when the true AR order is p.

[2] The purpose of Akaike's information criterion is to find a model closest to the true model about which we may never know. From the perspective of Akaike's information criterion, assuming that the true model is contained in a set of candidates models may be nonsensical. See Burnham and Anderson (2002) for related discussions.

as $T \to \infty$. That is, the divergence rate of $C(T)$ should be in between $\log(T)$ and T for the strong consistency. Obviously, $AIC(k)$, $BIC(k)$, and $\phi(k)$, introduced earlier do not satisfy this sufficiency condition.

Wei (1992) proposes another model selection criterion, the Fisher information criterion (FIC). For the AR model, it is defined as

$$FIC(k) = n\hat{\sigma}_u^2(k) + \hat{\sigma}_u^2(P)\log\left|\sum_{t=k+1}^{T} x_t x_t'\right|, \ 0 \leq k \leq P,$$

where $x_t = (y_{t-1}, \ldots, y_{t-k})'$. Here, the conventional penalty term is replaced by the log determinant of the Fisher information matrix. Whereas AIC and BIC are based on firm statistical theories, FIC appears to be an ad hoc, but intuitively appealing, procedure. Wei shows that his model selection criterion selects the true AR order with probability one as the sample size becomes infinite, for both stationary and nonstationary AR models.

Phillips and Ploberger (1994) derive a model selection criterion called the posterior odds criterion (PIC). Here I discuss only the case where the true model is the AR process possibly with a unit root, though extensions to the ARMA model are straightforward once Hannan and Rissanen's (1982) procedure is adopted as shown by Phillips and Ploberger. Assuming that the true AR order is less than or equal to P, PIC chooses the AR($\hat{k}$) model when a weighted LR between it and the AR(P) model is maximized. Like their unit root test, it is a hybrid of the classical and Bayesian approaches. The weighted LR is written as

$$PIC(k) = \left|\frac{A_T(k)}{\hat{\sigma}_u^2(P)}\right|^{-1/2} \left|\frac{A_T(P)}{\hat{\sigma}_u^2(P)}\right|^{-1/2}$$

$$\times \exp\left(\left(\frac{1}{\hat{\sigma}_u^2(P)}\right)\left(\hat{\alpha}(k)'A_T(k)\hat{\alpha}(k) - \hat{\alpha}(P)'A_T(P)\hat{\alpha}(P)\right)\right),$$

where $A_T(k)$ is the data moment matrix using k lagged variables, $\hat{\sigma}_u^2(P)$ is the usual estimator of error variance from the AR(P) model, and $\hat{\alpha}(k)$ is the OLS estimator of the vector of AR coefficients from the AR(k) model. The chosen AR order $\hat{k}$ maximizes $PIC(k)$ over k ($0 \leq k \leq P$). Phillips and Ploberger show by simulation that PIC has good finite-sample properties when compared to AIC and BIC. For stationary systems, PIC is asymptotically equivalent to BIC as shown by Phillips and Ploberger (1996, p. 398).

Observing that AIC and BIC tend to choose too small a lag for the ADF regression—which, in turn, leads to size distortions of the ADF test—Ng and Perron (2001) devise a modified Akaike information criterion. Its objective is to reduce size distortions of the GLS-based unit root tests. They consider the

ADF regression model,

$$\Delta y_t = d_t + \rho y_{t-1} + \sum_{j=1}^{k} \gamma_j \Delta y_{t-j} + u_t, \ (t = P + 1, \ldots, T),$$

where $d_t = \beta_0$ or $\beta_0 + \beta_1 t$ and P is the assumed upper bound for the AR order. Because the series starts at $P + 1$, all the competing models with different k are using the same number of effective observations. Assuming $\rho = 0$, Ng and Perron derive Akaike's information criterion along with ERS's GLS-detrending. Letting y_{t-1}^d be y_{t-1} detrended by ERS's GLS method (cf. Subsection 2.4.4), the modified AIC is written as

$$MAIC(k) = \log\left(\hat{\sigma}_u^2(k)\right) + \frac{2(\tau(k) + k)}{T - P},$$

where $\hat{\sigma}_u^2(k) = (T - P)^{-1} \sum_{t=P+1}^{T} \hat{u}_{tk}^2$, $\hat{u}_{tk}$ is the residual obtained by regressing $\{\Delta y_t^d\}$ on $\{y_{t-1}^d, \Delta y_{t-1}^d, \ldots, \Delta y_{t-k}^d\}$, $\tau(k) = \frac{1}{\hat{\sigma}_u^2(k)} \hat{\rho}^2 \sum_{t=P+1}^{T} (y_{t-1}^d)^2$ and $\hat{\rho}$ is the OLS estimator of ρ using the detrended data. This criterion is certainly different from the usual one because the null restriction of a unit root is imposed for its derivation. Moreover, it uses the GLS-detrending method with the chosen values of $\bar{c}$ in ERS. Based on $MAIC$, Ng and Perron also propose

$$MBIC(k) = \log\left(\hat{\sigma}_u^2(k)\right) + \frac{\log(T - P)(\tau(k) + k)}{T - P}.$$

Ng and Perron show via simulation that their information criteria deliver better size properties of the Dickey-Fuller-GLS test than BIC. However, they acknowledge that the modified model selection criteria may not perform well for the lag selection of the AR model because its main purpose is to reduce size distortions of the Dickey-Fuller-GLS test.

Burridge and Hristova (2008) study model selection criteria for the AR model containing a unit root and having i.i.d. errors in the domain of attraction of a stable law with index $0 < \alpha < 2$. They show that AIC, BIC, and Hannan and Quinn's (1979) model selection criterion estimate the true order consistently. Notice that the consistency of AIC they derive is in contrast to previous research results, which show that AIC is not a consistent lag selection criterion for the AR model.

5.3   Interval and Point Estimation for Unit Root Processes

This section introduces several methods of point and interval estimation for the AR model possibly with a unit root. The methods of interval estimation introduced here address Sims' (1988) criticism of the classical asymptotic theory for the unit root AR(1) model. According to Sims, that theory is problematic because the t-ratio has different asymptotic distributions depending on the location of the AR(1) coefficient (see Subsection 4.6.1). The interval estimation methods discussed in this section overcome Sims' criticism, though their approaches are obviously classical.

5.3.1 Interval Estimation Based on Local-to-Unity Asymptotics

Stock (1991) proposes confidence intervals of the AR process's largest root using the local-to-unity asymptotics of Bobkoski (1983), Phillips (1987b), and Chan and Wei (1987). He considers the unobserved components model

$$y_t = \mu + \beta t + x_t; \tag{5.1}$$

$$a(B)x_t = u_t, \quad a(B) = b(B)(1 - \alpha B),$$

where $b(z) = \sum_{j=0}^{k} b_j z^j$, $b_0 = 1$, $b(1) \neq 0$ and $\{u_t\}$ is a martingale difference sequence. Most importantly, α is specified as $\alpha = 1 + \frac{c}{T}$. To obtain confidence intervals for α, Stock devises those for the parameter c and transforms them for the confidence intervals of α. To this end, Model (5.1) is rewritten as

$$y_t = \tilde{\mu} + \tilde{\beta} t + \rho y_{t-1} + \sum_{j=1}^{k} \gamma_j \Delta y_{t-j} + u_t,$$

where $\rho = 1 + \frac{cb(1)}{T}$. The ADF test statistic, τ^*, for the null hypothesis $\rho = 1$ has the asymptotic distribution represented by

$$\left(\int_0^1 J^\tau(s)^2 \, ds \right)^{1/2} \left\{ \left(\int_0^1 J^\tau(s)^2 \, ds \right)^{-1} \int_0^1 J^\tau(s) \, dW(s) + c \right\}, \tag{5.2}$$

where $J^\tau(\lambda) = J_c(\lambda) - \int_0^1 (4 - 6s) J_c(s) \, ds - \lambda \int_0^1 (12s - 6) J_c(s) \, ds$ and $J_c(\cdot)$ is the Ornstein-Uhlenbeck process defined in Subsection 2.2.3. Note that this distribution depends only on c and that it is continuous in c. However, because the analytical forms of the pdf and cdf of this distribution are unknown, simulation methods should be used to find percentiles of this distribution for each value of c.

Assume for simplicity that the confidence level is fixed. Then, for each value of c, an acceptance interval for τ^* can be obtained from the asymptotic distribution (5.2). Let us denote this interval $f_l(c) \leq \tau^* \leq f_u(c)$, where $f_l(c)$ and $f_u(c)$ are, respectively, the lower and upper asymptotic percentiles of τ^* that yield the fixed confidence level. If $f_l(c)$ and $f_u(c)$ are strictly increasing in c, the critical values can be converted for the interval $f_l^{-1}(\tau^*) \leq c \leq f_u^{-1}(\tau^*)$, which is the desired confidence interval for the parameter c. The confidence interval for c is converted straightforwardly into that for α by using the relation

$\alpha = 1 + \frac{c}{T}$. Stock (1991) provides a table mapping the value of τ^* into a confidence interval for c. Applying his method to the Nelson-Plosser dataset, Stock finds that all the series except unemployment rate and bond yields contain a unit root in their 90% and 80% confidence intervals.

If one is interested in the confidence interval for ρ rather than for α,[3] the main hindrance is the unknown parameter $b(1)$. To estimate $b(1)$, we run an AR(1) regression, obtain residuals, and run an AR regression again using the residuals. Because the largest root is near to unity, the residuals from the first AR(1) regression are consistent estimators of $(1 - \alpha B)x_t$. Thus, regressing the residuals on their lagged values provides estimates of $b(1)$ (i.e., one minus the sum of the AR coefficients is equal to $b(1)$ asymptotically). Once $b(1)$ is estimated, asymptotic confidence intervals for ρ are obtained from the relation $\rho = 1 + \frac{cb(1)}{T}$.

Wright (2000) applies Stock's method to construct confidence intervals for the impulse response function of a univariate time series with a near unit root. He shows that these intervals show better coverage rates than other existing intervals when there is a near unit root.

Phillips (2012a) analyzes asymptotic properties of Stock's confidence interval using the stationary AR(1) model with coefficient α. He reports that Stock's confidence interval has zero coverage probability for α in the limit for fixed $|\alpha| < 1$ and all α for which $T^{1/3}(1 - \alpha) \to \infty$. He also reports that Stock's confidence interval is centered on $\ddot{\alpha} = \frac{3\alpha - 1}{\alpha + 1}$ and that the interval shrinks to $\ddot{\alpha}$ as $T \to \infty$. Phillips's analysis indicates that Stock's confidence interval works well only when the true value of α is close to one and fails to deliver proper confidence intervals for the stationary AR model. The main reason for the failure of Stock's confidence interval for the stationary AR(1) model is the use of the ADF test statistic, which imposes the null of a unit root. A modified version of Stock's confidence interval introduced in Mikusheva (2007) (see Subsection 5.3.8) has a uniform asymptotic coverage probability, overcoming the problem of Stock's original confidence interval.

5.3.2   Unbiased Estimation

Andrews (1993)[4] proposes median-unbiased estimation of the AR(1) model. He considers the unobserved components model

$$y_t = \mu + x_t, \; x_t = \alpha x_{t-1} + u_t, \; (t = 1, \ldots, T), \tag{5.3}$$

---

[3] Andrews and Chen (1994) argue that the sum of the AR coefficients is a more useful measure of persistence than the largest root, because the former is related to the cumulative impulse response and the spectral density at the zero frequency.

[4] According to Andrews (1993), the idea of median-unbiased estimation originates from Lehmann (1959). See also Rudebusch (1992) for a related idea.

where $\alpha \in (-1, 1]$, $u_t \sim \text{iid} \, N(0, \sigma_u^2)$, $x_0 \sim N(0, \frac{\sigma_u^2}{1-\alpha^2})$ if $\alpha \in (-1, 1)$, and x_0 is an arbitrary random variable if $\alpha = 1$. Because this model can be written as

$$y_t = \mu(1 - \alpha) + \alpha y_{t-1} + u_t, \tag{5.4}$$

$\{y_t\}$ is a strictly stationary, AR(1) process when $\alpha \in (-1, 1)$. In contrast, it is a random walk process when $\alpha = 1$. Andrews also considers the AR(1) model with an intercept and a linear time trend, but the median-unbiased estimation of the model is a straight extension of that of the AR(1) model with an intercept only and is not discussed here.

An estimator is median-unbiased if the median of the estimator is the true parameter. More precisely, an estimator, $\tilde{\beta}$, with a continuous distribution is median-unbiased for the true parameter β if and only if $P[\tilde{\beta} > \beta] = \frac{1}{2} = P[\tilde{\beta} < \beta]$. In this relation, β is the true parameter and, at the same time, the median of $\tilde{\beta}$. Thus, $\tilde{\beta}$ is median-unbiased.

Suppose that the least squares estimator of α, $\hat{\alpha}$, for the AR(1) model (5.4) has the median function $m_T(\alpha)$. This means that $m_T(\alpha)$ is the median of $\hat{\alpha}$ for each value of α at a given sample size T or, equivalently, $P[\hat{\alpha} > m_T(\alpha)] = \frac{1}{2} = P[\hat{\alpha} < m_T(\alpha)]$. The function $m_T(\cdot)$ is strictly increasing on the parameter space $(-1, 1]$, and its inverse function $m_T^{-1} : (m(-1), m(1)] \to (-1, 1]$ satisfying the relation $m_T^{-1}(m_T(\alpha)) = \alpha$ exists. Here, $m_T(-1)$ is defined by the relation $m_T(-1) = \lim_{\alpha \to -1} m_T(\alpha)$. Andrews (1993) introduces a median-unbiased estimator of α, $\hat{\alpha}_U$, defined by

$$\hat{\alpha}_U = \begin{cases} 1, & \text{if } \hat{\alpha} > m_T(1) \\ m_T^{-1}(\hat{\alpha}), & \text{if } m_T(-1) < \hat{\alpha} \leq m_T(1) \\ -1, & \text{if } \hat{\alpha} \leq m_T(-1). \end{cases}$$

The estimator $\hat{\alpha}_U$ is median-unbiased because

$$P[\hat{\alpha}_U > \alpha] = P[m_T(\hat{\alpha}_U) > m_T(\alpha)] = P[\hat{\alpha} > m_T(\alpha)] = \frac{1}{2} \tag{5.5}$$

and $P[\hat{\alpha}_U < \alpha] = \frac{1}{2}$. Note that the first equality of relation (5.5) holds because $m_T(\cdot)$ is strictly increasing, the second by the definition of $\hat{\alpha}_U$, and the third by the definition of $m_T(\cdot)$. A practical difficulty with the median-unbiased estimator, $\hat{\alpha}_U$, is that the function $m_T(\cdot)$ is unknown. Andrews employs simulation to overcome this difficulty. For each value of α at a given sample size, the median function $m_T(\cdot)$ is tabulated. Because the function $m_T(\cdot)$ is strictly increasing, its inverse function $m_T^{-1}(\cdot)$ is also empirically derivable from the simulated median function. Then the median-unbiased estimator, $\hat{\alpha}_U$, is calculated from the estimated inverse function.

In addition to the median-unbiased point estimation, Andrews (1993) also considers constructing two-sided 90% and one-sided 95% confidence intervals for the parameter α. For intervals at other confidence levels, more simulation is required. Andrews' confidence intervals can be constructed without knowing the precise location of α. Therefore, they overcome Sims' (1988) first criticism discussed earlier. Andrews applies the median-unbiased estimator to some real exchange-rate, velocity, and industrial production series and finds stronger evidence for a unit root than with the OLS estimator.

Andrews and Chen (1994) extend Andrews' (1993) median-unbiased estimation of the AR(1) model to the AR(p) model with an intercept and a linear time trend. They consider the AR(p) model

$$y_t = \mu + \beta t + \alpha y_{t-1} + \sum_{i=1}^{p-1} \rho_i \Delta y_{t-i} + u_t, \tag{5.6}$$

where α and $\{u_t\}$ satisfy corresponding assumptions given in Andrews. For the approximately median-unbiased estimation of α, the following iterative procedure is suggested.

Step 1: Obtain OLS estimators of the parameters in Model (5.6) denoted as $\hat{\mu}$, $\hat{\beta}, \hat{\alpha}, \hat{\rho}_1, \ldots, \hat{\rho}_{p-1}$.
Step 2: Treat the OLS estimators $\hat{\rho}_1, \ldots, \hat{\rho}_{p-1}$ as true parameters and run a simulation that regresses $y_t - \sum_{i=1}^{p-1} \hat{\rho}_i \Delta y_{t-i}$ on $\{1, t, y_{t-1}\}$ R times. This gives the median function of the OLS estimator of α given the true parameters $\hat{\rho}_1, \ldots, \hat{\rho}_{p-1}$. Use this median function to get the median-unbiased estimator of α, $\hat{\alpha}_U$, as in Andrews.

These steps are repeated either for a fixed number of times or until convergence by using the median-unbiased estimator $\hat{\alpha}_U$ from Step 2 in the renewed Step 1. That is, in the renewed Step 1, regress $y_t - \hat{\alpha}_U y_{t-1}$ on $\{1, t, \Delta y_{t-1}, \ldots, \Delta y_{t-(p-1)}\}$ to obtain new estimators of $\rho_1, \ldots, \rho_{p-1}$, which are then used in the new Step 2 to obtain the second median-unbiased estimator of α. In practice, this procedure will require computation on a massive scale.

The user of Andrews' (1993) and Andrews and Chen's (1993) median-unbiased estimator should bear in mind that it depends on a normality assumption, though Andrews demonstrates robustness of his estimator against nonnormal errors via simulation. Moreover, because the simulated median function depends on the sample size and the estimated parameter values for the lagged dependent variables in case of the AR(p) model, additional new simulation is required at each sample size and at each set of values for the estimated parameters. This aspect of Andrews' and Andrews and Chen's procedures makes them less attractive when massive computation is infeasible. Last, there is no theoretical formula available for the standard error of the median-unbiased estimator, though simulation can again be used to estimate it. Assessing the accuracy level of the median-unbiased estimator is not trivial for this reason.

An unbiased estimator of the parameter α is also studied by Roy and Fuller (2001). They calculate the bias of the parameter α in Model (5.6) under the assumption that the AR process has stationary roots only. Then, using the estimator of the bias, they correct the OLS estimator. The formula for this bias correction is quite complicated, so the interested reader is referred to the paper by Roy and Fuller (2001). They show that the median of the bias-corrected estimator is very close to the true parameter value even when the value of α is one or close to one. In other words, their estimator is nearly unbiased for the parameter α. But Roy and Fuller do not consider constructing confidence intervals for the parameter α.

5.3.3 Interval Estimation Using Overfitting

Choi (1993) considers interval estimation using an overfitted AR model. For example, if the true model is known to be AR(1), consider the AR(2) model

$$y_t = \alpha_1 y_{t-1} + \alpha_2 y_{t-2} + u_t, \ u_t \sim \text{iid}\left(0, \sigma_u^2\right),$$

where in fact $\alpha_2 = 0$. Because the OLS estimator of α_1, $\hat{\alpha}_1$, follows a normal distribution even when $\alpha_1 = 1$ (see Subsection 2.2.2), confidence intervals for α_1 can be devised in the usual manner using the t-ratio based on $\hat{\alpha}_1$. However, the presence of the insignificant variable, y_{t-2}, in the model will hurt the efficiency of the OLS estimator of α_1, which is the price to be paid in order to construct confidence intervals of α_1. In the limit, we have

$$\sqrt{T}(\hat{\alpha}_1 - \alpha_1) \Rightarrow N(0, 1),$$

which shows that $\hat{\alpha}_1$ is asymptotically more efficient than Phillips and Han's (2008) and Chen and Kuo's (2013) estimators that are discussed later. It is asymptotically equivalent to Gorodnichenko, Mikusheva, and Ng's (2012) with $K = 1$.

For the AR(p) model, confidence intervals for the sum of AR coefficients can be constructed using the augmented Dickey-Fuller regression further augmented by y_{t-p-1}. That is, run OLS on the model

$$y_t = \rho y_{t-1} + \sum_{j=1}^{p-1} \gamma_j \Delta y_{t-j} + \delta y_{t-p-1} + u_t, \ (t = p+1, \ldots, T) \quad (5.7)$$

and construct confidence intervals for the parameter ρ using the t-ratio along with a standard normal distribution. Choi (1993) reports via simulation that his confidence intervals work reasonably well for the AR(2) process when the sample size is as large as one hundred.

5.3.4   Resampling Methods

As discussed earlier in Section 4.5, the bootstrap method can fail for unit root testing. Similarly, conventional bootstrapping cannot be used to construct confidence intervals of the parameters of nonstationary AR processes. Hansen (1999), nonetheless, devises a bootstrap method that circumvents the problem of the conventional bootstrap.

For simplicity, consider the AR(1) model with an intercept,

$$y_t = \mu + \alpha y_{t-1} + u_t, \; u_t \sim \text{iid}(0, \sigma_u^2),$$

although Hansen's (1999) method is devised for a general, possibly nonstationary AR model with an intercept and a linear time trend. Let the OLS-based t-ratio for α be $t(\alpha)$. The conventional, asymptotic β-level confidence interval for α is constructed as

$$C_c = \{\alpha \mid q_1(\alpha) \le t(\alpha) \le q_2(\alpha)\},$$

where the quantiles $q_1(\alpha)$ and $q_2(\alpha)$ are chosen such that $P(C_c) \to \beta$ as the sample size increases. The interval is usually equal-tailed. The problem of this confidence interval is that the quantiles differ depending on α. In response to this problem, the conventional bootstrap method would generate bootstrap samples many times and estimate the quantiles. However, when $\alpha = 1$ and $\mu = 0$, the bootstrap and limiting distributions of the OLS estimator of α are not the same. This implies that the bootstrap method cannot be used for the construction of confidence intervals of α. Hansen, as a remedy to this problem, considers estimating $q_1(\alpha)$ and $q_2(\alpha)$ at each value of α using bootstrapping. That is, for a given value of $\alpha = \alpha^0$, we follow three steps:

Step 1: Regress $\{y_t - \alpha^0 y_{t-1}\}$ on $\{1\}$ and get the estimate of μ and residuals.
Step 2: Using the estimate of μ and residuals from Step 1, construct bootstrap samples $\{y_t^*(\alpha^0)\}$ B times.
Step 3: Using the B bootstrap samples from Step 2, calculate B t-ratios. Quantiles of these B t-ratios provide the bootstrap estimates of $q_1(\alpha^0)$ and $q_2(\alpha^0)$.

If these steps are repeated for many values of α, the functions $q_1(\alpha)$ and $q_2(\alpha)$ can be estimated reasonably well. Let these estimated functions be $q_1^*(\alpha)$ and $q_2^*(\alpha)$. Then, the grid bootstrap confidence interval for α is defined as

$$C_g = \{\alpha \mid q_1^*(\alpha) \le t(\alpha) \le q_2^*(\alpha)\}.$$

For a given OLS estimator of α and its standard error, $t(\alpha)$ is a monotonically decreasing function of α. Thus, the values of α at which $t(\alpha)$ equals the bootstrap quantiles are uniquely defined; these values constitute the grid bootstrap confidence interval for α. Hansen shows that the coverage rate of C_g converges to the confidence level β asymptotically. He also shows that his confidence intervals work reasonably well in finite samples.

Romano and Wolf (2001) use subsampling to construct confidence intervals of α in Model (5.6). The subsampling method and its applications are well introduced in Politis, Romano, and Wolf (1999). In the subsampling approach, the statistic of interest is computed at subsamples of the data (consecutive sample points in the case of the time series), and the subsampled values of the statistic are used to estimate its finite-sample distribution. The major strength of the subsampling method is that it can work even when the bootstrap method fails. In applying the subsampling method to time series, subsamples should use consecutive sample points in order to retain the structure of serial correlation. The main difference between bootstrap and subsampling is that the former uses resampling with replacements (e.g., resampling residuals with replacements in the regression models), whereas the latter does it without replacements. When bootstrapping works, it usually does better than subsampling.

To implement the subsampling procedure, these four steps need to be followed. We assume that the AR order p is known.

Step 1: Fix the block size b ($\geq p + 2$) and the confidence level.

Step 2: Using the subsamples $\{y_{p+1}, \ldots, y_{p+b}\}$, $\{y_{p+2}, \ldots, y_{p+b+1}\}$, ..., $\{y_{T-b+1}, \ldots, y_T\}$, calculate $T - b - p - 1$ OLS-based t-ratios for α that use the full-sample $\{y_{p+1}, \ldots, y_T\}$ OLS estimator of α as the true value of α.

Step 3: Calculate quantiles of the t-ratios from Step 2 at the given confidence level and denote them as (q_{s1}, q_{s2}).

Step 4: The subsampling-based confidence interval for α is given as $(\hat{\alpha} - q_{s2} \times \text{se}(\hat{\alpha}), \hat{\alpha} - q_{s1} \times \text{se}(\hat{\alpha}))$, where $\hat{\alpha}$ and $\text{se}(\hat{\alpha})$ are the OLS estimator of α and its standard error, respectively, that use the full sample $\{y_{p+1}, \ldots, y_T\}$.

Romano and Wolf show that the coverage rate of the subsampling-based confidence interval converges to the given confidence level as the sample size grows if $b \to \infty$ and $\frac{b}{T} \to 0$ as $T \to \infty$.

In practice, the choice of b should be made carefully: Romano and Wolf (2001) suggest the minimum volatility rule, which is easier to implement than other methods. Its algorithm for a fixed l is as follows:

Step 1: From $b_i = b_{small}$ to $b_i = b_{big}$, calculate the subsample confidence intervals $(q_{s1}^{b_i}, q_{s2}^{b_i})$.

Step 2: Calculate the standard deviations of $\{q_{s1}^{b_i}\}$ and $\{q_{s2}^{b_i}\}$ where i runs from $small + l$ to $big - l$, and add them up.

Step 3: Choose the block size that gives the minimum of the sum of the standard deviations of Step 2.

Romano and Wolf recommend a small number for l (2 or 3) in Step 2 and also note that the results are insensitive to b_{small} and b_{big}. They show via simulation that their subsampling confidence intervals work reasonably well in finite samples.

5.3.5   Instrumental Variables Estimation

So and Shin (1999) consider instrumental variables estimation of the AR process possibly with a unit root. For the AR(1) model (2.1) with i.i.d. errors, they propose the estimator of α using the sign of $\{y_{t-1}\}$ as an instrument. More precisely, their estimator is defined by

$$\hat{\alpha}_c = \frac{\sum_{t=2}^{T} \text{sign}(y_{t-1})y_t}{\sum_{t=2}^{T} |y_{t-1}|},$$

where $\text{sign}(y_{t-1}) = 1$ if $y_{t-1} \geq 0$ and $\text{sign}(y_{t-1}) = -1$ if $y_{t-1} < 0$. So and Shin call this the Cauchy estimator because they date its genesis to Cauchy. The standard error of $\hat{\alpha}_c$ is

$$\text{se}(\hat{\alpha}_c) = \frac{\sqrt{T\hat{\sigma}_u^2}}{\sum_{t=2}^{T} |y_{t-1}|},$$

where $\hat{\sigma}_u^2$ is a consistent estimator of σ_u^2 using the OLS residuals.
A striking fact found by So and Shin is that

$$\frac{\hat{\alpha}_c - \alpha}{\text{se}(\hat{\alpha}_c)} \xrightarrow{d} N(0, 1) \tag{5.8}$$

whatever the value of α. Thus, confidence intervals can be constructed in the usual manner when the Cauchy estimator is used. So and Shin report in a small simulation study that the performance of their confidence interval is comparable to that of Andrews (1993). So and Shin's method can easily be extended to higher order AR processes once $\{y_t\}$ and $\{y_{t-1}\}$ are regressed on nonstochastic terms and lagged differences, and the residuals are used instead of $\{y_t\}$ and $\{y_{t-1}\}$, respectively, in the formulas given earlier. However, the finite-sample properties of So and Shin's confidence interval for higher order AR processes are still unknown and need to be studied further.

Phillips, Park, and Chang (2004) extend So and Shin's (1999) result to other types of instruments. They find that such results as (5.8) can hold for other instrumental variables estimators and that the Cauchy estimator has better properties than the other estimators they consider.

5.3.6 Estimation Using Differences

Phillips and Han (2008)[5] employ Model (5.3) where $\alpha \in (-1, 1]$, $u_t \sim$ iid$(0, \sigma_u^2)$ and x_0 is any random variable. First-differencing of Model (5.3) yields $\Delta y_t = \alpha \Delta y_{t-1} + \Delta u_t$. Adding $\Delta y_t + \Delta y_{t-1}$ to both sides of this equation, we obtain

$$2\Delta y_t + \Delta y_{t-1} = \alpha \Delta y_{t-1} + \eta_t,$$

where $\eta_t = 2\Delta y_t + (1 - \alpha)\Delta y_{t-1}$. Because Δy_{t-1} and η_t are uncorrelated,[6] the OLS estimator of α, $\hat{\alpha}_{PH}$, has the following limiting distribution

$$\sqrt{T}(\hat{\alpha}_{PH} - \alpha) \Rightarrow N(0, 2(1 + \alpha)).$$

This result can be used to construct confidence intervals for α, which are valid for $\alpha \in (-1, 1]$. Unlike the OLS estimator for Model (5.3), the OLS estimator $\hat{\alpha}_{PH}$ has no discontinuity in its limiting distribution. However, for $\alpha \in (-1, 1)$, $\hat{\alpha}_{PH}$ has a larger variance than the usual OLS estimator based on Model (5.3); for $\alpha = 1$, it converges in probability to α at a slower rate than the OLS estimator. That is, $\hat{\alpha}_{PH}$ is asymptotically less efficient than the OLS estimator. In addition, it is not obvious how their method can be extended to higher order AR processes.

Phillip and Han (2008) also consider the case $a_T = \alpha_T - 1$, where $a_T \to 0$. Under the condition $a_T^{2T}/\sqrt{T} \to 0$, it is shown that

$$\sqrt{T}(\hat{\alpha}_{PH} - \alpha_T - a_T) \Rightarrow N(0, 4).$$

For example, if $\alpha_T = 1 + \frac{c}{T}$, this result enables us to construct a confidence interval for α that is mildly greater than one.

Chen and Kuo (2013) difference Model (5.3) twice to obtain

$$\Delta^2 y_t = \alpha \Delta^2 y_{t-1} + \Delta^2 u_t$$

$$= \frac{\alpha}{2}\Delta^2 y_{t-1} + \left(\frac{\alpha}{2}\Delta^2 y_{t-1} + \Delta^2 u_t\right)$$

$$= \frac{\alpha}{2}\Delta^2 y_{t-1} + \zeta_t.$$

Because $E(\Delta^2 y_{t-1}\zeta_t) = 0$, the OLS estimator of α, $\hat{\alpha}_{CK}$, has the limiting distribution

$$\sqrt{T}(\hat{\alpha}_{CK} - \alpha) \Rightarrow N(0, 2), \text{ for } \alpha \in (-1, 1].$$

This shows that $\hat{\alpha}_{CK}$ is more efficient than $\hat{\alpha}_{PH}$ for $\alpha > 0$, and less efficient than the OLS estimator.

---

[5] See Han, Phillips, and Sul (2011) for further extensions of Phillips and Han (2008).

[6] This follows because $E(\Delta y_{t-1})^2 = \frac{2\sigma_u^2}{1+\alpha}$ and $E(\Delta y_t \Delta y_{t-1}) = -\frac{\sigma_u^2(1-\alpha)}{1+\alpha}$.

5.3.7 Moments-Based Estimation

Gorodnichenko, Mikusheva, and Ng (2012) propose a moments-based non-linear estimator for the AR(1) model (2.1) with i.i.d. errors. The estimator is $\sqrt{T}$-consistent and has a normal distribution in the limit uniformly over $\alpha \in (-1, 1]$. Their idea is to quasi-difference the observations $\{y_t\}$ at some $\bar{\alpha}$ and then optimize over all possible values of $\bar{\alpha}$ by matching the sample autocovariances of the quasi-differenced data with those of the model evaluated under the assumption that $\bar{\alpha}$ is the true value.

To implement this idea, let $e_t = y_t - \bar{\alpha}y_{t-1}$ and $\hat{\gamma}_j(\bar{\alpha}) = \frac{1}{T}\sum_{t=j+1}^{T} e_t e_{t-j}$. Denoting $E_{\bar{\alpha}}(\cdot)$ as the expectation operator under the assumption that $\bar{\alpha}$ is the true value, we have $\gamma_j(\bar{\alpha}) = E_{\bar{\alpha}}(e_t e_{t-j}) = \mathbf{1}\{j = 0\}\sigma_u^2$. Then, $g_j(\bar{\alpha}) = \hat{\gamma}_j(\bar{\alpha}) - \gamma_j(\bar{\alpha})$ is close to zero when $\bar{\alpha}$ is α. Thus, for a fixed j, minimizing $(g_j(\bar{\alpha}))^2$ over $\bar{\alpha}$ would provide a consistent estimator of α. But $g_j(\bar{\alpha})$ is stochastically unbounded if $\alpha = 1$ and $\bar{\alpha} \neq 1$, which makes it generate a nonstandard limiting distribution when $\alpha = 1$. As a remedy, Gorodnichenko, Mikusheva, and Ng suggest using

$$h_j(\bar{\alpha}) = g_j(\bar{\alpha}) - (\hat{\gamma}_0(\bar{\alpha}) - \sigma_u^2)$$

for optimization. They show that this function is uniformly bounded in probability over $\alpha \in (-1, 1]$. However, because σ_u^2 is unknown, we need to replace σ_u^2 with its OLS-based estimator s^2. Then, the objective function that utilizes all the information in the data is

$$\left(s^2 - \sigma_u^2\right)^2 + \sum_{j=1}^{K} \left(\hat{h}_j(\bar{\alpha})\right)^2,$$

where $\hat{h}_j(\bar{\alpha})$ denotes $h_j(\bar{\alpha})$ using s^2 instead of σ_u^2 and K is a constant that has to be chosen. The first term in this function is added to estimate σ_u^2. The estimator of α resulting from minimizing this function over σ_u^2 and $\bar{\alpha}$, denoted here as $\hat{\alpha}_K$, is distributed in the limit as

$$\sqrt{T}(\hat{\alpha}_K - \alpha) \Rightarrow \mathbf{N}\left(0, \frac{1}{\sum_{j=1}^{K} \alpha^{2(j-1)}}\right) \tag{5.9}$$

uniformly over $\alpha \in (-1, 1]$. When $\alpha \in (-1, 1)$, the limiting variance is $(1 - \alpha^2)/(1 - \alpha^{2K})$, which is larger than that of the OLS estimator. When $\alpha = 1$, $\hat{\alpha}_K$ converges in probability to α at a slower rate than the OLS estimator. Thus, $\hat{\alpha}_K$ is asymptotically less efficient than the OLS estimator. But its uniform asymptotic distribution can be used to construct confidence intervals.

In practice, it is uncertain how we choose the parameter K. When it is large, the limiting distribution (5.9) shows that $\hat{\alpha}_K$ becomes more efficient, but there must be a price to be paid for large K. This issue requires more investigation.

Gorodnichenko, Mikusheva, and Ng extend their method to the AR(1) model with nonstochastic terms and to higher order AR models.

5.3.8   Confidence Intervals with Uniform Asymptotic Coverage Probabilities

Mikusheva (2007) studies asymptotic properties of the confidence intervals of Stock (1991), Andrews (1993), Hansen (1999), and Romano and Wolf (2001). A confidence interval $C(Y)$ for the parameter α is said to have a uniform asymptotic coverage probability $1 - \gamma$ if[7]

$$\lim_{T \to \infty} \inf_{\alpha \in \Theta} \inf P_\alpha[\alpha \in C(Y)] \geq 1 - \gamma, \tag{5.10}$$

where Θ is the parameter space of α and $P_\alpha[\cdot]$ denotes probability evaluated under the true value α. This condition guarantees that there is a sample size that provides the required accuracy for all values of the parameter α. By contrast, the condition for the pointwise convergence of coverage probabilities,

$$\lim_{T \to \infty} P_\alpha[\alpha \in C(Y)] \geq 1 - \gamma \text{ for every } \alpha \in \Theta,$$

does not do so. In fact, under the condition of pointwise convergence, we may find a part of the parameter space where the required accuracy is not achieved even for a large sample size. For this reason, Mikusheva claims that only the confidence interval satisfying condition (5.10) is valid. The distinction between the uniform and pointwise convergence is unimportant when the limiting distribution does not change over the parameter space. But when it does, as in Stock (1991), Andrews (1993), Hansen (1999), and Romano and Wolf (2001), it becomes important. In fact, Mikusheva shows that a modified version of Stock's (1991), Andrews' (1993), and Hansen's (1999) confidence intervals are asymptotically valid, whereas that of Romano and Wolf (2001) is not. Note that Stock's original confidence interval is not asymptotically valid as pointed out by Phillips (2012a). From her finding, Mikusheva concludes that Romano and Wolf's confidence interval should not be used in practice.

5.4   Improved Estimation of the AR(1) Model with a Unit Root

5.4.1   Indirect Inference Estimation

Phillips (2012b) applies the method of indirect inference (cf. Gourieroux, Monfort, and Renault, 1993) to the AR(1) model without nonstochastic variables (cf. equation (2.1)). The indirect inference method can be explained briefly as

---

[7]   See chapter 11 of Lehmann and Romano (2005) for further details.

follows. Suppose that we wish to estimate parameter θ, but it is more appropriate or easier to estimate an auxiliary parameter β, which is a function of θ. The extremum estimator of β is written as $\hat{\beta}_T = \arg\min_\beta Q_T(\beta; y)$, where y denotes the data vector. We assume that $\hat{\beta}_T \xrightarrow{p} \beta$ as $T \to \infty$. If the data vector can be simulated given a value of θ, the estimator of β using the h-th simulated data vector $y^h(\theta)$ is written similarly as $\tilde{\beta}_T^h(\theta) = \arg\min_\beta Q_T(\beta; y^h(\theta))$. The estimator $\hat{\beta}_T$ is consistent for β whatever value θ takes. But the estimator $\tilde{\beta}_T(\theta)$ is consistent for β only when θ takes the true value. Therefore, it is intuitively appealing to estimate parameter θ as

$$\hat{\theta}_T^H = \arg\min_\theta \left\| \hat{\beta}_T - \frac{1}{H} \sum_{h=1}^{H} \tilde{\beta}_T^h(\theta) \right\|, \tag{5.11}$$

for some metric $\|\cdot\|$. If a chosen value of θ is different from the true value, the objective function for $\hat{\theta}_T^H$ will take a large value, and vice versa. The estimator $\hat{\theta}_T^H$ is called the indirect inference estimator of θ. This estimation procedure requires performing nonlinear optimization $H+1$ times, which might be computationally demanding. Additionally, assumptions on the underlying distribution should be made to simulate data, which invites the issue of robustness. Asymptotic theory for the indirect inference estimator is given in Gourieroux, Monfort and Renault (1993) and Phillips (2012b).

Because it is anticipated that $\frac{1}{H} \sum_{h=1}^{H} \tilde{\beta}_T^h(\theta) \xrightarrow{p} E\tilde{\beta}_T^h(\theta) = b_T(\theta)$ as $H \to \infty$, the indirect inference estimator (5.11) can be written for infinite H as

$$\hat{\theta}_T = \arg\min_\theta \left\| \hat{\beta}_T - b_T(\theta) \right\|.$$

If $b_T(\theta)$ is invertible, the indirect inference estimator is written as

$$\hat{\theta}_T = b_T^{-1}(\hat{\beta}_T).$$

Note that this estimator does not require simulation. Phillips derives the asymptotic distribution of this estimator for the AR(1) Model (2.1) with $y_0 = 0$ assuming a normal distribution for the error terms. For the AR(1) model, there is no auxiliary parameter, so that $\beta = \theta = \alpha$. Moreover, $\hat{\beta}_T$ is the MLE (or, equivalently, the OLS estimator) of α. Phillips calculates $b_T(\theta)$ analytically, which is then used to derive the indirect inference estimator of parameter α. The indirect inference estimator has the same limiting distribution as the MLE for the case $|\alpha| < 1$, but its limiting distribution is different from that of MLE for the case $\alpha = 1 + \frac{c}{T}$. In fact, in the latter case, it is a function of $(\int_0^1 J_c^2(r)\,dr)^{-1} \int_0^1 J_c(r)\,dW(r)$ and c. Where $\alpha = 1$, Phillips shows that the indirect inference estimator is less biased and more concentrated than the MLE by simulation. But asymptotically, unit root tests based on the indirect inference estimator and MLE are equivalent because the latter is a monotonic transformation of the former. Finite-sample properties of the indirect inference estimator and its robustness to the assumptions on the initial variable and the error terms are not fully explored in Phillips (2012b) and await further research.

5.4.2 Fully Aggregated Estimator

Han, Phillips, and Sul (2011) observe that Model (5.3) yields

$$y_t - y_{t-2-l} = \alpha(y_{t-1} - y_{t-1-l}) + u_t - u^*_{t-2-l}, \ (l = 1, 2, \ldots, t - 3)$$

where $u^*_t = x_t - \alpha x_{t+1}$. Because $E(y_{t-1} - y_{t-1-l})(u_t - u^*_{t-2-l}) = 0$ for any $l \geq 1$, OLS can be used for this model. But a more reasonable estimator that utilizes all the information in the data would be

$$\hat{\alpha}_{fa} = \frac{\sum_{l=1}^{T-3} \sum_{t=3+l}^{T} (y_t - y_{t-2-l})(y_{t-1} - y_{t-1-l})}{\sum_{l=1}^{T-3} \sum_{t=3+l}^{T} (y_{t-1} - y_{t-1-l})^2},$$

which Han, Phillips, and Sul call the fully aggregated estimator. They find that for $\alpha = 1$,

$$T(\hat{\alpha}_{fa} - 1) \Rightarrow \left(\int_0^1 \overline{W}^2(r) \, dr \right)^{-1} \left(\int_0^1 \overline{W}(r) \, dW(r) + \int_0^1 W^2(r) \, dr \right),$$

which shows that $T(\hat{\alpha}_{fa} - 1)$ corrects the downward bias of the OLS estimator (or the MLE under a normality condition with $x_0 = 0$) through the almost surely positive term $\int_0^1 W^2(r) \, dr$. Indeed, Han, Phillips, and Sul show via simulation that the fully aggregated estimator performs better than the MLE for $\alpha \geq 0.5$ in terms of bias and root mean squared errors.

5.5 Distribution Theory for Unit Root Tests

White (1958) documents that the limiting distribution of the OLS estimator for the AR(1) model with a unit root is nonnormal. In practice, this does not pose any serious problem for hypothesis testing because asymptotic quantiles of unit root test statistics are easy to obtain by simulation. Still, analytical properties of the limiting distribution of the OLS estimator for the AR(1) model with a unit root are a research theme to which many theorists have applied their skills. Moreover, there have been some attempts to estimate the finite-sample quantiles of unit root test statistics. This section introduces research results from these endeavors.

5.5.1   Approaches Based on the Inversion of Characteristic and Moment-Generating Functions

For the AR(1) model,

$$y_t = \alpha y_{t-1} + u_t, \ (t = 2, \ldots, T),$$

the OLS estimator of the AR(1) coefficient is written as

$$\hat{\alpha} - \alpha = \frac{y'Ay}{y'By} = \frac{U_T}{V_T}$$

where $y = [y_1, \ldots, y_T]$,

$$A = -\frac{1}{2}\begin{bmatrix} 2\alpha & -1 & & & \\ -1 & 2\alpha & -1 & \mathbf{0} & \\ & \ddots & \ddots & \ddots & \\ & \mathbf{0} & -1 & 2\alpha & -1 \\ & & & -1 & 0 \end{bmatrix} \text{ and } B = \begin{bmatrix} I_{T-1} & \mathbf{0} \\ \mathbf{0} & 0 \end{bmatrix}.$$

Assuming $u_t \sim$ iid $N(0, \sigma_u^2)$ and $y_0 = 0$, White (1958) derives the limiting joint characteristic functions[8] of $\frac{U_T}{g(T)}$ and $\frac{V_T}{g(T)^2}$ with $g(T) = \frac{T}{\sqrt{2}}$ as

$$\Phi(u, v) = \left[\exp(\sqrt{2}\alpha i u) \left\{ \cos\left(2\sqrt{iv}\right) - \frac{\sqrt{2}\alpha i u \sin\left(2\sqrt{iv}\right)}{2\sqrt{iv}} \right\} \right]^{-1/2}$$

(5.12)

for the case $|\alpha| = 1$. He also reports the limiting joint moment-generating functions of $\frac{U_T}{g(T)}$ and $\frac{V_T}{g(T)}$ for the cases $|\alpha| < 1$ and $|\alpha| > 1$ using $g(T) = \sqrt{\frac{T}{1-\alpha^2}}$ for the former case and $g(T) = \frac{|\alpha|^T}{\alpha^2 - 1}$ for the latter. He inverts these moment-generating functions to obtain the cdf of $g(T)(\hat{\alpha} - \alpha)$, a standard normal distribution for $|\alpha| < 1$, and a Cauchy distribution for $|\alpha| > 1$. He reports that he fails to invert the moment-generating function for the case $|\alpha| = 1$, a problem tackled by Evans and Savin (1981) later.

Before moving on, let me make a digression from the main topic and explain Gurland's (1948) Theorem 1 because it is used by a paper to be discussed later. Gurland's Theorem 1 provides the cdf of the ratio of two random variables with the denominator being positive with probability one, given that the joint characteristic function of the two random variables is known. The essence of the technique used for Gurland's Theorem 1 can be explained as follows. Suppose

---

[8] True to the original paper, White derives the limiting joint moment functions of $\frac{U_T}{g(T)}$ and $\frac{V_T}{g(T)^2}$. But the difference is insignificant.

that we wish to find the distribution of $Z = \frac{X}{Y}$ and that the joint characteristic function of X and Y, $\mathrm{cf}_{X,Y}(u, v) = E(\exp(iXu + iYv))$, is known. Letting $W_z = X - zY$, we have

$$P(Z < z) = P\left(\frac{X}{Y} < z\right) = P(W_z < 0).$$

Because the characteristic function of W_z is given as

$$\mathrm{cf}(w) = E(\exp(i(X - zY)w))$$
$$= \exp(iXw - iYzw)$$
$$= \mathrm{cf}_{X,Y}(w, -zw),$$

the cdf of Z is obtained by inverting this characteristic function. The inversion formula is given in section 3 of Gurland.

Building on the joint characteristic function (5.12) and applying Gurland's (1948) method, Evans and Savin (1981) obtain the cdf and pdf of $g(T)(\hat\alpha - \alpha)$ for the case $|\alpha| = 1$, though not in closed forms. Evans and Savin confirm that the percentiles reported in Fuller (1976) are accurate in light of their own computational results. Evans and Savin (1984) extend the results of Evans and Savin (1981) to the AR(1) model with an intercept.

Abadir (1993) applies the Laplace inversion formula to Evans and Savin's (1981) cdf to derive the cdf and pdf of $g(T)(\hat\alpha - \alpha)$ for $\alpha = 1$. These formulas do not contain integrals and are expressed in terms of infinite series involving a parabolic cylinder function. Abadir (1992, 1995) uses the joint characteristic function (5.12) to derive the limiting joint pdf of $\frac{U_T}{g(T)}$ and $\frac{V_T}{g(T)^2}$ and transform the joint pdf to obtain the pdf and cdf of the Dickey-Fuller t-ratio. The resulting pdf and cdf are complex and contain infinite series.

Using the joint characteristic function (5.12) and Abadir's (1992, 1995) Laplace transform method, Larsson (1998) derives the cdf of the Dickey-Fuller t-ratio and approximates the resulting integral using the saddle-point method. See also Larsson (1995) for similar results related to the nearly integrated AR process of Chan and Wei (1987) and Phillips (1987b).

Perron (1996) derives the limiting moment-generating function of $T(\hat\alpha - \alpha)$ for the AR(1) model with a near unit root $\alpha = \exp(\frac{c}{T})$ and stationary errors using methods similar to those mentioned earlier. The limiting moment generating function is inverted to give the asymptotic cdf of $T(\hat\alpha - \alpha)$. He finds that the asymptotic distribution obtained in this way provides a poor approximation to the exact finite-sample distribution when the errors follow either the MA(1) process with its root close to -1 or the AR process with its root close to 1 or -1. This finding explains the finite-sample size distortions of the ADF and Phillips-Perron tests observed when the errors follow the MA(1) process with its root close to -1 (cf. Subsection 2.3.4).

The limiting distribution of the Dickey-Fuller coefficient test statistic can be represented using a weighted series of standard normal variates and squared standard normal variates as given in Subsection 2.2.1. Gönen, Puri, Ruymgaart, and van Zuijlen (2000) derive the joint characteristic function of the two series and derive their joint pdf. The latter is converted to obtain the limiting pdf of the Dickey-Fuller coefficient test statistic. The pdf is not in a closed form and is different from those of Rao (1978) and Abadir (1993). Gönen et al. also extend their methods to the nearly integrated AR(1) model and the AR(1) model with an intercept.

5.5.2 Fredholm Determinant Approach

Nabeya and Tanaka (1990a) employ the Fredholm determinant approach[9] to find the limiting characteristic function of the OLS estimator for the AR(1) model. Their approach can be used in a unified manner for the nearly integrated AR(1) model with nonstochastic trends and serially correlated errors; it yields more flexibility than the approach based on limiting characteristic and moment-generating functions.

For the AR(1) model with $\alpha = 1 - \frac{c}{T}$, for example, they first show that

$$P\left[T(\hat{\alpha} - 1)\right] \longrightarrow P\left[\int_0^1 \int_0^1 K_{c,x}(s, t)\, dW(s)\, dW(r) + 1 > 0\right],$$

where $K_{c,x}(s, t) = \frac{x}{c}\{\exp(-c\,|s - t|) - \exp(-c(2 - s - t))\}$. Expressing the limiting distribution as a double stochastic integral is essential in their approach. Then, they obtain the Fredholm determinant[10] associated with $K_{c,x}(s, t)$, which for the current case is

$$D_{c,x}(\lambda) = \exp(-c)\left[\cos\mu + (c + \lambda)\frac{\sin\mu}{\mu}\right]$$

with $\mu = \sqrt{2\lambda x - c^2}$. The limiting characteristic function of $T(\hat{\alpha} - 1)$ is obtained by using the Fredholm determinant as

$$\varphi_{c,x,r}(\theta) = \exp(ir\theta)\left[D_{c,x}(2i\theta)\right]^{-1/2}.$$

---

[9] Nabeya and Tanaka's (1990a) approach dates back to Anderson and Darling (1952), who use the Fredholm determinant approach to derive the characteristic functions of some goodness-of-fit test statistics.

[10] For a kernel function $K(s, t)$, consider the integral $f_i(t) = \lambda_i \int_0^1 K(s, t) f_i(s)\, ds$. The solutions of these equations are $\lambda_1, \lambda_2, \ldots$. The Fredholm determinant is defined by $D(\lambda) = \Pi_{i=1}^{\infty}(1 - \frac{\lambda}{\lambda_i})$. In many cases, it is impossible to obtain $\{\lambda_i\}$ explicitly, but the Fredholm determinant can be obtained by solving a differential equation with boundary conditions. Thus, in the Fredholm determinant approach, the problem of finding the characteristic function is reduced to that of finding the solution of a differential equation. See Section 5.3 of Tanaka (1996) for details.

For the relationship between the characteristic function and the Fredholm determinant, the reader is referred to Theorem 5.4 of Tanaka (1996). Nabeya and Tanaka apply Imhof's (1961) method to this limiting characteristic function to compute the cdf and pdf numerically.

Nabeya and Tanaka (1990b) use the Fredholm determinant approach to calculate the limiting power of some unit root tests. Nabeya and Sørensen (1994) extend Nabeya and Tanaka (1990a) to the case where $\frac{y_0}{\sqrt{T}}$ converges to a constant and the coefficients of trend terms go to zero as the sample size grows.

5.5.3 Simulation-Based Methods

MacKinnon (1994, 1996) suggests a simulation-based method for the calculation of the finite-sample quantiles, cdfs and p-values of unit root tests. MacKinnon's (1994) method involves the following steps.

Step 1: Generate the AR(1) process $y_t = y_{t-1} + u_t$ with $u_t \sim$ iid $N(0, 1)$[11] I times at $T = 50, 60, 75, 100, 125, 150, 200, 250, 300, 400, 500, 750, 1{,}000,$ 1,250, and calculate 199 equally spaced quantiles of a unit root test statistic (e.g., the Dickey-Fuller t-ratio). MacKinnon (1994) sets $I = 50{,}000$.

Step 2: Repeat Step 1 100 times and record the quantiles. This gives a 14×100 by 199 matrix (denoted $[q_j^p(T_k)]$ for $j = 1, \ldots, 1{,}400$ and $p = 0.005, 0.010, \ldots, 0.995$).

Step 3: Estimate the regression equation[12]

$$q^p(T_k) = \eta_\infty^p + \eta_1^p T_k^{-1} + \eta_2^p T_k^{-2} + \varepsilon_k, \ (k = 1, \ldots, 1400), \quad (5.13)$$

for each p using the GMM method, taking different variances at each T into consideration.

For example, the estimated 5% quantile of a unit root test statistic at sample size $T = 50$ is

$$\hat{q}^{0.05}(50) = \hat{\eta}_\infty^{0.05} + \hat{\eta}_1^{0.05} 50^{-1} + \hat{\eta}_2^{0.05} 50^{-2},$$

where $\hat{\eta}_\infty^{0.05}$, $\hat{\eta}_1^{0.05}$, and $\hat{\eta}_2^{0.05}$ are the corresponding coefficients in equation (5.13) obtained by the GMM estimation. If the true DGP follows a Gaussian AR(1) process, MacKinnon's method will provide better estimates of the finite-sample quantiles of unit root tests. However, if this condition is not met, there is no guarantee that his method provides more accurate quantiles than corresponding asymptotic ones. Using the simulated quantiles along with the cdf of a standard normal distribution, MacKinnon (1994, 1996) also reports approximate cdfs

---

[11] MacKinnon does not specify the initial value in his Monte Carlo study.
[12] Here, $T_k = 50$ for $k = 1, \ldots, 100$; $T_k = 60$ for $k = 101, \ldots, 200$, etc. MacKinnon (1996) adds T_k^{-3} to this equation.

of some unit root test statistics. The simulated quantiles can also be used to calculate p-values of unit root tests (e.g., linear interpolation can be used straightforwardly).

Adda and Gonzalo (1996) suggest a simulation-based, semi-nonparametric method for the estimation of the pdfs of the Dickey-Fuller test statistics. More specifically, they assume a general function for the pdfs of the Dickey-Fuller test statistics that involve unknown parameters. Then, they estimate these unknown parameters using simulated values of the test statistics. The estimated pdfs can be used for the calculation of approximate p-values on numerical integration.

5.6   Sampling Frequency and Tests for a Unit Root

One of the questions empirical researchers may have about unit root testing is how to choose a sampling frequency of the data in use. For instance, the choice between quarterly and annual GDP series or between daily and weekly stock prices can be a concern in empirical applications. This section introduces some works studying the issues of unit root testing in relation to sampling frequency. See also Stock (1994) for related discussions.

Sampling frequency has different meanings for flow and stock data. For stock data such as interest rates, stock prices, and monetary aggregates, sampling frequency implies how often the data are recorded. However, for flow data such as GDP and consumption, it is related to the interval of aggregation for data generation. Sampling frequencies for these two types of data have different implications for unit root testing and are dealt with separately in this section.

5.6.1   Stock Data

Shiller and Perron (1985) report via simulation that increasing the sampling frequency of stock data does not increase the power of unit root tests. The data they consider include stock prices and interest rates. Their claim implies that using daily data, rather than weekly or monthly data, does not result in a higher powered unit root test.

Perron (1991) provides a more rigorous treatment of the power of unit root tests and sampling frequency. He starts with the simple Ornstein-Uhlenbeck diffusion process

$$dy_t = \rho y_t \, dt + \sigma \, dW(t), \quad -\infty < \rho < \infty, \ 0 < t \leq S, \ y_0 = y(0), \quad (5.14)$$

where $W(\cdot)$ is a Wiener process and ρ, σ, and $y(0)$ are fixed constants. Here S represents the data span. He considers the null hypothesis of a unit root $H_0 : \rho = 0$ against the alternatives $H_1 : \rho < 0$ (stationary alternative) and $H_1' : \rho > 0$ (explosive alternative). I focus only on the former case here. A discrete time representation of the process (5.14) is

$$y_{th} = \alpha_h y_{(t-1)h} + v_{th}, \quad y_0 = y(0), \quad \left(t = 1, \dots, T = \frac{S}{h} \right), \quad (5.15)$$

where $\alpha_h = \exp(\rho h)$ and $v_{th} \sim \text{iid } N(0, \sigma^2(\exp(2\rho h) - 1)/2\rho)$ (cf. Bergstrom, 1990). Under the null hypothesis of a unit root, we have $\alpha_h = 1$. An interesting fact derivable from this representation is that $\alpha_h \to 1$ as $h \to 0$, even when $\rho \neq 0$. That is, the AR(1) coefficient converges to are 1 as sampling frequency increases, whatever true value the parameter ρ has. For asymptotic analyses, Perron assumes that T, S, and h are all indexed by n, which diverges to infinity (denoted by T_n, S_n, and h_n). Then, Model (5.15) can be written as

$$y_{nt} = \exp(\rho h_n) y_{n(t-1)} + u_{nt}, \quad y_0 = y(0), \quad (t = 1, \dots, T_n), \quad (5.16)$$

where $u_{nt} \sim \text{iid } N(0, \sigma^2(\exp(2\rho h) - 1)/2\rho)$ under the alternative hypothesis, $u_{nt} \sim \text{iid } N(0, \sigma^2 h_n)$ under the null hypothesis, and $T_n = \frac{S_n}{h_n}$. Using representation (5.16) with $y(0)$ having any fixed value, Perron shows that the Dickey-Fuller coefficient test is consistent if and only if $S_n \to \infty$ as $n \to \infty$. He also shows that the test is inconsistent when $S_n \to S$ (a positive constant) as $n \to \infty$.

We can expect from Perron's (1991) results that the finite-sample power of unit root tests for stock data depends on the span of the data, not on the sampling frequency of the data. Although this is a reasonable expectation, the finite-sample situation can be trickier. Choi and Chung (1995) show via simulation that the finite-sample power of the ADF test can significantly decrease[13] when sampling frequency decreases, whereas that of the Phillips-Perron tests does not change much with sampling frequency.

Boswijk and Klaassen (2012) also provide a contrarian view regarding the relationship between sampling frequency and the power of unit root tests. They show that increasing sampling frequency improves the power of unit roots when the data have fat tails and volatility clustering. This is based on the observation that high-frequency data often exhibit fat tails and volatility clustering that low-frequency data do not. Because the MLE-based unit root test in the presence of fat tails and volatility clustering has higher power with fatter tails and higher volatility clustering, using high-frequency data for the test can yield higher power. Boswijk and Klaassen verify this claim via simulation.

Choi and Chung (1995) and Boswijk and Klaassen (2012) confirm that using high-frequency data in practice may result in a power gain without sacrificing anything.

---

[13] They consider the data-generating scheme $m_t = \alpha m_{t-1} + e_t, (t = 1, \dots, 1, 200)$ and show that the power of the ADF test for $\{m_t\}_{t=1,\dots,1200}$ is significantly higher than that for $\{m_{12r}\}_{r=1,\dots,100}$.

5.6.2   Flow Data

Choi (1992b) considers the DGP

$$y_t = \alpha y_{t-1} + e_t, \ (t = 1, \ldots, T);$$

$$x_s = y_{4s} + y_{4s-1} + y_{4s-2} + y_{4s-3}, \ \left(s = 1, \ldots, \frac{T}{4}\right),$$

and reports the finite-sample power of the ADF and Phillips-Perron tests for $\{y_t\}$ and $\{x_s\}$. Note that this data-generating scheme is for flow data based on aggregation and that $x_s = \alpha^4 x_{s-1} + u_s$, where $\{u_s\}$ is an MA process. For both the ADF and Phillips-Perron tests, the finite-sample power increases substantially when $\{y_t\}$ is used, implying that using higher frequency data improves the finite-sample power of unit root tests. These results are in contrast to Shiller and Perron's (1985) findings and imply that Shiller and Perron's conclusion on the finite-sample power of unit root tests and sampling frequency may apply only to stock data. Ng (1995) reports results similar to those of Choi.

Using flow data, Chambers (2004)[14] derives some theoretical results for the relationship between test consistency and sampling frequency. He employs the Ornstein-Uhlenbeck diffusion process (5.14) as in Perron (1991), but considers the aggregation-based flow data

$$y_{th} = \int_{(t-1)h}^{th} y_r \, dr, \ (t = 1, \ldots, T).$$

The observed time series are, therefore, $y_h, y_{2h}, \ldots, y_{Th}$. Chambers shows that $\{y_{th}\}$ follows the ARIMA(0, 1, 1) and ARMA(1, 1) processes under the null of a unit root and the alternative of stationarity, respectively. This is in contrast to the case of stock data for which the error terms always follow a white noise process. As in Perron, Chambers assumes that the sample size, data span and sampling frequency are indexed by n, which goes to infinity. For the Dickey-Fuller coefficient test to be consistent against the alternative of stationarity, conditions $S_n \to \infty$ and $h_n S_n^{1/2} \to \infty$ are required. In particular, when the data span S_n is fixed, the Dickey-Fuller coefficient test is inconsistent. These results are in accordance with Perron's findings discussed earlier. Chambers also reports via simulation that the power of the Dickey-Fuller coefficient test increases with sampling frequency when S_n is not too short. But when S_n is short, it does not increase with the sampling frequency. The former result accords well with those of Choi (1992b), and the latter result for short S_n manifests test inconsistency for a fixed data span.

---

[14]   See Chambers (2008) for a corrigendum to Chambers (2004).

5.7 Effects of Seasonal Adjustments on Unit Root Testing

Seasonal adjustments are commonly made for quarterly and monthly time series. The most popular seasonal adjustment procedures are the U.S. Census Bureau X-11 method and its upgrade, the X-12-ARIMA method. This section introduces research results that show the effects of the X-11 seasonal adjustment on unit root testing.

The X-11 method consists of complex steps as explained in Ghysels and Osborn (2001). According to Ghysels and Perron (1993), those complex steps can be approximated by a linear filter when its default option is considered. Using this approximate filter, they study the limiting distributions of the augmented Dickey-Fuller and Phillips-Perron test statistics using the filtered series and show that their limiting distributions are the same as those using the unfiltered, original series that may contain seasonality. Thus, as far as limiting distributions are concerned, the seasonal adjustment entails no change. However, they also show that the filtering brings upward bias of the OLS estimator for stationary time series, making the unit root test statistics less powerful.[15]

If one is quite concerned about the reduced power of unit root tests for seasonally adjusted time series, an available remedy is to use unadjusted time series along with Hylleberg, Engle, Granger, and Yoo's (1990; HEGY hereafter) seasonal unit root test (see Subsection 6.2.2). HEGY's procedure allows one to test for a unit root present at an unadjusted, seasonal time series. Seasonal unit root tests are discussed in detail in the next chapter.

5.8 Summary and Further Remarks

This chapter introduced the topics of model selection, interval and point estimation for the AR model possibly with a unit root, distribution theory for the AR(1) model with a unit root, sampling frequency and tests for a unit root, and effects of seasonal adjustments on unit root testing.

It is comforting to find that such model selection methods as *AIC*, *BIC*, Hannan and Quinn's (1979), and Phillips and Ploberger's (1994) can be used for the AR model with a unit root. Unit roots do not pose any serious difficulties as far as model selection is concerned. If the model selection is made for subsequent unit root testing, Ng and Perron's (2001) information criteria are more useful than conventional ones and are recommended for use.

---

[15] Similar results are reported for unit root tests under structural change in Ghysels and Perron (1996). In addition, Ghysels (1990) shows that there is considerably less evidence supporting the hypothesis of the presence of a unit root in the U.S. postwar real GNP and real per capita GNP series when seasonally unadjusted data are used instead of the seasonally adjusted ones. Ghysels's finding can be explained by the analytic work by Ghysels and Perron (1993).

The interval and point estimation methods for the AR(1) model possibly with a unit root are useful when one wants to move beyond hypothesis testing. Among the various confidence intervals introduced in this chapter, it is difficult to decide which one stands out. Hansen's (1999) bootstrap-based confidence interval is conjectured to work best, but more thorough investigations are needed to arrive at a definitive conclusion.

The two estimation methods of Phillips (2012b) and Han, Phillips, and Sul (2011) are shown via simulation to improve on the MLE for the AR(1) model with a unit root. Essentially, they do so by reducing bias. Thus, their findings do not seem to be a counter example to the common notion that the MLE has the least asymptotic variance. But those are intriguing estimation methods that deserve further research.

Distribution theory for the AR(1) model with a unit root is useful for calculating quantiles and p-values of unit root tests. Moreover, historically, research on unit roots started from the investigation of the limiting distribution of the OLS estimator for the AR(1) model. The techniques used for deriving the pdfs and cdfs of this chapter will continue to be useful for other, related research problems. For example, some panel unit root test statistics use p-values of univariate unit root tests as discussed in Subsection 7.2.3, and hence the distribution theory of this chapter is also relevant to panel data analysis.

The issue of sampling frequency is practically important, so the research results summarized here should be helpful. The findings presented here support the use of high-frequency data in practice because it may bring a power gain in finite samples.

Seasonal adjustments are shown to affect the power of unit root tests in an adverse manner. Those who are concerned about this issue should study the next chapter in great detail.

6 Seasonal Unit Roots

6.1 Introduction

This chapter introduces inferential procedures for seasonal unit roots. Seasonality is a unique feature of time series, but it was ignored in the previous chapters, which implicitly assumed that there is no seasonality in the data. However, when it is present in the data, it is important to know how we can find an appropriate model for the data and how we perform inference on the chosen model. A popular model for seasonal time series is the seasonal ARIMA model due to Box and Jenkins (1976). One of the key elements of this model is seasonal differencing, which is required when seasonal unit roots are present. In this sense, testing for seasonal unit roots is an essential step in Box and Jenkin's modeling of seasonal time series. Albeit less popular than the seasonal ARIMA model, periodic autoregressive (PAR) models are also useful for modeling seasonal time series. Properties of the PAR model depend on the presence or absence of a unit root, so that testing for a unit root and for the null hypothesis of stationarity is important for the PAR model.

This chapter starts from Dickey, Hasza, and Fuller (1984; DHF hereafter), who use the AR(S) model (S denotes the number of seasons) to test for seasonal unit roots, and it discusses its extensions. Then, the testing procedures of HEGY and their extensions are introduced. HEGY's advantage over DHF is that it can test the presence of positive, negative, and complex unit roots separately. Seasonal stationarity tests that complement the seasonal unit root tests are introduced next. Seasonal unit root and stationarity tests under structural changes are also discussed. In addition, this chapter introduces several methods that can be used to test for a unit root in the PAR model. Last, empirical studies examining seasonal unit roots are discussed.

6.2   Testing for Seasonal Unit Roots

A time series $\{y_t\}$, observed at S equally spaced time intervals per year, is said to have seasonal unit roots if $\{(1 - B^S)y_t\}$ is a stationary process. If there are seasonal unit roots in a time series, using the usual regression model with seasonal dummies can lead to spurious regressions, as shown by Abeysinghe (1991, 1994) and Franses, Hylleberg, and Lee (1995). In addition, knowledge of seasonal unit roots is required when the seasonal ARIMA model is used. Thus, detecting seasonal unit roots can be important in empirical applications.

Tests for seasonal unit roots have been developed using methods similar to those for a positive unit root discussed in Chapter 2. However, they tend to be more complex because of the presence of complex unit roots. Broadly speaking, there have been two approaches in testing for seasonal unit roots. One is based on the AR(S) regression, and the other uses a component-wise testing strategy. This section introduces various tests belonging in these two categories.

6.2.1   Tests Using the AR(S) Regression and Its Variants

DHF's Test
DHF study the AR model

$$y_t = \alpha_S y_{t-S} + u_t, \ (t = S + 1, \dots, T), \tag{6.1}$$

where $\alpha_S = 1$ and $u_t \sim \text{iid}(0, \sigma_u^2)$. In this model, S denotes the number of seasons (i.e., $S = 4$ for quarterly data and $S = 12$ for monthly data). The time series $\{y_t\}$ has seasonal unit roots, because the characteristic equation $1 - z^S = 0$ has roots on the unit circle.

DHF's main interest lies in testing the null hypothesis $H_0 : \alpha_S = 1$ against the alternative $H_1 : \alpha_S < 1$. To estimate the coefficient α_S, DHF use the OLS and weighted symmetric estimators (see Subsection 2.4.6 for the latter estimator). Because their simulation results favor the OLS estimator and the t-test using it, I focus on the OLS estimation. DHF derive the limiting distribution of the OLS estimator $\hat{\alpha}_S = \left(\sum_{t=S+1}^{T} y_{t-S}^2 \right)^{-1} \sum_{t=S+1}^{T} y_{t-S} y_t$, which can be represented[1] as

$$S^{-1} T(\hat{\alpha}_S - 1) \Rightarrow \left(\sum_{s=1}^{S} \int_0^1 W_s^2(r) \, dr \right)^{-1} \sum_{s=1}^{S} \int_0^1 W_s(r) \, dW_s(r), \tag{6.2}$$

---

[1]   DHF do not use the functional central limit theorem for their results, and the limiting distributions they derive are not expressed in terms of the standard Brownian motion. But it is shown later (e.g., Ghysels and Osborn, 2001) that their limiting distributions are expressible in terms of Brownian motion as here.

Table 6.1. *Asymptotic critical values of the DHF test*

	Coefficient test statistic significance level			t-ratio significance level		
	1%	5%	10%	1%	5%	10%
$S = 4$						
Model (6.1)	-15.27	-9.16	-6.59	-2.56	-1.90	-1.53
Model (6.3)	-36.19	-27.88	-24.00	-4.61	-4.04	-3.73
Model (6.4)	-19.50	-12.62	-9.65	-3.05	-2.38	-2.03
$S = 12$						
Model (6.1)	-17.99	-11.58	-8.72	-2.49	-1.80	-1.44
Model (6.3)	-70.04	-59.45	-53.95	-6.35	-5.82	-5.49
Model (6.4)	-20.56	-13.65	-10.44	-2.74	-2.06	-1.66

Note: If the computed values of DHF's test statistics are smaller than the corresponding critical values, reject the null hypothesis.

where $\{W_s(r)\}$ denotes independent Brownian motions. To understand the intuition behind this result, let $y_t = y_{s\tau}$, where index s is for season and τ for year $(s = 1, \ldots, S; \ \tau = 1, \ldots, T_\tau$ and $T = ST_\tau)$. Then, we can rewrite the OLS estimator as

$$\hat{\alpha}_S - 1 = \left(\sum_{s=1}^{S} \sum_{\tau=1}^{T_\tau} y_{s(\tau-1)}^2 \right)^{-1} \sum_{s=1}^{S} \sum_{\tau=1}^{T_\tau} y_{s(\tau-1)} u_{s\tau}.$$

Applying the functional central limit theorem as in Section 2.3 by sending T_τ to infinity, we can obtain the asymptotic distribution (6.2). The t-ratio using $\hat{\alpha}_S$ is formulated in the usual manner, and DHF derive its limiting distribution. The moment-generating function of the limiting distribution is reported in Pitarakis (1998) and Nabeya (2000, 2001). Nabeya (2001) also considers the model with nonstochastic, polynomial regressors.

DHF extend their analysis to the models

$$y_t = \sum_{s=1}^{S} \theta_s D_{st} + \alpha_S y_{t-S} + u_t; \tag{6.3}$$

$$y_t = \mu + \alpha_S y_{t-S} + u_t, \tag{6.4}$$

where $D_{st} = 1$ if t corresponds to season s and $D_{st} = 0$ otherwise. The limiting distributions of the coefficient and t-test statistics for Models (6.1), (6.3), and (6.4) are reported in Table 6.1.

DHF also consider the model

$$\phi(B)(y_t - \alpha_S y_{t-S}) = u_t, \ u_t \sim \text{iid}(0, \sigma_u^2), \tag{6.5}$$

where roots of the characteristic equation $\phi(z) = 1 - \phi_1 z - \cdots - \phi_p z^p = 0$ lie outside the unit circle. Letting $\Delta_S = 1 - B^S$, we may write

$$y_t - \alpha_S y_{t-S} = \Delta_S y_t + (1 - \alpha_S) y_{t-S} = \Delta_S y_t + \rho_S y_{t-S}. \tag{6.6}$$

Plugging relation (6.6) into (6.5) yields

$$\Delta_S y_t = \rho_S(y_{t-S} + \phi_1 y_{t-S-1} + \cdots + \phi_p y_{t-S-p})$$
$$+ \phi_1 \Delta_S y_{t-1} + \cdots + \phi_p \Delta_S y_{t-p} + u_t.$$

Using this model, we may test the null hypothesis $H_0 : \alpha_S = 1$ because it is equivalent to $H_0 : \rho_S = 0$. Because $\phi_1, \cdots, \phi_p$ are not known, the first regressor in this equation is replaced with $y_{t-S} + \hat{\phi}_1 y_{t-S-1} + \cdots + \hat{\phi}_p y_{t-S-p}$, where the coefficient estimates are obtained by regressing $\Delta_S y_t$ on $\{\Delta_S y_{t-1}, \ldots, \Delta_S y_{t-p}\}$. Then, the t-ratio for ρ_S can be constructed in the usual manner and its critical values are the same as those in Table 6.1.

Extensions of DHF

Hasza and Fuller (1982) and Li (1991) study the null hypothesis $H_0 : \alpha_1 = \alpha_S = 1$ for the model

$$\phi(B)(1 - \alpha_1 B)(1 - \alpha_S B^S) y_t = u_t, \ u_t \sim \text{iid}(0, \sigma_u^2), \tag{6.7}$$

where all the roots of the equation $\phi(z) = 0$ lie outside the unit circle. Interest in the null hypothesis stems from Box and Jenkins (1976), who advocate using the filter $(1 - B)(1 - B^S)$ for seasonal time series. Assuming $\phi(B) = 1$, Hasza and Fuller consider the model

$$y_t = \omega_1 y_{t-1} + \omega_2 y_{t-S} + \omega_3 y_{t-S-1} + u_t$$

and devise an F-test for the null hypothesis $H_0 : \omega_1 = 1, \omega_2 = 1, \omega_3 = -1$ because this is equivalent to the null hypothesis $H_0 : \alpha_1 = \alpha_S = 1$. Li develops an LM test statistic[2] for the null against various alternatives. Li's model also involves a constant, a linear time trend, and seasonal dummies.

Using Hasza and Fuller's (1982) model, Osborn, Chui, Smith, and Birchenhall (1988) develop t-ratios for a nonseasonal positive unit root and seasonal unit roots. As in DHF, they rewrite equation (6.7) as

$$\Delta \Delta_S y_t = \rho_{s1}(\Delta_S y_t + \phi_1 \Delta_S y_{t-1} + \cdots + \phi_p \Delta_S y_{t-p})$$
$$+ \rho_{s2}(\Delta y_t + \phi_1 \Delta y_{t-1} + \cdots + \phi_p \Delta y_{t-p})$$
$$+ \phi_1 \Delta \Delta_S y_{t-1} + \cdots + \phi_p \Delta \Delta_S y_{t-p} + e_t,$$

---

[2] See also Barthélémy and Lubrano (1996) for related test statistics based on the Dickey-Fuller-type transformation of the AR model.

where $\Delta = 1 - B$. Because the ϕ's are not known, the first and second regressors in this equation are replaced with $\Delta_S y_t + \hat{\phi}_1 \Delta_S y_{t-1} + \cdots + \hat{\phi}_p \Delta_S y_{t-p}$ and $\Delta y_t + \hat{\phi}_1 \Delta \Delta_S y_{t-1} + \cdots + \hat{\phi}_p \Delta \Delta_S y_{t-p}$, where the coefficient estimates are obtained by regressing $\Delta \Delta_S y_t$ on $\{\Delta \Delta_S y_{t-1}, \ldots, \Delta \Delta_S y_{t-p}\}$. The t-ratios for the significance of ρ_{s1} and ρ_{s2} test the nulls of a nonseasonal positive unit root and seasonal unit roots, respectively. Osborn, Chui, Smith, and Birchenhall apply their and Hasza and Fuller's tests to UK nondurable consumption, income, wealth, and inflation data, finding evidence of both nonseasonal and seasonal unit roots only for the consumption series. The others do not seem to contain seasonal unit roots, although they do appear to have a nonseasonal, positive unit root.

Ahn and Cho (1993)[3] consider the unobserved components model

$$y_t = \sum_{s=1}^{S} (\theta_s + \zeta_s \gamma) D_{st} + x_t; (t = S+1, \ldots, T)$$

$$x_t = \alpha_S x_{t-S} + u_t, \ u_t \sim \text{iid}(0, \sigma_u^2),$$

where $\{D_{st}\}$ denotes seasonal dummies and $\gamma = [(t-1)/S + 1]$. Coefficients $\{\theta_s\}$ are seasonal intercepts that do not vary across seasons, and γ denotes a trend that is upward year by year, but stays constant within a year. Ahn and Cho devise an LM test for the null hypothesis $H_0 : \alpha_S = 1$.

Kunst (1997) augments DHF's regression model with intervening variables and performs a joint hypothesis test. Namely, Kunst assumes the DGP in its simplest form as

$$y_t - y_{t-S} = \phi_1 y_{t-1} + \cdots + \phi_S y_{t-S} + u_t, \ u_t \sim \text{iid}\left(0, \sigma_u^2\right)$$

and tests the null hypothesis $H_0 : \phi_1 = \cdots = \phi_S = 0$ using the likelihood principle. Under this null hypothesis, seasonal differencing $1 - B^S$ is justified. Kunst tabulates quantiles of his test statistics for various values of S using simulation.

There are some demerits and merits to Kunst's (1997) test. First, because his model does not contain any deterministic regressors, his test has limited applicability. Second, as pointed out by Ghysels and Osborn (2001, p. 66) and Osborn and Rodrigues (2002), his test is virtually the same as Ghysels, Lee, and Noh's (1994) F-test using HEGY's framework (see Subsection 6.2.2). Last, it is not intuitively clear why those intervening variables should be included in the Kunst regression but not in DHF. Adding more variables is not a good strategy because it will certainly result in a test with lower power. However, there is a

---

[3] Cho, Park, and Ahn (1995) consider an analogous model and devise a Dickey-Fuller test for seasonal unit roots.

virtue in his approach. When the true DGP has only a positive unit root, Kunst's test statistic will diverge in probability because his test can differentiate the null hypothesis of seasonal unit root from the alternative $H_1 : \phi_1 = 1, \phi_2 = \cdots = \phi_{S-1} = 0, \phi_S = -1$ (i.e., a positive unit root). Thus, if the Kunst test does not reject the null hypothesis, it means that there is no positive unit root and that seasonal differencing is justified. Taylor (2003b) demonstrates that we cannot interpret the DHF test in this way.

Taylor (2003b) derives the limiting distributions of DHF's test statistics when the true DGP is a random walk process. He finds that the test statistics have nondegenerate distributions in this case, implying that the DHF test is not consistent when the alternative is a random walk process. This also means that DHF's test cannot distinguish between unit roots at zero frequency and seasonal frequencies. This is in contrast to the HEGY test, discussed in Subsection 6.2.2. Castro (2006) extends Taylor's result to processes with negative and complex unit root. Castro's result implies that the DHF test is inconsistent when the DGP under the alternative is a process with negative or complex unit roots. As discussed earlier, however, the problems of the DHF test indicated by Taylor and Castro can be overcome if we add intervening variables in the regression equation and perform the joint hypothesis test of Kunst (1997).

Lee and Dickey (2004) use unconditional maximum likelihood estimation (see Pantula, Gonzalez-Farias, and Fuller, 1994) for Model (6.1) and devise seasonal unit root tests. A downside of this approach is the complicated algorithm, though it may show improved power compared to other tests. See Subsection 2.4.6 for related discussions.

Shin and Oh (2000) assume that the errors in Model (6.1) follow a mixing process and derive the limiting distribution of the OLS estimator. It depends on nuisance parameters in a complicated manner, so that Phillips's (1987a) semiparametric correction does not work properly. As a remedy, Shin and So (2000) suggest a semiparametric GLS estimator with the same limiting distribution as the OLS estimator for Model (6.1).

Last, one can also consider resampling methods for Model (6.1). Using Ferretti and Romo's (1996) method (see Subsection 4.5.2), Psaradakis (2000) applies bootstrapping to Model (6.1) and establishes its validity.

6.2.2   Component-Wise Testing for Seasonal Unit Roots

HEGY's Test

When $S = 4$, the characteristic equation for Model (6.1) has roots $1, -1$, and $\pm i$. HEGY consider testing the presence of all of these roots in a single framework. I explain HEGY's testing procedure here using Ghysels and Osborn's (2001) exposition, which is more intuitive than that of HEGY. Following Ghysels and Osborn, construct

$$y_t^{(1)} = y_t + y_{t-1} + y_{t-2} + y_{t-3}; \tag{6.8}$$

$$y_t^{(2)} = y_t - y_{t-1} + y_{t-2} - y_{t-3};$$

$$y_t^{(3)} = y_t - y_{t-2}.$$

When $\alpha_S = 1$ in Model (6.1), it is easy to see that

$$(1 - B)y_t^{(1)} = u_t;$$

$$(1 + B)y_t^{(2)} = u_t;$$

$$(1 + B^2)y_t^{(3)} = u_t.$$

That is, $y_t^{(1)}$, $y_t^{(2)}$, and $y_t^{(3)}$ have roots 1, -1, and $\pm i$, respectively. To test for a positive unit root against the alternative of stable roots, we may test the null hypothesis $H_0 : \alpha = 1$ in the regression equation

$$y_t^{(1)} = \alpha y_{t-1}^{(1)} + u_t$$

or, equivalently, $H_0 : \rho_1 = 0$ in the regression equation

$$(1 - B)y_t^{(1)} = \rho_1 y_{t-1}^{(1)} + u_t$$

against the alternative $H_1 : \rho_1 < 0$. Because $(1 - B)y_t^{(1)} = \Delta_4 y_t$ ($\Delta_4 = 1 - B^4$), this equation can also be written as

$$\Delta_4 y_t = \rho_1 y_{t-1}^{(1)} + u_t. \tag{6.9}$$

For a negative unit root, noting that $(1 + B)y_t^{(2)} = \Delta_4 y_t$, we consider testing the null of $H_0 : \rho_2 = 0$ in the regression equation

$$\Delta_4 y_t = \rho_2 y_{t-1}^{(2)} + u_t. \tag{6.10}$$

Because the alternative hypothesis is stationarity, it is written as $H_1 : \rho_2 > 0$. Likewise, for the case of complex unit roots, we consider the regression equation

$$\Delta_4 y_t = \rho_3 y_{t-2}^{(3)} + u_t, \tag{6.11}$$

and test the null of $H_0 : \rho_3 = 0$ against the alternative of stationarity $H_1 : \rho_3 > 0$. We can also consider the regression equation

$$\Delta_4 y_t = \rho_4 y_{t-1}^{(3)} + u_t, \tag{6.12}$$

which uses $y_{t-1}^{(3)}$ instead of $y_{t-2}^{(3)}$. Obviously, when $\rho_4 = 0$, $\{y_t\}$ has complex unit roots. But when it is not, stochastic properties of $\{y_t^{(3)}\}$ depend on the location of ρ_4. It can be either stable or explosive. Thus, the alternative in this case is taken as $\rho_4 \neq 0$.

Combining equations (6.9)–(6.10), HEGY consider the model

$$\Delta_4 y_t = \pi_1 x_{t-1}^{(1)} + \pi_2 x_{t-1}^{(2)} + \pi_3 x_{t-2}^{(3)} + \pi_4 x_{t-1}^{(3)} + u_t, \tag{6.13}$$

where $x_t^{(1)} = y_t^{(1)}$, $x_t^{(2)} = -y_t^{(2)}$, and $x_t^{(3)} = -y_t^{(3)}$. The sign changes of the regressors are made to make all the t-ratios for the coefficients π_1, π_2, and π_3 use the left tails of their limiting distributions. HEGY suggest testing the presence of seasonal unit roots by testing the null hypotheses $H_0 : \pi_2 = 0$ and $H_0 : \pi_3 = \pi_4 = 0$ using the t-ratio and F-statistic, respectively. Note that the former hypothesis corresponds to the presence of a negative unit root, and the latter to the presence of complex unit roots. Asymptotic critical values for the t-ratio and F-statistic in the presence of an intercept, seasonal dummies, and a linear time trend are reported in Table 6.2. When $\{u_t\}$ is not a white noise process, lagged variables of $\Delta_4 y_t$ should be added as additional regressors. The critical values in Table 6.2 can also be used in this case.

Model (6.13) can also be obtained by the expansion of $1 - \alpha z^4$. Factor $1 - \alpha z^4$ at seasonal frequencies $\omega = \frac{2\pi k}{4}$ ($k = 0, 1, 2, 3$) such that

$$1 - \alpha z^4 = (1 - \alpha_1 z)(1 + \alpha_2 z)(1 + (\alpha_3 - \alpha_4)iz)(1 - (\alpha_3 - \alpha_4)iz)$$

$$= (1 - \alpha_1 z)(1 + \alpha_2 z)(1 + 2\alpha_4 z + (\alpha_3^2 + \alpha_4^2)z^2)$$

$$= f(\alpha_1, \alpha_2, \alpha_3, \alpha_4), \text{ say.}$$

Then, ignoring the remainder term, consider a first-order Taylor expansion of $f(\alpha_1, \alpha_2, \alpha_3, \alpha_4)$ around $\alpha_1 = 1$, $\alpha_2 = 1$, $\alpha_3 = 1$, and $\alpha_4 = 0$, which corresponds to $\alpha = 1$. The Taylor expansion yields

$$f(\alpha_1, \alpha_2, \alpha_3, \alpha_4) = (1 - z^4) - \pi_1 z(1 + z + z^2 + z^3)$$

$$+ \pi_2 z(1 - z + z^2 - z^3) + \pi_3 z^2(1 - z^2) + \pi_4 z(1 - z^2),$$

where $\pi_k = \alpha_k - 1$ ($k = 1, 2$), $\pi_3 = 2(\alpha_3 - 1)$, and $\pi_4 = 2\alpha_4$. This expansion also provides HEGY's equation (6.13). See Burke (1996) for a more rigorous treatment of the expansion given here.

Extensions of HEGY

There are many extensions of the HEGY procedure. Using Model (6.13), Ghysels, Lee, and Noh (1994) develop asymptotic theory for the joint null

Table 6.2. *Asymptotic critical values of the HEGY tests*

	t-ratio significance level			F-statistic significance level		
	1%	5%	10%	1%	5%	10%
Int.	−2.58	−1.92	−1.59	4.76	3.12	2.37
Int. & sea. dum.	−3.50	−2.89	−2.60	8.93	6.61	5.56
Int. & lin. trnd.	−2.59	−1.95	−1.62	4.66	3.07	2.34
Int., lin. trnd. & sea. dum.	−3.52	−2.91	−2.60	8.96	6.57	5.56

Note: If the computed value of the t-ratio (F-statistic) is smaller (larger) than the critical value, reject the null hypothesis.

hypotheses

$$H_0 : \pi_1 = \pi_2 = \pi_3 = \pi_4 = 0; \tag{6.14}$$

$$H_0' : \pi_2 = \pi_3 = \pi_4 = 0. \tag{6.15}$$

When the first null hypothesis is rejected, there are no unit roots at all. When the second is rejected, there are neither negative nor complex unit roots though there might be a positive unit root. Thus, it is straightforward to interpret their test results.

Beaulieu and Miron (1993) extend the HEGY test to monthly time series and develop relevant asymptotic theory. Their model and theory are much more complex than HEGY's; their model contains 12 regressors. Beaulieu and Miron apply their method to some U.S. monthly aggregate data and find no evidence of seasonal unit roots.

Using HEGY's framework, Smith and Taylor (1998)[4] propose regression-based tests for seasonal unit roots that permit the drift in the seasonal random walk to differ across seasons. The differential seasonal drift allows the amplitude of seasonal variation to vary through time. Their approach is to replace the single time trend variable in the HEGY regression with trend variables that can vary in impact across the seasons. More specifically, Smith and Taylor consider the model

$$\alpha(B)(y_{4\tau+s} - \mu_s^* - \beta_s^*(4\tau + s)) = u_{4\tau+s}, \ u_t \sim \text{iid}(0, \sigma_u^2),$$

$$(s = -3, \ldots, 0; \ \tau = 1, 2, \ldots, T_\tau), \tag{6.16}$$

where τ is an index for year, s is for season, and $\alpha(z) = 1 - \sum_{j=1}^{4} \alpha_j z^j$. Furthermore, $B^{4j+k}\mu_s^* = \mu_{s-k}^*$ and $B^{4j+k}\beta_s^* = \beta_{s-k}^*$ if $-3 \leq q - k \leq 0$, and

---

[4] Taylor (1998) extends Smith and Taylor (1998) to monthly time series. Smith, Taylor, and Castro (2009) further generalize Smith and Taylor (1998), assuming AR errors.

$B^{4j+k}\mu_s^* = \mu_{4+s-k}^*$ and $B^{4j+k}\beta_s^* = \beta_{4+s-k}^*$ if $q - k < -3$, so that the intercept and trend parameters do not vary across the seasons.

The AR(4) process (6.16) can be rewritten as

$$\alpha(B)y_{4\tau+s} = \mu_s + \beta_s(4\tau + s) + u_{4\tau+s}, \tag{6.17}$$

where $\mu_s = \mu_s^* - \sum_{j=1}^4 \alpha_j \mu_{s-j}^* + \sum_{j=1}^4 j\alpha_j \beta_{s-j}^*$ and $\beta_s = \beta_s^* - \sum_{j=1}^4 \alpha_j \beta_{s-j}^*$. Under the null hypothesis $H_0 : \alpha(z) = 1 - z^4$, $\mu_s = 4\beta_s^*$ and $\beta_s = 0$, implying

$$\Delta_4 y_{4\tau+s} = \mu_s + u_{4\tau+s}$$

or equivalently

$$y_{4\tau+s} = y_s + \mu_s \tau + \sum_{r=1}^{\tau} u_{4r+s}. \tag{6.18}$$

This representation of $\{y_{4\tau+s}\}$ illustrates that the drift changes across the seasons. Relations (6.17) and (6.18) show that the level process $\{y_{4\tau+s}\}$ will display similar deterministic trending behavior whether or not the null hypothesis holds.

As in HEGY, Smith and Taylor (1998) rewrite Model (6.17) as

$$\Delta_4 y_{4\tau+s} = \mu_s + \beta_s(4\tau + s) + \pi_1 y_{1,4\tau+s-1} + \pi_2 y_{2,4\tau+s-1}$$

$$+ \pi_3 y_{3,4\tau+s-2} + \pi_4 y_{3,4\tau+s-1} + u_{4\tau+s},$$

where $y_{1,4\tau+s} = (1 + B + B^2 + B^3)y_{4\tau+s}$, $y_{2,4\tau+s} = -(1 - B + B^2 - B^3)y_{4\tau+s}$, and $y_{3,4\tau+s} = -(1 - B^2)y_{4\tau+s}$. This model contains various HEGY models as special cases. The inclusion of the heterogeneous seasonal trend dummies with the null restriction $\beta_s = 0$ makes unit root test statistics invariant to the coefficients of the seasonal intercept dummies. The intuition for this follows from the Dickey-Fuller test for a unit root with drift against the alternative hypothesis of trend stationarity; this requires including a linear time trend in the regression model with a zero restriction on its coefficient to make the Dickey-Fuller test statistics invariant to the values of the intercept term (see Subsection 2.3.1 for further discussion). Smith and Taylor derive the limiting distributions of the t-ratios and F-statistics for the null hypotheses $H_0 : \pi_1 = 0$, $H_0 : \pi_2 = 0$, $H_0 : \pi_3 = 0$, $H_0 : \pi_4 = 0$, $H_0 : \pi_1 = \pi_2 = \pi_3 = \pi_4 = 0$, $H_0 : \pi_2 = \pi_3 = \pi_4 = 0$, and $H_0 : \pi_3 = \pi_4 = 0$.

Burridge and Taylor (2001a) study the limiting distributions of the t-ratios and F-statistics in Smith and Taylor (1998) when the errors follow AR processes. Even when the regression equation is augmented with appropriately lagged differences, limiting distributions of the t-ratios for complex unit roots depend on nuisance parameters that originate from the serial correlation of the errors. However, the t-ratios for positive and negative unit roots and the

F-statistics for null hypotheses (6.14) and (6.15) have limiting distributions invariant to the serial correlation of the errors. As a remedy to the sensitivity of the HEGY t-ratios to the serial correlation, Burridge and Taylor (2004) suggest using bootstrapping. The bootstrap method yields a correct size for the t-ratios and, additionally, improves size properties of the F-test under the null hypothesis.

Castro and Osborn (2011) study the asymptotic distributions of HEGY's test statistics when the errors follow MA processes. When the regression equation is augmented with enough number of lagged differences, the t-ratios for positive and negative unit roots and the F-statistics for null hypotheses (6.14) and (6.15) are found to be pivotal, but the t-ratios for complex unit roots are not. This is concordant with Burridge and Taylor's (2001a) result.

Burridge and Taylor (2001b) employ the same model as Burridge and Taylor (2001a), but assume that the innovation process $\{u_{4\tau+s}\}$ is periodically heteroskedastic. That is, $u_{4\tau+s} = \sigma_s e_{4\tau+s}$ where σ_s is a positive constant and $e_{4\tau+s} \sim$ iid$(0, 1)$. The limiting distributions of the unit root test statistics for positive and negative unit roots are not affected by the periodic heteroskedasticity. However, those for complex unit roots do depend on nuisance parameters that stem from the periodic heteroskedasticity.[5]

Using the trigonometric representations of deterministic seasonal components, Smith and Taylor (1999) devise seasonal unit root tests. They assume the DGP

$$
\left(1 - \alpha_S B^S \right) \left(y_{S\tau+s} - \left\{ \sum_{j=0}^{[S/2]} \gamma_j^a \sin\left(s\omega_j\right) + \gamma_j^b \cos\left(s\omega_j\right) \right\} \right.
$$

$$
\left. - \left\{ \sum_{j=0}^{[S/2]} \delta_j^a \sin\left(s\omega_j\right) + \delta_j^b \cos\left(s\omega_j\right) \right\} (S\tau + s) \right)
$$

$$
= u_{S\tau+1}, \ (s = 1 - S, \ldots, 0; \ \tau = 1, \ldots, T_\tau), \tag{6.19}
$$

where $\omega_j = \frac{2\pi j}{S}$, the index s is for season, and τ is for year. The variable $S\tau + s$ denotes a trend that moves up season by season and year by year. The trigonometric functions in the DGP (6.19) have often been used to model deterministic seasonal components. When Model (6.19) is rewritten as an AR model, the seasonal trend term disappears under the null hypothesis $\alpha_S = 1$. The details for this are given in Smith and Taylor. Using Model (6.19) along with HEGY's method, Smith and Taylor devise F-statistics for the null hypotheses of various combinations of unit roots and develop their asymptotic distributions.

---

[5] Taylor (2005) proposes variance ratio tests that overcome this problem.

Rodrigues and Taylor (2004b)[6] derive the asymptotic local power of the HEGY test under the sequence of alternatives

$$H_1 : \alpha_S = 1 - \frac{c}{T} \; (c > 0). \tag{6.20}$$

According to them, the asymptotic local power of the t-test for coefficients π_3 and π_4 in equation (6.13) depends on the serial correlation structure of the data, whereas that of the F-test for the joint null hypothesis on π_3 and π_4 does not. Based on this observation, they recommend the use of the F-test rather than the t-test.

Castro (2007) derives the limiting distributions of the t-ratios and F-statistic introduced in HEGY when not all of the unit roots, 1, -1, $\pm i$, are present. This study shows that the t-ratio for π_1 in equation (6.13) has the same limiting distribution as in HEGY when the DGP contains only a positive unit root. The same holds true for the t-ratio for π_2 and the F-statistic for complex unit roots. Thus, these statistics can be used for their original purposes even when some of the unit roots are absent as long as respective unit roots are present. However, the t-ratios for complex unit roots—those corresponding to π_3 and π_4 in equation (6.13)—have limiting distributions that depend on nuisance parameters even when the DGP contains only complex unit roots. Furthermore, when the DGP has complex and negative unit roots, the limiting distributions of the t-ratios for complex unit roots are different from those in HEGY. This analysis alerts us, in accordance with Burridge and Taylor (2001b) and Rodrigues and Taylor (2004b), that care should be taken when using the t-ratios for complex unit roots in the HEGY regression.

Power Improvements of the HEGY Test

Some studies have aimed at improving the power of the HEGY test. As we have seen in Section 2.4, there must be many ways to improve its power if other estimation methods and testing procedures are employed. To devise individual and joint tests for seasonal unit roots, Breitung and Franses (1998) use the LM principle as in SP (see Subsection 2.4.1) along with the Phillips-Perron-type nonparametric treatment of serial correlation. They report some power improvement over the HEGY test. However, they consider only nonseasonal drift, which may hinder its use in practice. Rodrigues (2002) extends SP's method to the HEGY regression with seasonal dummies and a linear time trend, overcoming Breitung and Franses's limitation.

Because Leybourne's (1995) MAX test shows some power gain over the Dickey-Fuller test (see Subsection 2.4.3 for related discussion), it may also do so for seasonal unit root testing. Leybourne and Taylor (2003) explore this

---

[6] See also Rodrigues (2001) for related results.

possibility. Using the HEGY regression model, they calculate the t-ratios and F-statistics for both the original and reversed data. In the case of the t-ratios, the maximum of the forward and reverse regressions is taken, whereas the minimum is taken in the case of F-statistics. Leybourne and Taylor develop asymptotic theory for these test statistics and report finite-sample power gain over the original HEGY test.

Rodrigues and Taylor (2004a) opt to use the weighted symmetric estimator of Park and Fuller (1995)—see Subsection 2.4.6 for a related discussion—to estimate the parameters of Model (6.13)[7] and report higher finite-sample power of the associated t- and F-tests than those of HEGY.

Rodrigues and Taylor (2007) apply the point-optimal test (see Subsection 4.7.3) and the GLS-detrending method of ERS (see Subsection 2.4.4) to devise test statistics for seasonal unit roots. Again, the starting point is the HEGY regression model, and the null hypotheses of a positive unit root, a negative unit root, and unit roots at seasonal frequencies are considered. For each null hypothesis, a sequence of local alternatives of the form similar to (6.20) are constructed. Then, assuming the presence of various deterministic components (e.g., seasonal intercept, seasonal trend, etc.), Rodrigues and Taylor construct the most powerful invariant tests for each null hypothesis at the chosen alternatives as in ERS and derive their asymptotic distributions. In addition, they detrend the time series using the ERS GLS method and use the detrended data to construct various t- and F-statistics for the null hypotheses of unit roots. Rodrigues and Taylor report that their new testing procedure demonstrates a power gain over that of HEGY.

Taylor (2002) estimates the deterministic component of the model recursively (see Subsection 2.4.7 for related discussions) to construct seasonal unit root tests. For example, in Model (6.16), Taylor estimates $y_{S\tau+s} - \mu_s - \beta_s(S\tau + s)$ using the recursive estimation method:

$$\tilde{y}_{S\tau+s} = y_{S\tau+s} - (\tau - \overline{\tau})\left(\sum_{k=0}^{\tau}(k - \overline{\tau})^2\right)^{-1}\sum_{k=0}^{\tau}(k - \overline{\tau})(y_{S\tau+s} - \overline{y}_{\tau,s}),$$

where $\overline{\tau} = (\tau + 1)^{-1}\sum_{k=0}^{\tau} k = \frac{\tau}{2}$ and $\overline{y}_{\tau,s} = (\tau + 1)^{-1}\sum_{k=0}^{\tau} y_{S\tau+s}$, and he uses $\{\tilde{y}_{S\tau+s}\}$ to construct seasonal unit root tests as in HEGY. Notice that the parameters μ_s and β_s are estimated using the data up to year τ. Taylor derives the asymptotic distributions of the t- and F-statistics in the HEGY regression and tabulates their critical values. He also shows via simulation that the test based on the recursive estimation has good finite-sample properties compared to the HEGY test using the OLS or weighted symmetric estimator.

---

[7] Because Rodrigues and Taylor's (2004a) model has serially correlated errors, it is in fact more complex than Model (6.13).

Shin and So (2000)[8] combine the recursive estimation of deterministic components and the Cauchy estimation of stochastic components to devise seasonal unit root tests. They report that the test combining the recursive estimation and OLS performs better than the test they propose.

The HEGY Test Under Measurement Errors and Outliers

Extending Franses and Haldrup (1994) (see Section 3.4), to seasonal unit root testing, Haldrup, Montañés, and Sanso (2005) study the HEGY test under measurement errors and outliers. They consider the DGP

$$y_t = x_t + w_t,$$ (6.21)

where $\Delta_S x_t = u_t$, $u_t \sim \mathrm{iid}(0, \sigma_u^2)$ and

$$w_t = \frac{\theta}{(1 - \alpha B)} \delta_t + \eta_t.$$ (6.22)

As in Franses and Haldrup, δ_t is a Bernoulli random variable that takes the value 1 or -1 with a given probability π and is zero otherwise. If $|\theta|$ is large and π is small, this model will generate infrequent outliers with large magnitudes. Additionally, $\{\eta_t\}$ are i.i.d. random variables that represent measurement errors. Under the DGP (6.21) and (6.22), Haldrup, Montañés, and Sanso derive limiting distributions of the HEGY test statistics and show that they involve location and scale factors that depend on the outliers and measurement errors. Thus, ignoring the outliers and measurement errors leads to size distortions of the HEGY test statistics. Haldrup, Montañés, and Sanso suggest a stepwise procedure that identifies the outliers and adjusts the HEGY test statistics accordingly. However, the procedure does not seem to completely overcome the size distortions of the HEGY test statistics, though it tends to reduce it.

6.2.3 Seasonal Unit Root Tests Using a Random-Coefficient Process

Extending the idea of LMT (see Subsection 3.6.3) to seasonal time series, Taylor and Smith (2001) test the null hypothesis of a seasonal random walk against the alternative of a heteroskedastic seasonally integrated process. The model they consider is

$$\alpha_{S\tau+s}(B) y_{S\tau+s} = u_{S\tau+s}, \quad u_t \sim \mathrm{iid}(0, \sigma_u^2),$$
$$(s = 1 - S, \ldots, 0; \ \tau = 1, 2, \ldots, T_\tau),$$ (6.23)

---

[8] See also Kuzin (2005) for a similar idea.

where $\alpha_{S\tau+s}(z) = 1 - \alpha_{S\tau+s}z^S$. The process defining the random-coefficients $\{\alpha_{S\tau+s}\}$ is given by

$$\alpha_{S\tau+s} = 1 + \delta_{S\tau+s}, \qquad (6.24)$$

where $\{\delta_{S\tau+s}\}$ follows the process

$$\delta_{S\tau+s} = \rho\delta_{S(\tau-1)+s} + \xi_{S\tau+s}, \ 0 \le \rho \le 1, \ \delta_s = 0.$$

It is assumed that $\begin{pmatrix} u_{S\tau+s} \\ \xi_{S\tau+s} \end{pmatrix} \sim \text{iid}\, N\left(0, \begin{bmatrix} \sigma_u^2 & 0 \\ 0 & \sigma_\xi^2 \end{bmatrix}\right)$. From relations (6.23) and (6.24),

$$\Delta_S y_{S\tau+s} = \delta_{S\tau+s} y_{S(\tau-1)+s} + u_{S\tau+s}.$$

This representation shows that $\{\Delta_S y_{S\tau+s}\}$ is a heteroskedastic seasonally integrated process if $\sigma_\xi^2 > 0$, whereas it is a seasonal random walk process if $\sigma_\xi^2 = 0$. Taylor and Smith consider testing the null hypothesis $H_0 : \sigma_\xi^2 = 0$ against the alternative $H_1 : \sigma_\xi^2 > 0$. For the two cases $\rho = 0$ and $\rho = 1$, they derive the locally most powerful test statistics for the null hypothesis and their limiting destitutions. They also consider the DGP with a seasonal intercept and a linear time trend as in Smith and Taylor (1998).

6.2.4 Sampling Frequency and Seasonal Unit Root Tests

Pons (2006) considers sampling quarterly data from monthly data for both flow and stock variables. He shows that the quarterly data have seasonal unit roots when the monthly data have them as well. More specifically, suppose that the monthly time series $\{y_t\}$ is represented by

$$(1 - B)^{d_0}\left(1 - \sqrt{3}B + B^2\right)^{d_1}\left(1 - B + B^2\right)^{d_2}$$

$$\times \left(1 + B^2\right)^{d_3}\left(1 + B + B^2\right)^{d_4}\left(1 + \sqrt{3}B + B^2\right)^{d_5}$$

$$\times (1 + B)^{d_6} y_t = x_t, \ (t = 1, 2, \ldots, T), \quad (6.25)$$

where $d_k = 0, 1$ ($k = 1, \ldots, 6$) and $\{x_t\}$ is a stationary and invertible ARMA process. When $d_k = 1$ for all k, this relation reduces to $(1 - B^{12})y_t = x_t$. Then, if $\{y_t\}$ is a stock variable, the quarterly data sampled from it are represented by

$$Y_v^i = y_{3(v-1)+i} \ (v = 1, 2, 3, 4; \ i = 1, 2, 3)$$

where v denotes the index for quarter and i for each month in a season. For example, Y_1^2 is the observation for the first quarter taken from the second month of the quarter. When $\{y_t\}$ is a flow variable, the quarterly data formulated by aggregation are represented by

$$Y_v^a = \sum_{i=1}^{3} Y_v^i.$$

Pons (2006) shows that

$$(1 - B)^{D_0}(1 + B^2)^{D_1}(1 + B)^{D_2} Y_v^i = U_v^i, \ (i = 1, 2, 3) \qquad (6.26)$$

and that

$$(1 - B)^{E_0}(1 + B^2)^{D_1}(1 + B)^{D_2} Y_v^a = U_v^a, \qquad (6.27)$$

where $D_0 = \max\{d_0, d_4\}$, $D_1 = \max\{d_1, d_3, d_5\}$, $D_2 = \max\{d_2, d_6\}$, $E_0 = d_0$, $U_v^i = u_{3(v-1)+i}$, and $U_v^a = \sum_{i=1}^{3} U_v^i$. According to relations (6.25) and (6.26), the quarterly data $\{Y_v^i\}$ may have a real, positive unit root while the monthly data $\{y_t\}$ do not if $d_0 = 0$ and $d_4 = 1$. This phenomenon is also reported in Granger and Siklos (1995), who use the frequency domain approach. But in the case of aggregation, a real, positive unit root in $\{y_t\}$ implies one in $\{Y_v^a\}$, and vice versa.

Relations (6.26) and (6.27) show that information on the presence of unit roots for monthly data can also be found from quarterly data. Using this idea, Pons (2006) suggests combining the HEGY statistics for monthly and quarterly data to test for seasonal unit roots in the monthly data. He demonstrates via simulation that his test sometimes yields higher power than Beaulieu and Miron's (1993).

6.3   Seasonal Stationarity Tests

This section introduces tests that take the null as stationarity with seasonal elements. Ideas of these tests stem from the stationarity tests considered in Section 4.7.

6.3.1   Tests for Parameter Constancy

Canova and Hansen (1995; CH hereafter) develop a test for the null hypothesis of no unit roots at seasonal frequencies against the alternative of a unit root at either a single seasonal frequency or at a set of seasonal frequencies. Assume for simplicity that the number of seasons, S, is even. CH consider the model

$$y_t = \mu + x_t'\varepsilon + f_t'\gamma_t + e_t, \ (t = 1, \ldots, T), \qquad (6.28)$$

where x_t is a vector of explanatory variables, $f_t = [f_{1t}', \ldots, f_{\frac{S}{2}t}']'$ with $f_{jt} = \left[\cos\left(\frac{2\pi jt}{S}\right), \sin\left(\frac{2\pi jt}{S}\right)\right]'$ for $j < \frac{S}{2}$; $f_{\frac{S}{2}t} = (-1)^t$; and $\{e_t\}$ is a stationary process. Here, f_{jt} corresponds to the seasonal frequency $2\pi j/S$. When $\{\gamma_t\}$ do not change over time, $f_t' \gamma_t$ in Model (6.28) is mathematically equivalent to the sum of seasonal dummies with unknown coefficients due to the theory of Fourier transformation (see, for example, Fuller, 1976).

CH assume $\gamma_t = \gamma_{t-1} + u_t$, where γ_0 is a fixed constant. To select particular frequencies, define a $(S-1) \times a$ matrix A. For example, to select all the frequencies for quarterly data, we should have $A = I_3$. Using the matrix A, we have

$$A'\gamma_t = A'\gamma_{t-1} + w_t.$$

CH take $E(w_t w_t') = \tau^2 G$ with $G = \tau^2 (A'\Omega^f A)^{-1}$, $\Omega^f = \lim_{T\to\infty} \frac{1}{T} E(F_T F_T')$, and $F_T = \sum_{j=1}^{T} f_j e_j$. The choice of the matrix G is innocuous and helps develop asymptotic theory. CH test the null hypothesis $H_0 : \tau^2 = 0$ with the LM principle. Under the null hypothesis, the DGP has no unit roots at the chosen frequencies. The test statistic takes the form

$$L = \frac{1}{T^2} \sum_{t=1}^{T} \hat{F}_t' A \left(A'\hat{\Omega}^f A \right)^{-1} A' \hat{F}_t,$$

where $\hat{\Omega}^f$ is an estimator of the long-run variance of $f_t e_t$ given by

$$\hat{\Omega}^f = \sum_{k=-m}^{m} w\left(\frac{k}{m}\right) \frac{1}{T} \sum_{t=1}^{T-k} f_{t+k} f_t' \hat{e}_{t+k} \hat{e}_t,$$

where $w(\cdot)$ is a kernel function and $\hat{e}_t$ is the OLS residual obtained by regressing y_t on $(1, x_t', f_t)$. Note that the use of the estimator $\hat{\Omega}^f$ allows for seasonal heteroskedasticity. CH report that

$$L \Rightarrow \int_0^1 W_a(r) W_a(r)' \, dr,$$

where $W_a(r)$ is an a-dimensional standard vector Brownian motion. Quantiles of the asymptotic distribution for some chosen a are reported in Table 6.3.

Hylleberg (1995) compares properties of the CH test in finite samples to those of HEGY. He finds that the HEGY test performs better when the DGP for experiments is the same as that for the test derivation, and vice versa. Thus, the two tests complement each other as unit root and stationarity tests do.

Caner (1998) extends the CH test using the parametric approach in the spirit of Leybourne and McCabe (1994). His test performs better via simulation when the DGP follows some parametric structures covered by his model for the test derivation.

Busetti and Harvey (2003b) complement the CH test in various ways. They show that the model may contain a deterministic linear time trend and even stochastic regressors with nonseasonal unit roots without bringing any changes

Table 6.3. *Asymptotic critical values of the Canova-Hansen test*

	Significance level		
	2.5%	5%	10%
1	0.748	0.470	0.353
2	1.070	0.749	0.610
3	1.350	1.010	0.846

Note: If the computed value of the L statistic is larger than the critical value, reject the null of stationarity.

in the test statistic's asymptotic distributions. Also, they modify the CH test statistic, adopting a nonparametric correction of serial correlation based on the estimates of the spectrum at seasonal frequencies. The modified test statistic, however, does not allow seasonal heteroskedasticity. Busetti and Harvey report that their test statistic compares well with other existing tests.

Taylor (2003a) considers the same model as CH, adding a linear time trend. Applying the testing principle of King and Wu's (1997) locally mean most powerful invariant test, he develops tests for joint and separate hypotheses of unit roots that are essentially the same as those of CH and other related works.

6.3.2   Locally Best Tests for an MA Unit Root

Tam and Reinsel (1997) use the idea that seasonal differencing induces seasonal unit roots in the MA component under the null hypothesis of no seasonal unit roots. This idea has been repeatedly used for stationarity tests as we see in Section 4.7. Using the same ideas as in Tanaka (1990) and Saikkonen and Luukkonen (1993a, 1993b), Tam and Reinsel devise locally best invariant and point-optimal test statistics for seasonal unit roots. Extensions to the model with a linear time trend are reported in Tam and Reinsel (1998). However, the alternative hypothesis of Tam and Reinsel's tests is the presence of unit roots at all seasonal frequencies. Properties of their tests with unit roots at particular frequencies are not yet known.

6.4   Seasonal Unit Root and Stationarity Tests under Structural Changes

This section discusses the effects of structural changes on seasonal unit root testing and introduces methods of seasonal unit root and stationarity testing under structural changes. Tests for seasonal unit roots and stationarity follow the intuition and ideas of the unit root and stationarity tests introduced in Sections 3.2 and 4.8.

6.4.1 Effects of Structural Changes on Unit Root Testing

Lopes and Montañés (2005)[9] study asymptotic properties of the HEGY test statistics when the data are generated by

$$y_t = \sum_{s=1}^{4} \mu_s D_{st} + \sum_{s=1}^{4} \kappa_s DU_{st} + \beta t + u_t, \ u_t \sim \text{iid}(0, \sigma_u^2),$$

where $\{D_{st}\}$ is a sequence of seasonal dummies, $DU_{st} = D_{st}\mathbf{1}\{t > T_B\}$, and $\{\kappa_s\}$ are finite constants. Note that this DGP has no unit roots and that the seasonal levels shift up at the date T_B. When the HEGY test statistics are computed using Model (6.13) with seasonal dummies and a linear time trend, the t-ratios for the coefficients π_1, π_2, and π_3 diverge to $-\infty$ in probability and that for π_4 converges to zero in probability. Thus, the t-ratios for π_1, π_2, and π_3 behave correctly because the null hypotheses of unit roots are rejected. Moreover, the F-statistics for the null hypotheses $H_0 : \pi_1 = \pi_2 = \pi_3 = \pi_4 = 0$, $H_0 : \pi_2 = \pi_3 = \pi_4 = 0$, and $H_0 : \pi_3 = \pi_4 = 0$ all diverge to ∞ in probability, again making the HEGY test consistent. In addition, Lopes and Montañés show that the finite-sample power of the HEGY test statistics becomes lower as the magnitudes of structural change increase. This is in accordance with Perron (1989), who reports that the Dickey-Fuller test is consistent but has low finite-sample power in the presence of a level shift. If there is structural change in the linear trend term, however, the HEGY test is expected to be inconsistent once we follow the intuition given in Perron, though the issue has not been studied formally.

Hassler and Rodrigues (2004)[10] consider the DGP

$$y_t = \sum_{s=1}^{4} \mu_s D_{st} + \sum_{s=1}^{4} \kappa_s DU_{st} + \beta t + x_t; \tag{6.29}$$

$$\Delta_4 x_t = u_t, \ u_t \sim \text{iid}(0, \sigma_u^2)$$

and derive the limiting distribution of the HEGY test statistics when the change date, T_B, is known. To compute the test statistics, $\{y_t\}$ is regressed on the nonstochastic regressors in Model (6.29), and the resulting residuals $\{\hat{x}_t\}$ are used as for (6.13). When $\{\kappa_s\}$ are bounded, the limiting distributions of the HEGY test statistics do not change. But when $\kappa_s = O(\sqrt{T})$, the

---

[9] See also Smith and Otero (1997), who study a closely related problem with simulation.

[10] Hassler and Rodrigues (2004) also study an LM-type test for seasonal unit roots based on SP.

distributions depend on nuisance parameters originating from the change date, T_B. These results indicate that the HEGY test's size distortions are expected when the magnitudes of structural changes are large.

In practice, it is hard to know the magnitudes of structural changes. Thus, determining the dates of structural changes correctly and using appropriate methods based on the estimated change dates are important for seasonal unit root testing. This issue is discussed in the next subsection.

6.4.2   Methods of Seasonal Unit Root Testing in the Presence of Structural Changes

Franses and Vogelsang (1998) consider testing for seasonal unit roots in the presence of a structural change in the level both for the additive and innovative outlier models (see Section 3.4 for these models). The date of change is assumed to be unknown. Letting T_B denote the date of change, the additive outlier model is written as

$$y_t = x_t + \sum_{s=1}^{4} \mu_s D_{st} + \sum_{s=1}^{4} \kappa_s DU_{st},$$

where $\{D_{st}\}$ is a sequence of seasonal dummies and $DU_{st} = D_{st}\mathbf{1}\{t > T_B\}$. In this model, the effects of structural changes on $\{y_t\}$ are immediate and represented by the parameters $\{\kappa_s\}$. Franses and Vogelsang are concerned with testing for seasonal unit roots in $\{x_t\}$. Assuming for the moment that T_B is known, the HEGY test statistics for seasonal unit roots are constructed as follows.

Step 1: Run the OLS regression

$$y_t = \sum_{s=1}^{4} \hat{\mu}_s D_{st} + \sum_{s=1}^{4} \hat{\kappa}_s DU_{st} + \hat{x}_t$$

and retain the residuals $\{\hat{x}_t\}$.

Step 2: Using the residuals $\{\hat{x}_t\}$, run the HEGY regression

$$\Delta_4 \hat{x}_t = \hat{\pi}_1 \hat{x}_{t-1}^{(1)} + \hat{\pi}_2 \hat{x}_{t-1}^{(2)} + \hat{\pi}_3 \hat{x}_{t-2}^{(3)} + \hat{\pi}_4 \hat{x}_{t-1}^{(3)} + \sum_{j=1}^{k} \hat{c}_j \Delta_4 \hat{x}_{t-j}$$

$$+ \sum_{s=1}^{4} \hat{\phi}_s \Delta_4 DU_{st} + \sum_{i=1}^{4} \hat{\eta}_i \Delta_4 DU_{4,t-i} + \hat{u}_t,$$

Table 6.4. *Asymptotic critical values of the Franses-Vogelsang test*

	t_{π_1}		t_{π_2}		F_{34}	
Significance level	5%	10%	5%	10%	5%	10%
AO model (min t, max F_{34})	−4.34	−4.11	−4.39	−4.12	13.52	12.19
IO model (min t, max F_{34})	−4.39	−4.11	−4.39	−4.12	13.52	12.19
AO model (using max F_δ)	−3.48	−3.18	−3.48	−3.18	9.88	8.62
IO model (using max F_δ)	−4.19	−3.83	−4.19	−3.84	12.89	11.38

Note: If the computed value of t-ratio (F-statistic) is smaller (larger) than the critical value, reject the null of seasonal unit roots.

where $\hat{x}_t^{(1)} = (1 + B + B^2 + B^3)\hat{x}_t$, $\hat{x}_t^{(2)} = -(1 - B + B^2 - B^3)\hat{x}_t$, and $\hat{x}_t^{(3)} = -(1 - B^2)\hat{x}_t$. The dummy variables are included to make the limiting distributions of the t-ratios and F-statistics for seasonal unit roots free of nuisance parameters.

Step 3: Calculate the t-ratios for the null hypotheses $H_0 : \pi_1 = 0$ and $H_0 : \pi_2 = 0$ and the F-statistic for the null hypothesis $H_0 : \pi_3 = \pi_4 = 0$.

Because T_B is unknown in practice, Franses and Vogelsang (1998) suggest repeating Steps 1–3 for various values of the change date and employing the minimums of the t-ratios and the maximum of the F-statistic. Asymptotic distributions of the resulting test statistics are reported in the first row of Table 6.4. An extension of Franses and Vogelsang to the case of a structural change in trend is made in Nunes and Rodrigues (2011). They consider the null hypothesis of seasonal unit roots under the presence or absence of structural changes.

Franses and Vogelsang (1998) also consider the innovation outlier model, the simplest form of which is

$$(1 - \alpha B^4)\left(y_t - \sum_{s=1}^{4} \mu_s D_{st} - \sum_{s=1}^{4} \kappa_s DU_{st} \right) = u_t, \ u_t \sim \text{iid}(0, \sigma_u^2).$$

In this model, the effects of structural changes are gradual and depend on the dynamics represented by the polynomial $1 - \alpha z^4$. Under $\alpha = 1$,

$$y_t = y_{t-4} + \sum_{s=1}^{4} \kappa_s \Delta_4 DU_{st} + u_t,$$

whereas under $|\alpha| < 1$

$$y_t = \alpha y_{t-4} + (1 - \alpha B^4)^{-1}\left(\sum_{s=1}^{4} \mu_s D_{st} - \sum_{s=1}^{4} \kappa_s DU_{st} \right) + u_t.$$

When serial correlations are introduced into $\{y_t\}$, these two models are nested into

$$\Delta_4 y_t = \pi_1 x_{t-1}^{(1)} + \pi_2 x_{t-1}^{(2)} + \pi_3 x_{t-2}^{(3)} + \pi_4 x_{t-1}^{(3)}$$

$$+ \sum_{j=1}^{k} \hat{c}_j \Delta_4 y_{t-j} + \sum_{s=1}^{4} \mu_s D_{st} + \sum_{s=1}^{4} \delta_s DU_{st} + \sum_{s=1}^{4} \omega_s \Delta_4 DU_{st} + u_t,$$

$$(6.30)$$

where $x_{t-1}^{(1)}$, $x_{t-1}^{(2)}$, and $x_{t-1}^{(3)}$ are defined as for equation (6.13). As in the additive model, the minimums of the t-ratios and the maximum of the F-statistic are used to test for seasonal unit roots. Asymptotic distributions of these test statistics are reported in the second row of Table 6.4.

Using Model (6.30), Franses and Vogelsang (1998) suggest estimating T_B by maximizing the F-statistic for the coefficients $\{\delta_s\}$ over various values of the change date (i.e., the estimated T_B is $\arg\max_{T_B} F_\delta(T_B)$). Using this estimated change date, the t-ratios and F-statistics can be calculated. Their limiting distributions are reported in Table 6.4 for both the additive and innovation outlier models. The relative merits of the method using the maximum F-statistic for the coefficients $\{\delta_s\}$ over the one described earlier are not reported in Franses and Vogelsang. However, Harvey, Leybourne, and Newbold (2002), make the following three claims: (i) Franses and Vogelsang's minimum t-ratios and maximum F-statistic are severely oversized for both the additive and innovation outlier models, especially when the magnitudes of structural changes are large; (ii) the t-ratios and F-statistic using the estimated change data perform well under the null for the additive outlier model; and (iii) the t-ratios and F-statistic using the estimated change data tend to be oversized for the innovation outlier model. For the innovation outlier model, Harvey, Leybourne, and Newbold report improved size properties when $4 + \arg\max F_\delta(T_B)$ is used as an estimator of T_B.[11]

Balcombe (1999) studies the same problem as Franses and Vogelsang (1998), but considers models with structural changes in trend. Following Zivot and Andrews (1992) (see Subsection 3.2.1), he proposes using the minimum t-ratios and maximum F-statistics of the HEGY regression.

Following the spirit of BLS (see Subsection 3.2.1), Smith and Taylor (2001) propose recursive and rolling tests of the seasonal unit root hypothesis. Assuming $\alpha(z) = 1 - \sum_{j=1}^{4} \alpha_{j,4\tau+s} z^j$ for Model (6.16),[12] they consider the null

---

[11] See also Popp (2007) for similar results.
[12] In fact, Smith and Taylor (2001) consider the model with an arbitrary number of seasons. For expositional convenience, it is assumed here that the number of seasons is four.

hypothesis $H_0 : \alpha(z) = 1 - z^4$ against the alternative hypothesis that the seasonal process $\{y_{4\tau+s}\}$ displays stationary autoregressive behavior over part of its history at either the zero or seasonal frequencies. The test statistics they consider are similar to those of BLS.

Franses, Hoek, and Paap (1997) take a Bayesian approach to seasonal unit root testing under mean shifts. They consider the model

$$y_t = \sum_{s=1}^{4} \mu_s D_{st} + \sum_{s=1}^{4} \kappa_s DU_{st} + \beta t + x_t$$

and devise posterior odds ratio tests for seasonal unit roots using the HEGY framework for $\{x_t\}$. They assume a normal pdf for the initial observations, but adopt flat priors for the other parameters including those for the mean shifts $\{\kappa_s\}$. They show that neglecting seasonal mean shifts may incorrectly suggest the presence of seasonal unit roots as in classical approaches and that the inclusion of an unknown change point provides more appropriate results. Applications of their method to three aggregate consumption series demonstrate that the hypothesis of seasonal unit roots can be rejected for two of them when seasonal mean shifts are allowed. However, it should be noted that criticisms of the Bayesian approach discussed in Section 4.6 also apply to these results: therefore care must be taken in interpreting these results.

6.4.3 Seasonal Stationarity Tests in the Presence of Structural Changes

Busetti and Harvey (2003b) assume the DGP

$$y_t = \mu + x_t'\varepsilon + f_t'\gamma_t + \mathbf{1}\{t > \lambda T\}f_t'\theta + e_t, \ (t = 1, \ldots, T; \ 0 < \lambda < 1),$$

$$(6.31)$$

which is the same as equation (6.28) if the dummy variable $\mathbf{1}\{t > \lambda T\}$ is absent. For the cases of both a known and unknown change fraction λ, Busetti and Harvey introduce a test statistic for the null hypothesis $H_0 : \tau^2 = 0$ and derive its limiting distribution. The main idea behind their test statistic is to combine the evidence in the two subsamples $\{1, \ldots, [\lambda T]\}$ and $\{[\lambda T] + 1, \ldots, T\}$.

Busetti and Taylor (2003a) consider Model (6.31). They find that the locally most powerful invariant test statistic for the null hypothesis $H_0 : \tau^2 = 0$ follows in the limit the well-known Cramér-von Mises limiting distribution multiplied by a factor stemming from the presence of a structural change. Using the least squares estimator of λ, they modify the test statistic such that it has the Cramér-von Mises distribution in the limit.

6.5   Periodic Integration

Autoregressive models that have seasonally varying parameters are called PAR models. The PAR model has been used to capture seasonality present in the data and is regarded as a viable alternative to the seasonal ARIMA model, though there are far fewer applications of the PAR model in the literature. The reader is referred to Franses (1996) and Ghysels and Osborn (2001) for an introduction to the PAR process. This section introduces several methods that can be used to test for a unit root and for the null hypothesis of stationarity in the PAR model.

Boswijk and Franses (1995)[13] consider the PAR model of order one,

$$y_t = \alpha_s y_{t-1} + u_t, \; u_t \sim \text{iid}(0, \sigma_u^2), \; (s = 1, \ldots, 4; \; t = 1, \ldots, T), \quad (6.32)$$

where the AR coefficients $\{\alpha_s\}$ change over s. Letting $Y_\tau = (Y_{1\tau}, Y_{2\tau}, Y_{3\tau}, Y_{4\tau})'$ where $Y_{s\tau}$ is the observation from season s in year τ, this model can be written as

$$A_0 Y_\tau = A_1 Y_{\tau-1} + u_\tau, \quad (6.33)$$

where

$$A_0 = \begin{bmatrix} 1 & 0 & 0 & 0 \\ -\alpha_2 & 1 & 0 & 0 \\ 0 & -\alpha_3 & 1 & 0 \\ 0 & 0 & -\alpha_4 & 1 \end{bmatrix}, \; A_1 = \begin{bmatrix} 0 & 0 & 0 & \alpha_1 \\ 0 & 0 & 0 & 0 \\ 0 & 0 & 0 & 0 \\ 0 & 0 & 0 & 0 \end{bmatrix}.$$

The vector process $\{Y_\tau\}$ is said to be periodically integrated if the characteristic equation

$$|A_0 - A_1 z| = 1 - \alpha_1 \alpha_2 \alpha_3 \alpha_4 z = 0$$

has a root equal to one. That is, the vector process is periodically integrated when $\alpha_1 \alpha_2 \alpha_3 \alpha_4 = 1$. When periodically integrated, both $\{Y_{i\tau}\}$ $(i = 1, \ldots, 4)$ and $\{y_t\}$ show trending behavior that is found in unit root processes (see Figures 1.8 and 1.9 of Ghysels and Osborn, 2001).

Model (6.33) can be rewritten as

$$Y_\tau = \Phi(B)^{-1} u_\tau, \; \text{with} \; \Phi(B) = A_0 - A_1 B$$

or equivalently as

$$\det(\Phi(B)) Y_\tau = \Phi(B)^* u_\tau,$$

where $\Phi(B)^*$ is the adjoint matrix of $\Phi(B)$. For Model (6.33),

$$\det(\Phi(z)) = 1 - \alpha_1 \alpha_2 \alpha_3 \alpha_4 z^4$$

---

[13]   See also Boswijk and Franses (1996) for a related discussion.

and

$$
\Phi(z)^* = \begin{bmatrix} 1 & \alpha_1\alpha_3\alpha_4 z^4 & \alpha_1\alpha_4 z^4 & \alpha_1 z^4 \\ \alpha_2 & 1 & \alpha_1\alpha_2\alpha_4 z^4 & \alpha_1\alpha_2 z^4 \\ \alpha_2\alpha_3 & \alpha_3 & 1 & \alpha_1\alpha_2\alpha_3 z^4 \\ \alpha_2\alpha_3\alpha_4 & \alpha_3\alpha_4 & \alpha_4 & 1 \end{bmatrix}.
$$

These relations show that each component of ΔY_τ $(= Y_\tau - Y_{\tau-1})$ is a stationary process when $\alpha_1\alpha_2\alpha_3\alpha_4 = 1$. However, this does not imply that $\{\Delta Y_\tau\}$ is a stationary and invertible vector process. Because $\Phi(1)^*$ is a singular matrix, $\{\Delta Y_\tau\}$ is indeed a noninvertible vector process. By contrast, when the nonstationary seasonal process (considered in Section 6.2)

$$
y_t = \alpha_S y_{t-S} + u_t, \ \alpha_S = 1, \ (t = S+1, \ldots, T)
$$

is written in a vector format as for relation (6.33), the seasonal differencing results in a stationary and invertible vector process. Thus, seasonal and periodic integration should be distinguished. Ghysels and Osborn (2001) discuss this point in greater detail.

Boswijk and Franses (1995) consider testing the null hypothesis $H_0 : g(\alpha) = \alpha_1\alpha_2\alpha_3\alpha_4 = 1$ against the alternative $H_0 : |g(\alpha)| < 1$. To this end, Boswijk and Franses rewrite Model (6.32) as

$$
y_t = \sum_{s=1}^{4} D_{st}\alpha_s y_{t-1} + u_t, \tag{6.34}
$$

where D_{st} is the quarterly dummy that takes the value one when t corresponds to season s and is zero otherwise. This model can be written under the null restriction as

$$
y_t = D_{1t}\alpha_1 y_{t-1} + D_{2t}\alpha_2 y_{t-1} + D_{3t}\alpha_3 y_{t-1} + D_{4t}(\alpha_1\alpha_2\alpha_3)^{-1} y_{t-1} + u_t, \tag{6.35}
$$

which can be estimated by the nonlinear least squares method. The LR test statistic for the null hypothesis is formulated as

$$
LR = T \log\left(\frac{SSR_R}{SSR_U}\right),
$$

where SSR_R is the sum of squared residuals from the restricted model (6.35) and SSR_U that from the unrestricted model (6.34). A one-sided version of this test statistic is

$$
LR_\tau = \text{sign}\,(g(\hat{a}) - 1) LR^{1/2},
$$

where $\text{sign}(x) = 1$ if $x \geq 0$ and $\text{sign}(x) = -1$ if $x < 0$. Boswijk and Franses show that the one-sided LR test statistic has the same limiting distribution as the Dickey-Fuller t-ratio.

Franses (1994) rewrites Model (6.33) as

$$\Delta Y_\tau = A Y_{\tau-1} + v_\tau, \tag{6.36}$$

where $A = A_0^{-1} A_1 - I$ and $v_\tau = A_0^{-1} u_\tau$. Observing that the rank of matrix A is three when $\alpha_1 \alpha_2 \alpha_3 \alpha_4 = 1$, he suggests using Johansen's (1988) test for cointegration to test the null hypothesis $H_0 : \alpha_1 \alpha_2 \alpha_3 \alpha_4 = 1$. However, because Franses's approach involves more parameters than that of Boswijk and Franses (1995), it is expected to yield lower power. Boswijk, Franses, and Haldrup (1997) further study implications of the rank of matrix A in Model (6.36). They show that the rank is equivalent to the number of cointegrating relations among the components of Y_τ.

Using HEGY's framework, Ghysels, Hall, and Lee (1996) propose test statistics that allow a researcher to test for the presence of zero and seasonal frequency unit roots in the PAR model. They consider the model

$$\Delta_4 y_t = \sum_{s=1}^{4} D_{st} \pi_{s1} x_{t-1}^{(1)} + \sum_{s=1}^{4} D_{st} \pi_{s2} x_{t-1}^{(2)} + \sum_{s=1}^{4} D_{st} \pi_{s3} x_{t-2}^{(3)}$$

$$+ \sum_{s=1}^{4} D_{st} \pi_{s4} x_{t-1}^{(3)} + u_t, \quad u_t \sim \text{iid}(0, \sigma_u^2),$$

where $\{D_{st}\}$ is a sequence of quarterly dummies and $x_t^{(1)}$, $x_t^{(2)}$, and $x_t^{(3)}$ are as defined right after equation (6.13). Lagged differences of $\Delta_4 y_t$, with seasonal coefficients can be added as regressors to incorporate further serial correlations in $\{y_t\}$. Ghysels, Hall, and Lee consider the null hypothesis $H_0 : \pi_{si} = 0$ ($s = 1, \ldots, 4; i = 1, \ldots, 4$) and propose using the Wald test principle for this null hypothesis. Under the null hypothesis, seasonal differencing yields a periodic-stationary process. Ghysels, Hall, and Lee also consider the null hypothesis $H_0 : \pi_{si} = 0$ ($s = 1, \ldots, 4; i = 2, 3, 4$), which corresponds to the presence of seasonal roots -1, $\pm i$. An intercept and a linear time trend with seasonal coefficients can also be added to their model with some changes in the limiting distributions of the Wald test statistics. Because the Wald test statistics are based on an overly parametrized model, Ghysels, Hall, and Lee also test the null hypotheses of real and complex unit roots using less parametrized models. The reader is referred to Ghysels, Hall, and Lee for details.

Castro and Osborn (2008) study the limiting distributions of the HEGY test statistics when the true DGP is a periodically integrated process. Each of them is shown to be a function of the limiting distribution of the Dickey-Fuller t-ratio.

Kurozumi (2002a) tests the null of periodic stationarity against the alternative of periodic integration. The simplest model he considers is

$$y_t = r_t + e_t;$$

$$r_t = \alpha_s r_{t-1} + u_t, \ u_t \sim \text{iid}(0, \sigma_u^2),$$

where $\{e_t\}$ is a periodically stationary process. Assuming $\alpha_1\alpha_2\alpha_3\alpha_4 = 1$, he devises an LM test for the null hypothesis $H_0 : \sigma_u^2 = 0$ along the same lines as in KPSS. Under the null hypothesis, $\{y_t\}$ is periodically stationary. But when the null hypothesis is violated, $\{y_t\}$ is periodically nonstationary. His test statistics depend on the values of α_1, α_2, α_3, and α_4. To overcome this difficulty, he suggests using the estimators of these parameters under the restriction $\alpha_1\alpha_2\alpha_3\alpha_4 = 1$ or, alternatively, taking the supremum of the LM statistics over the parameter spaces of α_1, α_2, α_3, and α_4 again with the restriction $\alpha_1\alpha_2\alpha_3\alpha_4 = 1$. In finite samples, Kurozumi's test statistics show reasonable power and size.

6.6 Evidence on Seasonal Unit Roots

When using seasonally unadjusted data, one may rightfully wonder whether the data have seasonal unit roots that warrant seasonal differencing as recommended by Box and Jenkins (1976). There are a few related results, though the list here is admittedly incomplete. Otto and Wirjanto (1990) apply the HEGY test to Canadian macroeconomic time series and find some evidence supporting the presence of seasonal unit roots. By contrast, applying the same method, Lee and Siklos (1991) find little evidence supporting the presence of seasonal unit roots in Canadian macroeconomic time series. Of course, the data used for both the studies are different in terms of kinds and sampling periods. In addition, HEGY report evidence of seasonal unit roots for several of 14 GDP series, but the evidence weakens when structural changes in the level are incorporated according to Franses and Vogelsang (1998).

6.7 Summary and Further Remarks

This chapter introduced testing procedures for seasonal unit roots: DHF, HEGY, and their extensions. Seasonal stationarity tests and seasonal unit root and stationarity tests under structural changes were also introduced. In addition, this chapter introduced several methods that can be used to test for a unit root in the PAR model, as well as empirical results examining seasonal unit roots.

Among the seasonal unit root tests introduced in this chapter, HEGY seems to be the most famous and popular. Because Smith and Taylor's test (1998) improves on HEGY, it also deserves attention in applications. Unfortunately, DHF's test cannot distinguish between unit roots at zero frequency and seasonal frequencies. When DHF's test does not reject the null, it is difficult to interpret the results.

If one wants to test the null hypothesis of stationarity in the presence of seasonality, CH's procedure is recommended. It tests the null hypothesis of no unit roots at seasonal frequencies against the alternative of a unit root at either a single seasonal frequency or at a set of seasonal frequencies.

To test for seasonal unit roots in the presence of structural changes, Franses and Vogelsang (1998) provide fairly comprehensive procedures that are notably useful in applications. Busetti and Harvey's (2003b) approach can test the null of stationarity in the presence of structural changes and seasonality and is complementary to Franses and Vogelsang's tests.

The PAR model is a viable alternative to the seasonal ARIMA model. To test for a unit root in the PAR model, procedures due to Boswijk and Franses (1995) and Ghysels, Hall, and Lee (1996) are useful. When the null hypothesis is stationarity, Kurozumi's (2002a) test can be used.

7 Panel Unit Roots

7.1 Introduction

In recent years, there has been much interest in nonstationary panels at both the theoretical and empirical levels. Today in macroeconomics, international finance, and other areas it is quite common to use panel data rather than individual time series, probably because of the developments of econometric tools for nonstationary panels. The initial, main motivation for using panel data was to increase the power of unit root tests because univariate unit root tests have low power as discussed briefly in Subsection 2.3.4. Indeed, Levin and Lin's (1992) and subsequent panel unit root tests demonstrate by simulation the power advantage of using panel data.

The literature on nonstationary panels that began from the power consideration has developed beyond that motivation and brought up some challenging issues that could not be conceived in univariate testing. In conventional panel data analysis, cross-sectional units are assumed to be independent, a reasonable approximation to reality. In using macropanels, however, independence is an obviously unrealistic assumption, and much effort has been expended to cope with this challenge. New, useful tools have emerged along the way, which will also help conventional, micropanel data analysis when the assumption of independence is deemed to be inappropriate. Moreover, in nonstationary panels, there is the possibility of cross-sectional cointegration, which complicates inferential procedures considerably. Some procedures have been developed to deal with this situation, but none is totally successful in my opinion.

The developments of the literature on panel unit roots resemble those of univariate, nonstationary time series that we have seen in Chapter 2. From reading Chapter 2, one may realize that the research paradigm for nonstationary panels is similar to that for univariate nonstationary time series. However, the literature on panel unit roots is still much thinner than that on univariate unit roots. Whether the panel literature will become as mature as that on univariate unit roots in the future remains to be seen.

This chapter discusses developments in the econometrics of panel unit roots. Earlier survey papers such as Banerjee (1999), Baltagi and Kao (2001), Phillips and Moon (2000), Choi (2006a), and Breitung and Pesaran (2008) supplement this chapter. This chapter is an expanded and updated version of Choi (2006a). It begins with discussions on panel unit roots and stationarity tests for independent panels and extends these discussions to cross-sectionally correlated panels. Panel unit roots and stationarity tests under structural changes are then introduced, and those for seasonal panel unit roots are also be discussed.

There are many empirical papers that use methods introduced in this chapter. Research topics that have used methods for panel unit roots include tests of the purchasing power parity hypothesis (e.g., Oh, 1996), growth and convergence (e.g., Estrin, Urga, and Lazarova, 2001), inflation-rate convergence (e.g., Culver and Papell, 1997), health care expenditures (e.g., McCoskey and Selden, 1998) and hysteresis in unemployment (e.g., Song and Wu, 1997). Admittedly, this list is very incomplete, but the full list is beyond the scope of this book.

7.2 Unit Root Tests for Independent Panels

This section introduces unit root tests for independent panels that have often been cited in the literature. These tests are often called the first-generation panel unit root tests. In practice, panels from macroeconomics and international finance are seldom cross-sectionally independent. However, as seen in Section 7.5, panel unit root tests for cross-sectionally correlated panels are extensions of those for independent panels. Therefore, it is important to study unit root tests for independent panels.

The three major tests considered in this section are the pooled t-test proposed by Levin, Lin, and Chu (2002; LLC hereafter),[1] the averaged t-test of Im, Pesaran, and Shin (2003; IPS hereafter), and the combination tests of Maddala and Wu (1999; MW hereafter) and Choi (2001). These tests are developed under the assumption of large numbers of time series observations and cross-sectional units (i.e., large T and large N). Quah (1994) also studies panel unit root tests under the same assumption, but the model he considers seems to be quite specialized compared to those considered in the aforementioned works.

In addition to the tests mentioned thus far, several other panel unit root tests are designed for finite T and large N, such as in the conventional dynamic panel literature.[2] Breitung and Meyer (1994); Harris and Tzavalis (1999, 2004);

---

[1] The LLC test is based on Levin and Lin (1992) but improves on it in the sense that heterogeneity of cross-sectional units is allowed.

[2] See Baltagi (2005) and Hsiao (2003) for the literature on dynamic panels.

Binder, Hsiao, and Pesaran (2005); De Wachter, Harris, and Tzavalis (2007); Kruiniger (2008); and De Blander and Dhaene (2012) belong to this category.[3] For these tests, homogeneity of slope coefficients should be imposed. The three tests mentioned in the previous paragraph retain more general specifications while requiring a large number of time series observations.

The three tests can be introduced in a unified manner using the AR models

$$\Delta y_{it} = \rho_i y_{i,t-1} + \sum_{j=1}^{k_i} \varphi_{ij} \Delta y_{i,t-j} + \mu_i + u_{it},$$

$$(i = 1, \ldots, N; t = k_i + 2, \ldots, T), \tag{7.1}$$

and

$$\Delta y_{it} = \rho_i y_{i,t-1} + \sum_{j=1}^{k_i} \varphi_{ij} \Delta y_{i,t-j} + \mu_i + \beta_i t + u_{it},$$

$$(i = 1, \ldots, N; t = k_i + 2, \ldots, T), \tag{7.2}$$

where $u_{it} \sim \text{iid}(0, \sigma_i^2)$ for every i and t. Note that $\{y_{it}\}_{t=k_i+2}^{T}, i \in \{1, \ldots, N\}$ are independent. Although LLC use the AR(1) models with ARMA residuals, the AR models here and their ARMA models do not have any differences for unit root testing because LLC also use the AR models as approximations to their ARMA models. The AR orders $\{k_i\}$ are assumed to be known, and in practice, can be estimated using information criteria and/or sequential testing. In addition, for all i, the characteristic roots of Models (7.1) and (7.2) are assumed to lie outside the unit circle with possibly one root taking value one.

In matrix notation, Model (7.1) is written as

$$\Delta \mathbf{y}_{iT} = \rho_i \mathbf{y}_{i,-1,T} + \mathbf{Q}_{iT} \gamma_i + u_{iT}, \ (i = 1, \ldots, N),$$

$\Delta \mathbf{y}_{iT} = [\Delta y_{i,k_i+2}, \ldots, \Delta y_{i,T}]', \ \mathbf{Q}_{iT} = (\mathbf{1}, \Delta \mathbf{y}_{i,-1,T}, \Delta \mathbf{y}_{i,-2,T}, \ldots, \Delta \mathbf{y}_{i,-k_i,T}),$
$\mathbf{1} = [1, \ldots, 1]', \mathbf{y}_{i,-l,T} = [y_{i,k_i+2-l}, \ldots, y_{i,T-l}]',$ and $\gamma_i = (\mu_i, \varphi_{i1}, \ldots, \varphi_{ik_i})'.$
In the same manner, Model (7.2) is written as

$$\Delta \mathbf{y}_{iT} = \rho_i \mathbf{y}_{i,-1,T} + \ddot{\mathbf{Q}}_{iT} \delta_i + u_{iT}, \ (i = 1, \ldots, N),$$

where $\ddot{\mathbf{Q}}_{iT} = (\mathbf{1}, \mathbf{t}, \Delta \mathbf{y}_{i,-1,T}, \Delta \mathbf{y}_{i,-2,T}, \ldots, \Delta \mathbf{y}_{i,-k_i,T}), \ \mathbf{t} = [k_i + 2, \ldots, T]',$ and $\delta_i = (\mu_i, \beta_i, \varphi_{i1}, \ldots, \varphi_{ik_i})'.$
The null hypothesis for the panel unit root tests is

$$H_0 : \rho_i = 0 \text{ for all } i. \tag{7.3}$$

---

[3] Madsen (2010) derives the asymptotic local power of Breitung and Meyer's (1994) and Harris and Tzavalis's (1999) tests. He reports that Breitung and Meyer's test has higher asymptotic local power than that of Harris and Tzavalis'

The alternative hypothesis is different depending on the test. For the LLC test, it is

$$H_1 : \rho_1 = \cdots = \rho_N = \rho \text{ and } \rho < 0 \qquad (7.4)$$

and for the IPS test

$$H_1 : \rho_i < 0 \text{ for } i \leq N_0 \text{ and } \rho_i = 0 \text{ for } i \geq N_0 + 1, \ldots, N. \qquad (7.5)$$

Because the LLC test has discriminating power for alternative hypothesis (7.5), the distinction between the alternative hypotheses may not be important. However, it is important to realize that the rejection of the null hypothesis does not imply an alternative hypothesis (7.4) for the LLC test. Indeed, when the null hypothesis is rejected, we can only say that a large number of individual time series do not have a unit root. This is discussed further in Subsection 7.2.4.

This section mainly uses the so-called sequential asymptotics, where $T \to \infty$ and then $N \to \infty$, because this approach is intuitive, practical, and easy to understand. The joint asymptotics where T and N are sent to infinity simultaneously or the diagonal asymptotics where N is assumed to be a function of T can also be considered. However, the limiting results from these approaches are essentially the same as those of the sequential asymptotics for the asymptotic results we discuss in this chapter, but require more stringent moment conditions. The reader is referred to Phillips and Moon (1999) for discussions of the sequential, joint, and diagonal asymptotics in relation to panel data analysis.

7.2.1   LLC Test

I introduce the LLC test for Model (7.1) first and then discuss its extension to Model (7.2). For the LLC test, I estimate the variance of the error terms, σ_i^2, by the time series OLS regression on each individual. This gives an estimator of σ_i^2

$$\hat{\sigma}_{iT}^2 = \frac{1}{T - k_i - 1} \left(\mathbf{M}_{Q_{iT}} \Delta \mathbf{y}_{iT} - \hat{\rho}_{iT} \mathbf{M}_{Q_{iT}} \mathbf{y}_{i,-1,T} \right)'$$
$$\times \left(\mathbf{M}_{Q_{iT}} \Delta \mathbf{y}_{iT} - \hat{\rho}_{iT} \mathbf{M}_{Q_{iT}} \mathbf{y}_{i,-1,T} \right), \qquad (7.6)$$

where $\mathbf{M}_{Q_{iT}} = I - \mathbf{Q}_{iT} \left(\mathbf{Q}_{iT}' \mathbf{Q}_{iT} \right)^{-1} \mathbf{Q}_{iT}'$ and $\hat{\rho}_{iT} = \frac{\mathbf{y}_{i,-1,T}' \mathbf{M}_{Q_{iT}} \Delta \mathbf{y}_{iT}}{\mathbf{y}_{i,-1,T}' \mathbf{M}_{Q_{iT}} \mathbf{y}_{i,-1,T}}$. Once normalized by $\hat{\sigma}_{iT}$, every individual time series has a common residual variance equal to one. LLC consider the following t-statistic using the normalized data

$$t_{NT} = \frac{\hat{\rho}_{NT}^p}{\sqrt{\hat{\sigma}_{NT}^2 \left(\sum_{i=1}^{N} \mathbf{y}_{i,-1,T}' \mathbf{M}_{Q_{iT}} \mathbf{y}_{i,-1,T} / \hat{\sigma}_{iT}^2 \right)^{-1}}} \qquad (7.7)$$

for null hypothesis (7.3). In (7.7), $\hat{\rho}_{NT}^{p}$ is the pooled OLS estimator of ρ $(= \rho_1 = \cdots = \rho_N)$ defined by

$$\hat{\rho}_{NT}^{p} = \frac{\sum_{i=1}^{N} \mathbf{y}_{i,-1,T}' \, \mathbf{M}_{Q_{iT}} \, \Delta \mathbf{y}_{iT} / \hat{\sigma}_{iT}^{2}}{\sum_{i=1}^{N} \mathbf{y}_{i,-1,T}' \mathbf{M}_{Q_{iT}} \mathbf{y}_{i,-1,T} / \hat{\sigma}_{iT}^{2}}$$

and

$$\hat{\sigma}_{NT}^{2} = \frac{1}{N\left(T - \overline{k} - 1\right)} \sum_{i=1}^{N} \left(\mathbf{M}_{Q_{iT}} \, \Delta \mathbf{y}_{iT} - \hat{\rho}_{NT}^{p} \mathbf{M}_{Q_{iT}} \mathbf{y}_{i,-1,T}\right)'$$

$$\times \left(\mathbf{M}_{Q_{iT}} \, \Delta \mathbf{y}_{iT} - \hat{\rho}_{NT}^{p} \mathbf{M}_{Q_{iT}} \mathbf{y}_{i,-1,T}\right) / \hat{\sigma}_{iT}^{2},$$

with $\overline{k}$ denoting the sample mean of $\{k_i\}$. It follows that $\hat{\rho}_{NT}^{p} \xrightarrow{p} 0$ and $\hat{\sigma}_{NT}^{2} \xrightarrow{p} 1$ under null hypothesis (7.3) as $T \to \infty$ and $N \to \infty$.

It is convenient for later analysis to rewrite (7.7) as

$$t_{NT} = \frac{\sum_{i=1}^{N} \mathbf{y}_{i,-1,T}' \mathbf{M}_{Q_{iT}} \, \Delta \mathbf{y}_{iT} / \hat{\sigma}_{iT}^{2}}{\sqrt{\hat{\sigma}_{NT}^{2} \sum_{i=1}^{N} \mathbf{y}_{i,-1,T}' \mathbf{M}_{Q_{iT}} \mathbf{y}_{i,-1,T} / \hat{\sigma}_{iT}^{2}}}.$$

Using this formula, we obtain under null hypothesis (7.3), as $T \to \infty$,

$$t_{NT} \Rightarrow \frac{\sum_{i=1}^{N} s_i \int_0^1 \overline{W}_i(r) \, dW_i(r)}{\sqrt{\hat{\sigma}_N^2 \sum_{i=1}^{N} s_i^2 \int_0^1 \overline{W}_i^2(r) \, dr}} = \zeta_N, \text{ say}, \tag{7.8}$$

where $\overline{W}_i(r) = W_i(r) - \int_0^1 W_i(s) \, ds$, $W_i(r)$ is Brownian motion, $\hat{\sigma}_N^2$ is the weak limit of $\hat{\sigma}_{NT}^2$ as $T \to \infty$, and $s_i = \sigma_{li}/\sigma_i$ with σ_{li}^2 being the long-run variance of Δy_{it}. Because $E\left(\int_0^1 \overline{W}_i(r) \, dW_i(r)\right) = -\frac{1}{2}$,

$$\frac{1}{N} \sum_{i=1}^{N} s_i \int_0^1 \overline{W}_i(r) \, dW_i(r) \xrightarrow{p} \lim_{N \to \infty} \left(-\frac{1}{2N} \sum_{i=1}^{N} s_i\right) \text{ as } N \to \infty \tag{7.9}$$

by the law of large numbers for a sequence of independent random variables. In addition, the law of large numbers applied to the denominator in relation (7.8) gives

$$\frac{1}{N} \sum_{i=1}^{N} s_i^2 \int_0^1 \overline{W}_i^2(r) \, dr \xrightarrow{p} \lim_{N \to \infty} \frac{1}{6N} \sum_{i=1}^{N} s_i^2 \tag{7.10}$$

because $E\left(\int_0^1 \overline{W}_i^2(r) \, dr\right) = \frac{1}{6}$. Assuming that the limits in relations (7.9) and (7.10) exist, we infer from (7.9) and (7.10) that the pooled t-statistic diverges in probability. Thus, the t-ratio cannot be used as it is and requires a modification.

To pursue a modification of the pooled t-test, apply the central limit theorem to the demeaned numerator in relation (7.8). This yields, as $N \to \infty$,

$$\frac{1}{\sqrt{N}} \sum_{i=1}^{N} s_i \left(\int_0^1 \overline{W}_i(r) \, dW_i(r) - E \left(\int_0^1 \overline{W}_i(r) \, dW_i(r) \right) \right)$$

$$= \frac{1}{\sqrt{N}} \sum_{i=1}^{N} s_i \left(\int_0^1 \overline{W}_i(r) \, dW_i(r) + \frac{1}{2} \right)$$

$$\Rightarrow N \left(0, \lim_{N \to \infty} \frac{1}{12N} \sum_{i=1}^{N} s_i^2 \right). \quad (7.11)$$

Note that $\text{Var} \left(\int_0^1 \overline{W}_i(r) \, dW_i(r) \right) = \frac{1}{12}$. Relations (7.10) and (7.11) imply

$$\zeta_N + \frac{1}{2} \frac{\sum_{i=1}^{N} s_i \int_0^1 \overline{W}_i(r) \, dW_i(r)}{\sqrt{\hat{\sigma}_N^2 \sum_{i=1}^{N} s_i^2 \int_0^1 \overline{W}_i^2(r) \, dr}} \Rightarrow N \left(0, \frac{1}{2} \right). \quad (7.12)$$

Asymptotic results (7.10), (7.11), and (7.12) indicate that the mean adjustment alone is not sufficient for the pooled t-ratio to have a standard normal distribution in the limit and that a scale adjustment is also needed. If we assume $T = \infty$, the full modification should be of the form[4]

$$\frac{\sum_{i=1}^{N} \left(\mathbf{y}_{i,-1,T}' \mathbf{M}_{Q_{iT}} \Delta \mathbf{y}_{iT} / \hat{\sigma}_{iT}^2 + \frac{1}{2} T \hat{s}_i \right)}{\sqrt{\frac{1}{2}} \sqrt{\hat{\sigma}_{NT}^2 \sum_{i=1}^{N} \mathbf{y}_{i,-1,T}' \mathbf{M}_{Q_{iT}} \mathbf{y}_{i,-1,T} / \hat{\sigma}_{iT}^2}}$$

$$= \frac{t_{NT}}{\sqrt{\frac{1}{2}}} - \frac{\left(-\frac{1}{2} \right) T \sum_{i=1}^{N} \hat{s}_i}{\sqrt{\frac{1}{2}} \sqrt{\hat{\sigma}_{NT}^2 \sum_{i=1}^{N} \mathbf{y}_{i,-1,T}' \mathbf{M}_{Q_{iT}} \mathbf{y}_{i,-1,T} / \hat{\sigma}_{iT}^2}}, \quad (7.13)$$

where $\hat{s}_i = \hat{\sigma}_{iT} / \hat{\sigma}_{li}$, with $\hat{\sigma}_{li}^2$ being a consistent estimator of the long-run variance σ_{li}^2 that uses $\Delta y_{it} - \frac{1}{T-1} \sum_{i=2}^{T} \Delta y_{it}$. Using the same methods as earlier, we can show that the test statistic (7.13) has a standard normal distribution in the limit.

For the case of finite-sample time series, LLC propose to use the mean and variance adjustment factors calculated by simulation. Using μ_T^* as a mean adjustment factor instead of $-\frac{1}{2}$, and σ_T^* as a variance adjustment factor instead

---

[4] LLC use $T - \bar{k} - 1$ instead of T. Using T simplifies the discussion without bringing any changes in the limiting distribution.

Table 7.1. *Mean and standard deviation adjustments for the LLC test*

		Model (7.1)		Model (7.2)	
T	$\overline{k}$	μ_T^*	σ_T^*	μ_T^*	σ_T^*
30	10	-0.546	0.889	-0.674	0.949
50	12	-0.531	0.826	-0.614	0.818
100	15	-0.518	0.776	-0.566	0.695
250	20	-0.509	0.742	-0.533	0.603
∞		-0.500	0.707	-0.500	0.500

Note: reject null hypothesis (7.3) when the LLC test statistic is smaller than a critical value from the lower tail of a standard normal distribution.

of $\sqrt{\frac{1}{2}}$ in relation (7.13), the LLC test statistic for Model (7.1) using the finite-sample mean and variance adjustments is defined by

$$
LLC = \frac{t_{NT}}{\sigma_T^*} - \frac{\mu_T^* T \sum_{i=1}^{N} \hat{s}_i}{\sigma_T^* \sqrt{\hat{\sigma}_{NT}^2 \sum_{i=1}^{N} \mathbf{y}_{i,-1,T}' \mathbf{M}_{Q_{iT}} \mathbf{y}_{i,-1,T} / \hat{\sigma}_{iT}^2}}.
$$

Values of μ_T^* and σ_T^* for various T and $\overline{k}$ are simulated using generated normal numbers and reported in table 2 of LLC. Some of these values are reproduced in Table 7.1. Note that the reported values are for particular values of $\overline{k}$ and may not be accurate for other values.

The LLC test statistic for Model (7.2) is obtained in exactly the same manner by replacing $\mathbf{Q}_{iT}$ with $\ddot{\mathbf{Q}}_{iT}$, but the mean and variance adjustment factors should change because the demeaned and detrended Brownian motion emerges instead of the demeaned Brownian motion when T is sent to infinity. Values of the adjustment factors for various T and $\overline{k}$ are also reported in table 2 of LLC, some of which are reproduced in Table 7.1.

7.2.2 IPS Test

IPS employ the average of individual t-ratios for null hypothesis (7.3). LLC's assumption $u_{it} \sim \text{iid}(0, \sigma_i^2)$ is strengthened to $u_{it} \sim \text{iid} \, \mathbf{N}(0, \sigma_i^2)$, and the individual t-ratio is defined by

$$
t_{iT} = \frac{\hat{\rho}_{iT}}{\sqrt{\hat{\sigma}_{iT}^2 \left(\mathbf{y}_{i,-1,T}' \mathbf{M}_{Q_{iT}} \mathbf{y}_{i,-1,T} \right)^{-1}}},
$$

where $\hat{\rho}_{iT} = \frac{\mathbf{y}_{i,-1,T}' \mathbf{M}_{Q_{iT}} \Delta \mathbf{y}_{iT}}{\mathbf{y}_{i,-1,T}' \mathbf{M}_{Q_{iT}} \mathbf{y}_{i,-1,T}}$ and $\hat{\sigma}_{iT}^2$ is a consistent estimator of σ_i^2 defined by (7.6). The IPS $\bar{t}$-test statistic is the average of the individual augmented

Dickey-Fuller test statistics and is defined by

$$\bar{t}_{NT} = \frac{1}{N} \sum_{i=1}^{N} t_{iT}. \tag{7.14}$$

For fixed N, as $T \to \infty$,

$$\bar{t}_{NT} \Rightarrow \frac{1}{N} \sum_{i=1}^{N} \frac{\int_0^1 \overline{W}_i(r) \, dW_i(r)}{\sqrt{\int_0^1 \overline{W}_i^2(r) \, dr}}$$

under null hypothesis (7.3). This can be shown to have a degenerate distribution when N goes to infinity using the same arguments as for the LLC test. For the case of large N and T, IPS propose a modified averaged t-ratio

$$W_{\text{tbar}} = \frac{\sqrt{N} \left(\bar{t}_{NT} - \frac{1}{N} \sum_{i=1}^{N} E \left(t_{iT}(k_i, 0) \mid \rho_i = 0 \right) \right)}{\sqrt{\frac{1}{N} \sum_{i=1}^{N} \text{Var} \left(t_{iT}(k_i, 0) \mid \rho_i = 0 \right)}},$$

where $t_{iT}(k_i, 0)$ denotes the individual t-ratio using the AR order k_i and the restrictions $\varphi_{i1} = \ldots = \varphi_{ik_i} = 0$. In finite samples, the latter restrictions do not affect W_{tbar}. IPS report the moments $E \left(t_{iT}(k_i, 0) \mid \rho_i = 0 \right)$ and $\text{Var} \left(t_{iT}(k_i, 0) \mid \rho_i = 0 \right)$ for some fixed AR orders obtained by simulation for the case $\rho_i = 0$ for all i. Table 7.2 reproduces some of these figures. Because the moment estimates are calculated using a fixed AR order for every individual, heterogeneous AR orders may bring finite-sample size distortions. However, according to simulation results in IPS, the IPS test works reasonably well in finite samples unless the AR order for the t-ratios is taken too small. IPS show that

$$W_{\text{tbar}} \Rightarrow \mathbf{N}(0, 1) \text{ as } T \to \infty \text{ and } N \to \infty.$$

In using W_{tbar}, we reject the null hypothesis (7.3) when W_{tbar} takes a value smaller than a critical value from the lower tail of a standard normal distribution. For Model (7.2), we follow the same procedure, but use the moment estimates reported in table 3 of IPS (reproduced in Table 7.2 here).

IPS use the augmented Dickey-Fuller test statistic, but other test statistics can also be considered. Smith, Leybourne, Kim, and Newbold (2004) report that the MAX and weighted symmetric test statistics (see Subsection 2.4.3 and 2.4.6, respectively) yield higher power than the augmented Dickey-Fuller test statistic.

Table 7.2. *Simulated mean and variance for the IPS $\bar{t}$-test statistic*

		Model (7.1)		Model (7.2)	
T	k	Mean	Variance	Mean	Variance
30	0	−1.526	0.789	−2.172	0.690
	2	−1.460	0.865	−2.095	0.756
	4	−1.394	0.946	−2.009	0.845
	6	−1.331	1.023	−1.923	0.945
50	0	−1.527	0.760	−2.176	0.633
	2	−1.493	0.798	−2.137	0.661
	4	−1.454	0.842	−2.091	0.705
	6	−1.418	0.886	−2.042	0.753
100	0	−1.532	0.735	−2.177	0.597
	2	−1.514	0.754	−2.158	0.613
	4	−1.495	0.771	−2.135	0.629
	6	−1.476	0.795	−2.113	0.650

7.2.3   Combination Test

A panel unit root test that uses combination of p-values has been proposed independently by MW and Choi (2001). The main idea of the test is to combine the p-values obtained from applying a unit root test to each individual. Using p-values to devise test statistics has a long history in meta-analysis, which is concerned with quantitative methods for combining statistical evidence across independent studies. Hedges and Olkin (1985) provide an excellent introduction to meta-analysis.

Suppose that we reject the null hypothesis $H_0 : \rho_i = 0$ when a realized value of the unit root test statistic G_{iT} is smaller than a constant. The asymptotic p-value of G_{iT} is defined by

$$p_i = F(G_{iT}),$$

where $F(\cdot)$ denotes the distribution function of G_{iT} when T is sent to infinity. MW propose using Fisher's test statistic defined by

$$P = -2 \sum_{i=1}^{N} \log(p_i). \tag{7.15}$$

Choi (2001) considers various test statistics including the inverse chi-square test statistic, but the most promising one is the inverse normal test statistic defined by

$$Z = \frac{1}{\sqrt{N}} \sum_{i=1}^{N} \Phi^{-1}(p_i), \tag{7.16}$$

where $\Phi(\cdot)$ is the standard normal cdf.
For fixed N, as $T \to \infty$,

$$P \Rightarrow \chi_{2N}^2 \tag{7.17}$$

and

$$Z \Rightarrow N(0, 1). \tag{7.18}$$

Under null hypothesis (7.3) as $T \to \infty$ and then $N \to \infty$, we have

$$P \overset{p}{\to} \infty, \tag{7.19}$$

which implies that P does not have a nondegenerate distribution in the limit. Relation (7.19) indicates that we should modify P such that it has a nondegenerate limiting distribution. $E(-2\log(p_i)) = 2$ and $\text{Var}(-2\log(p_i)) = 4$, so Choi (2001) modifies the test statistic P as

$$P_{\mathrm{m}} = \frac{1}{2\sqrt{N}} \sum_{i=1}^{N} (-2\log(p_i) - 2) = -\frac{1}{\sqrt{N}} \sum_{i=1}^{N} (\log(p_i) + 1). \tag{7.20}$$

Applying the Lindeberg–Lévy central limit theorem to (7.20) gives under the null as $T \to \infty$ and then $N \to \infty$,

$$P_{\mathrm{m}} \Rightarrow N(0, 1).$$

The test statistic Z can be used for any N because relation (7.18) continues to hold when $N \to \infty$.

Critical values for the P and P_{m} test statistics are taken from the upper tail of the chi-square distribution and the lower tail of a standard normal distribution, respectively. In using Z, we reject null hypothesis (7.3) when its value is smaller than a critical value from the lower tail of a standard normal distribution.

For the underlying test statistic, G_{iT}, MW use the augmented Dickey-Fuller test statistic, whereas Choi (2001) uses ERS's Dickey-Fuller-GLS test statistic. Simulation results in Choi indicate that the Z test is more powerful in finite samples than other tests such as IPS when the Dickey-Fuller-GLS test statistic is used.

Advantages of the combination test are its flexibility and ease: the test can be used for heterogeneous panels without any difficulties, and moment calculations are not needed, unlike with the LLC and IPS tests. However, because calculation of the p-values entails errors, finite-sample size distortions can be observed. Choi (2006b) uses the simulation method of MacKinnon (1994) for the calculation of the p-values and finds that it improves size properties of the combination test significantly. See also Hanck (2008) for related discussion. Data for Choi's (2006b) simulation are generated according to

$$x_t = x_{(t-1)} + u_t, x_0 = 0, \ u_t \sim \text{iid} \, N(0, 1), \ (t = 1, \dots, T + 30),$$

and the last T data points are used. The following steps summarize MacKinnon's (1994) method for the combination test.

Step 1: Generate $\{x_t\}$ I times at $T = 30$, 50, 75, 100, 250, 500, and $1,000$ and calculate 399 equally spaced percentiles of the Dickey-Fuller-GLS$^\mu$ (or Dickey-Fuller-GLS$^\tau$) test. Choi (2006b) uses $I = 50,000$ at $T = 30, 50, 75, 100$; $I = 30,000$ at $T = 250, 500$; and $I = 20,000$ at $T = 1,000$.

Step 2: Repeat Step 1 50 times and record the percentiles. This gives a 7×50 by 399 matrix (denoted as $[q_j^p(T_k)]$ for $j = 1, \dots, 350$ and $p = 0.0025, 0.0050, \dots, 0.9975$). The first 50 rows of this matrix (corresponding to $k = 1$) are the percentiles at $T = 30$, for example.

Step 3: Estimate the regression equation

$$q_j^p(T_k) = \eta_\infty^p + \eta_1^p T_k^{-1} + \eta_2^p T_k^{-2} + \varepsilon_j, \ (j = 1, \dots, 350), \quad (7.21)$$

for each p using the GLS method that takes account of different variances at each T. This step gives a 399 by 3 coefficient matrix for equation (7.21).

For the Dickey-Fuller-GLS$^\mu$ test, for example, the 20th row of the coefficient matrix in Step 3 gives

$$\eta_\infty^{0.05} = -1.948; \ \eta_1^{0.05} = -19.36; \ \eta_2^{0.05} = 143.4.$$

Using these, the 5% percentile for the Dickey-Fuller-GLS$^\mu$ test at $T = 100$ is calculated as

$$-1.948 - \frac{19.36}{100} + \frac{143.4}{100^2} = -2.1273.$$

Thus, at any T, we may obtain 399 percentiles using the coefficient matrix from Step 3. These percentiles coupled with interpolation give p-values of the Dickey-Fuller-GLS test statistic.

7.2.4   Test Consistency

This subsection studies consistency of panel unit root tests.[5] It uses the statistic P_m as an example, but this analysis can easily be extended to other test statistics.

---

[5] This subsection is excerpted from Choi (2001).

Under alternative hypothesis (7.5), we have

$$P_{\mathrm{m}} = \sqrt{N} \left\{ \frac{1}{N} \sum_{i=1}^{N} (-\log(p_i)) - 1 \right\}$$

$$= \sqrt{N} \left\{ \frac{N_0}{N} \frac{1}{N_0} \sum_{i=1}^{N_0} (-\log(p_i)) - \frac{N - N_0}{N} \frac{1}{N - N_0} \sum_{i=N_0+1}^{N} \log(p_i) - 1 \right\}$$

$$= \sqrt{N} \left\{ \frac{N_0}{N} A_{N_0} - \frac{N - N_0}{N} B_{N_0} - 1 \right\}, \text{ say.} \qquad (7.22)$$

But $-\log(p_i) \xrightarrow{p} \infty$ for $i = 1, \ldots, N_0$ under the alternative as $T \to \infty$, which implies that $A_{N_0} \geq \min\{-\log(p_1), \ldots, -\log(p_{N_0})\} = \infty$. Moreover, by the law of large numbers $B_{N_0} \to_p E(\log(p_i)) = -1$. Therefore, if $\frac{N_0}{N} \to c$ (a constant) as $N \to \infty$, we have under alternative hypothesis (7.5)

$$P_{\mathrm{m}} \xrightarrow{p} \infty$$

as $T \to \infty$ and then $N \to \infty$. This shows that the combination test using the P_{m} test statistic is consistent when the condition $\frac{N_0}{N} \to c$ (a constant) is satisfied. In other words, a large fraction of individuals should be stationary for the test to be consistent. Relation (7.22) also implies that the P_{m} test statistic diverges quickly when N_0 is large relative to N and when N is large. This relation is in accordance with the common perception that larger data sets and stronger evidence against the null yield higher power of tests. It also implies that the null of a unit root may be true for some individuals even when a panel unit root test rejects null hypothesis (7.3). In other words, rejection of the null hypothesis does not imply that every individual is stationary when N is large. In a related study, Karlsson and Löthgren (2000) show through simulation that the acceptance or rejection of the unit root null (7.3) is not sufficient evidence to conclude that all series have a unit root or that all are stationary.

7.2.5 Asymptotic Power Analysis of Panel Unit Root Tests

Moon and Perron (2008) consider the model of independent panels

$$y_{it} = \mu_i + x_{it}; \qquad (7.23)$$

$$x_{it} = \alpha_i x_{i,t-1} + u_{it},$$

where $u_{it} \sim \text{iid}(0, \sigma_u^2)$, $\alpha_i = 1 - \frac{\theta_i}{N^{1/2}T}$, and θ_i is a sequence of i.i.d. random variables with mean μ_θ and variance σ_θ^2 on a nonnegative bounded interval $[0, M_\theta]$. For this model, they derive the asymptotic distribution of the LLC test statistic under the sequence of local alternatives, which is $\mathrm{N}\left(-\frac{3}{2}\sqrt{\frac{5}{51}}\mu_\theta, 1\right)$.

This gives $\Phi\left(\frac{3}{2}\sqrt{\frac{5}{51}}\mu_\theta - z_\alpha\right)$ as the asymptotic local power function, where $\Phi(\cdot)$ is the standard normal cdf and z_α is the α-level critical value from a standard normal distribution. The asymptotic local power function shows that the asymptotic local power of the LLC test depends only on the mean of θ_i and not on heterogeneity of the local alternative around the mean.

For Model (7.23), Moon, Perron, and Phillips (2007; MPP hereafter) derive the asymptotic power envelope for the null hypothesis

$$H_0 : \theta_i = 0 \text{ a.s. for all } i, \tag{7.24}$$

against the alternative

$$H_1 : \theta_i \neq 0 \text{ for some } i \tag{7.25}$$

under the assumption of zero initial variables.[6] MPP show that the asymptotic local power of the LLC test is below the power envelope.

Breitung (2000) and MPP consider a model of independent panels,

$$y_{it} = \mu_i + \beta_i t + x_{it}; \tag{7.26}$$

$$x_{it} = \alpha_i x_{i,t-1} + u_{it},$$

where $u_{it} \sim \text{iid}(0, \sigma_i^2)$, $\alpha_i = 1 - \frac{\theta_i}{N^\kappa T}$, and θ_i is a sequence of i.i.d. random variables with mean μ_θ. This model is called the fixed effects model with incidental trends. Breitung considers the case $\kappa = \frac{1}{2}$ and reports that the LLC test has zero asymptotic power against the sequence of local alternatives.

Noticing that the zero asymptotic power results from LLC's bias correction, Breitung suggests a test statistic that does not require a bias correction. It is based on transforming the data such that

$$y_{it}^* = s_t \left[\Delta y_{it} - \frac{1}{T-t}(\Delta y_{i,t+1} + \cdots + \Delta y_{iT}) \right], \quad s_t = \frac{T-t}{T-t+1}$$

$$x_{it}^* = y_{i,t-1} - y_{i0} - \frac{t-1}{T}(y_{it} - y_{i0}).$$

Because y_{it}^* and x_{it}^* are orthogonal to each other, the t-ratio using the pooled OLS estimator

$$UB_{NT} = \frac{\sum_{i=1}^{N}\sum_{t=2}^{T-1}\sigma_i^{-2}y_{it}^*x_{it}^*}{\sqrt{\sum_{i=1}^{N}\sum_{t=2}^{T-1}\sigma_i^{-2}y_{it}^*x_{it}^*}}$$

does not require a bias correction. MPP show[7] that the asymptotic distribution of UB_{NT} under the sequence of local alternatives with $\kappa = \frac{1}{4}$ is $\mathbf{N}(-6.80 \times$

---

[6] It does not seem to be easy to relax this restrictive condition. MPP explain how complicated it is to extend the case of zero initial conditions to the cases considered in the univariate unit root literature (see Subsection 2.4.10).

[7] See also Moon, Perron, and Phillips (2006) for a similar study.

$10^{-2}\mu_\theta$, 1). In contrast, MPP show that the asymptotic distribution of the LLC test statistic under the sequence of local alternatives with $\kappa = \frac{1}{4}$ is $N(-5.27 \times 10^{-2}\mu_\theta, 1)$. Thus, Breitung's test has higher asymptotic local power than the LLC test, which is also confirmed by Breitung's simulation results. The fact that κ should be $\frac{1}{4}$ for nonnegligible asymptotic local power indicates that detecting unit roots becomes more difficult in the presence of heterogeneous trends. In the case of the model with heterogeneous intercepts only, note that it was $\frac{1}{2}$.

Using the Neyman-Pearson framework for Model (7.26), MPP derive the asymptotic power envelope for the null hypothesis (7.24) against the alternative (7.25) under the assumption of zero initial variables. The power envelope is found to depend on $E(\theta_i^4)$. Under the heterogeneous alternative (7.25), powers of the five tests they consider—Ploberger and Phillips (2002),[8] Moon and Phillips (2004), Breitung (2000), LLC, and Moon and Perron (2008)—are found to be below the power envelope. Among the five tests, Ploberger and Phillips's (2002) has the highest asymptotic local power. The second best is Breitung's (2000), but this ordering is at best tentative because the asymptotic local power depends on the initial variable, which is set to be zero in MPP. The IPS and combination tests cannot be studied within the MPP's framework, but MPP show via simulation that Ploberger and Phillips's and Breitung's tests tend to perform better than that of IPS.

IPS's asymptotic local power is studied by Harris, Harvey, Leybourne, and Sakkas (2010). They assume Model (7.23) with

$$x_{i1} = \eta_i \sqrt{\frac{\sigma_i^2}{1 - \alpha_i^2}},$$

where $\eta_i \sim \text{iid}(\mu_\eta, \sigma_\eta^2)$ across i and $\sigma_i^2 = \text{Var}(u_{it})$ for all t.[9] Under the local alternatives $\alpha_i = 1 - \frac{\theta_i}{N^{1/2}T}$ ($\theta_i \geq 0$ for all i), they derive the asymptotic local power function of IPS's test statistic, finding that the power decreases monotonically as the magnitude of the initial variables increases, in contrast to what is usually observed in the univariate case.

7.3   Tests for the Null of Stationarity

This section introduces tests for the null of stationarity designed for independent panels: the LM test of Hadri (2000) and the combination test of Yin and Wu

---

[8] It is defined by $\frac{1}{\sqrt{N}} \sum_{i=1}^{N} \left(\frac{1}{T\sigma_i^2} \sum_{t=1}^{T} X_{it,T}^2 - \omega_T \right)$, where $X_{it,T} = \frac{1}{\sqrt{T}}[(x_{it} - x_{i0}) - \frac{t}{T}(x_{it} - x_{i0})]$ and $\omega_T = \frac{1}{T} \sum_{i=1}^{N} \frac{t}{T}\left(1 - \frac{t}{T}\right)$.

[9] Under the local alternatives $\alpha_i = 1 - \frac{\theta_i}{N^{1/2}T}$, $x_{i1} = O_p(N^{1/4}T^{1/2})$, which Harris, Harvey, Leybourne, and Sakkas (2010) admit is unrealistic, but they argue that the assumption is suitable for deriving the asymptotic local power function of the IPS test.

(2000) and Choi (2001). The tests are based on Models (7.23) and (7.26). Assuming that u_{it} are $I(0)$ for all i and that u_{it} are cross-sectionally independent, the null hypothesis of the tests is

$$H_0 : |\alpha_i| < 1 \text{ for all } i. \tag{7.27}$$

As discussed in Subsection 4.7.9, time series tests for the null of stationarity tend to have serious size distortions when the null is close to the alternative of a unit root. Because panel tests for the null of stationarity share the same property, caution should be exercised when interpreting the results of panel stationarity tests.

7.3.1 Hadri's Test

Hadri's (2000) LM test statistics for null hypothesis (7.27) are based on the "random walk plus noise" model and are defined using the regression residuals from Models (7.23) and (7.26). Letting $r_{it} = \sum_{k=1}^{t}(y_{ik} - \bar{y}_i)$ with $\bar{y}_i = \frac{1}{T}\sum_{t=1}^{T} y_{it}$, Hadri's test statistic for Model (7.23) is defined by

$$LM_{NT} = \frac{1}{N}\sum_{i=1}^{N}\frac{1}{T^2\hat{\sigma}_i^2}\sum_{t=1}^{T}r_{it}^2, \tag{7.28}$$

where $\hat{\sigma}_i^2$ estimates the long-run variance of y_{it}: $\hat{\sigma}_i^2 = \sum_{j=-l}^{l} C_i(j)k(\frac{j}{l})$ with $C_i(j) = \frac{1}{T}\sum_{t=1}^{T-j}(y_{it} - \bar{y}_i)(y_{i,t+j} - \bar{y}_i)$ and $k(\cdot)$ a lag window. The lag length, l, is assumed to satisfy $l/T \to 0$ as $T \to \infty$. This test may be considered the average of KPSS's test of level stationarity for each individual.

Because

$$LM_{NT} \Rightarrow \frac{1}{N}\sum_{i=1}^{N}\int (W_i(r) - rW_i(1))^2 \, dr \text{ as } T \to \infty$$

under some regularity conditions on $\{u_{it}\}$ and $E\int(W_i(r) - rW_i(1))^2 \, dr = \frac{1}{6}$, Hadri proposes a modifications of the LM test for large N along the lines of IPS. The modified test is defined by

$$W_{\text{LMbar}} = \frac{\sqrt{N}\left(LM_{NT} - \frac{1}{6}\right)}{\sqrt{\frac{1}{45}}}. \tag{7.29}$$

As $T \to \infty$ and $N \to \infty$, we have $W_{\text{LMbar}} \Rightarrow N(0, 1)$. We reject null hypothesis (7.27) when W_{LMbar} takes a larger value than the critical value from the right-hand side of a standard normal distribution.

For Model (7.26), using the demeaned and detrended y_{it} for r_{it}, we replace $\frac{1}{6}$ and $\frac{1}{45}$ in formula (7.29) with $\frac{1}{15}$ and $\frac{11}{6300}$, respectively, to reflect the different weak limit of LM_{NT} when $T \to \infty$. The limiting distribution of the test statistic is $N(0, 1)$ as for Model (7.23). When T is small, the mean and variance adjustments for (7.29) introduced so far may not be appropriate. To cope with this problem, Hadri and Larsson (2005) provide finite-sample mean and variance adjustments for Hadri's test statistic.

The asymptotic normality of W_{LMbar} is based on sequential asymptotics. Y. Shin and Snell (2006) study W_{LMbar} under joint asymptotics $N, T \to \infty$ and find that the condition $\frac{N}{T} \to 0$ is required for asymptotic normality. This indicates that N should be small relative to T for Hadri's test to have good size performance in finite samples.

Now we study the consistency property of Hadri's test. For this, let the number of individuals having a unit root be N_0 and assume $\frac{N_0}{N} \to c$ (a constant). Also, let $LM_{NT} = \frac{1}{N} \sum_{i=1}^{N} \eta_{iT}$, and assume $\alpha_i = 1$ for $i = 1, \ldots, N_0$. Then,

$$
\begin{aligned}
W_{\text{LMbar}} &= \frac{\sqrt{N} \left(\frac{1}{N} \left(\sum_{i=1}^{N_0} \eta_{iT} + \sum_{i=N_0+1}^{N} \eta_{iT} \right) - \frac{1}{6} \right)}{\sqrt{\frac{1}{45}}} \\
&= \frac{\sqrt{\frac{N_0}{N}} \frac{1}{\sqrt{N_0}} \sum_{i=1}^{N_0} \eta_{iT}}{\sqrt{\frac{1}{45}}} + \frac{\sqrt{N} \left(\frac{1}{N} \sum_{i=N_0+1}^{N} \eta_{iT} - \frac{1}{6} \right)}{\sqrt{\frac{1}{45}}} \\
&= A_{NT} + B_{NT}, \text{ say.}
\end{aligned}
$$

Because $\eta_{iT} = O_p(T/l)$ for $i = 1, \ldots, N_0$ (cf. KPSS, p. 169), $A_{NT} = O_p\left(\frac{T\sqrt{N}}{l}\right)$ and it diverges to plus infinity in probability as long as l diverges slower than $T\sqrt{N}$. Moreover,

$$
\begin{aligned}
B_{NT} &= \frac{\sqrt{N} \left(\frac{N-N_0}{N} \frac{1}{N-N_0} \sum_{i=N_0+1}^{N} \eta_{iT} - \frac{1}{6} \right)}{\sqrt{\frac{1}{45}}} \\
&= \frac{\sqrt{N} \left(\frac{N-N_0}{N} \bar{\eta} - \frac{1}{6} \right)}{\sqrt{\frac{1}{45}}} \\
&= \sqrt{\frac{N}{N-N_0}} \frac{\sqrt{N-N_0} \left(\bar{\eta} - \frac{1}{6} \right)}{\sqrt{\frac{1}{45}}} - \frac{\frac{N_0}{\sqrt{N}}}{6\sqrt{\frac{1}{45}}} \\
&= O_p(1) + O_p\left(\sqrt{N} \right)
\end{aligned}
$$

because $\sqrt{N-N_0}\left(\bar{\eta} - \frac{1}{6}\right) = O_p(1)$. Thus, $B_{NT} \xrightarrow{p} -\infty$ as $T \to \infty$ and $N \to \infty$ when $\frac{N_0}{N} \to c$ (a constant). But A_{NT} dominates B_{NT} if $\frac{T}{l} \to \infty$.

Thus, it follows that $W_{\text{LMbar}} \xrightarrow{p} \infty$ when the null hypothesis is violated under the conditions $\frac{N_0}{N} \to c$ (a constant) and $\frac{T}{T} \to \infty$. The latter two conditions are required for the consistency of Hadri's test.

7.3.2 Combination Test

Suppose that we reject the null hypothesis, $H_0 : |\alpha_i| < 1$, when a realized value of the stationarity test statistic G_{iT} is greater than a constant. Then, the asymptotic p-value for the G_{iT} test is defined as

$$p_i = 1 - F(G_{iT_i}),$$

where $F(\cdot)$ denotes the asymptotic distribution function of G_{iT}. Yin and Wu (2000) employ KPSS's and Leybourne and McCabe's (1994) test statistics for G_{iT} and combine the resulting p-values using Fisher's test statistic defined in (7.15). Its limiting distribution for a fixed N is given in (7.17). When N is large, its modified version P_{m} should be used. Instead of Fisher's test statistic, the Z test statistic defined by (7.16) may also be used as discussed in Choi (2001). Its distribution is standard normal for both finite and infinite N.

7.4   Unit Root and Stationarity Tests under Structural Changes

This section introduces unit root and stationarity tests under structural changes. The methods introduced in this section are extensions of the related methods for univariate time series discussed in Sections 3.2 and 4.8. Im, Lee, and Tieslau (2005) develop a panel unit root test under structural change.[10] They consider the model with a level shift

$$y_{it} = \mu_i + \beta_i t + \delta_i \mathbf{1}\{t > T_{\text{B}i}\} + x_{it},$$

$$x_{it} = \alpha_i x_{i,t-1} + u_{it}, \ u_{it} \sim \text{iid}\,\mathbf{N}(0, \sigma_i^2), \ (t = 1, \ldots, T)$$

for the observations $\{y_{it}\}$ and propose a panel unit root test based on scores following the methods of SP (see Subsection 2.4.1 for the Schmidt-Phillips test). As in SP and Amsler and Lee (1995), Im, Lee, and Tieslau consider the OLS regression

$$\Delta y_{it} = intercept + \delta_i \Delta \mathbf{1}\{t > T_{\text{B}i}\} + \phi_i \tilde{x}_{i,t-1} + error,$$

where

$$\tilde{x}_{i,t-1} = y_{i,t-1} - \tilde{\beta}_i(t-1) - \tilde{\delta}_i \Delta \mathbf{1}\{t > T_{\text{B}i}\}$$

---

[10]   I mention in passing that Murray and Papell (2000) and Breitung and Candelon (2005) consider the same problem as in Im, Lee, and Tieslau (2005).

and $\tilde{\beta}_i$ and $\tilde{\delta}_i$ are obtained by regressing $\{\Delta y_{it}\}$ on $\{1, \Delta 1\{t > T_{Bi}\}\}$. The t-ratio from this regression for the null hypothesis $H_0 : \phi_i = 0$ is denoted as t_{iT}. Im, Lee, and Tieslau construct the sample mean of the t-ratios and adjust it as in IPS. The limiting distribution of their test statistic is standard normal and does not depend on the change points $\{T_{Bi}\}$.

Carrion-i-Silvestre, Del Barrio-Castro, and López-Bazo (2005) consider the model with both level and trend shifts

$$y_{it} = \mu_i + \sum_{k=1}^{m_i} \delta_{ik} 1\{t > T_{Bki}\} + \beta_i t + \sum_{k=1}^{m_i} \gamma_{ik}(t - T_{Bki}) 1\{t > T_{Bki}\} + u_{it}$$

(7.30)

and test the null hypothesis that all of $\{u_{it}\}$ are $I(0)$. Model (7.30) is similar to one of the models considered in Subsection 4.8.1. In Model (7.30), level and trend shifts may occur m_i times simultaneously for individual i at time points $\{T_{Bki}\}$. Note that each individual has a different structural change point. Assume that the structural change points are known and let $\lambda_i = \left[\frac{T_{B1i}}{T}, \ldots, \frac{T_{Bm_i i}}{T} \right]'$. The OLS regression residuals from equation (7.30) are denoted $\{\hat{u}_{it}(\lambda_i)\}$. Denoting KPSS's test statistic using $\{\hat{u}_{it}(\lambda_i)\}$ as $\eta_{iT}(\lambda_i)$, Carrion-i-Silvestre, Del Barrio-Castro, and López-Bazo suggest using the test statistic

$$W_{\text{LMbar}}(\lambda) = \frac{\sqrt{N}\left(LM_{NT} - \bar{\varsigma}\right)}{\varsigma}$$

(7.31)

as in Hadri (2000), where $LM_{NT} = \frac{1}{N} \sum_{i=1}^{N} \eta_{iT}(\lambda_i)$, $\bar{\varsigma} = \frac{1}{N} \sum_{i=1}^{N} \varsigma_i$, $\bar{\varsigma}^2 = \frac{1}{N} \sum_{i=1}^{N} \varsigma_i^2$, $\varsigma_i = A \sum_{k=1}^{m_i} (\lambda_{i,k} - \lambda_{i,k-1})^2$, and $\varsigma_i = B \sum_{k=1}^{m_i} (\lambda_{i,k} - \lambda_{i,k-1})^4$. The constants A and B are equal to $\frac{1}{6}$ and $\frac{1}{45}$, respectively, for Model (7.30) without the time trend variables (i.e., regressors t and $1\{t > T_{Bki}\}$ are not present), and they are equal to $\frac{1}{15}$ and $\frac{11}{6300}$, respectively, for Model (7.30) with the time trend variables. In practice, $\{\lambda_i\}$ are unknown. Carrion-i-Silvestre, Del Barrio-Castro, and López-Bazo propose estimating the change points by minimizing the sum of squared residuals from equation (7.30) and plugging the estimates into (7.31). The resulting limiting distribution is $N(0, 1)$.

Hadri and Rao (2008) extend Carrion-i-Silvestre, Del Barrio-Castro, and López-Bazo (2005) to some other types of changing trends and propose similar methods for testing the null of stationarity. They also suggest using bootstrap methods for cross-sectionally correlated errors as in MW.

Costantini and Gutierrez (2007) consider the model

$$\Delta y_{it} = \mu_{it} + \beta_{it} t + \rho_i y_{i,t-1} + u_{it}$$

and test the null hypothesis $H_0 : \rho_i = 0$ for all i against the alternative $H_1 : \rho_i < 0$ for $t = 1, \ldots, T_B$ and for $i = 1, \ldots, N_1$ and $\rho_i = 0$ for $t = T_B + 1, \ldots, T$

and for $i = N_1 + 1, \ldots, N$. That is, they test for changes in the persistence of the observations. They use BLS's and Leybourne, Kim, Smith, and Newbold's (2003) t-ratios introduced in Sections 3.2 and 4.9, respectively, and combine their p-values using the inverse normal statistic (7.16).

7.5 Unit Root Tests for Cross-Sectionally Correlated Panels

This section introduces unit root tests for cross-sectionally correlated panels. These are often called second-generation panel unit root tests. The tests introduced so far assume cross-sectionally independent panels, and—according to the simulation results of O'Connell (1998), MW, and Strauss and Yigit (2003)—panel unit root tests are seriously oversized when errors are cross-sectionally correlated. Additionally, Banerjee, Marcellino, and Osbat (2005) report that cross-sectional cointegration results in oversized panel unit root tests. At the more intuitive level, it is hard to believe that data from countries or from companies belonging to the same industry are independent. All these factors point to the need for unit root tests designed for cross-sectionally correlated panels.

7.5.1 Tests Using Common Factors

Bai and Ng (2004; BN hereafter), Moon and Perron (2004; MP hereafter), Phillips and Sul (2003), and Pesaran (2007) model cross-sectional correlation by common factors and develop tests using large-T and large-N asymptotics. Phillips and Sul's and Pesaran's panel unit root tests use Models (7.1) and (7.2),[11] but assume a one-factor structure

$$u_{it} = \gamma_i f_t + \varepsilon_{it}, \tag{7.32}$$

where f_t is an unobserved common factor, γ_i is a factor-loading coefficient and ε_{it} are idiosyncratic errors. Phillips and Sul and Pesaran assume that $\{f_t\}$ and $\{\varepsilon_{it}\}$ are white noise processes. This assumption is reasonable enough when there are enough lagged variables in Models (7.1) and (7.2), although their theories are expected to work for stationary f_t as well. Because ε_{it} is assumed independent of ε_{js} and f_s for all i and j ($i \neq j$) and for all s and t, cross-sectional correlation originates from the common factor f_t. If $\gamma_i = 0$ for all i, there will be no cross-sectional correlation. The main idea of Phillips and Sul's and Pesaran's tests is to eliminate the common factor f_t and apply the panel unit root tests developed for independent panels.

Phillips and Sul (2003) estimate $[\gamma_1, \ldots, \gamma_N]$ and $[\sigma_1^2, \ldots, \sigma_N^2]$ by the method of moments under the assumption $\mathrm{Var}(f_t) = 1$ for all t, which gives the variance-covariance matrix of $[u_{1t}, \ldots, u_{Nt}]'$. Phillips and Sul use this matrix

[11] Pesaran (2007) assumes homogeneous AR processes.

to make a GLS-type transformation of the data such that the transformed data are cross-sectionally uncorrelated. They recommend using the inverse normal test (7.16) for the transformed time series and show by simulation that their method works reasonably well in finite samples.

Pesaran (2007) uses regressions augmented by the cross-sectional averages of lagged levels and first differences whose presence eliminates the cross-sectional correlation embodied in $\gamma_i f_t$. To understand this idea, consider the cross-sectional average of the homogeneous AR model with one lagged difference,

$$\frac{1}{N}\sum_{i=1}^{N}\Delta y_{it} = \frac{\rho}{N}\sum_{i=1}^{N}y_{i,t-1} + \varphi\frac{1}{N}\sum_{i=1}^{N}\Delta y_{i,t-1} + \frac{f_t}{N}\sum_{i=1}^{N}\gamma_i + \frac{1}{N}\sum_{i=1}^{N}\varepsilon_{it}$$

$$\approx \frac{\rho}{N}\sum_{i=1}^{N}y_{i,t-1} + \frac{\varphi}{N}\sum_{i=1}^{N}\Delta y_{i,t-1} + \frac{f_t}{N}\sum_{i=1}^{N}\gamma_i,$$

where the approximate relation holds for large N by the law of large numbers. This relation shows that f_t is expressible as a linear combination of cross-sectional averages of the lagged level $y_{i,t-1}$ and the differences Δy_{it} and $\Delta y_{i,t-1}$, as long as $\frac{1}{N}\sum_{i=1}^{N}\gamma_i \neq 0$. Thus, if we run the time series OLS regression for each i,

$$\Delta y_{it} = \hat{\rho}y_{i,t-1} + \hat{\varphi}\Delta y_{i,t-1} + \hat{\alpha}_1\bar{y}_{t-1} + \hat{\alpha}_2\Delta\bar{y}_t + \hat{\alpha}_3\Delta\bar{y}_{t-1} + \hat{u}_{it},$$

where $\bar{}$ denotes the cross-sectional average, the residual $\hat{u}_{it}$ will be devoid of $\gamma_i f_t$ in the limit. Using this regression, the Dickey-Fuller t-ratios are devised—called the cross-sectionally augmented (CADF) test—and combined as in IPS. The t-ratios' limiting distributions are different from the Dickey-Fuller distribution due to the presence of the cross-sectional average of the lagged level. Pesaran uses a truncated version of the IPS test statistic that avoids the problem of moment calculation. In addition, the t-ratios are also used to formulate combination test statistics. His experimental results show that the IPS test using truncation and the combination test using the inverse normal principle perform well. A limitation of the model Pesaran uses is that it imposes homogeneity across cross-sectional units. Certainly, this is a restriction that empirical researchers do not wish to entertain. A major novelty of Pesaran's approach is that the cross-sectional correlation is eliminated by simple OLS without estimating factors and factor-loading coefficients as other approaches require.

BN use the models

$$y_{it} = c_i + \lambda_i' f_t + x_{it} \tag{7.33}$$

and

$$y_{it} = c_i + \beta_i t + \lambda_i' f_t + x_{it}, \qquad (7.34)$$

where $\{y_{it}\}$ are observed panel data, f_t is a vector of unobserved common factors, γ_i is a vector of factor-loading coefficients, and x_{it} are idiosyncratic components and independent across cross-sectional units. Cross-sectional correlation of $\{y_{it}\}$ originates from the common factor f_t in these models. In BN, the number of factors is assumed to be unknown and is allowed to be greater than one, unlike in Phillips and Sul (2003) and Pesaran (2007). In practice, the number of factors can be estimated by various methods as surveyed by Breitung and Choi (2013). Furthermore, the factors $\{f_t\}$ may contain unit roots in BN.

BN difference their models first and then apply the principal components method to estimate $\{\Delta f_t\}$ and $\{\lambda_i\}$. This effectively handles the possible presence of unit roots in $\{f_t\}$. The partial sum of the factor estimates serves as an estimator of f_t. Using the estimates of $\lambda_i' f_t$, often called the common components, those of $\{x_{it}\}$ can be obtained. The modified Fisher test statistic (7.20), using the Dickey-Fuller test as an underlying test, is then applied to the estimates of $\{x_{it}\}$ to test for unit roots in $\{x_{it}\}$.[12] Furthermore, they suggest using Stock and Watson's (1988) procedure to test for the number of unit roots in f_t. In BN's procedure, nonstationarity of the panel data may stem from the factors or the idiosyncratic components or from both. In this sense, it is more flexible than the other procedures. Only when the null of unit roots is rejected for both the factors and the idiosyncratic components can the observed data $\{y_{it}\}$ be statistically concluded to be stationary. If only the factors contain unit roots, using panel data does not bring any power gain in unit root testing because the unit root testing uses only the time series information in $\{f_t\}$ under that circumstance. Experimental results in BN confirm that the their methods work reasonably well in finite samples.

Whereas BN estimate the factor and factor loading by the principal components method, Kapetanios (2007) considers using Kapetanios and Marcellino's (2009) and Forni, Hallin, Lippi, and Reichlin's (2004) factor-estimation methods. His Monte Carlo study shows that persistent factors cannot be extracted easily and that the resulting panel unit root test seems to work poorly as a result. In addition, he demonstrates that multiple factors are less easily extracted and have a further adverse impact on inference. He concludes that factor-based methods seem to have considerable problems and that more work is needed for these methods to come into standard practice.

MP's test for panel unit roots is based on models similar to (7.33) and (7.34), but f_t appears as part of the error term of the observed time series. In MP's

---

[12] Bai and Ng (2010) study additional test statistics using pooled estimation. See also Westerlund and Larsson (2009) for a related proof.

procedure, the common factors should be stationary, unlike in BN. MP consider the model

$$y_{it} = \alpha_i y_{i,t-1} + u_{it}, \; u_{it} = \lambda_i' f_t + \varepsilon_{it}. \tag{7.35}$$

As earlier, ε_{it} is assumed to be independent of ε_{js} and f_s for all i and j ($i \neq j$) and for all s and t. Thus, cross-sectional correlation stems from the common factor f_t. Using pooled OLS for Model (7.35), MP obtain the estimates of $\{u_{it}\}$. Using these estimates, MP estimate the number of factors and the common components, $\lambda_i' f_t$, by the principal components method. The estimates of the common components are eliminated from the observed data $\{y_{it}\}$, and semiparametric, pooled panel t-ratios for unit roots are applied to the de-factored data. The t-ratios have a standard normal distribution in the limit. These test statistics are also extended to models with individual effects and heterogeneous time trends. However, MP's experimental results show that their test statistics are subject to serious size distortions, particularly when the number of factors is estimated.

7.5.2   Combination Tests

The combination test of Subsection 7.2.3 depends on the assumption of independence of all individual time series, which is certainly not desirable for some applications. Demetrescu, Hassler, and Tarcolea[13] (2006) propose an approach that can overcome this problem, using Hartung's (1999) idea. Demetrescu, Hassler, and Tarcolea focus on the inverse normal test statistic (7.16) and, letting $t_i = \Phi^{-1}(p_i)$ with p_i denoting p-value from the Dickey-Fuller test, suggest a modified inverse normal test statistic

$$t(\hat{\rho}, \kappa) = \frac{\sum_{i=1}^{N} t_i}{\sqrt{N + (N^2 - N)\left(\hat{\rho}^* + \kappa\sqrt{\frac{2}{N+1}(1 - \hat{\rho}^*)}\right)}},$$

where $\hat{\rho}^* = \max\left(-\frac{1}{N-1}, \hat{\rho}\right)$ with $\hat{\rho} = 1 - \frac{1}{N-1}\sum_{i=1}^{N}\left(t_i - \frac{1}{N}\sum_{i=1}^{N} t_i\right)^2$ and κ is a constant. In their simulation, Demetrescu, Hassler, and Tarcolea use $\kappa = 0.2$. They show that their test statistic has a standard normal distribution in the limit when two conditions are satisfied,

(i) $\displaystyle\lim_{N\to\infty} \frac{1}{N(N-1)} \sum\sum_{i\neq j} \delta_{ij} = \tilde{\delta}, \; \tilde{\delta} \in (0, 1)$;

(ii) $\displaystyle\lim_{N\to\infty} \frac{1}{N(N-1)} \sum\sum_{i\neq j} \left(\delta_{ij} - \tilde{\delta}\right)^2 = 0,$

---

[13]   See also Costantini and Lupi (2012) who use Hansen's (1995) covariate augmented Dickey-Fuller test (see Subsection 2.4.5) in Demetrescu, Hassler, and Tarcolea's (2006) framework.

where δ_{ij} is the covariance of t_i and t_j. The second condition implies that $\{\delta_{ij}\}$ should vary very little from its asymptotic mean. Demetrescu, Hassler, and Tarcolea show that their test statistic works well for the case where Ω (the variance-covariance matrix of the error terms) has constant off-diagonal elements and also that their test statistic performs better than MW's (i.e., test statistic (7.15)) and Chang's (2002) under that circumstance.

Sheng and Yang (2013) employ Zaykin, Zhivotovsky, and Weir's (2002) truncated product method for panel unit root testing. Their statistic is

$$\Pi_{i=1}^{N} p_i^{1\{p_i \le \tau\}},$$

which is the product of all the p-values that do not exceed some prescribed value τ. The truncation reduces the impact of some large p-values and may induce higher power. Sheng and Yang assume either constant correlation between p-values or general forms of cross-sectional dependence in the panel units. Because the limiting null distributions are unknown, they use bootstrap methods for their test statistic. Sheng and Yang's test sometimes outperforms Pesaran's (2007) and Demetrescu, Hassler, and Tarcolea's (2006) tests according to their simulation results with $\tau = 0.1$.

Choi (2006b) considers the two-way error component model

$$y_{it} = \beta_0 + x_{it}, (i = 1, \ldots, N; t = 1, \ldots, T), \tag{7.36}$$

where

$$x_{it} = \mu_i + \lambda_t + v_{it},$$

$$v_{it} = \sum_{l=1}^{p_i} \alpha_{il} v_{i(t-l)} + e_{it},$$

and $\{v_{it}\}$ are independent across cross-sections. Assuming that the largest root of v_{it} is $\left(1 + \frac{c}{T}\right)$ for all i, Choi regresses $\left[y_{i1}, y_{i2} - \left(1 + \frac{c}{T}\right)y_{i1}, \ldots, y_{iT} - \left(1 + \frac{c}{T}\right)y_{i(T-1)}\right]'$ on $\left[1, 1 - \left(1 + \frac{c}{T}\right), \ldots, 1 - \left(1 + \frac{c}{T}\right)\right]'$ to obtain the GLS estimator of parameter β_0 in Model (7.36) as in ERS.[14] Denoting the GLS estimator of β_0 using sample $[y_{i1}, \ldots, y_{iT}]'$ as $\hat{\beta}_{0i}$, the demeaned series can be written for large T as

$$y_{it} - \hat{\beta}_{0i} \simeq \lambda_t - \lambda_1 + v_{it} - v_{i1}. \tag{7.37}$$

Demeaning $y_{it} - \hat{\beta}_{0i}$ cross-sectionally for large T yields

$$z_{it} = y_{it} - \hat{\beta}_{0i} - \frac{1}{N} \sum_{i=1}^{N} (y_{it} - \hat{\beta}_{0i}) \simeq v_{it} - v_{i1} - \overline{v}_{.t} + \overline{v}_{.1}, \tag{7.38}$$

[14] Choi uses $c = -7$ for all i.

where $\frac{1}{N}\sum_{i=1}^{N} q_{ia} = \overline{q}_{.a}$. Relation (7.38) shows that β_0, μ_i, and λ_t were eliminated from y_{it} by the time series and cross-sectional demeanings. Relation (7.38) also shows that z_{it} are independent across i for large T and N because $\overline{v}_{.t}$ and $\overline{v}_{.1}$ converge to zero in probability as $N \rightarrow \infty$ for any T. Choi uses $\{z_{it}\}$ to formulate combination test statistics as in Choi (2001). He also extends it to a model with a linear time trend.

7.5.3   GLS-Based and Robust t-Ratios

When errors are cross-sectionally correlated, it is natural to consider SUR (or GLS) estimation for Models (7.1) and (7.2). O'Connell (1998)[15] and Taylor and Sarno (1998) use the SUR approach for panel unit root testing in relation to the purchasing power parity hypothesis, but they do so without any theoretical analysis of the approach. Due to Chang (2004) and Breitung and Das (2005; BD hereafter), it is now known that the limiting distributions of the SUR-based panel unit root test statistics depend on nuisance parameters unless the AR order is one across all cross-sectional units. To cope with this problem, Chang uses bootstrapping. However, whether bootstrapped or not, the SUR method requires the condition $T \geq N$ because the estimator of the variance-covariance matrix becomes singular otherwise, which may be too restrictive in some applications. Even if the condition is satisfied, BD report via simulation that the SUR method does not work properly unless T is substantially larger than N.

BD introduce methods that can circumvent the problems associated with the SUR approach.[16] To explain their approach, start from the panel AR(1) model

$$\Delta y_{it} = \rho y_{i,t-1} + u_{it}, \quad (i = 1, \ldots, N; t = 2, \ldots, T), \tag{7.39}$$

where $\{u_{it}\}$ is a cross-sectionally correlated white noise process. Let $u_t = [u_{i1}, \ldots, u_{iN}]'$ and assume $E(u_t u_t') = \Omega \ (> 0)$. Thus, cross-sectional correlations are embodied in the nondiagonal elements of Ω. BD show that the usual OLS-based t-ratio,

$$t_{ols} = \frac{\sum_{t=2}^{T} y_{t-1}' \Delta y_t}{\hat{\sigma}\sqrt{\sum_{t=2}^{T} y_{t-1}' y_{t-1}}},$$

where $y_t = [y_{1t}, \ldots, y_{Nt}]'$ and $\hat{\sigma}^2 = \frac{1}{NT}\sum_{i=1}^{N}\sum_{t=2}^{T}(\Delta y_{it} - \hat{\rho} y_{i,t-1})^2$ with $\hat{\rho}$ denoting the pooled OLS estimator, does not have a standard normal distribution in the limit (as $T \rightarrow \infty$ and $N \rightarrow \infty$). As a remedy, noticing that a valid

---

[15] O'Connell (1998) considers only the AR(1) model.

[16] See Jönsson (2005) for a similar idea, but his analysis is confined to the panel AR(1) model and therefore is less general than BD's.

estimator of the variance of the OLS estimator is

$$v_{\hat{\rho}} = \frac{\sum_{t=2}^{T} y_{t-1}' \hat{\Omega} y_{t-1}}{\left(\sum_{t=2}^{T} y_{t-1}' y_{t-1}\right)^2},$$

where $\hat{\Omega} = \frac{1}{T-1} \sum_{t=2}^{T} (\Delta y_t - \hat{\rho} y_{t-1})(\Delta y_t - \hat{\rho} y_{t-1})'$, BD suggest a robust t-ratio,

$$t_{\text{rob}} = \frac{\sum_{t=2}^{T} y_{t-1}' \Delta y_t}{\sqrt{\sum_{t=2}^{T} y_{t-1}' \hat{\Omega} y_{t-1}}}.$$

In addition, BD suggest the GLS-based t-ratio

$$t_{\text{gls}} = \frac{\sum_{t=2}^{T} y_{t-1}' \Omega^{-1} \Delta y_t}{\sqrt{\sum_{t=2}^{T} y_{t-1}' \Omega^{-1} y_{t-1}}}.$$

Both t_{rob} and t_{gls} are shown to have a standard normal distribution in the limit as $T \to \infty$ and $N \to \infty$, but the feasible version of t_{gls} requires $T \geq N$ because $\hat{\Omega}$ is singular otherwise.

For Models (7.1) and (7.2), the following steps calculate the robust t-ratio and the GLS-based t-ratio. We assume $k_i = k$ for all i.[17]

Step 1: Run the vector autoregression

$$\Delta y_t = \hat{\Psi} y_{t-1} + \hat{\Gamma}_1 y_{t-1} + \cdots + \hat{\Gamma}_k y_{t-k} + \hat{u}_t.$$

Step 2: Calculate

$$y_t^* = y_t - \sum_{j=1}^{k} \hat{\Gamma}_j y_{t-j}.$$

This behaves like a vector unit root process under the null of unit roots.[18]
Step 3: The robust t-ratio and the GLS-based t-ratio are calculated using $\{y_t^*\}$.

BD also consider these extensions of the t-ratios to the models with heterogeneous intercepts and linear time trends using Breitung's (2000) methods.[19] According to BD's simulation results, t_{rob} seems to be promising in finite samples.

Breitung and Das (2008) further study the properties of t_{ols}, t_{rob}, and t_{gls} under the factor structure (7.33) without the heterogeneous intercepts. They find that

---

[17] If this condition is not satisfied, the maximum AR order may be used as the common AR order.
[18] Suppose for simplicity that $\Delta y_t = \Psi y_{t-1} + \Gamma_1 \Delta y_{t-1} + u_t$. Then, $y_t - \Gamma_1 y_{t-1} = y_{t-1} - \Gamma_1 y_{t-2} + u_t$ under $\Psi = 0$, which shows that $y_t - \Gamma_1 y_{t-1}$ is a vector unit root process. BD show that $y_t - \hat{\Gamma}_1 y_{t-1}$ resembles a unit root process in the limit.
[19] See Subsection 7.2.5 for the case of heterogeneous intercepts and trends.

t_{ols} and t_{rob} either diverge in probability or depend on nuisance parameters when $\{f_t\}$ or $\{x_{it}\}$ (or both) contain unit roots. The GLS-based t-ratio, t_{gls}, has a standard normal distribution in the limit when both the common and idiosyncratic components are nonstationary and when the common factors are $I(0)$ and the idiosyncratic components are $I(1)$. This analysis indicates that it is hard to use these test statistics under the factor structure.

7.5.4   IV Approach

Chang (2002) considers the panel AR(1) Model (7.39) and devises an IV estimator using the instrument $z_{i,t-1} = y_{i,t-1} \exp(-c_i |y_{i,t-1}|)$, where c_i is a constant. Chang claims that her test using the IV estimator is robust to cross-sectional correlation. Although her test is based on an intriguing idea, Demetrescu, Hassler, and Tarcolea's (2006) and Shin and Kang's (2006) simulation results show that it is subject to serious size distortions when strong cross-sectional correlation is present or when N is large relative to T. Moreover, Im and Pesaran (2003) indicate that her asymptotic theory is based on $\frac{N \log T}{T} \to 0$, a condition requiring quite a small N relative to T.

Using the panel AR(1) Model (7.39), Shin and Kang (2006)[20] devise an IV estimator for the transformed data $\breve{y}_t = \Omega^{-1/2} y_t$. So and Shin (1999) use a similar idea for univariate time series as we have seen in Subsection 5.3.5. The IV estimator is defined by

$$\hat{\rho}_{\text{IV}} = \left(\sum_{t=2}^{T} H_t \breve{y}_t' \right) \sum_{t=2}^{T} H_t \Delta \breve{y}_t',$$

where $H_t = \text{diag}(h_{1t}, \dots, h_{Nt})$, $h_{it} = h_m(\sigma_{ii}^{-1/2} y_{i,t-1})$, $h_m(x) = 1$ if $x > m$, $h_m(x) = x/m$ if $|x| \le m$, $h_m(x) = -1$ if $x < -m$, σ_{ii} is the (i, i)-th element of Ω, and m is a positive real number. In their simulation, Shin and Kang consider $m = 0, 1, 2$. They devise a Wald test using the estimator $\hat{\rho}_{\text{IV}}$ and show that it has a chi-square distribution in the limit as $T \to \infty$ for a fixed N. They also extend their test to the models with serial correlation and deterministic regressors. Because Shin and Kang's test uses a transformation based on the estimated variance-covariance matrix, it requires $T \ge N$ and is expected to work well only when T is much larger than N.

Demetrescu and Hanck (2012) extend Shin and Kang (2006) to the case of large N, assuming a factor structure for the error terms. They consider an IV-based test statistic similar to (7.14) and show that it has a standard normal distribution as N and T go to infinity simultaneously. Because Demetrescu and

---

[20]   See also Oh and So (2004) for a similar idea applied to independent panels.

Hanck's test statistic requires the same transformation as for Shin and Kang's, it is expected to work well only when T is much larger than N.

Noticing that Chang's (2002) test is not robust to cross-sectional cointegration, Chang and Song (2009) consider the regression model

$$y_{it} = \alpha_i y_{i,t-1} + \sum_{j=1}^{k_i} \varphi_{ij} \Delta y_{i,t-j} + \sum_{j=1}^{m_i} \beta'_{ij} w_{i,t-j} + u_{it},$$

where $\{w_{i,t-j}\}$ are covariates and $\{u_{it}\}$ are cross-sectionally correlated, and use the IV estimation as in Chang. They then combine the t-ratios for $H_0 : \alpha_i = 1$ as in Chang and claim that a standard normal distribution can be used for the resulting test statistic. If the covariates include lagged differences of all the units and all of the cointegration errors from the N-dimensional system, the model becomes a single equation in a vector error-correction system. However, it is not possible to include all the lagged differences and cointegration errors in practice, and it is hard to decide which variables should be included in the covariates in the absence of knowledge on short-run dynamics and cointegration relations, especially when N is large. Chang and Song's simulation and empirical examples do not fully address this issue, so more needs to be shown to convince the reader of the practicability of their approach.

7.5.5 Resampling Methods

All the tests introduced so far in this section deal properly with cross-sectional correlation at least in theory. However, none except BN and Chang and Song (2009) assume cointegration among the individual units, even though—as Banerjee, Marcellino, and Osbat (2005) report—cross-sectional cointegration results in oversized panel unit root tests. This subsection introduces two procedures that can accommodate cross-sectional cointegration and correlation, both of which use resampling methods.

Choi and Chue (2007) propose using subsampling for cross-sectionally correlated and cointegrated panels. In the subsampling approach, the statistic of interest is computed at subsamples of the data, and the subsampled values of the statistic are used to estimate its finite-sample distribution. The reader is referred to Politis, Romano, and Wolf (1999) for an introduction to subsampling. In applying the subsampling method to time series, subsamples should use consecutive sample points in order to retain the structure of serial correlation.

Let ξ_{NT} be a panel unit root test statistic that uses the whole sample. Its limiting distribution depends on nuisance parameters for cross-sectionally correlated and cointegrated panels. As a way to approximate the limiting distribution, letting ξ_{Nbs} be a panel unit root test that uses the subsample $\{y_{is}, \ldots, y_{i,s+b-1}\}_{i=1}^{N}$, consider the statistic

$$L_{NTb}^{\xi}(x) = \frac{1}{T - b + 1} \sum_{s=1}^{T-b+1} 1\{\xi_{Nbs} \leq x\}, \tag{7.40}$$

where $1\{\xi_{Nbs} \leq x\} = 1$ if $\xi_{Nbs} \leq x$ and $1\{\xi_{Nbs} \leq x\} = 0$ if $\xi_{Nbs} > x$. If $b \to \infty$ and $b/T \to 0$ as $T \to \infty$, $L_{NTb}^{\xi}(x)$ approximates the limiting cdf uniformly in x for a fixed N and can thus be used for panel unit root testing. Choi and Chue (2007) employ test statistics (7.7), (7.14), and (7.16) in Section 7.2 for subsampling. Choi and Chue also show that the tests using the subsample critical values are consistent. For the choice of the block size b, they introduce simulation-based calibration rules. Though they assume N to be finite, they show that the subsampling method with the calibration rules via simulation works well for N as large as 100 for both cointegrated and noncointegrated panels. By contrast, Pesaran's and MP's test show serious size distortions for cointegrated panels.

Palm, Smeekes, and Urbain (2011) consider the model

$$y_t = \Lambda F_t + x_t,$$

which is a multivariate version of BN's Model (7.33) that does not have heterogeneous intercepts. In their setup, $\{F_t\}$ and $\{x_t\}$ are allowed to be contemporaneously and dynamically correlated, and $\{x_{it}\}$ are allowed to be cross-sectionally correlated. This is a more general setup than in BN. BN provide separate procedures for detecting unit roots in the factors and in the idiosyncratic term $\{x_t\}$, but Palm, Smeekes, and Urbain simply test for unit roots in $\{y_t\}$. They consider two test statistics

$$\tau_{\mathrm{p}} = T \frac{\sum_{i=1}^{N} \sum_{t=2}^{T} y_{i,t-1} \Delta y_{it}}{\sum_{i=1}^{N} \sum_{t=2}^{T} y_{i,t-1}^2};$$

$$\tau_{\mathrm{gm}} = \frac{1}{N} \sum_{i=1}^{N} T \frac{\sum_{t=2}^{T} y_{i,t-1} \Delta y_{it}}{\sum_{t=2}^{T} y_{i,t-1}^2}$$

and show that these test statistics have limiting distributions (as $T \to \infty$ for a fixed N) that depend on nuisance parameters. Thus, Palm, Smeekes, and Urbain employ Künsch's (1989) block bootstrapping (see Section 4.5.2 for the bootstrapping of univariate, nonstationary time series) and show that the bootstrap procedure is consistent. Simulation results in Palm, Smeekes, and Urbain confirm that the bootstrap procedure works well. However, their model does not contain nonstochastic terms, which may limit its use in practice.

7.6   Stationarity Tests for Cross-Sectionally Correlated Panels

Bai and Ng (2005) extend the method of BN for panel unit root testing to tests for the null of stationarity. Using Models (7.33) and (7.34), they defactor and detrend the series and apply KPSS's test and the modified Fisher test (cf. equation (7.20)) to test the null of stationarity for idiosyncratic errors. They also apply KPSS's tests to the estimated factors.

Harris, Leybourne, and McCabe (2005) consider the model

$$y_{it} = \alpha_i y_{i,t-1} + u_{it},$$

where $\{u_{it}\}$ are $I(0)$ and cross-sectionally correlated. Harris, Leybourne, and McCabe propose the test statistic

$$S_k = \frac{C_k}{\hat{\sigma}_{la}},$$

where $C_k = \frac{1}{\sqrt{T}} \sum_{t=k+1}^{T} a_{kt}$, $a_{kt} = \sum_{i=1}^{N} y_{it} y_{i,t-k}$ and $\hat{\sigma}_{la}^2$ is the usual long-run variance estimator using $\{a_{kt}\}$ for the null hypothesis $H_0 : |\alpha_i| < 1$ for all i against the alternative $H_1 : \alpha_i = 1$ for at least one i. Harris, Leybourne, and McCabe show that S_k has a standard normal distribution in the limit for $k = [\sqrt{\delta T}]$ (δ is a constant) as $T \to \infty$. In Harris, Leybourne, and McCabe, N is a fixed constant. They further show $S_k \xrightarrow{p} \infty$ under H_1 and extend S_k to models with deterministic terms and $\{y_{it}\}$ having a factor structure. Simulation results in Harris, Leybourne, and McCabe with $\delta = 3$ show that their test works reasonably well when $N \leq 40$.

If N is small, Choi and Ahn's (1999) multivariate tests for stationarity can be used for cross-sectionally correlated panels. In addition, Choi and Chue's (2007) subsampling method can also be used, although additional simulation for the calibration rule is required. To use this method, simply replace ξ_{Nbs} in relation (7.40) with a panel test statistic for the null of stationarity, and this provides the critical values of the test statistic under cross-sectional correlation.

7.7   Tests for Seasonal Panel Unit Roots

Otero, Smith, and Giulietti (2005) combine HEGY's and IPS's tests (See Subsection 6.2.2 for HEGY's test). They consider the model

$$\Delta_4 y_{it}$$
$$= \mu_{it} + \beta_i t + \sum_{j=1}^{S-1} \gamma_{is} D_{st} + \pi_1 x_{i,t-1}^{(1)} + \pi_2 x_{i,t-1}^{(2)} + \pi_3 x_{i,t-2}^{(3)} + \pi_4 x_{i,t-1}^{(3)} + u_{it},$$

where $x_{it}^{(1)} = y_{it} + y_{i,t-1} + y_{i,t-2} + y_{i,t-3}$, $x_{it}^{(2)} = -y_{it} + y_{i,t-1} - y_{i,t-2} + y_{i,t-3}$, and $x_{it}^{(3)} = y_{it} - y_{i,t-2}$; they use t-ratios and F-statistics for the null hypotheses $H_0 : \pi_1 = 0$, $H_0 : \pi_2 = 0$, $H_0 : \pi_3 = \pi_4 = 0$, and $H_0 : \pi_2 = \pi_3 = \pi_4 = 0$ to formulate IPS's test statistics. Required mean and variance adjustments obtained by simulation are also reported. Otero, Smith, and Giulietti (2007) extend the test statistics in Otero, Smith, and Giulietti (2005) to the case of cross-sectionally correlated panels. To this end, they use bootsrapping and Pesaran's (2007) method.

Lee and Shin (2006) consider the model

$$\Delta_d y_{it} = \rho_i(y_{i,t-d} - \mu_{i,t-d}) + \sum_{j=1}^{k_i} \varpi_{ij} \Delta_d y_{i,t-j} + u_{it}$$

and test the null hypothesis $H_0 : \rho_1 = \cdots = \rho_N = 0$ with Shin and Kang's (2006) IV-based test statistics introduced in Subsection 7.5.4. They derive the limiting distributions of the test statistic for a fixed N as $T \to \infty$.

7.8 Simulation Studies

MW, Choi (2001), and Hlouskova and Wagner (2006) report simulation results for the first-generation panel unit root tests. For heterogeneous alternatives, the combination test seems to perform well according to MW and Choi (2001). Hlouskova and Wagner study the performance of LLC, Harris and Tzavalis (1999), Breitung (2000), IPS, and the Fisher statistic of MW under homogeneous alternatives. They report size and power performance of the tests. But it is difficult to tell which test is most powerful in this experimental setup because the considered alternatives are homogeneous. Hlouskova and Wagner also report finite-sample performance of Hadri's (2000) and Hadri and Larsson's (2005) tests. These tests sometimes have serious size distortion as we would expect from similar univariate studies.

Gutierrez (2006) studies the size and power properties of Choi's (2006b), BN's, MP's and Phillips and Sul's (2003) tests by simulation. He assumes factor structures for the errors. Regarding BN's procedure, he finds that the pooled Dickey-Fuller-GLS test provides higher power than the pooled augmented Dickey-Fuller test for the analysis of the nonstationary properties of the idiosyncratic components. Choi's test is shown to be oversized under the factor structure, which is expected because the test assumes a two-way error component.

Gengenbach, Palm, and Urbain (2009) study the finite-sample properties of Pesaran's (2003), MP's, and BN's tests. Based on their simulation results, they recommend using Pesaran's or MP's test in a first step to determine if there are unit roots in the data. In a second step, they recommend using BN's test to determine whether the unit roots arise in the common factors or in the idiosyncratic components.

Baltagi, Bresson, and Pirotte (2007) study the finite-sample performance of the tests of LLC, Breitung (2000), IPS, MW, Choi (2001, 2006b), Chang (2002), Pesaran (2007), and Phillips and Sul (2003). They show that these tests can have considerable size distortions when the true specification exhibits spatial error correlation. These results indicate that each test is quite sensitive to aberrations of its model specification.

7.9   Other Studies

This section introduces some other works worth our attention that do not relate to the previous sections. Moon and Phillips (1999, 2004) study the dynamic panel data model with near unit roots. Moon and Phillips (1999) study the MLE, whereas Moon and Phillips (2004) the GMM estimator.

Shin, Kang, and Oh (2004) use the recursive mean adjustment for the pooled t-test (see Subsection 2.4.7 for the recursive mean adjustment) and show that it has higher power than tests based on OLS.

Breuer, McNown, and Wallace (2002) estimate a system of AR equations using the SUR method and test the null of a unit root for each series by the Dickey-Fuller test. They find that this test has higher power than the usual Dickey-Fuller test. Because the limiting distribution of this test is different from that of Dickey and Fuller (1979), they use simulation to tabulate the critical values. But performing the simulation requires choosing some unknown parameter values, which makes it difficult to use their procedure in practice.

Ng (2008) devises a method to estimate the fraction of a panel that has an AR unit root. Ng aggregates observations over a cross-section and finds that the variance of the aggregated time series has a linear time trend with a coefficient equal to the fraction of the panel that has an AR unit root. Using the latter fact, Ng proposes an estimator of the fraction. The estimator is reported to be $\sqrt{N}$ consistent.

Gutierrez (2009) shows, using Monte Carlo simulation, that panel data with a high sampling frequency can provide significant improvement in the finite empirical power of panel unit root tests, especially when the panel has a small N. These results are consistent with Choi and Chung's (1995) univariate results. The tests he considers are IPS, Pesaran (2007), and MP.

Westerlund and Larsson (2012) devise an LM test for a unit root in random-coefficient panel data model. Their test essentially tests the null of an exact unit root for all individuals against the alternative that there is a unit root on average. This alternative is obviously different from the fixed alternatives considered in Section 7.2. It is not certain yet whether Westerlund and Larsson's alternative is relevant to empirical studies.

7.10   Summary and Further Remarks

This chapter introduced various tests for panel unit roots and stationarity. It began with the first-generation unit root and stationarity tests for independent panels and then moved to the second-generation tests that allow cross-sectional correlations. Panel unit root and stationarity tests under structural changes were introduced, and those for seasonal panel unit roots were also considered.

The literature on panel unit roots and stationarity is still developing, although not as quickly as ten years ago. There seems be no consensus yet on how best we can test for unit roots and stationarity for dependent panels. Each method developed thus far works well within its model specification, but it becomes less appealing under other specifications. Resampling methods may be most robust to model misspecifications, but the downside is that they need much more computation. Convenient, simple, and robust panel unit root and stationarity tests for cross-sectionally correlated and possibly cointegrated panels are most desired, but no one seems to have devised them yet.

Epilogue

I have discussed research on unit roots conducted over the last few decades. It began with White (1958), but the related literature has grown to be immense and rich over the years. It is quite amazing that so many researchers have exerted their efforts to understand the problems related to unit roots. Why is it so, and how could this research effort be possible? There are several reasons. First, the models used for the literature on unit roots are simple. They are the AR(1) model and its extensions. It means that there is no entry barrier to understanding the models in use. If an individual has a new idea and is equipped with relevant techniques, he or she can readily work on a paper related to unit roots. Second, the literature on unit roots is empirically relevant. A large number of empirical papers using unit root tests and related methods have been written in economics and other branches of social science, and this trend is expected to continue. In fact, unit root tests have become a standard tool in time series analysis, as indicated by the numbers of citations of such papers as Dickey and Fuller (1979) and Phillips (1987a). The empirical relevance of unit roots has motivated many researchers to work on the related problems. Third, the functional central limit theory that Phillips (1986, 1987a) introduced to the literature made it possible to analyze various linear and nonlinear regression models without running into methodological difficulties. Equipped with the proper basic tool, researchers could develop their own theories in diverse directions, which expanded the literature on unit roots.

Regression analysis has a long history starting arguably from Galton's (1889) study on the relationship between children's and their parents' heights. During its long history, however, no one could have imagined that the stochastic nature of regressors could fundamentally change the way regression results are interpreted until White (1958), Dickey and Fuller (1979), Phillips (1986, 1987a), Engle and Granger (1987), and others pointed it out. Indeed, the literature on unit roots (and cointegration) brought everlasting changes in the way regression results are examined in time series and panel data analyses. When the research results on regressions with nonstationary variables were first known, so many empirical researchers vigorously reexamined economic propositions hitherto known using newly developed methods that they produced massive amounts of empirical research in macroeconomics, international finance, corporate finance, and other areas over the last 30 years. This was an exciting and rare situation in which econometric theorists and empiricists benefited enormously from each other's research and where econometric theory had profound impacts on empirical practice. It is no wonder that some people call it the "unit roots revolution."

Is the unit roots revolution over now? It may seem so, because there are fewer papers on unit roots in journals these days and there are fewer remaining questions in the area of unit roots compared to 20 years ago. This seems natural as the literature becomes mature. However, methodology from the unit roots literature and empirical facts found using the methodology will have permanent impacts on econometric theory and practice. Moreover, there are still many unknown questions related to unit roots, some of which were mentioned in this book, and they are waiting to be tackled by new and old researchers alike. A well-written paper on unit roots will always get immediate attention from the "unit roots tribe"[1] and will be appreciated and recognized. In this sense, the unit roots revolution is not over yet; it is only being perfected.

The approach I took in writing this book is to include as many papers as possible to record developments in the literature while emphasizing important ones. However, I had to omit some works. Those decisions do not mean that those works are unimportant or uninteresting, but simply reflect the limitations of time and my efforts. If someone alerts me to an important omission, I will try to include it in a future revision of this book.

---

[1] Anyone who has written at least one paper related to unit roots, either theoretical or empirical, belongs to this tribe. This is my definition of the unit roots tribe.

References

Abadir, K. M. (1992). "A Distribution Generating Equation for Unit-Root Statistics," *Oxford Bulletin of Economics and Statistics*, 54, 305–323.

Abadir, K. M. (1993). "On the Asymptotic Power of Unit Root Tests," *Econometric Theory*, 9, 189–221.

Abadir, K. M. (1995). "The Limiting Distribution of the *t* Ratio under a Unit Root," *Econometric Theory*, 11, 775–793.

Abeysinghe, T. (1991). "Inappropriate Use of Seasonal Dummies in Regression," *Economics Letters*, 36, 175–179.

Abeysinghe, T. (1994). "Deterministic Seasonal Models and Spurious Regressions," *Journal of Econometrics*, 61, 259–272.

Adda, J., and J. Gonzalo. (1996). "*P*-Values for Non-Standard Distributions with an Application to the DF Test," *Economics Letters*, 50, 155–160.

Agiakloglou, C., and P. Newbold. (1992). "Empirical Evidence on Dickey-Fuller-Type Tests," *Journal of Time Series Analysis*, 13, 471–483.

Agiakloglou, C., and P. Newbold. (1994). "Lagrange Multiplier Tests for Fractional Difference," *Journal of Time Series Analysis*, 15, 253–262.

Agiakloglou, C., and P. Newbold. (1996). "The Balance between Size and Power in Dickey-Fuller Tests with Data-Dependent Rules for the Choice of Truncation Lag," *Economics Letters*, 52, 229–234.

Ahn, S. K. (1993). "Some Tests for Unit Roots in Autoregressive Integrated Moving-Average Models with Deterministic Trends," *Biometrika*, 80, 855–868.

Ahn, S. K., and S. Cho. (1993). "Some Tests for Unit Roots in Seasonal Time Series with Deterministic Trends," *Statistics & Probability Letters*, 16, 85–95.

Ahn, S. K., S. Fotopoulos, and L. He. (2001). "Unit Root Tests with Infinite Variance Errors," *Econometric Reviews*, 20, 461–483.

Ahtola, J., and G. C. Tiao. (1987). "Distributions of Least Squares Estimators of Autoregressive Parameters for a Process with Complex Roots on the Unit Circle," *Journal of Time Series Analysis*, 8, 1–14.

Akaike, H. (1973). "Information Theory and an Extension of the Maximum Likelihood Principle," presented at the Second International Symposium on Information Theory, Tsahkadsor, Armenia; September, pp. 267–281.

Akgiray, V., and G. G. Booth. (1988). "The Stable-Law Model of Stock Returns," *Journal of Business & Economic Statistics*, 6, 51–57.

Akgiray, V., G. G. Booth, and B. Seifert. (1988). "Distribution Properties of Latin American Black Market Exchange Rates," *Journal of International Money and Finance*, 7, 37–48.

Altonji, J., and Ashenfelter, O. (1980). "Wage Movements and the Labour Market Equilibrium Hypothesis," *Economica*, 47, 217–45.

Amsler, C., and J. Lee. (1995). "An LM Test for a Unit Root in the Presence of a Structural Change," *Econometric Theory*, 11, 359–368.

Amsler, C., and P. Schmidt. (2012). "Tests of Short Memory with Thick-Tailed Errors," *Journal of Business & Economic Statistics*, 30, 381–390.

Anderson, R. L. (1942). "Distribution of the Serial Correlation Coefficient," *Annals of Mathematical Statistics*, 13, 1–13.

Anderson, T. W., and D. A. Darling. (1952). "Asymptotic Theory of Certain 'Goodness of Fit' Criteria Based on Stochastic Processes," *Annals of Mathematical Statistics*, 23, 193–212.

Andrews, D. W. K. (1991). "Heteroskedasticity and Autocorrelation Consistent Covariance Matrix Estimation," *Econometrica*, 59, 817–858.

Andrews, D. W. K. (1993). "Exactly Median-Unbiased Estimation of First Order Autoregressive/Unit Root Models," *Econometrica*, 61, 139–165.

Andrews, D. W. K., and H. Chen. (1994). "Approximately Median-Unbiased Estimation of Autoregressive Models," *Journal of Business & Economic Statistics*, 12, 187–204.

Andrews, D. W. K., and P. Guggenberger. (2008). "Asymptotics for Stationary Very Nearly Unit Root Processes," *Journal of Time Series Analysis*, 29, 203–212.

Andrews, D. W. K., and W. Ploberger. (1994). "Optimal Tests When a Nuisance Parameter Is Present Only under the Alternative," *Econometrica*, 62, 1383–1414.

Arellano, C., and S. G. Pantula. (1995). "Testing for Trend Stationarity versus Difference Stationarity," *Journal of Time Series Analysis*, 16, 147–164.

Arnold, L. (1974). *Stochastic Differential Equations: Theory and Applications*. New York: Wiley.

Astill, S., D. I. Harvey, and A. M. R Taylor. (2013). "A Bootstrap Test for Additive Outliers in Non-Stationary Time Series," *Journal of Time Series Analysis*, 34, 454–465.

Aue, A. (2008). "Near-Integrated Random Coefficient Autoregressive Time Series," *Econometric Theory*, 24, 1343–1372.

Aue, A., and L. Horváth. (2007). "A Limit Theorem for Mildly Explosive Autoregression with Stable Errors," *Econometric Theory*, 23, 201–220.

Aue, A., and L. Horváth. (2013). "Structural Breaks in Time Series," *Journal of Time Series Analysis*, 34, 1–16.

Bai, J., and S. Ng. (2004). "A Panic Attack on Unit Roots and Cointegration," *Econometrica*, 72, 1127–1177.

Bai, J., and S. Ng. (2005). "A New Look at Panel Testing of Stationarity and the PPP Hypothesis," in *Identification and Inference in Econometric Models: Essays in Honor of Thomas J. Rothenberg*, edited by D. W. K. Andrews and J. Stock, pp. 426–450. New York: Cambridge University Press.

Bai, J., and S. Ng. (2010). "Panel Unit Root Tests With Cross-Section Dependence: A further Investigation," *Econometric Theory*, 26, 1088–1114.

Baillie, R. T. (1996). "Long Memory Processes and Fractional Integration in Econometrics," *Journal of Econometrics*, 73, 5–59.

Balcombe, K. (1999). "Seasonal Unit Root Tests with Structural Breaks in Deterministic Seasonality," *Oxford Bulletin of Economics and Statistics*, 61, 569–582.

Baltagi, B. H. (2005). *Econometric Analysis of Panel Data*. New York: Wiley.

Baltagi, B. H., G. Bresson, and A. Pirotte. (2007). "Panel Unit Root Tests and Spatial Dependence," *Journal of Applied Econometrics*, 22, 339–360.

Baltagi, B. H., and C. Kao. (2001). "Nonstationary Panels, Cointegration in Panels and Dynamic Panels: A Survey," in *Advances in Econometrics* vol. 15, edited by B.H. Baltagi, pp. 7–51. Amsterdam: JAI.

Balvers, R., Y. Wu, and E. Gilliland. (2000). "Mean Reversion across National Stock Markets and Parametric Contrarian Investment Strategies," *Journal of Finance*, 55, 745–772.

Banerjee, A. (1999). "Panel Data Unit Roots and Cointegration: An Overview," *Oxford Bulletin of Economics and Statistics*, 61, 607–629.

Banerjee, A., J. Dolado, J. W. Galbraith, and D. F. Hendry. (1993). *Co-Integration, Error-Correction, and the Econometric Analysis of Non-Stationary Data*. New York: Oxford University Press.

Banerjee, A., R. L. Lumsdaine, and J. H. Stock. (1992). "Recursive and Sequential Tests of the Unit-Root and Trend-Break Hypotheses: Theory and International Evidence," *Journal of Business & Economic Statistics*, 10, 271–287.

Banerjee, A., M. Marcellino, and C. Osbat. (2005). "Testing for PPP: Should We Use Panel Methods?" *Empirical Economics*, 30, 77–91.

Barthélémy, F., and M. Lubrano. (1996). "Unit Roots Tests and SARIMA Models," *Economics Letters*, 50, 147–154.

Basawa, I. V., A. K. Mallik, W. P. McCormick, J. H. Reeves, and R. L. Taylor. (1991a). "Bootstrap Test of Significance and Sequential Bootstrap Estimation for Unstable First Order Autoregressive Processes," *Communications in Statistics—Theory and Methods*, 20, 1015–1026.

Basawa, I. V., A. K. Mallik, W. P. McCormick, J. H. Reeves, and R. L. Taylor. (1991b). "Bootstrapping Unstable First-Order Autoregressive Processes," *Annals of Statistics*, 19, 1098–1101.

Basawa, I. V., A. K. Mallik, W. P. McCormick, and R. L. Taylor. (1989). "Bootstrapping Explosive Autoregressive Processes," *Annals of Statistics*, 17, 1479–1486.

Baumol, W. J. (1986). "Productivity Growth, Convergence, and Welfare: What the Long-Run Data Show," *American Economic Review*, 76, 1072–1085.

Beaulieu, J., and J. A. Miron. (1993). "Seasonal Unit Roots in Aggregate U.S. Data," *Journal of Econometrics*, 55, 305–328.

Bec, F., M. Ben Salem, and M. Carrasco. (2004). "Tests for Unit-Root versus Threshold Specification with an Application to the Purchasing Power Parity Relationship," *Journal of Business & Economic Statistics*, 22, 382–395.

Bec, F., A. Guay, and E. Guerre. (2008). "Adaptive Consistent Unit-Root Tests Based on Autoregressive Threshold Model," *Journal of Econometrics*, 142, 94–133.

Becker, R., W. Enders, and J. Lee. (2006). "A Stationarity Test in the Presence of an Unknown Number of Smooth Breaks," *Journal of Time Series Analysis*, 27, 381–409.

Beran, J. (1994). *Statistics for Long-memory Processes*. Vol. 61 of *Monographs on Statistics and Applied Probability*. New York: Chapman & Hall/CRC.

Berger, J. O. (1985). *Statistical Decision Theory and Bayesian Analysis*. New York: Springer-Verlag.

Berger, J. O., and R. Yang. (1994). "Noninformative Priors and Bayesian Testing for the AR(1) Model," *Econometric Theory*, 10, 461–482.

Bergstrom, A. R. (1990). *Continuous Time Econometric Modelling*. New York: Oxford University Press.

Berk, K. N. (1974). "Consistent Autoregressive Spectral Estimates," *Annals of Statistics*, 2, 489–502.

Bernard, A. B., and S. N. Durlauf. (1995). "Convergence in International Output," *Journal of Applied Econometrics*, 10, 97–108.

Bernardo, J. M., and A. F. M. Smith. (1994). *Bayesian Theory*. New York: Wiley.

Beveridge, S., and C. R. Nelson. (1981). "A New Approach to Decomposition of Economic Time Series into Permanent and Transitory Components with Particular Attention to Measurement of the 'Business Cycle,'" *Journal of Monetary Economics*, 7, 151–174.

Bierens, H. J. (1997). "Testing the Unit Root with Drift Hypothesis against Nonlinear Trend Stationarity, with an Application to the U.S. Price Level and Interest Rate," *Journal of Econometrics*, 81, 29–64.

Bierens, H. J. (2001). "Complex Unit Roots and Business Cycles: Are They Real?" *Econometric Theory*, 17, 962–983.

Billingsley, P. (1999). *Convergence of Probability Measures*. 2nd edition. New York: John Wiley.

Binder, M., C. Hsiao, and M. H. Pesaran. (2005). "Estimation and Inference in Short Panel Vector Autoregressions with Unit Roots and Cointegration," *Econometric Theory*, 21, 795–837.

Blanchard, O. J., and L. H. Summers. (1986). "Hysteresis and the European Unemployment Problem," in *NBER Macroeconomics Annual*, edited by S. Fischer, pp. 15–90. Cambridge, MA: MIT Press.

Blanchard, O. J., and L. H. Summers. (1987). "Hysteresis in Unemployment," *European Economic Review*, 31, 288–295.

Blood, D. J., and P. C. B. Phillips. (1995)." Recession Headline News, Consumer Sentiment, the State of the Economy and Presidential Popularity: A Time Series Analysis 1989–1993," *International Journal of Public Opinion Research*, 7, 2–22.

Bloomfield, P. (1973). "An Exponential Model for the Spectrum of a Scalar Time Series," *Biometrika*, 60, 217–226.

Bobkoski, M. J. (1983). "Hypothesis Testing in Nonstationary Time Series." PhD diss., University of Wisconsin–Madison.

Bose, A. (1988). "Edgeworth Correction by Bootstrap in Autoregressions," *Annals of Statistics*, 16, 1709–1722.

Boswijk, H. P., and P. H. Franses. (1995). "Testing for Periodic Integration," *Economics Letters*, 48, 241–248.

Boswijk, H. P., and P. H. Franses. (1996). "Unit Roots in Periodic Autoregressions," *Journal of Time Series Analysis*, 17, 221–245.

Boswijk, H. P., P. H. Franses, and N. Haldrup. (1997). "Multiple Unit Roots in Periodic Autoregression," *Journal of Econometrics*, 80, 167–193.

Boswijk, H. P., and F. Klaassen, F. (2012). "Why Frequency Matters for Unit Root Testing in Financial Time Series," *Journal of Business & Economic Statistics*, 30, 351–357.

Box, G. E. P., and G. M. Jenkins. (1976). *Time Series Analysis: Forecasting and Control*. San Francisco: Holden-Day.

Box-Steffensmeier, J. M., and R. M. Smith. (1996). "The Dynamics of Aggregate Partisanship," *American Political Science Review*, 90, 567–580.

Bradley, R. C. (1988). "A Central Limit Theorem for Stationary ρ-Mixing Sequences with Infinite Variance," *Annals of Probability*, 16, 313–332.

Breitung, J. (2000). "The Local Power of Some Unit Root Tests for Panel Data," in *Advances in Econometrics*, vol. 15, edited by B. Baltagi, pp. 161–178. Amsterdam: JAI.

Breitung, J. (2002). "Nonparametric Tests for Unit Root and Cointegration," *Journal of Econometrics*, 108, 343–363.

Breitung, J., and B. Candelon. (2005). "Purchasing Power Parity during Currency Crises: A Panel Unit Root Test under Structural Breaks," *Review of World Economics*, 141, 124–140.

Breitung, J., and I. Choi. (2013). "Factor Models," in *Handbook of Research Methods and Applications in Empirical Macroeconomics*, edited by N. Hashimzade, and M. A. Thornton, pp. 249–265. Northampton, MA: Edward Elgar.

Breitung, J., and S. Das. (2005). "Panel Unit Root Tests under Cross-Sectional Dependence," *Statistica Neerlandica*, 59, 414–433.

Breitung, J., and S. Das. (2008). "Testing for Unit Roots in Panels with a Factor Structure," *Econometric Theory*, 24, 88–108.

Breitung, J., and P. H. Franses. (1998). "On Phillips-Perron-Type Tests for Seasonal Unit Roots," *Econometric Theory*, 14, 200–221.

Breitung, J., and C. Gouriéroux. (1997). "Rank Tests for Unit Roots," *Journal of Econometrics*, 81, 7–27.

Breitung, J., and W. Meyer. (1994). "Testing for Unit Roots in Panel Data: Are Wages on Different Bargaining Levels Cointegrated?" *Applied Economics*, 26, 353–361.

Breitung, J., and M. H. Pesaran. (2008). "Unit Roots and Cointegration in Panels," in *The Econometrics of Panel Data*, edited by L. Mátyás and P. Sevestre, pp. 279–322. Berlin: Springer.

Breuer, J. B., R. McNown, and M. Wallace. (2002). "Series-Specific Unit Root Tests with Panel Data," *Oxford Bulletin of Economics and Statistics*, 64, 527–546.

Brockwell, P. J., and R. A. Davis. (1991). *Time Series: Theory and Methods*. New York: Springer-Verlag.

Brunello, G. (1990). "Hysteresis and 'The Japanese Unemployment Problem': A Preliminary Investigation," *Oxford Economic Papers*, 42, 483–500.

Bühlmann, P. (1997). "Sieve Bootstrap for Time Series," *Bernoulli*, 3, 123–148.

Burke, S.P. (1996). "Some Reparameterizations of Large Polynomials for Dynamic Analysis," *Oxford Bulletin of Economics and Statistics*, 58, 373–389.

Burnham, K. P., and D. R. Anderson. (2002). *Model Selection and Multi-Model Inference: A Practical Information-Theoretic Approach*. 2nd edition. New York: Springer-Verlag.

Burridge, P., and E. Guerre. (1996). "The Limit Distribution of Level Crossings of a Random Walk, and a Simple Unit Root Test," *Econometric Theory*, 12, 705–723.

Burridge, P., and D. Hristova. (2008). "Consistent Estimation and Order Selection for Nonstationary Autoregressive Processes with Stable Innovations," *Journal of Time Series Analysis*, 29, 695–718.

Burridge, P., and A. M. R. Taylor. (2000). "On the Power of GLS-Type Unit Root Tests," *Oxford Bulletin of Economics and Statistics*, 62, 633–645.

Burridge, P., and A. M. R. Taylor. (2001a). "On the Properties of Regression-Based Tests for Seasonal Unit Roots in the Presence of Higher-Order Serial Correlation," *Journal of Business & Economic Statistics*, 19, 374–379.

Burridge, P., and A. M. R. Taylor. (2001b). "On Regression-Based Tests for Seasonal Unit Roots in the Presence of Periodic Heteroscedasticity," *Journal of Econometrics*, 104, 91–117.

Burridge, P., and A. M. R. Taylor. (2004). "Bootstrapping the HEGY Seasonal Unit Root Tests," *Journal of Econometrics*, 123, 67–87.

Busetti, F., L. Forni, A. Harvey, and F. Venditti. (2007). "Inflation Convergence and Divergence within the European Monetary Union," *International Journal of Central Banking*, 3(2), 95–121.

Busetti, F., and A. Harvey. (2001). "Testing for the Presence of a Random Walk in Series with Structural Breaks," *Journal of Time Series Analysis*, 22, 127–150.

Busetti, F., and A. Harvey. (2003a). "Further Comments on Stationarity Tests in Series with Structural Breaks at Unknown Points," *Journal of Time Series Analysis*, 24, 137–140.

Busetti, F., and A. Harvey. (2003b). "Seasonality Tests," *Journal of Business & Economic Statistics*, 21, 420–436.

Busetti, F., and A. M. R. Taylor. (2003a). "Variance Shifts, Structural Breaks, and Stationarity Tests," *Journal of Business & Economic Statistics*, 21, 510–531.

Busetti, F., and A. M. R. Taylor. (2003b). "Testing against Stochastic Trend and Seasonality in the Presence of Unattended Breaks and Unit Roots," *Journal of Econometrics*, 117, 21–53.

Busetti, F., and A. M. R. Taylor. (2004). "Tests of Stationarity against a Change in Persistence," *Journal of Econometrics*, 123, 33–66.

Busetti, F., and A. M. R. Taylor. (2005). "Stationarity Tests for Irregularly Spaced Observations and the Effects of Sampling Frequency on Power," *Econometric Theory*, 21, 757–794.

Callegari, F., N. Cappuccio, and D. Lubian. (2003). "Asymptotic Inference in Time Series Regressions with a Unit Root and Infinite Variance Errors," *Journal of Statistical Planning and Inference*, 116, 277–303.

Caner, M. (1998). "A Locally Optimal Seasonal Unit-Root Test," *Journal of Business & Economic Statistics*, 16, 349–356.

Caner, M., and B. E. Hansen. (2001). "Threshold Autoregression with a Unit Root," *Econometrica*, 69, 1555–1596.

Caner, M., and L. Kilian. (2001). "Size Distortions of Tests of the Null Hypothesis of Stationarity: Evidence and Implications for the PPP Debate," *Journal of International Money and Finance*, 20, 639–657.

Canova, F., and B. E. Hansen. (1995). "Are Seasonal Patterns Constant over Time? A Test for Seasonal Stability," *Journal of Business & Economic Statistics*, 13, 237–252.

Caporale, G. M., and N. Pittis. (1999). "Unit Root Testing Using Covariates: Some Theory and Evidence," *Oxford Bulletin of Economics and Statistics*, 61, 583–595.

Cappuccio, N., and D. Lubian. (2006). "Local Asymptotic Distributions of Stationarity Tests," *Journal of Time Series Analysis*, 27, 323–345.

Carrion-i-Silvestre, J. L., T. Del Barrio-Castro, and E. López-Bazo. (2005). "Breaking the Panels: An Application to the GDP Per Capita," *Econometrics Journal*, 8, 159–175.

Carrion-i-Silvestre, J. L., D. Kim, and P. Perron. (2009). "GLS-Based Unit Root Tests with Multiple Structural Breaks under Both the Null and the Alternative Hypotheses," *Econometric Theory*, 25, 1754–1792.

Casella, G., and R. L. Berger. (1990). *Statistical Inference*. Belmont, CA: Duxbury Press.

Castro, T. D. B. (2006). "On the Performance of the DHF Tests against Nonstationary Alternatives," *Statistics & Probability Letters*, 76, 291–297.

Castro, T. D. B. (2007). "Using the HEGY Procedure When Not All Roots Are Present," *Journal of Time Series Analysis*, 28, 910–922.

Castro, T. D. B., and D. R. Osborn. (2008). "Testing for Seasonal Unit Roots in Periodic Integrated Autoregressive Processes," *Econometric Theory*, 24, 1093–1129.

Castro, T. D. B., and D. R. Osborn. (2011). "HEGY Tests in the Presence of Moving Averages," *Oxford Bulletin of Economics and Statistics*, 73, 691–704.

Cavaliere, G. (2001). "Testing the Unit Root Hypothesis Using Generalized Range Statistics," *Econometrics Journal*, 4, 70–88.

Cavaliere, G. (2004). "Unit Root Tests under Time-Varying Variances," *Econometric Reviews*, 23, 259–292.

Cavaliere, G., D. I. Harvey, S. J. Leybourne, and A. R. Taylor. (2011). "Testing for Unit Roots in the Presence of a Possible Break in Trend and Nonstationary Volatility," *Econometric Theory*, 27, 957–991.

Cavaliere, G., and I. Georgiev. (2007). "Testing for Unit Roots in Autoregressions with Multiple Level Shifts," *Econometric Theory*, 23, 1162–1215.

Cavaliere, G., and A. M. R. Taylor. (2007). "Testing for Unit Roots in Time Series Models with Non-Stationary Volatility," *Journal of Econometrics*, 140, 919–947.

Cavaliere, G., and A. M. R. Taylor. (2008). "Bootstrap Unit Root Tests for Time Series with Nonstationary Volatility," *Econometric Theory*, 24, 43–71.

Chambers, M. J. (2004). "Testing for Unit Roots with Flow Data and Varying Sampling Frequency," *Journal of Econometrics*, 119, 1–18.

Chambers, M. J. (2008). "Corrigendum to: 'Testing for Unit Roots with Flow Data and Varying Sampling Frequency' [*J. Econom.* 119 (1) (2004) 1–18]," *Journal of Econometrics*, 144, 524–525.

Chan, N. H. (1990). "Inference for Near-Integrated Time Series with Infinite Variance," *Journal of the American Statistical Association*, 85, 1069–1074.

Chan, N. H., and N. Terrin. (1995). "Inference for Unstable Long-memory Processes with Applications to Fractional Unit Root Autoregressions," *Annals of Statistics*, 23, 1662–1683.

Chan, N. H., and L. T. Tran. (1989). "On the First-Order Autoregressive Process with Infinite Variance," *Econometric Theory*, 5, 354–362.

Chan, N. H., and C. Z. Wei. (1987). "Asymptotic Inference for Nearly Nonstationary AR(1) Processes," *Annals of Statistics*, 15, 1050–1063.

Chan, N. H., and C. Z. Wei. (1988). "Limiting Distributions of Least Squares Estimates of Unstable Autoregressive Processes," *Annals of Statistics*, 16, 367–401.

Chan, N. H., and R. Zhang. (2012). "Non-Stationary Autoregressive Processes with Infinite Variance," *Journal of Time Series Analysis*, 33, 916–934.

Chang, Y. (2002). "Nonlinear IV Unit Root Tests in Panels with Cross-Sectional Dependency," *Journal of Econometrics*, 110, 261–292.

Chang, Y. (2004). "Bootstrap Unit Root Tests in Panels with Cross-Sectional Dependency," *Journal of Econometrics*, 120, 263–293.

Chang, Y., and J. Y. Park. (2002). "On the Asymptotics of ADF Tests for Unit Roots," *Econometric Reviews*, 21, 431–447.

Chang, Y., and J. Y. Park. (2003). "A Sieve Bootstrap for the Test of a Unit Root," *Journal of Time Series Analysis*, 24, 379–400.

Chang, Y., and W. Song. (2009). "Testing for Unit Roots in Small Panels with Short-Run and Long-Run Cross-Sectional Dependencies," *Review of Economic Studies*, 76, 903–935.

Chen, J. G., and B. S. Kuo. (2013). "Gaussian Inference in General AR(1) Models Based on Difference," *Journal of Time Series Analysis*, 34, 447–453.

Cho, S., Y. J. Park, and S. K. Ahn. (1995). "Unit Root Tests for Seasonal Models with Deterministic Trends," *Statistics & Probability Letters*, 25, 27–35.

Choi, I. (1992a). "Durbin-Hausman Tests for a Unit Root," *Oxford Bulletin of Economics and Statistics*, 54, 289–304.

Choi, I. (1992b). "Effects of Data Aggregation on the Power of Tests for a Unit Root: A Simulation Study," *Economics Letters*, 40, 397–401.

Choi, I. (1993). "Asymptotic Normality of the Least-Squares Estimates for Higher Order Autoregressive Integrated Processes with Some Applications," *Econometric Theory*, 9, 263–282.

Choi, I. (1994). "Residual-Based Tests for the Null of Stationarity with Applications to U.S. Macroeconomic Time Series," *Econometric Theory*, 10, 720–746.

Choi, I. (2001). "Unit Root Tests for Panel Data," *Journal of International Money and Finance*, 20, 249–272.

Choi, I. (2006a). "Nonstationary Panels," in *Palgrave Handbook of Econometrics*, vol. 1, edited by T. C. Mills and K. Patterson, pp. 511–539. New York: Palgrave Macmillan.

Choi, I. (2006b). "Unit Root Tests for Cross-Sectionally Correlated Panels," in *Econometric Theory and Practice: Frontiers of Analysis and Applied Research*, edited by D. Corbae, S. Durlauf, and B. Hansen, pp. 311–333. New York: Cambridge University Press.

Choi, I. (2009). "Improving Empirical Size of the KPSS Test of Stationarity," *Journal of Economic Theory and Econometrics*, 1, 1–14.

Choi, I., and B. C. Ahn. (1999). "Testing the Null of Stationarity for Multiple Time Series," *Journal of Econometrics*, 88, 41–77.

Choi, I., and T. K. Chue. (2007). "Subsampling Hypothesis Tests for Nonstationary Panels with Applications to Exchange Rates and Stock Prices," *Journal of Applied Econometrics*, 22, 233–264.

Choi, I., and B. S. Chung. (1995). "Sampling Frequency and the Power of Tests for a Unit Root: A Simulation Study," *Economics Letters*, 49, 131–136.

Choi, I., and P. C. B. Phillips. (1993). "Testing for a Unit Root by Frequency Domain Regression," *Journal of Econometrics*, 59, 263–286.

Chowdhury, A. R. (1991). "A Causal Analysis of Defense Spending and Economic Growth," *Journal of Conflict Resolution*, 35, 80–97.

Christiano, L. J. (1992). "Searching for a Break in GNP," *Journal of Business & Economic Statistics*, 10, 237–250.

Clarke, H. D., and M. C. Stewart. (1994). "Prospections, Retrospections, and Rationality: The 'Bankers' Model of Presidential Approval Reconsidered," *American Journal of Political Science*, 38, 1104–1123.

Cochrane, J. H. (2005). *Asset Pricing*. Princeton, NJ: Princeton University Press.

Cook, S. (2003). "Modified Unit Root Tests and Momentum Threshold Autoregressive Processes," *Statistics & Probability Letters*, 64, 83–88.

Costantini, M., and L. Gutierrez. (2007). "Simple Panel Unit Root Tests to Detect Changes in Persistence," *Economics Letters*, 96, 363–368.

Costantini, M., and C. Lupi. (2012). "A Simple Panel-CADF Test for Unit Roots," *Oxford Bulletin of Economics and Statistics*, 75, 276–296.

Cox, D. D. (1991). "Gaussian Likelihood Estimation for Nearly Nonstationary AR(1) Processes," *Annals of Statistics*, 19, 1129–1142.

Cox, D. D., and I. Llatas. (1991). "Maximum Likelihood Type Estimation for Nearly Nonstationary Autoregressive Time Series," *Annals of Statistics*, 19, 1109–1128.

Culver, S. E., and D. H. Papell. (1997). "Is There a Unit Root in the Inflation Rate? Evidence from Sequential Break and Panel Data Models," *Journal of Applied Econometrics*, 12, 435–444.

Davidson, J. (1994). *Stochastic Limit Theory*. New York: Oxford University Press.

Davis, A. W. (1976). "Statistical Distributions in Univariate and Multivariate Edgeworth Populations," *Biometrika*, 63, 661–670.

Davison, A. C., and D. V. Hinkley. (1997). *Bootstrap Methods and Their Application*. Cambridge: Cambridge University Press.

De Blander, R., and G. Dhaene. (2012). "Unit Root Tests for Panel Data With AR(1) Errors and Small T," *Econometrics Journal*, 15, 101–124.

de Jong, R. M., C. Amsler and P. Schmidt. (2007). "A Robust Version of the KPSS Test Based on Indicators," *Journal of Econometrics*, 137, 311–333.

DeJong, D. N., J. C. Nankervis, N. E. Savin, and C. H. Whiteman. (1992a). "Integration versus Trend Stationary in Time Series," *Econometrica*, 60, 423–433.

DeJong, D. N., J. C. Nankervis, N. E. Savin, and C. H. Whiteman. (1992b). "The Power Problems of Unit Root Test in Time Series with Autoregressive Errors," *Journal of Econometrics*, 53, 323–343.

DeJong, D. N., and C. H. Whiteman. (1991a). "The Case for Trend-Stationarity Is Stronger than We Thought," *Journal of Applied Econometrics*, 6, 413–421.

DeJong, D. N., and C. H. Whiteman. (1991b). "On Robustness," *Journal of Monetary Economics*, 28, 265–270.

DeJong, D. N., and C. H. Whiteman. (1991c). "Reconsidering 'Trends and Random Walks in Macroeconomic Time Series,'" *Journal of Monetary Economics*, 28, 221–254.

DeLong, J. B. (1988). "Productivity Growth, Convergence, and Welfare: Comment," *American Economic Review*, 78, 1138–1154.

Demetrescu, M., and C. Hanck. (2012). "Unit Root Testing in Heteroscedastic Panels Using the Cauchy Estimator," *Journal of Business & Economic Statistics*, 30, 256–264.

Demetrescu, M., U. Hassler, and A. Tarcolea. (2006). "Combining Significance of Correlated Statistics with Application to Panel Data," *Oxford Bulletin of Economics and Statistics*, 68, 647–663.

Demetrescu, M., and R. Kruse. (2013). "The Power of Unit Root Tests against Nonlinear Local Alternatives," *Journal of Time Series Analysis*, 34, 40–61.

Demetrescu, M., V. Kuzin, and U. Hassler. (2008). "Long Memory Testing in the Time Domain," *Econometric Theory*, 24, 176–215.

Dent, W. (1977). "Computation of the Exact Likelihood Function of an ARIMA Process," *Journal of Statistical Computation and Simulation*, 5, 193–206.

De Wachter, S., R. D. F. Harris, and E. Tzavalis. (2007). "Panel Data Unit Roots Tests: The Role of Serial Correlation and the Time Dimension," *Journal of Statistical Planning and Inference*, 137, 230–244.

Dickey, D. A., and W. A. Fuller. (1979). "Distribution of the Estimators for Autoregressive Time Series with a Unit Root," *Journal of the American Statistical Association*, 74, 427–431.

Dickey, D. A., and W. A. Fuller. (1981). "Likelihood Ratio Statistics for Autoregressive Time Series with a Unit Root," *Econometrica*, 49, 1057–1072.

Dickey, D. A., D. P. Hasza, and W. A. Fuller. (1984). "Testing for Unit Roots in Seasonal Time Series," *Journal of the American Statistical Association*, 79, 355–367.

Diebold, F. X. and G. D. Rudebusch. (1991). "On the Power of Dickey-Fuller Tests against Fractional Alternatives," *Economics Letters*, 35, 155–160.

Distaso, W. (2008). "Testing for Unit Root Processes in Random-Coefficient Autoregressive Models," *Journal of Econometrics*, 142, 581–609.

Dolado, J. J., J. Gonzalo, and L. Mayoral. (2002). "A Fractional Dickey-Fuller Test for Unit Roots," *Econometrica*, 70, 1963–2006.

Donsker, M. D. (1951). "An Invariance Principle for Certain Probability Limit Theorems," *Memoirs of the American Mathematical Society*, 6, 1–12.

Dufour, J., and M. L. King. (1991). "Optimal Invariant Tests for the Autocorrelation Coefficient in Linear Regressions with Stationary or Nonstationary AR(1) Errors," *Journal of Econometrics*, 47, 115–143.

Efron, B., and R. Tibshirani. (1993). *An Introduction to the Bootstrap*. New York: Chapman & Hall.

Elliott, G. (1999). "Efficient Tests for a Unit Root When the Initial Observation is Drawn from Its Unconditional Distribution," *International Economic Review*, 40, 767–783.

Elliott, G., and M. Jansson. (2003). "Testing for Unit Roots with Stationary Covariates," *Journal of Econometrics*, 115, 75–89.

Elliott, G., and U. K. Müller. (2006). "Minimizing the Impact of the Initial Condition on Testing for Unit Roots," *Journal of Econometrics*, 135, 285–310.

Elliott, G., T. J. Rothenberg, and J. H. Stock. (1996). "Efficient Tests for an Autoregressive Unit Root," *Econometrica*, 64, 813–836.

Elliott, G., and J. H. Stock. (2001). "Confidence Intervals for Autoregressive Coefficients Near One," *Journal of Econometrics*, 103, 155–181.

Enders, W., and C. W. J. Granger. (1998). "Unit-Root Tests and Asymmetric Adjustment with an Example Using the Term Structure of Interest Rates," *Journal of Business & Economic Statistics*, 16, 304–311.

Enders, W., and J. Lee. (2012a). "A Unit Root Test Using a Fourier Series to Approximate Smooth Breaks," *Oxford Bulletin of Economics and Statistics*, 74, 574–599.

Enders, W., and J. Lee. (2012b). "The Flexible Fourier Form and Dickey-Fuller Type Unit Root Tests," *Economics Letters*, 117, 196–199.

Engle, R. F., and C. W. J. Granger. (1987). "Co-Integration and Error Correction: Representation, Estimation, and Testing," *Econometrica*, 55, 251–276.

Estrin, S., G. Urga, and S. Lazarova. (2001). "Testing for Ongoing Convergence in Transition Economies, 1970 to 1998," *Journal of Comparative Economics*, 29, 677–691.

Evans, G. B. A., and N. E. Savin. (1981). "Testing for Unit Roots: 1," *Econometrica*, 49, 753–779.

Evans, G. B. A., and N. E. Savin. (1984). "Testing for Unit Roots: 2," *Econometrica*, 52, 1241–1269.

Falk, B., and C. Wang. (2003). "Testing Long-Run PPP with Infinite-Variance Returns," *Journal of Applied Econometrics*, 18, 471–484.

Fama, E. F., and K. R. French. (1988). "Permanent and Temporary Components of Stock Prices," *Journal of Political Economy*, 96, 246–273.

Fan, Y., and R. Gençay. (2010). "Unit Root Tests with Wavelets," *Econometric Theory*, 26, 1305–1331.

Ferguson, T. S. (1967). *Mathematical Statistics: A Decision Theoretic Approach*. New York: Academic Press.

Ferretti, N., and J. Romo. (1996). "Unit Root Bootstrap Tests for AR(1) Models," *Biometrika*, 83, 849–860.

Forni, M., M. Hallin, M. Lippi, and L. Reichlin. (2004). "The Generalized Dynamic Factor Model Consistency and Rates," *Journal of Econometrics*, 119, 231–255.

Fossati, S. (2013). "Unit Root Testing with Stationary Covariates and a Structural Break in the Trend Function," *Journal of Time Series Analysis*, 34, 368–384 .

Fotopoulos, S. B., and S. K. Ahn. (2003). "Rank Based Dickey-Fuller Test Statistics," *Journal of Time Series Analysis*, 24, 647–662.

Franses, P. H. (1994). "A Multivariate Approach to Modeling Univariate Seasonal Time Series," *Journal of Econometrics*, 63, 133–151.

Franses, P. H. (1996). *Periodicity and Stochastic Trends in Economic Time Series.* Oxford: Oxford University Press.

Franses, P. H., and N. Haldrup. (1994). "The Effects of Additive Outliers on Tests for Unit Roots and Cointegration," *Journal of Business & Economic Statistics*, 12, 471–478.

Franses, P. H., H. Hoek, and R. Paap. (1997). "Bayesian Analysis of Seasonal Unit Roots and Seasonal Mean Shifts," *Journal of Econometrics*, 78, 359–380.

Franses, P. H., S. Hylleberg, and H. S. Lee. (1995). "Spurious Deterministic Seasonality," *Economics Letters*, 48, 249–256.

Franses, P. H., and T. J. Vogelsang. (1998). "On Seasonal Cycles, Unit Roots, and Mean Shifts," *Review of Economics and Statistics*, 80, 231–240.

Fuller, W. A. (1976). *Introduction to Statistical Time Series.* New York: John Wiley & Sons.

Galbraith, J. W., and V. Zinde-Walsh. (1999). "On the Distributions of Augmented Dickey-Fuller Statistics in Processes with Moving Average Components," *Journal of Econometrics*, 93, 25–47.

Galton, F. (1889). *Natural Inheritance.* London: Macmillan.

Gao, J. and P. M. Robinson. (2013). "Inference on Nonstationary Time Series with Moving Mean," Working Paper, London School of Economics.

Gao, J., D. Tjostheim, D., and J. Yin. (2013). "Estimation in Threshold Autoregressive Models with a Stationary and a Unit Root Regime," *Journal of Econometrics*, 172, 1–13.

García, A., and A. Sansó. (2006). "A Generalization of the Burridge-Guerre Nonparametric Unit Root Test," *Econometric Theory*, 22, 756–761.

Gengenbach, C., F. C. Palm, and J. Urbain. (2009). "Panel Unit Root Tests in the Presence of Cross-Sectional Dependencies: Comparison and Implications for Modelling," *Econometric Reviews*, 29, 111–145.

Ghysels, E. (1990). "Unit-Root Tests and the Statistical Pitfalls of Seasonal Adjustment: The Case of U.S. Postwar Real Gross National Product," *Journal of Business & Economic Statistics*, 8, 145–152.

Ghysels, E., A. Hall, and H. S. Lee. (1996). "On Periodic Structures and Testing for Seasonal Unit Roots," *Journal of the American Statistical Association*, 91, 1551–1559.

Ghysels, E., H. S. Lee, and J. Noh. (1994). "Testing for Unit Roots in Seasonal Time Series: Some Theoretical Extensions and a Monte Carlo Investigation," *Journal of Econometrics*, 62, 415–442.

Ghysels, E., and D. R. Osborn. (2001). *The Econometric Analysis of Seasonal Time Series.* New York: Cambridge University Press.

Ghysels, E., and P. Perron. (1993). "The Effect of Seasonal Adjustment Filters on Tests for a Unit Root," *Journal of Econometrics*, 55, 57–98.

Ghysels, E., and P. Perron. (1996). "The Effect of Linear Filters on Dynamic Time Series with Structural Change," *Journal of Econometrics*, 70, 69–97.

Gil-Alana, L. A., and P. M. Robinson (1997). "Testing of Unit Root and Other Nonstationary Hypotheses in Macroeconomic Time Series," *Journal of Econometrics*, 80, 241–268.

Gönen, M., M. L. Puri, F. H. Ruymgaart, and M. C. A. van Zuijlen. (2000). "The Limiting Density of Unit Root Test Statistics: A Unifying Technique," *Journal of Time Series Analysis*, 21, 249–260.

Gonzalo, J., and T. H. Lee. (1996). "Relative Power of *t* Type Tests for Stationary and Unit Root Processes," *Journal of Time Series Analysis*, 17, 37–47.

Gorodnichenko, Y., A. Mikusheva, and S. Ng. (2012). "Estimators for Persistent and Possibly Nonstationary Data with Classical Properties," *Econometric Theory*, 28, 1003–1036.

Gourieroux, C., Monfort, A., and Renault, E. (1993). "Indirect Inference," *Journal of Applied Econometrics*, 8(S1), S85–S118.

Granger, C. W. J., and J. J. Hallman. (1991). "Nonlinear Transformations of Integrated Time Series," *Journal of Time Series Analysis*, 12, 207–224.

Granger, C. W. J., and R. Joyeux (1980). "An Introduction to Long-Memory Time Series Models and Fractional Differencing," *Journal of Time Series Analysis*, 1, 15–29.

Granger, C. W. J., and P. Newbold (1974). "Spurious Regressions in Econometrics," *Journal of Econometrics*, 2, 111–120.

Granger, C. W. J., and P. L. Siklos. (1995). "Systematic Sampling, Temporal Aggregation, Seasonal Adjustment, and Cointegration Theory and Evidence," *Journal of Econometrics*, 66, 357–369.

Granger, C. W. J., and N. R. Swanson. (1997). "An Introduction to Stochastic Unit-Root Processes," *Journal of Econometrics*, 80, 35–62.

Granger, C. W. J., and T. Teräsvirta. (1993). *Modelling Nonlinear Economic Relationships*. Oxford: Oxford University Press.

Green, D., B. Palmquist, and E. Schickler. (1998). "Macropartisanship: A Replication and Critique," *American Political Science Review*, 92, 883–899.

Gregoir, S. (2006). "Efficient Tests for the Presence of a Pair of Complex Conjugate Unit Roots in Real Time Series," *Journal of Econometrics*, 130, 45–100.

Grenander, U., and M. Rosenblatt. (1957). *Statistical Analysis of Stationary Time Series*. New York: John Wiley.

Gurland, J. (1948). "Inversion Formulae for the Distribution of Ratios," *Annals of Mathematical Statistics*, 19, 228–237.

Gutenbrunner, C., and J. Jurečková. (1992). "Regression Rank Scores and Regression Quantiles," *Annals of Statistics*, 20, 305–330. ·

Gutenbrunner, C., J. Jurečková, R. Koenker, and S. Portnoy. (1993). "Tests of Linear Hypotheses Based on Regression Rank Scores," *Journal of Nonparametric Statistics*, 2, 307–331.

Gutierrez, L. (2006). "Panel Unit-Root Tests for Cross-Sectionally Correlated Panels: A Monte Carlo Comparison," *Oxford Bulletin of Economics and Statistics*, 68, 519–540.

Gutierrez, L. (2009). "Sampling at Different Frequencies, and the Power of Panel Unit Root Tests," *Economics Letters*, 102, 59–61.

Hadri, K. (2000). "Testing for Stationarity in Heterogeneous Panel Data," *Econometrics Journal*, 3, 148–161.

Hadri, K., and R. Larsson. (2005). "Testing for Stationarity in Heterogeneous Panel Data Where the Time Dimension Is Finite," *Econometrics Journal*, 8, 55–69.

Hadri, K., and Y. Rao. (2008). "Panel Stationarity Test with Structural Breaks*," *Oxford Bulletin of Economics and Statistics*, 70, 245–269.

Haldrup, N., A. Montañés, and A. Sanso. (2005). "Measurement Errors and Outliers in Seasonal Unit Root Testing," *Journal of Econometrics*, 127, 103–128.

Hall, A. (1989). "Testing for a Unit Root in the Presence of Moving Average Errors," *Biometrika*, 76, 49–56.

Hall, A. (1992). "Testing for a Unit Root in Time Series Using Instrumental Variable Estimators with Pretest Data Based Model Selection," *Journal of Econometrics*, 54, 223–250.

Hall, A. (1994). "Testing for a Unit Root in Time Series with Pretest Data-Based Model Selection," *Journal of Business & Economic Statistics*, 12, 461–470.

Hall, A., and T. Y. Lee. (1996). "Instrumental Variable Based Unit Root Tests When Both ARMA (p, q) Orders Are Chosen to Be Too Large," *Economics Letters*, 52, 247–255.

Hall, P. (1992). *The Bootstrap and Edgeworth Expansion*. New York: Springer-Verlag.

Hall, P., and C. C. Heyde. (1980). *Martingale Limit Theory and Its Application*. New York: Academic Press.

Hallin, M., R. Van den Akker, and B. J. Werker. (2011). "A Class of Simple Distribution-Free Rank-Based Unit Root Tests," *Journal of Econometrics*, 163, 200–214.

Halunga, A. G., and D. R. Osborn. (2012). "Ratio-Based Estimators for a Change Point in Persistence," *Journal of Econometrics*, 171, 24–31.

Hamilton, J. D. (1994). *Time Series Analysis*. Princeton, NJ: Princeton University Press.

Hamori, S., and A. Tokihisa. (1997). "Testing for a Unit Root in the Presence of a Variance Shift," *Economics Letters*, 57, 245–253.

Han, C., P. C. B. Phillips, and D. Sul. (2011). "Uniform Asymptotic Normality in Stationary and Unit Root Autoregression," *Econometric Theory*, 27, 1117–1151.

Hanck, C. (2008). "The Error-in-Rejection Probability of Meta-Analytic Panel Tests," *Economics Letters*, 101, 27–30.

Hannan, E. J. (1963). "Regression for *Time Series*," in *Time Series Analysis*, edited by M. Rosenblatt, pp. 17–37. New York: Wiley.

Hannan, E. J., and M. Deistler. (1988). *The Statistical Theory of Linear Systems*. New York: John Wiley.

Hannan, E. J., and B. G. Quinn. (1979). "The Determination of the Order of an Autoregression," *Journal of the Royal Statistical Society: Series B (Methodological)*, 41, 190–195.

Hannan, E. J., and J. Rissanen. (1982). "Recursive Estimation of Mixed Autoregressive-Moving Average Order," *Biometrika*, 69, 81–94.

Hansen, B. E. (1995). "Rethinking the Univariate Approach to Unit Root Testing: Using Covariates to Increase Power," *Econometric Theory*, 11, 1148–1171.

Hansen, B. E. (1999). "The Grid Bootstrap and the Autoregressive Model," *Review of Economics and Statistics*, 81, 594–607.

Harris, D., D. I. Harvey, S. J. Leybourne, and N. D. Sakkas. (2010). "Local Asymptotic Power of the Im–Pesaran–Shin Panel Unit Root Test and the Impact of Initial Observations," *Econometric Theory*, 26, 311–324.

Harris, D., D. I. Harvey, S. J. Leybourne, and A. R. Taylor. (2009). "Testing for a Unit Root in the Presence of a Possible Break in Trend," *Econometric Theory*, 25, 1545–1588.

Harris, D., S. Leybourne, and B. McCabe. (2005). "Panel Stationarity Tests for Purchasing Power Parity with Cross-Sectional Dependence," *Journal of Business & Economic Statistics*, 23, 395–409.

Harris, D., B. Mccabe and S. Leybourne. (2008). "Testing for Long Memory," *Econometric Theory*, 24, 143–175.

Harris, R. D. F., and E. Tzavalis. (1999). "Inference for Unit Roots in Dynamic Panels Where the Time Dimension Is Fixed," *Journal of Econometrics*, 91, 201–226.

Harris, R. D. F., and E. Tzavalis. (2004). "Testing for Unit Roots in Dynamic Panels in the Presence of a Deterministic Trend: Re-Examining the Unit Root Hypothesis for Real Stock Prices and Dividends," *Econometric Reviews*, 23, 149–166.

Hartung, J. (1999). "A Note on Combining Dependent Tests of Significance," *Biometrical Journal*, 41, 849–855.

Harvey, A. C. (1989). *Forecasting, Structural Time Series Models and the Kalman Filter*. Cambridge: Cambridge University Press.

Harvey, D. I., and S. J. Leybourne. (2005). "On Testing for Unit Roots and the Initial Observation," *Econometrics Journal*, 8, 97–111.

Harvey, D. I., and S. J. Leybourne. (2006). "Power of a Unit-Root Test and the Initial Condition," *Journal of Time Series Analysis*, 27, 739–752.

Harvey, D. I., S. J. Leybourne, and P. Newbold. (2002). "Seasonal Unit Root Tests with Seasonal Mean Shifts," *Economics Letters*, 76, 295–302.

Harvey, D. I., S. J. Leybourne, and A. M. Taylor. (2009). "Unit Root Testing in Practice: Dealing with Uncertainty over the Trend and Initial Condition," *Econometric Theory*, 25, 587–667.

Harvey, D. I., S. J. Leybourne, and A. M. Taylor. (2012a). "Unit Root Testing under a Local Break in Trend," *Journal of Econometrics*, 167, 140–167.

Harvey, D. I., S. J. Leybourne, and A. M. Taylor. (2012b). "Testing for Unit Roots in the Presence of Uncertainty over Both the Trend and Initial Condition," *Journal of Econometrics*, 169, 188–195.

Harvey, D. I., S. J. Leybourne, and A. M. Taylor. (2013). "Unit Root Testing under a Local Break in Trend Using Partial Information on the Break Date," *Oxford Bulletin of Economics and Statistics*, doi: 10.1111/obes.12013.

Harvey, D. I., and T. C. Mills. (2004). "Tests for Stationarity in Series with Endogenously Determined Structural Change," *Oxford Bulletin of Economics and Statistics*, 66, 863–893.

Hasan, M. N. (2001). "Rank Tests of Unit Root Hypothesis with Infinite Variance Errors," *Journal of Econometrics*, 104, 49–65.

Hasan, M. N., and R. W. Koenker. (1997). "Robust Rank Tests of the Unit Root Hypothesis," *Econometrica*, 65, 133–161.

Hasegawa, H., A. Chaturvedi, and T. van Hoa. (2000). "Bayesian Unit Root Test in Nonnormal AR(1) Model," *Journal of Time Series Analysis*, 21, 261–280.

Hassler, U., and P. M. M. Rodrigues. (2004). "Seasonal Unit Root Tests under Structural Breaks," *Journal of Time Series Analysis*, 25, 33–53.

Hassler, U., P. M. M. Rodrigues, and A. Rubia. (2009). "Testing for General Fractional Integration in the Time Domain," *Econometric Theory*, 25, 1793–1828.

Hassler, U., and J. Wolters. (1994). "On the Power of Unit Root Tests against Fractional Alternatives," *Economics Letters*, 45, 1–5.

Hasza, D. P., and W. A. Fuller. (1982). "Testing for Nonstationary Parameter Specifications in Seasonal Time Series Models," *Annals of Statistics*, 10, 1209–1216.

Hatanaka, M. (1996). *Time-Series-Based Econometrics: Unit Roots and Co-Integrations*. New York: Oxford University Press.

He, C., and R. Sandberg. (2006). "Dickey-Fuller Type of Tests against Nonlinear Dynamic Models," *Oxford Bulletin of Economics and Statistics*, 68, 835–861.

Hedges, L. V., and I. Olkin. (1985). *Statistical Methods for Meta-Analysis*. San Diego: Academic Press.

Heimann, G., and J. Kreiss. (1996). "Bootstrapping General First Order Autoregression," *Statistics & Probability Letters*, 30, 87–98.

Heo, U., and R. J. Eger (2005). "Paying for Security: The Security-Prosperity Dilemma in the United States," *Journal of Conflict Resolution*, 49, 792–817.

Herce, M. A. (1996). "Asymptotic Theory of 'LAD' Estimation in a Unit Root Process with Finite Variance Errors," *Econometric Theory*, 12, 129–153.

Herrndorf, N. (1984). "A Functional Central Limit Theorem for Weakly Dependent Sequences of Random Variables," *Annals of Probability*, 12, 141–153.

Herwartz, H., and J. Roestel. (2011). "Convergence of Real Capital Market Interest Rates? Evidence from Inflation Indexed Bonds," *Journal of Money, Credit and Banking*, 43, 1523–1541.

Hlouskova, J., and M. Wagner. (2006). "The Performance of Panel Unit Root and Stationarity Tests: Results from a Large Scale Simulation Study," *Econometric Reviews*, 25, 85–116.

Homm, U., and J. Breitung, J. (2012). "Testing for Speculative Bubbles in Stock Markets: A Comparison of Alternative Methods," *Journal of Financial Econometrics*, 10, 198–231.

Hosking, J. R. M. (1981). "Fractional Differencing," *Biometrika*, 68, 165–176.

Hosseinkouchack, M. (2013). "Local Asymptotic Power of Breitung's Test," *Oxford Bulletin of Economics and Statistics*, 75, 624–636.

Hsiao, C. (2003). *Analysis of Panel Data*. New York: Cambridge University Press.

Huber, P. (1967). The Behavior of the Maximum Likelihood Estimates under Nonstandard Conditions. *Proceedings of the Fifth Berkeley Symposium on Mathematical Statistics and Probability*, 1, 221–233.

Huber, P. (1981). *Robust Statistics*. New York: Wiley.

Hylleberg, S. (1995). "Tests for Seasonal Unit Roots: General to Specific or Specific to General?" *Journal of Econometrics*, 69, 5–25.

Hylleberg, S., R. F. Engle, C. W. J. Granger, and B. S. Yoo. (1990). "Seasonal Integration and Cointegration," *Journal of Econometrics*, 44, 215–238.

Ibragimov, I. A., and Y. V. Linnik. (1971). *Independent and Stationary Sequences of Random Variables*. Groningen, The Netherlands: Wolters-Noordhoff.

Im, K. S., J. Lee, and M. Tieslau. (2005). "Panel LM Unit-Root Tests with Level Shifts," *Oxford Bulletin of Economics and Statistics*, 67, 393–419.

Im, K. S., and M. H. Pesaran. (2003). "On the Panel Unit Root Tests Using Nonlinear Instrumental Variables," Working Paper, University of Cambridge.

Im, K. S., M. H. Pesaran, and Y. Shin. (2003). "Testing for Unit Roots in Heterogeneous Panels," *Journal of Econometrics*, 115, 53–74.

Imhof, J. P. (1961). "Computing the Distribution of Quadratic Forms in Normal Variables," *Biometrika*, 48, 419–426.

Jacobs, D., and R. Helms. (2001). "Racial Politics and Redistribution: Isolating the Contingent Influence of Civil Rights, Riots, and Crime on Tax Progressivity," *Social Forces*, 80, 91–121.

Jacobs, D., and S. L. Kent. (2007). "The Determinants of Executions since 1951: How Politics, Protests, Public Opinion, and Social Divisions Shape Capital Punishment," *Social Problems*, 54, 297–318.

Jandhyala, V., S. Fotopoulos, I. MacNeill, and P. Liu. (2013). "Inference for Single and Multiple Change-Points in Time Series," *Journal of Time Series Analysis*, 34, 423-446.

Jansson, M. (2004). "Stationarity Testing with Covariates," *Econometric Theory*, 20, 56–94.

Jansson, M. (2008). "Semiparametric Power Envelopes for Tests of the Unit Root Hypothesis," *Econometrica*, 76, 1103–1142.

Jansson, M., and M. O. Nielsen. (2012a). "Nearly Efficient Likelihood Ratio Tests of the Unit Root Hypothesis," *Econometrica*, 80, 2321–2332.

Jansson, M., and M. O. Nielsen. (2012b). "Supplement to 'Nearly Efficient Likelihood Ratio Tests of the Unit Root Hypothesis,'" *Econometrica Supplemental Material*, 80, http://www.econometricsociety.org/ecta/Supmat/10306_Simulations.pdf.

Jeffreys, H. (1961). *Theory of Probability*. London: Oxford University Press.

Johansen, S. (1988). "Statistical Analysis of Cointegration Vectors," *Journal of Economic Dynamics and Control*, 12, 231–254.

Jönsson, K. (2005). "Cross-Sectional Dependency and Size Distortion in a Small-Sample Homogeneous Panel Data Unit Root Test," *Oxford Bulletin of Economics and Statistics*, 67, 369–392.

Juhl, T., and Z. Xiao. (2003). "Power Functions and Envelopes for Unit Root Tests," *Econometric Theory*, 19, 240–253.

Kapetanios, G. (2005). "Unit-Root Testing against the Alternative Hypothesis of up to m Structural Breaks," *Journal of Time Series Analysis*, 26, 123–133.

Kapetanios, G. (2007). "Dynamic Factor Extraction of Cross-Sectional Dependence in Panel Unit Root Tests," *Journal of Applied Econometrics*, 22, 313–338.

Kapetanios, G., and M. Marcellino. (2009). "A Parametric Estimation Method for Dynamic Factor Models of Large Dimensions," *Journal of Time Series Analysis*, 30, 208–238.

Kapetanios, G., and Y. Shin. (2006). "Unit Root Tests in Three-Regime SETAR Models," *Econometrics Journal*, 9, 252–278.

Kapetanios, G., Y. Shin, and A. Snell. (2003). "Testing for a Unit Root in the Nonlinear STAR Framework," *Journal of Econometrics*, 112, 359–379.

Karatzas, I., and S. E. Shreve. (1991). *Brownian Motion and Stochastic Calculus*. 2nd edition. New York: Springer-Verlag.

Karlsson, S., and M. Löthgren. (2000). "On the Power and Interpretation of Panel Unit Root Tests," *Economics Letters*, 66, 249–255.

Kejriwal, M., P. Perron, and J. Zhou. (2013). "Wald Tests for Detecting Multiple Structural Changes in Persistence," *Econometric Theory*, 29, 289–323.

Kew, H., and D. Harris. (2009). "Heteroskedasticity-Robust Testing for a Fractional Unit Root," *Econometric Theory*, 25, 1734–1753.

Kim, D., and P. Perron. (2009). "Unit Root Tests Allowing for a Break in the Trend Function at an Unknown Time under Both the Null and Alternative Hypotheses," *Journal of Econometrics*, 148, 1–13.

Kim, I. M., and G. S. Maddala. (1991). "Flat Priors vs. Ignorance Priors in the Analysis of the AR(1) Model," *Journal of Applied Econometrics*, 6, 375–380.

Kim, J. Y. (1998). "Large Sample Properties of Posterior Densities, Bayesian Information Criterion and the Likelihood Principle in Nonstationary Time Series Models," *Econometrica*, 66, 359–380.

Kim, J. Y. (2000). "Detection of Change in Persistence of a Linear Time Series," *Journal of Econometrics*, 95, 97–116.

Kim, J. Y., J. Belaire-Franch, and R. B. Amador. (2002). "Corrigendum to 'Detection of Change in Persistence of a Linear Time Series' [*J. Econom.* 95 (2000) 97–116]," *Journal of Econometrics*, 109, 389–392.

Kim, K., and P. Schmidt. (1993). "Unit Root Tests with Conditional Heteroskedasticity," *Journal of Econometrics*, 59, 287–300.

Kim, T. H., S. Leybourne, and P. Newbold. (2002). "Unit Root Tests with a Break in Innovation Variance," *Journal of Econometrics*, 109, 365–387.

King, M. L. (1987). "Towards a Theory of Point Optimal Testing," *Econometric Reviews*, 6, 169–218.

King, M. L., and G. H. Hillier. (1985). "Locally Best Invariant Tests of the Error Covariance Matrix of the Linear Regression Model," *Journal of the Royal Statistical Society: Series B (Methodological)*, 47, 98–102.

King, M. L., and P. X. Wu. (1997). "Locally Optimal One-Sided Tests for Multiparameter Hypotheses," *Econometric Reviews*, 16, 131–156.

Knight, K. (1989). "Limit Theory for Autoregressive-Parameter Estimates in an Infinite-Variance Random Walk," *Canadian Journal of Statistics/La Revue Canadienne De Statistique*, 17, 261–278.

Knight, K. (1991). "Limit Theory for M-Estimates in an Integrated Infinite Variance Process," *Econometric Theory*, 7, 200–212.

Koedijk, K. G., and C. J. M. Kool. (1992). "Tail Estimates of East European Exchange Rates," *Journal of Business & Economic Statistics*, 10, 83–96.

Kocenda, E., and D. H. Papell. (1997). "Inflation Convergence within the European Union: A Panel Data Analysis," *International Journal of Finance & Economics*, 2, 189–198.

Koenker, R. (2005). *Quantile Regresssion*. New York: Cambridge University Press.

Koenker, R., and G. Bassett Jr. (1978). "Regression Quantiles," *Econometrica*, 46, 33–50.

Koenker, R., and Z. Xiao. (2004). "Unit Root Quantile Autoregression Inference," *Journal of the American Statistical Association*, 99, 775–787.

Koop, G. (1992). "'Objective' Bayesian Unit Root Tests," *Journal of Applied Econometrics*, 7, 65–82.

Koop, G., D. J. Poirier, and J. L. Tobias. (2007). *Bayesian Econometric Methods*. New York: Cambridge University Press.

Koop, G., and M. F. J. Steel. (1994). "A Decision-Theoretic Analysis of the Unit-Root Hypothesis Using Mixtures of Elliptical Models," *Journal of Business & Economic Statistics*, 12, 95–107.

Koopmans, T. (1942). "Serial Correlation and Quadratic Forms in Normal Variables," *Annals of Mathematical Statistics*, 13, 1–42.

Koul, H. L., and A. Schick. (1996). "Adaptive Estimation in a Random-Coefficient Autoregressive Model," *Annals of Statistics*, 24, 1025–1052.

Kourogenis, N., and N. Pittis. (2008). "Testing for a Unit Root under Errors with Just Barely Infinite Variance," *Journal of Time Series Analysis*, 29, 1066–1087.

Krämer, W. (1998). "Fractional Integration and the Augmented Dickey-Fuller Test," *Economics Letters*, 61, 269–272.

Kreiss, J. (1987). "On Adaptive Estimation in Stationary ARMA Processes," *Annals of Statistics*, 15, 112–133.

Kristal, T. (2010). "Good Times, Bad Times: Postwar Labor's Share of National Income in Capitalist Democracies," *American Sociological Review*, 75, 729–763.

Kruiniger, H. (2008). "Maximum Likelihood Estimation and Inference Methods for the Covariance Stationary Panel AR(1)/Unit Root Model," *Journal of Econometrics*, 144, 447–464.

Künsch, H. R. (1989). "The Jackknife and the Bootstrap for General Stationary Observations," *Annals of Statistics*, 17, 1217–1241.

Kunst, R. M. (1997). "Testing for Cyclical Non-Stationarity in Autoregressive Processes," *Journal of Time Series Analysis*, 18, 123–135.

Kurozumi, E. (2002a). "Testing for Periodic Stationarity," *Econometric Reviews*, 21, 243–270.

Kurozumi, E. (2002b). "Testing for Stationarity with a Break," *Journal of Econometrics*, 108, 63–99.

Kurozumi, E. (2005). "Detection of Structural Change in the Long-Run Persistence in a Univariate Time Series," *Oxford Bulletin of Economics and Statistics*, 67, 181–206.

Kurozumi, E., and S. Tanaka. (2010). "Reducing the Size Distortion of the KPSS Test," *Journal of Time Series Analysis*, 31, 415–426.

Kuzin, V. (2005). "Recursive Demeaning and Deterministic Seasonality," *Statistics & Probability Letters*, 72, 195–204.

Kwiatkowski, D., P. C. B. Phillips, P. Schmidt, and Y. Shin. (1992). "Testing the Null Hypothesis of Stationarity against the Alternative of a Unit Root: How Sure Are We that Economic Time Series Have a Unit Root?" *Journal of Econometrics*, 54, 159–178.

Lai, T. L., and D. Siegmund. (1983). "Fixed Accuracy Estimation of an Autoregressive Parameter," *Annals of Statistics*, 11, 478–485.

Lanne, M., H. Lütkepohl, and P. Saikkonen. (2002). "Comparison of Unit Root Tests for Time Series with Level Shifts," *Journal of Time Series Analysis*, 23, 667–685.

Lanne, M., H. Lütkepohl, and P. Saikkonen. (2003). "Test Procedures for Unit Roots in Time Series with Level Shifts at Unknown Time," *Oxford Bulletin of Economics and Statistics*, 65, 91–115.

Lanne, M., and P. Saikkonen. (2003). "Reducing Size Distortions of Parametric Stationarity Tests," *Journal of Time Series Analysis*, 24, 423–439.

Larsson, R. (1995). "The Asymptotic Distributions of Some Test Statistics in Near-Integrated AR Processes," *Econometric Theory*, 11, 306–330.

Larsson, R. (1998). "Distribution Approximation of Unit Root Tests in Autoregressive Models," *Econometrics Journal*, 1, 10–26.

Lau, A. H., H. Lau, and J. R. Wingender. (1990). "The Distribution of Stock Returns: New Evidence against the Stable Model," *Journal of Business & Economic Statistics*, 8, 217–223.

Lee, H. S., and P. L. Siklos. (1991). "Unit Roots and Seasonal Unit Roots in Macroeconomic Time Series: Canadian Evidence," *Economics Letters*, 35, 273–277.

Lee, J. (1996). "On the Power of Stationarity Tests Using Optimal Bandwidth Estimates," *Economics Letters*, 51, 131–137.

Lee, J. (1999). "Stationarity Tests with Multiple Endogenized Breaks," in *Nonlinear Time Series Analysis of Economic and Financial Data: Dynamic Modeling and Econometrics in Economics and Finance*, vol. 1, edited by P. Rothman, pp. 143–163. New York: Springer.

Lee, J., C. J. Huang, and Y. Shin. (1997). "On Stationary Tests in the Presence of Structural Breaks," *Economics Letters*, 55, 165–172.

Lee, J., and P. Schmidt. (1994). "Unit Root Tests Based on Instrumental Variables Estimation," *International Economic Review*, 35, 449–462.

Lee, J., and M. C. Strazicich. (2001). "Testing the Null of Stationarity in the Presence of a Structural Break," *Applied Economics Letters*, 8, 377–382.

Lee, J., and M. C. Strazicich. (2003). "Minimum Lagrange Multiple Unit Root Test with Two Structural Breaks," *Review of Economics & Statistics*, 85, 1082–1089.

Lee, T., and D. A. Dickey. (2004). "Limiting Distributions of Unconditional Maximum Likelihood Unit Root Test Statistics in Seasonal Time-Series Models," *Journal of Time Series Analysis*, 25, 551–561.

Lee, Y., and D. W. Shin. (2006). "Unit Root Tests for Cross-Sectionally Dependent Seasonal Panels," *Economics Letters*, 93, 311–317.

Lehmann, E. L. (1959). *Testing Statistical Hypotheses*. New York: John Wiley and Sons.

Lehmann, E. L., and J. P. Romano, J. P. (2005). *Testing Statistical Hypotheses*. New York: Springer.

Lettau, M., and S. Ludvigson. (2001). "Consumption, Aggregate Wealth, and Expected Stock Returns," *Journal of Finance*, 56, 815–849.

Levin, A., and C. F. Lin. (1992). "Unit Root Tests in Panel Data: Asymptotic and Finite-Sample Properties," Working Paper, UCSD.

Levin, A., C. Lin, and C. J. Chu. (2002). "Unit Root Tests in Panel Data: Asymptotic and Finite-Sample Properties," *Journal of Econometrics*, 108, 1–24.

Leybourne, S. J. (1995). "Testing for Unit Roots Using Forward and Reverse Dickey-Fuller Regressions," *Oxford Bulletin of Economics and Statistics*, 57, 559–571.

Leybourne, S. J., T. H. Kim, and P. Newbold. (2005). "Examination of Some More Powerful Modifications of the Dickey-Fuller Test," *Journal of Time Series Analysis*, 26, 355–369.

Leybourne, S. J., T. H. Kim, V. Smith, and P. Newbold. (2003). "Tests for a Change in Persistence against the Null of Difference-Stationarity," *Econometrics Journal*, 6, 291–311.

Leybourne, S. J., and B. P. M. McCabe. (1994). "A Consistent Test for a Unit Root," *Journal of Business & Economic Statistics*, 12, 157–166.

Leybourne, S. J., and B. P. M. McCabe. (1999). "Modified Stationarity Tests with Data-Dependent Model Selection Rules," *Journal of Business & Economic Statistics*, 17, 264–270.

Leybourne, S. J., B. P. M. McCabe, and A. R. Tremayne. (1996). "Can Economic Time Series Be Differenced to Stationarity?" *Journal of Business & Economic Statistics*, 14, 435–446.

Leybourne, S. J., T. C. Mills, and P. Newbold. (1998). "Spurious Rejections by Dickey-Fuller Tests in the Presence of a Break under the Null," *Journal of Econometrics*, 87, 191–203.

Leybourne, S. J., and P. Newbold. (1999). "On the Size Properties of Phillips-Perron Tests," *Journal of Time Series Analysis*, 20, 51–61.

Leybourne, S. J., and P. Newbold. (2000). "Behaviour of the Standard and Symmetric Dickey-Fuller-Type Tests When There Is a Break under the Null Hypothesis," *Econometrics Journal*, 3, 1–15.

Leybourne, S. J., P. Newbold, and D. Vougas. (1998). "Unit Roots and Smooth Transitions," *Journal of Time Series Analysis*, 19, 83–97.

Leybourne, S. J., and A. M. R. Taylor. (2003). "Seasonal Unit Root Tests Based on Forward and Reverse Estimation," *Journal of Time Series Analysis*, 24, 441–460.

Leybourne, S. J., and A. M. R. Taylor. (2004). "On Tests for Changes in Persistence," *Economics Letters*, 84, 107–115.

Leybourne, S. J., A. M. R. Taylor, and T. H. Kim. (2007). "CUSUM of Squares-Based Tests for a Change in Persistence," *Journal of Time Series Analysis*, 28, 408–433.

Li, G., and Li, W. K. (2009). "Least Absolute Deviation Estimation for Unit Root Processes with GARCH Errors," *Econometric Theory*, 25, 1208–1227.

Li, H. (1995). "The Power of Modified Instrumental Variables Tests for Unit Roots," *Biometrika*, 82, 660–666.

Li, W. K. (1991). "Some Lagrange Multiplier Tests for Seasonal Differencing," *Biometrika*, 78, 381–387.

Lindley, D. V. (1957). "A Statistical Paradox," *Biometrika*, 44, 187–192.

Ling, S., and W. K. Li. (1998). "Limiting Distributions of Maximum Likelihood Estimators for Unstable Autoregressive Moving-Average Time Series with General Autoregressive Heteroscedastic Errors," *Annals of Statistics*, 26, 84–125.

Ling, S., and W. K. Li. (2001). "Asymptotic Inference for Nonstationary Fractionally Integrated Autoregressive Moving–Average Models," *Econometric Theory*, 17, 738–764.

Ling, S. and W. K. Li. (2003). "Asymptotic Inference for Unit Root Processes with GARCH (1, 1) Errors," *Econometric Theory*, 19, 541–564.

Ling, S., W. K. Li, and M. McAleer. (2003). "Estimation and Testing for Unit Root Processes with GARCH (1, 1) Errors: Theory and Monte Carlo Evidence," *Econometric Reviews*, 22, 179–202.

Ling, S., and M. McAleer. (2003). "Asymptotic Theory for a Vector ARMA–GARCH Model," *Econometric Theory*, 19, 280–310.

Linton, O. (1993). "Adaptive Estimation in ARCH Models," *Econometric Theory*, 9, 539–569.

Liu, H., and G. Rodríguez. (2006). "Unit Root Tests and Structural Change When the Initial Observation Is Drawn from Its Unconditional Distribution," *Econometrics Journal*, 9, 225–251.

Liu, R. Y., and K. Singh. (1992). "Moving Blocks Jackknife and Bootstrap Capture Weak Dependence," in *Exploring the Limit of Bootstrap*, edited by R. LePage and L. Billard, pp. 225–248. New York: Wiley.

Lobato, I. N., and C. Velasco. (2006). "Optimal Fractional Dickey-Fuller Tests," *Econometrics Journal*, 9, 492–510.

Lobato, I. N., and C. Velasco. (2007). "Efficient Wald Tests for Fractional Unit Roots," *Econometrica*, 75, 575–589.

Lobato, I. N. and C. Velasco. (2008). "Power Comparison among Tests for Fractional Unit Roots," *Economics Letters*, 99, 152–154.

Lopes, A. C. B. d.S., and A. Montañés. (2005). "The Behavior of HEGY Tests for Quarterly Time Series with Seasonal Mean Shifts," *Econometric Reviews*, 24, 83–108.

Lubrano, M. (1995). "Testing for Unit Roots in a Bayesian Framework," *Journal of Econometrics*, 69, 81–109.

Lucas, A. (1995a). "An Outlier Robust Unit Root Test with an Application to the Extended Nelson–Plosser Data," *Journal of Econometrics*, 66, 153–173.

Lucas, A. (1995b). "Unit Root Tests Based on M-Estimators," *Econometric Theory*, 11, 331–346.

Lumsdaine, R. L., and D. H. Papell. (1997). "Multiple Trend Breaks and the Unit-Root Hypothesis," *Review of Economics and Statistics*, 79, 212–218.

Luukkonen, R., P. Saikkonen, and T. Teräsvirta. (1988). "Testing Linearity against Smooth Transition Autoregressive Models." *Biometrika*, 75, 491–499.

MacKinnon, J. G. (1994). "Approximate Asymptotic Distribution Functions for Unit-Root and Cointegration Tests," *Journal of Business & Economic Statistics*, 12, 167–176.

MacKinnon, J. G. (1996). "Numerical Distribution Functions for Unit Root and Cointegration Tests," *Journal of Applied Econometrics*, 11, 601–618.

MacNeill, I.B. (1978). "Properties of Sequences of Partial Sums of Polynomial Regression Residuals with Applications to Tests for Change of Regression at Unknown Times," *Annals of Statistics*, 6, 422–433.

Maddala, G. S., and I. Kim. (1998). *Unit Roots, Cointegration, and Structural Change*. Cambridge: Cambridge University Press.

Maddala, G. S., and S. Wu. (1999). "A Comparative Study of Unit Root Tests with Panel Data and a New Simple Test," *Oxford Bulletin of Economics and Statistics*, 61, 631–652.

Madsen, E. (2010). "Unit Root Inference in Panel Data Models Where the Time-Series Dimension Is Fixed: A Comparison of Different Tests," *Econometrics Journal*, 13, 63–94.

Magdalinos, T. (2012). "Mildly Explosive Autoregression under Weak and Strong Dependence," *Journal of Econometrics*, 169, 179–187.

Mann, H. B., and A. Wald. (1943). "On the Statistical Treatment of Linear Stochastic Difference Equations," *Econometrica*, 11, 173–200.

Marinucci, D., and P. M. Robinson (1999). "Alternative Forms of Fractional Brownian Motion," *Journal of Statistical Planning and Inference*, 80, 111–122.

Marriott, J., and P. Newbold. (2000). "The Strength of Evidence for Unit Autoregressive Roots and Structural Breaks: A Bayesian Perspective," *Journal of Econometrics*, 98, 1–25.

McCoskey, S. K., and T. M. Selden. (1998). "Health Care Expenditures and GDP: Panel Data Unit Root Test Results," *Journal of Health Economics*, 17, 369–376.

Meffert, M. F., H. Norpoth, and A. V. S. Ruhil. (2001). "Realignment and Macropartisanship," *American Political Science Review*, 95, 953–962.

Mikusheva, A. (2007). "Uniform Inference in Autoregressive Models," *Econometrica*, 75, 1411–1452.

Montañés, A., and M. Reyes. (1998). "Effect of a Shift in the Trend Function on Dickey-Fuller Unit Root Tests," *Econometric Theory*, 14, 355–363.

Moon, H. R., and B. Perron. (2004). "Testing for a Unit Root in Panels with Dynamic Factors," *Journal of Econometrics*, 122, 81–126.

Moon, H. R., and B. Perron. (2008). "Asymptotic Local Power of Pooled t-Ratio Tests for Unit Roots in Panels with Fixed Effects," *Econometrics Journal*, 11, 80–104.

Moon, H. R., B. Perron, and P. C. B. Phillips. (2006). "On the Breitung Test for Panel Unit Roots and Local Asymptotic Power," *Econometric Theory*, 22, 1179–1190.

Moon, H. R., B. Perron, and P. C. B. Phillips. (2007). "Incidental Trends and the Power of Panel Unit Root Tests," *Journal of Econometrics*, 141, 416–459.

Moon, H. R., and P. C. B. Phillips. (1999). "Maximum Likelihood Estimation in Panels with Incidental Trends," *Oxford Bulletin of Economics and Statistics*, 61, 711–747.

Moon, H. R., and P. C. B. Phillips. (2004). "GMM Estimation of Autoregressive Roots Near Unity with Panel Data," *Econometrica*, 72, 467–522.

Moreno, M., and J. Romo. (2000). "Bootstrap Tests for Unit Roots Based on LAD Estimation," *Journal of Statistical Planning and Inference*, 83, 347–367.

Moreno, M., and J. Romo. (2012). "Unit Root Bootstrap Tests under Infinite Variance," *Journal of Time Series Analysis*, 33, 32–47.

Müller, U. K. (2005). "Size and Power of Tests of Stationarity in Highly Autocorrelated Time Series," *Journal of Econometrics*, 128, 195–213.

Müller, U. K. (2011). "Efficient Tests under a Weak Convergence Assumption," *Econometrica*, 79, 395–435.

Müller, U. K., and G. Elliott. (2003). "Tests for Unit Roots and the Initial Condition," *Econometrica*, 71, 1269–1286.

Murray, C. J., and D. H. Papell. (2000). "Testing for Unit Roots in Panels in the Presence of Structural Change with an Application to OECD Unemployment," in *Advances in Economics*, vol. 15, edited by B. H. Baltagi, pp. 223–238. Amsterdam: JAI.

Nabeya, S. (2000). "Asymptotic Distributions for Unit Root Test Statistics in Nearly Integrated Seasonal Autoregressive Models," *Econometric Theory*, 16, 200–230.

Nabeya, S. (2001). "Unit Root Seasonal Autoregressive Models with a Polynomial Trend of Higher Degree," *Econometric Theory*, 17, 357–385.

Nabeya, S., and B. E. Sørensen. (1994). "Asymptotic Distributions of the Least-Squares Estimators and Test Statistics in the Near Unit Root Model with Non-Zero Initial Value and Local Drift and Trend," *Econometric Theory*, 10, 937–966.

Nabeya, S., and K. Tanaka. (1990a). "A General Approach to the Limiting Distribution for Estimators in Time Series Regression with Nonstable Autoregressive Errors," *Econometrica*, 58, 145–163.

Nabeya, S., and K. Tanaka. (1990b). "Limiting Power of Unit-Root Tests in Time-Series Regression," *Journal of Econometrics*, 46, 247–271.

Nelson, C. R., and C. R. Plosser. (1982). "Trends and Random Walks in Macroeconomic Time Series: Some Evidence and Implications," *Journal of Monetary Economics*, 10, 139–162.

Newey, W. K., and K. D. West. (1987). "A Simple, Positive Semi-Definite, Heteroskedasticity and Autocorrelation Consistent Covariance Matrix," *Econometrica*, 55, 703–708.

Newey, W. K., and K. D. West. (1994). "Automatic Lag Selection in Covariance Matrix Estimation," *Review of Economic Studies*, 61, 631–653.

Ng, S. (1995). "Testing for Unit Roots in Flow Data Sampled at Different Frequencies," *Economics Letters*, 47, 237–242.

Ng, S. (2008). "A Simple Test for Nonstationarity in Mixed Panels," *Journal of Business & Economic Statistics*, 26, 113–127.

Ng, S., and P. Perron. (1995). "Unit Root Tests in ARMA Models with Data-Dependent Methods for the Selection of the Truncation Lag," *Journal of the American Statistical Association*, 90, 268–281.

Ng, S., and P. Perron. (2001). "Lag Length Selection and the Construction of Unit Root Tests with Good Size and Power," *Econometrica*, 69, 1519–1554.

Nielsen, M. O. (2004a). "Efficient Likelihood Inference in Nonstationary Univariate Models," *Econometric Theory*, 20, 116–146.

Nielsen, M. O. (2004b). "Efficient Inference in Multivariate Fractionally Integrated Time Series Models," *Econometrics Journal*, 7, 63–97.

Nielsen, M. O. (2005). "Multivariate Lagrange Multiplier Tests for Fractional Integration," *Journal of Financial Econometrics*, 3, 372–398.

Nielsen, M. O. (2009). "A Powerful Test of the Autoregressive Unit Root Hypothesis Based on a Tuning Parameter Free Statistic," *Econometric Theory*, 25, 1515–1544.

Nunes, L. C., P. Newbold, and C. M. Kuan. (1997). "Testing for Unit Roots with Breaks: Evidence on the Great Crash and the Unit Root Hypothesis Reconsidered," *Oxford Bulletin of Economics and Statistics*, 59, 435–448.

Nunes, L. C., and P. M. M. Rodrigues. (2011). "On LM-Type Tests for Seasonal Unit Roots in the Presence of a Break in Trend," *Journal of Time Series Analysis*, 32, 108–134.

Nyblom, J. (1989). "Testing for the Constancy of Parameters over Time," *Journal of the American Statistical Association*, 84, 223–230.

O'Connell, P. G. J. (1998). "The Overvaluation of Purchasing Power Parity," *Journal of International Economics*, 44, 1–19.

Oh, K.-Y. (1996). "Purchasing Power Parity and Unit Root Tests Using Panel Data," *Journal of International Money and Finance*, 15, 405–418.

Oh, Y. J., and B. S. So. (2004). "Robust Tests for Unit Roots in Heterogeneous Panels," *Economics Letters*, 84, 35–41.

Osborn, D. R., A. P. L. Chui, J. P. Smith, and C. R. Birchenhall. (1988). "Seasonality and the Order of Integration for Consumption," *Oxford Bulletin of Economics and Statistics*, 50, 361–377.

Osborn, D. R., and P. M. M. Rodrigues. (2002). "Asymptotic Distributions of Seasonal Unit Root Tests: A Unifying Approach," *Econometric Reviews*, 21, 221–241.

Otero, J., J. Smith, and M. Giulietti. (2005). "Testing for Seasonal Unit Roots in Heterogeneous Panels," *Economics Letters*, 86, 229–235.

Otero, J., J. Smith, and M. Giulietti. (2007). "Testing for Seasonal Unit Roots in Heterogeneous Panels in the Presence of Cross Section Dependence," *Economics Letters*, 97, 179–184.

Otto, G., and T. S. Wirjanto. (1990). "Seasonal Unit-Root Tests on Canadian Macroeconomic Time Series," *Economics Letters*, 34, 117–120.

Oya, K., and H. Toda. (1998). "Dickey-Fuller, Lagrange Multiplier and Combined Tests for a Unit Root in Autoregressive Time Series," *Journal of Time Series Analysis*, 19, 325–347.

Palm, F. C., S. Smeekes, and J. Urbain. (2008). "Bootstrap Unit-Root Tests: Comparison and Extensions," *Journal of Time Series Analysis*, 29, 371–401.

Palm, F. C., S. Smeekes, and J. Urbain. (2011). "Cross-Sectional Dependence Robust Block Bootstrap Panel Unit Root Tests," *Journal of Econometrics*, 163, 85–104.

Pantula, S. G. (1991). "Asymptotic Distributions of Unit-Root Tests When the Process Is Nearly Stationary," *Journal of Business & Economic Statistics*, 9, 63–71.

Pantula, S. G., G. Gonzalez-Farias, and W. A. Fuller. (1994). "A Comparison of Unit-Root Test Criteria," *Journal of Business & Economic Statistics*, 12, 449–459.

Pantula, S. G., and A. Hall. (1991). "Testing for Unit Roots in Autoregressive Moving Average Models: An Instrumental Variable Approach," *Journal of Econometrics*, 48, 325–353.

Paparoditis, E., and D. N. Politis. (2003). "Residual-Based Block Bootstrap for Unit Root Testing," *Econometrica*, 71, 813–855.

Park, H. J., and W. A. Fuller. (1995). "Alternative Estimators and Unit Root Tests for the Autoregressive Process," *Journal of Time Series Analysis*, 16, 415–429.

Park, J. Y. (2003). "Bootstrap Unit Root Tests," *Econometrica*, 71, 1845–1895.

Parker, C., E. Paparoditis, and D. N. Politis. (2006). "Unit Root Testing via the Stationary Bootstrap," *Journal of Econometrics*, 133, 601–638.

Patterson, K. (2010) *A Primer for Unit Root Testing*. New York: Palgrave Macmillan.

Patterson, K. (2011) *Unit Root Tests in Time Series*. New York: Palgrave Macmillan.

Pelagatti, M. M., and P. K. Sen. (2013). "Rank Tests for Short Memory Stationarity," *Journal of Econometrics*, 172, 90–105.

Percival, D. B., and A. T. Walden. (2000). *Wavelet Methods for Time Series Analysis*. New York: Cambridge University Press.

Perron, P. (1989). "The Great Crash, the Oil Price Shock, and the Unit Root Hypothesis," *Econometrica*, 57, 1361–1401.

Perron, P. (1990). "Testing for a Unit Root in a Time Series with a Changing Mean," *Journal of Business & Economic Statistics*, 8, 153–162.

Perron, P. (1991). "Test Consistency with Varying Sampling Frequency," *Econometric Theory*, 7, 341–368.

Perron, P. (1996). "The Adequacy of Asymptotic Approximations in the Near-Integrated Autoregressive Model with Dependent Errors," *Journal of Econometrics*, 70, 317–350.

Perron, P. (2006). "Dealing with Structural Breaks," in *Palgrave Handbook of Econometrics*, vol. 1, edited by T. C. Mills and K. Patterson, pp. 278–352. New York: Palgrave Macmillan.

Perron, P., and S. Ng. (1996). "Useful Modifications to Some Unit Root Tests with Dependent Errors and Their Local Asymptotic Properties," *Review of Economic Studies*, 63, 435–463.

Perron, P., and S. Ng. (1998). "An Autoregressive Spectral Density Estimator at Frequency Zero for Nonstationarity Tests," *Econometric Theory*, 14, 560–603.

Perron, P., and G. Rodríguez. (2003). "Searching for Additive Outliers in Nonstationary Time Series," *Journal of Time Series Analysis*, 24, 193–220.

Perron, P., and T. J. Vogelsang. (1992). "Nonstationarity and Level Shifts with an Application to Purchasing Power Parity," *Journal of Business & Economic Statistics*, 10, 301–320.

Pesaran, M. H. (2003). "Aggregation of Linear Dynamic Models: An Application to Life-Cycle Consumption Models under Habit Formation," *Economic Modelling*, 20, 227–435.

Pesaran, M. H. (2007). "A Simple Panel Unit Root Test in the Presence of Cross-Section Dependence," *Journal of Applied Econometrics*, 22, 265–312.

Phillips, P. C. B. (1986). "Understanding Spurious Regressions in Econometrics," *Journal of Econometrics*, 33, 311–340.

Phillips, P. C. B. (1987a). "Time Series Regression with a Unit Root," *Econometrica*, 55, 277–301.

Phillips, P. C. B. (1987b). "Towards a Unified Asymptotic Theory for Autoregression," *Biometrika*, 74, 535–547.

Phillips, P. C. B. (1990). "Time Series Regression with a Unit Root and Infinite-Variance Errors," *Econometric Theory*, 6, 44–62.

Phillips, P. C. B. (1991). "To Criticize the Critics: An Objective Bayesian Analysis of Stochastic Trends," *Journal of Applied Econometrics*, 6, 333–364.

Phillips, P. C. B. (1998). "Impulse Response and Forecast Error Variance Asymptotics in Nonstationary VARs," *Journal of Econometrics*, 8, 21–56.

Phillips, P. C. B. (2007). "Unit Root Log Periodogram Regression," *Journal of Econometrics*, 138, 104–124.

Phillips, P. C. B. (2012a). "On Confidence Intervals for Autoregressive Roots and Predictive Regression," Working Paper, Yale University.

Phillips, P. C. B. (2012b). "Folklore Theorems, Implicit Maps, and Indirect Inference," *Econometrica*, 80, 425–454.

Phillips, P. C. B., and S. N. Durlauf. (1986). "Multiple Time Series Regression with Integrated Processes," *Review of Economic Studies*, 53, 473–495.

Phillips, P. C. B., and C. Han. (2008). "Gaussian Inference in AR (1) Time Series with or without a Unit Root," *Econometric Theory*, 24, 631–650.

Phillips, P. C. B., and S. Jin. (2002). "The KPSS Test with Seasonal Dummies," *Economics Letters*, 77, 239–243.

Phillips, P. C. B., and T. Magdalinos. (2007). "Limit Theory for Moderate Deviations from a Unit Root," *Journal of Econometrics*, 136, 115–130.

Phillips, P. C. B., and T. Magdalinos. (2009). "Unit Root and Cointegrating Limit Theory When Initialization Is in the Infinite Past," *Econometric Theory*, 25, 1682–1715.

Phillips, P. C. B., and R. H. Moon. (1999). "Linear Regression Limit Theory for Nonstationary Panel Data," *Econometrica*, 67, 1057–1111.

Phillips, P. C. B., and R. H. Moon. (2000). "Nonstationary Panel Data Analysis: An Overview of Some Recent Developments," *Econometric Reviews*, 19, 263–286.

Phillips, P. C. B., J. Y. Park, and Y. Chang. (2004). "Nonlinear Instrumental Variable Estimation of an Autoregression," *Journal of Econometrics*, 118, 219–246.

Phillips, P. C. B., and P. Perron. (1988). "Testing for a Unit Root in Time Series Regression," *Biometrika*, 75, 335–346.

Phillips, P. C. B., and W. Ploberger. (1994). "Posterior Odds Testing for a Unit Root with Data-Based Model Selection," *Econometric Theory*, 10, 774–808.

Phillips, P. C. B., and W. Ploberger. (1996). "An Asymptotic Theory of Bayesian Inference for Time Series," *Econometrica*, 64, 381–412.

Phillips, P. C. B., and Shimotsu, K. (2004). "Local Whittle Estimation in Nonstationary and Unit Root Cases," *Annals of Statistics*, 32, 656–692.

Phillips, P. C. B., and V. Solo. (1992). "Asymptotics for Linear Processes," *Annals of Statistics*, 20, 971–1001.

Phillips, P. C. B., and D. Sul. (2003). "Dynamic Panel Estimation and Homogeneity Testing under Cross Section Dependence," *Econometrics Journal*, 6, 217–259.

Phillips, P. C. B., Y. Wu, and J. Yu (2011). "Explosive Behavior in the 1990s NASDAQ: When Did Exuberance Escalate Asset Values?" *International Economic Review* 71, 421–436.

Pitarakis, J. Y. (1998). "Moment Generating Functions and Further Exact Results for Seasonal Autoregressions," *Econometric Theory*, 14, 770–782.

Ploberger, B., and P. C. B. Phillips. (2002). "Optimal Testing for Unit Roots in Panel Data," Working Paper, Yale University.

Politis, D. N., and J. P. Romano. (1994). "The Stationary Bootstrap," *Journal of the American Statistical Association*, 89, 1303–1313.

Politis, N., J. Romano, and M. Wolf. (1999). *Subsampling*. New York: Springer Verlag.

Pons, G. (2006). "Testing Monthly Seasonal Unit Roots with Monthly and Quarterly Information," *Journal of Time Series Analysis*, 27, 191–209.

Popp, S. (2007). "Modified Seasonal Unit Root Test with Seasonal Level Shifts at Unknown Time," *Economics Letters*, 97, 111–117.

Poterba, J. M., and L. H. Summers. (1988). "Mean Reversion in Stock Prices: Evidence and Implications," *Journal of Financial Economics*, 22, 27–59.

Pötscher, B. M. (1989). "Model Selection under Nonstationarity: Autoregressive Models and Stochastic Linear Regression Models," *Annals of Statistics*, 17, 1257–1274.

Price, S., and D. Sanders. (1993). "Modeling Government Popularity in Postwar Britain: A Methodological Example," *American Journal of Political Science*, 37, 317–334.

Priestley, M.B. (1981). *Spectral Analysis and Time Series*, Vol. 1. London: Academic Press.

Psaradakis, Z. (2000). "Bootstrap Tests for Unit Roots in Seasonal Autoregressive Models," *Statistics & Probability Letters*, 50, 389–395.

Psaradakis, Z. (2001a). "Bootstrap Tests for an Autoregressive Unit Root in the Presence of Weakly Dependent Errors," *Journal of Time Series Analysis*, 22, 577–594.

Psaradakis, Z. (2001b). "Markov Level Shifts and the Unit-Root Hypothesis," *Econometrics Journal*, 4, 225–241.

Psaradakis, Z. (2002). "On the Asymptotic Behaviour of Unit-Root Tests in the Presence of a Markov Trend," *Statistics & Probability Letters*, 57, 101–109.

Psaradakis, Z. (2003). "A Sieve Bootstrap Test for Stationarity," *Statistics & Probability Letters*, 62, 263–274.

Psaradakis, Z. (2006). "Blockwise Bootstrap Testing for Stationarity," *Statistics & Probability Letters*, 76, 562–570.

Quah, D. (1994). "Exploiting Cross-Section Variation for Unit Root Inference in Dynamic Data," *Economics Letters*, 44, 9–19.

Quandt, R. E. (1960). "Tests of the Hypothesis That a Linear Regression System Obeys Two Separate Regimes," *Journal of the American Statistical Association*, 55, 324–330.

Rao, C. R., and Y. Wu. (2001). "On Model Selection," in *Lecture Notes-Monograph Series*, vol. 38, *Model Selection*, edited by C. R. Rao, Y. Wu, S. Konishi, and R. Mukerjee, pp. 1–64. Beachwood, OH: Institute of Mathematical Statistics.

Rao, M. M. (1978). "Asymptotic Distribution of an Estimator of the Boundary Parameter of an Unstable Process," *Annals of Statistics*, 6, 185–190.

Rappoport, P., and L. Reichlin. (1989). "Segmented Trends and Non-Stationary Time Series," *Economic Journal*, 99, 168–177.

Resnick, S. I. (1986). "Point Processes, Regular Variation and Weak Convergence," *Advances in Applied Probability*, 18, 66–138.

Robinson, P. M. (1994). "Efficient Tests of Nonstationary Hypotheses," *Journal of the American Statistical Association*, 89, 1420–1437.

Robinson, P. M. (2003). "Long-Memory Time Series," in *Time Series with Long Memory*, edited by P. M. Robinson, pp. 4–32. New York: Oxford University Press.

Rodrigues, P. M. M. (2001). "Near Seasonal Integration," *Econometric Theory*, 17, 70–86.

Rodrigues, P. M. M. (2002). "On LM Type Tests for Seasonal Unit Roots in Quarterly Data," *Econometrics Journal*, 5, 176–195.

Rodrigues, P. M. M. (2006). "Properties of Recursive Trend-Adjusted Unit Root Tests," *Economics Letters*, 91, 413–419.

Rodrigues, P. M. M. (2013). "Recursive Adjustment, Unit Root Tests and Structural Breaks," *Journal of Time Series Analysis*, 34, 62–82.

Rodrigues, P. M. M., and A. M. R. Taylor. (2004a). "Alternative Estimators and Unit Root Tests for Seasonal Autoregressive Processes," *Journal of Econometrics*, 120, 35–73.

Rodrigues, P. M. M., and A. M. R. Taylor. (2004b). "Asymptotic Distributions for Regression-Based Seasonal Unit Root Test Statistics in a Near-Integrated Model," *Econometric Theory*, 20, 645–670.

Rodrigues, P. M. M., and A. M. R. Taylor. (2007). "Efficient Tests of the Seasonal Unit Root Hypothesis," *Journal of Econometrics*, 141, 548–573.

Rodrigues, P. M. M, and A. M. R. Taylor. (2012). "The Flexible Fourier Form and Local Generalised Least Squares De-Trended Unit Root Tests," *Oxford Bulletin of Economics and Statistics*, 74, 736–759.

Romano, J. P., and M. Wolf. (2001). "Subsampling Intervals in Autoregressive Models with Linear Time Trend," *Econometrica*, 69, 1283–1314.

Romer, D. (2001). *Advanced Macroeconomics*. 2nd edition. New York: McGraw Hill.

Rothenberg, T. J., and J. H. Stock. (1997). "Inference in a Nearly Integrated Autoregressive Model with Nonnormal Innovations," *Journal of Econometrics*, 80, 269–286.

Roy, A., and W. A. Fuller. (2001). "Estimation for Autoregressive Time Series with a Root Near 1," *Journal of Business & Economic Statistics*, 19, 482–493.

Rudebusch, G. D. (1992). "Trends and Random Walks in Macroeconomic Time Series: A Re-Examination," *International Economic Review*, 33, 661–680.

Said, S. E., and D. A. Dickey. (1984). "Testing for Unit Roots in Autoregressive-Moving Average Models of Unknown Order," *Biometrika*, 71, 599–607.

Said, S. E., and D. A. Dickey. (1985). "Hypothesis Testing in ARIMA(p, 1, q) Models," *Journal of the American Statistical Association*, 80, 369–374.

Saikkonen, P., and H. Lütkepohl. (2002). "Testing for a Unit Root in a Time Series with a Level Shift at Unknown Time," *Econometric Theory*, 18, 313–348.

Saikkonen, P., and R. Luukkonen. (1993a). "Point Optimal Tests for Testing the Order of Differencing in ARIMA Models," *Econometric Theory*, 9, 343–362.

Saikkonen, P., and R. Luukkonen. (1993b). "Testing for a Moving Average Unit Root in Autoregressive Integrated Moving Average Models," *Journal of the American Statistical Association*, 88, 596–601.

Saikkonen, P., and R. Luukkonen. (1996). "Testing the Order of Differencing in Time Series Regression," *Journal of Time Series Analysis*, 17, 481–496.

Samorodnitsky, G., and M. S. Taqqu. (1994). *Stable Non-Gaussi6an Random Processes*. New York: Chapman & Hall.

Samuelson, P. A. (1965). "Proof that Properly Discounted Present Values of Assets Vibrate Randomly," *Bell Journal of Economics and Management Science*, 4, 369–374.

Sargan, J. D., and A. Bhargava. (1983). "Testing Residuals from Least Squares Regression for Being Generated by the Gaussian Random Walk," *Econometrica*, 51, 153–174.

Sarno, L., and M. P. Taylor. (2002). *The Economics of Exchange Rates*. New York: Cambridge University Press.

Schmidt, P., and J. Lee. (1991). "A Modification of the Schmidt-Phillips Unit Root Test," *Economics Letters*, 36, 285–289.

Schmidt, P., and P. C. B. Phillips. (1992). "LM Tests for a Unit Root in the Presence of Deterministic Trends," *Oxford Bulletin of Economics and Statistics*, 54, 257–287.

Schotman, P. C., and H. K. van Dijk. (1991a). "A Bayesian Analysis of the Unit Root in Real Exchange Rates," *Journal of Econometrics*, 49, 195–238.

Schotman, P. C., and H. K. van Dijk. (1991b). "On Bayesian Routes to Unit Roots," *Journal of Applied Econometrics*, 6, 387–401.

Schwarz, G. (1978). "Estimating the Dimension of a Model," *Annals of Statistics*, 6, 461–464.

Schwert, G. W. (1989). "Tests for Unit Roots: A Monte Carlo Investigation," *Journal of Business & Economic Statistics*, 7, 147–159.

Sen, P. K. (1980). "Asymptotic Theory of Some Tests for a Possible Change in the Regression Slope Occurring at an Unknown Time Point," *Zeitschrift Fur Wahrscheinlichkeitstheorie Und Verwandte Gebiete*, 52, 203–218.

Sen, P. K. (2001). "Behaviour of Dickey-Fuller F-Tests under the Trend-Break Stationary Alternative," *Statistics & Probability Letters*, 55, 257–268.

Sen, P. K. (2007). "On the Distribution of Dickey-Fuller Unit Root Statistics When There Is a Break in the Innovation Variance," *Statistics & Probability Letters*, 77, 63–68.

Seo, B. (1999). "Distribution Theory for Unit Root Tests with Conditional Heteroskedasticity," *Journal of Econometrics*, 91, 113–144.

Seo, M. H. (2008). "Unit Root Test in a Threshold Autoregression: Asymptotic Theory and Residual-Based Block Bootstrap," *Econometric Theory*, 24, 1699–1716.

Serfling, R. J. (1980). *Approximation Theorems of Mathematical Statistics*. New York: John Wiley.

Shao, J., and D. Tu. (1995). *The Jackknife and Bootstrap*. New York: Springer-Verlag.

Sheng, X., and J. Yang. (2013). "Truncated Product Methods for Panel Unit Root Tests," *Oxford Bulletin of Economics and Statistics*, 75, 624–636.

Shibata, R. (1976). "Selection of the Order of an Autoregressive Model by Akaike's Information Criterion," *Biometrika*, 63, 117–126.

Shiller, R. J., and P. Perron. (1985). "Testing the Random Walk Hypothesis: Power versus Frequency of Observation," *Economics Letters*, 18, 381–386.

Shin, D. W., and S. Kang. (2006). "An Instrumental Variable Approach for Panel Unit Root Tests under Cross-Sectional Dependence," *Journal of Econometrics*, 134, 215–234.

Shin, D. W., S. Kang, and M. S. Oh. (2004). "Recursive Mean Adjustment for Panel Unit Root Tests," *Economics Letters*, 84, 433–439.

Shin, D. W., and O. Lee. (2003). "An Instrumental Variable Approach for Tests of Unit Roots and Seasonal Unit Roots in Asymmetric Time Series Models," *Journal of Econometrics*, 115, 29–52.

Shin, D. W., and M. S. Oh. (2000). "Semiparametric Tests for Seasonal Unit Roots Based on a Semiparametric Feasible GLSE," *Statistics & Probability Letters*, 50, 207–218.

Shin, D. W., S. Sarkar, and J. H. Lee. (1996). "Unit Root Tests for Time Series with Outliers," *Statistics & Probability Letters*, 30, 189–197.

Shin, D. W., and B. S. So. (1999a). "New Tests for Unit Roots in Autoregressive Processes with Possibly Infinite Variances," *Statistics & Probability Letters*, 44, 387–397.

Shin, D. W., and B. S. So. (1999b). "Unit Root Tests Based on Adaptive Maximum Likelihood Estimation," *Econometric Theory*, 15, 1–23.

Shin, D. W., and B. S. So. (2000). "Gaussian Tests for Seasonal Unit Roots Based on Cauchy Estimation and Recursive Mean Adjustments," *Journal of Econometrics*, 99, 107–137.

Shin, D. W., and B. S. So. (2001). "Recursive Mean Adjustment for Unit Root Tests," *Journal of Time Series Analysis*, 22, 595–612.

Shin, Y., and A. Snell. (2006). "Mean Group Tests for Stationarity in Heterogeneous Panels," *Econometrics Journal*, 9, 123–158.

Sibbertsen, P., and R. Kruse. (2009). "Testing for a Break in Persistence under Long-Range Dependencies," *Journal of Time Series Analysis*, 30, 263–285.

Sims, C. A. (1988). "Bayesian Skepticism on Unit Root Econometrics," *Journal of Economic Dynamics and Control*, 12, 463–474.

Sims, C. A., and H. Uhlig. (1991). "Understanding Unit Rooters: A Helicopter Tour," *Econometrica*, 59, 1591–1599.

Smeekes, S., and A. M. Taylor. (2012). "Bootstrap Union Tests for Unit Roots in the Presence of Nonstationary Volatility," *Econometric Theory*, 28, 422–456.

Smith, J., and J. Otero. (1997). "Structural Breaks and Seasonal Integration," *Economics Letters*, 56, 13–19.

Smith, L. V., S. J. Leybourne, T. H. Kim, and P. Newbold. (2004). "More Powerful Panel Data Unit Root Tests with an Application to Mean Reversion in Real Exchange Rates," *Journal of Applied Econometrics*, 19, 147–170.

Smith, R. J., and A. M. R. Taylor. (1998). "Additional Critical Values and Asymptotic Representations for Seasonal Unit Root Tests," *Journal of Econometrics*, 85, 269–288.

Smith, R. J., and A. M. R. Taylor. (1999). "Likelihood Ratio Tests for Seasonal Unit Roots," *Journal of Time Series Analysis*, 20, 453–476.

Smith, R. J., and A. M. R. Taylor. (2001). "Recursive and Rolling Regression-Based Tests of the Seasonal Unit Root Hypothesis," *Journal of Econometrics*, 105, 309–336.

Smith, R. J., A. M. R. Taylor, and T. D. B. Castro. (2009). "Regression-Based Seasonal Unit Root Tests," *Econometric Theory*, 25, 527–560.

So, B. S., and D. W. Shin. (1999). "Cauchy Estimators for Autoregressive Processes with Applications to Unit Root Tests and Confidence Intervals," *Econometric Theory*, 15, 165–176.

Sollis, R., S. Leybourne, and P. Newbold. (1999). "Unit Roots and Asymmetric Smooth Transitions," *Journal of Time Series Analysis*, 20, 671–677.

Solo, V. (1984). "The Order of Differencing in ARIMA Models," *Journal of the American Statistical Association*, 79, 916–921.

Song, F. M., and Y. Wu. (1997). "Hysteresis in Unemployment: Evidence from 48 U.S. States," *Economic Inquiry*, 35, 235–243.

Sowell, F. (1990). "The Fractional Unit Root Distribution," *Econometrica*, 48, 495–505.

Sowell, F. (1991). "On DeJong and Whiteman's Bayesian Inference for the Unit Root Model," *Journal of Monetary Economics*, 28, 255–263.

Stock, J. H. (1991). "Confidence Intervals for the Largest Autoregressive Root in U.S. Macroeconomic Time Series," *Journal of Monetary Economics*, 28, 435–459.

Stock, J. H. (1994). "Unit Roots, Structural Breaks and Trends," in *Handbook of Econometrics*, Vol. 4, edited by R. F. Engle and D. L. McFadden, pp. 2739–2841. Amsterdam: Elsevier.

Stock J. H. (1999) "A Class of Tests for Integration and Cointegration," in *Cointegration, Causality and Forecasting: A Festschrift for Clive W. J. Granger*, edited by R. F. Engle and H. White, pp. 135–167. Oxford: Oxford University Press.

Stock, J. H., and M. W. Watson. (1988). "Testing for Common Trends," *Journal of the American Statistical Association*, 83, 1097–1107.

Strauss, J., and T. Yigit. (2003). "Shortfalls of Panel Unit Root Testing," *Economics Letters*, 81, 309–313.

Sul, D., P. C. B. Phillips, and C. Y. Choi. (2005). "Prewhitening Bias in HAC Estimation," *Oxford Bulletin of Economics and Statistics*, 67, 517–546.

Swensen, A. R. (2003). "Bootstrapping Unit Root Tests for Integrated Processes," *Journal of Time Series Analysis*, 24, 99–126.

Tam, W., and G. C. Reinsel. (1997). "Tests for Seasonal Moving Average Unit Root in ARIMA Models," *Journal of the American Statistical Association*, 92, 725–738.

Tam, W., and G. C. Reinsel. (1998). "Seasonal Moving-Average Unit Root Tests in the Presence of a Linear Trend," *Journal of Time Series Analysis*, 19, 609–625.

Tanaka, K. (1990). "Testing for a Moving Average Unit Root," *Econometric Theory*, 6, 433–444.

Tanaka, K. (1996). *Time Series Analysis: Nonstationary and Noninvertible Distribution Theory*. New York: Wiley.

Tanaka, K. (1998). "Analysis of Models with Complex Roots on the Unit Circle," *Journal of the Japanese Statistical Society*, 38, 145–155.

Tanaka, K. (1999). "The Nonstationary Fractional Unit Root," *Econometric Theory*, 15, 549–582.

Tanaka, K. (2008). "On Various Applications of Wavelet Analysis to Statistics," in *Selected Papers on Analysis and Related Topics*, American Mathematical Society Translations, Series 2, vol. 223, pp. 137–157. Providence: American Mathematical Society.

Taylor, A. M. R. (1998). "Testing for Unit Roots in Monthly Time Series," *Journal of Time Series Analysis*, 19, 349–368.

Taylor, A. M. R. (2002). "Regression-Based Unit Root Tests with Recursive Mean Adjustment for Seasonal and Nonseasonal Time Series," *Journal of Business & Economic Statistics*, 20, 269–281.

Taylor, A. M. R. (2003a). "Locally Optimal Tests against Unit Roots in Seasonal Time Series Processes," *Journal of Time Series Analysis*, 24, 591–612.

Taylor, A. M. R. (2003b). "On the Asymptotic Properties of Some Seasonal Unit Root Tests," *Econometric Theory*, 19, 311–321.

Taylor, A. M. R. (2005). "Variance Ratio Tests of the Seasonal Unit Root Hypothesis," *Journal of Econometrics*, 124, 33–54.

Taylor, A. M. R., and R. J. Smith. (2001). "Tests of the Seasonal Unit-Root Hypothesis against Heteroscedastic Seasonal Integration," *Journal of Business & Economic Statistics*, 19, 192–207.

Taylor, M. P., and L. Sarno. (1998). "The Behavior of Real Exchange Rates during the Post-Bretton Woods Period," *Journal of International Economics*, 46, 281–312.

Toda, H. Y., and P. C. B. Phillips. (1993). "Vector Autoregressions and Causality," *Econometrica*, 61, 1367–1393.

Tong, H. (1983). *Threshold Models in Non-Linear Time Series Analysis*. New York: Springer-Verlag.

Tong, H. (1993). *Non-Linear Time Series: A Dynamical System Approach*. Oxford: Oxford University Press.

Tsay, R. S. (1984). "Order Selection in Nonstationary Autoregressive Models," *Annals of Statistics*, 12, 1425–1433.

Tsay, R. S. (1993). "Testing for Noninvertible Models with Applications," *Journal of Business & Economic Statistics*, 11, 225–233.

Uhlig, H. (1994). "On Jeffreys Prior When Using the Exact Likelihood Function," *Econometric Theory*, 10, 633–644.

van der Vaart, A. W. (1998). *Asymptotic Statistics*. New York: Cambridge University Press.

Velasco, C. (2006). "Semiparametric Estimation of Long-Memory Models," in *Palgrave Handbook of Econometrics*, vol. 1, edited by T. C. Mills and K. Patterson, pp. 353–395. New York: Palgrave Macmillan.

Velasco, C. and P. M. Robinson. (2000). "Whittle Pseudo-Maximum Likelihood Estimation for Nonstationary Time Series," *Journal of the American Statistical Association*, 95, 1229–1243.

Vogelsang, T. J. (1999). "Two Simple Procedures for Testing for a Unit Root When There Are Additive Outliers," *Journal of Time Series Analysis*, 20, 237–252.

Vogelsang, T. J., and P. Perron. (1998). "Additional Tests for a Unit Root Allowing for a Break in the Trend Function at an Unknown Time," *International Economic Review*, 39, 1073–1100.

Wang, G. (2006). "A Note on Unit Root Tests with Heavy-Tailed GARCH Errors," *Statistics & Probability Letters*, 76, 1075–1079.

Wei, C. Z. (1992). "On Predictive Least Squares Principles," *Annals of Statistics*, 20, 1–42.

West, K. D. (1988). "Asymptotic Normality, When Regressors Have a Unit Root," *Econometrica*, 56, 1397–1417.

West, M., and J. Harrison. (1989). *Bayesian Forecasting and Dynamic Models*. New York: Springer-Verlag.

Westerlund, J., and R. Larsson. (2009). "A Note on the Pooling of Individual PANIC Unit Root Tests," *Econometric Theory*, 25, 1851–1868.

Westerlund, J., and R. Larsson. (2012). "Testing for a Unit Root in a Random Coefficient Panel Data Model," *Journal of Econometrics*, 167, 254–273.

White, H. (1980). "A Heteroskedasticity-Consistent Covariance Matrix Estimator and a Direct Test for Heteroskedasticity," *Econometrica*, 48, 817–838.

White, J. S. (1958). "The Limiting Distribution of the Serial Correlation Coefficient in the Explosive Case," *Annals of Mathematical Statistics*, 29, 1188–1197.

Wright, J. H. (2000). "Confidence Intervals for Univariate Impulse Responses with a Near Unit Root," *Journal of Business & Economic Statistics*, 18, 368–373.

Xiao, Z. (2001). "Testing the Null Hypothesis of Stationarity against an Autoregressive Unit Root Alternative," *Journal of Time Series Analysis*, 22, 87–105.

Xiao, Z., and P. C. B. Phillips. (1998). "An ADF Coefficient Test for a Unit Root in ARMA Models of Unknown Order with Empirical Applications to the U.S. Economy," *Econometrics Journal*, 1, 27–43.

Yin, Y., and S. Wu. (2000). "Stationarity Tests in Heterogeneous Panels," in *Advances in Econometrics* vol. 15, edited by B. Baltagi, pp. 275–296. Amsterdam: JAI.

Yoon, G. (2006). "A Note on some Properties of STUR Processes," *Oxford Bulletin of Economics and Statistics*, 68, 253–260.

Zaykin, D. V., L. A. Zhivotovsky, P. H. Westfall, and B. S. Weir. (2002). "Truncated Product Method for Combining P-Values," *Genetic Epidemiology*, 22, 170–185.

Zellner, A. (1971). *An Introduction to Bayesian Inference in Econometrics*. New York: John Wiley.

Zellner, A. (1986). "On Assessing Prior Distributions and Bayesian Regression Analysis with *g* Prior Distributions," in *Bayesian Inference and Decision Techniques—Essays in Honor of Bruno De Finetti*, edited by P. K. Goel and A. Zellner, pp. 233–243. Amsterdam: North-Holland.

Zellner, A., and A. Siow. (1980). "Posterior Odds Ratios for Selected Regression Hypotheses," *Trabajos De Estadística y De Investigación Operativa*, 31, 585–603.

Zhang, R. M., and N. H. Chan. (2012). "Maximum Likelihood Estimation for Nearly Non-Stationary Stable Autoregressive Processes," *Journal of Time Series Analysis*, 33, 542–553.

Zivot, E. (1994). "A Bayesian Analysis of the Unit Root Hypothesis within an Unobserved Components Model," *Econometric Theory*, 10, 552–578.

Zivot, E., and D. W. K. Andrews. (1992). "Further Evidence on the Great Crash, the Oil-Price Shock, and the Unit-Root Hypothesis," *Journal of Business & Economic Statistics*, 10, 251–270.

Zivot, E., and P. C. B. Phillips. (1994). "A Bayesian Analysis of Trend Determination in Economic Time Series," *Econometric Reviews*, 13, 291–336.

Index

Printed in the United States
by Baker & Taylor Publisher Services